Sensory Biographies

ETHNOGRAPHIC STUDIES IN SUBJECTIVITY

Tanya Luhrmann and Steven Parish, Editors

1. *Forget Colonialism? Sacrifice and the Art of Memory in Madagascar,* by Jennifer Cole
2. *Sensory Biographies: Lives and Deaths among Nepal's Yolmo Buddhists,* by Robert Desjarlais
3. *Culture and the Senses: Bodily Ways of Knowing in an African Community,* by Kathryn Linn Geurts
4. *Sins Between Cultures: Christianity, Cultural Change, and Moral Torment in a Papua New Guinea Society,* by Joel Robbins

Sensory Biographies

Lives and Deaths among Nepal's Yolmo Buddhists

Robert Desjarlais

UNIVERSITY OF CALIFORNIA PRESS

Berkeley / Los Angeles / London

Grateful acknowledgment is made to the following publishers for permission to reprint quotations from these works: Sheep Meadow Press, *Poems of Jerusalem and Love Poems: A Bilingual Edition,* by Yehuda Amichai, copyright © 1988 by Yehuda Amichai; Bantam Dell Publishing Group, *The Tibetan Book of the Dead,* composed by Padma Sambhava and translated by Robert Thurman, copyright © 1994 by Robert A. F. Thurman; Snow Lion Publications, *Living in the Face of Death: The Tibetan Tradition,* by Glenn H. Mullin, copyright © 1986 by Glenn H. Mullin, and *Introduction to Tibetan Buddhism,* by John Powers, copyright © 1995 by John Powers; Kensington Publishing Group, *The One Hundred Thousand Songs of Milarepa,* by Garma Chen-Chi Chang, copyright © 1962 by the Oriental Studies Foundation, all rights reserved, reprinted by permission of Citadel Press/Kensington Publishing Corp.; Oxford University Press, *The Buddha,* by Michael Carrithers, copyright © 1996 by Michael Carrithers; Penguin Books U.S.A. and Far West Translations, *The Life of Milarepa,* by Lobsang P. Lhalungpa, copyright © 1977 by Far West Translations, used by permission of Dutton, a division of Penguin Putnam Inc.

University of California Press
Berkeley and Los Angeles, California

University of California Press, Ltd.
London, England

© 2003 by The Regents of the University of California

Library of Congress Cataloging-in-Publication Data

Desjarlais, Robert R.
    Sensory biographies : lives and deaths among Nepal's Yolmo Buddhists / Robert Desjarlais.
        p.   cm. — (Ethnographic studies in subjectivity ; 2)
    Includes bibliographical references and index.
    ISBN 0-520-23587-8 (cloth : alk. paper). — ISBN 0-520-23588-6 (pbk. : alk. paper)
    1. Ghang Lama.   2. Kisang Omu.   3. Lamas — Nepal — Biography.
4. Buddhists — Nepal — Biography.   5. Death — Religious aspects —
Buddhism.   6. Nepal — Religious life and customs.   7. Helambu Sherpa
(Nepalese people) — Religion.   I. Title.
BQ962.H35 D47   2003
294.3′923′09225496 — dc21
[B]   2002016553

Manufactured in the United States of America

12   11   10   09   08   07   06   05   04   03
10   9   8   7   6   5   4   3   2   1

The paper used in this publication is both acid-free and totally chlorine-free (TCF). It meets the minimum requirements of ANSI/NISO Z39.48-1992 (R 1997) *(Permanence of Paper).* ⊚

Contents

List of Illustrations   vii

Note on Transliteration   ix

Kurāgraphy   1

Hardship, Comfort   20

Twenty-Seven Ways of Looking at Vision   54

Startled into Alertness   102

A Theater of Voices   133

"I've Gotten Old"   152

Essays on Dying   161

"Dying Is This"   176

The Painful Between   182

Desperation   189

The Time of Dying   201

Death Envisioned   206

To Phungboche, by Force   219

Staying Still   230

Mirror of Deeds   236

Here and There   245

"So: Ragged Woman"   255

Echoes of a Life   275
A Son's Death   309
The End of the Body   315
Last Words   328

Notes   353
Glossary of Terms   375
References   379
Acknowledgments   389
Index   393

Illustrations

Figures

1. Ghang Lama (Mheme), 1997   21
2. Thodong as seen from the south, 1998   33
3. Surje Lama, 1998   49
4. A page of a Tibetan religious text, the Bardo Thedol   68
5. The chhorten in Boudhanath   77
6. The view from Thodong, 1998: Lhatul Lama, the author, and Surje Lama   88
7. Kisang Omu, 2001   103
8. A wedding in Malemchi, 1989   111
9. Women working in the fields below Thodong, 1989   162
10. Kisang Omu in her early fifties   220
11. Phur Gyalmu with her sister and grandson, 1998   268
12. Ghang Lama, 1998   276
13. The two sides of a "purification print"   300
14. Ritual cleansing of the deceased, Thodong, 1988   301

Maps

1. Location of Yolmo region in Nepal   9
2. Map of Yolmo region   10

Table

1. Yolmo people noted in this book   16

Note on Transliteration

Most Yolmo *wa,* or "Yolmo people" (*Yolmo wa* is nowadays usually pronounced as "yhol-mo wa," with an aspirated *y* leading into "ol-mo"), speak their national language, Nepali, as well as a distinct Tibetan-derived language known to them today as Yolmo. Linguists have identified this unwritten language as Kagate, a Tibetan dialect that acquired its name because it was first recorded as spoken among a group of *kāgate,* or "paper-makers," in eastern Nepal.[1] It is now clear that earlier generations of this group of kāgate originated from the Yolmo region of Nepal. The grammar, syntax, and lexicons of the Yolmo language are quite similar to those of many Tibetan dialects, especially classical Tibetan. A majority of Yolmo wa rely on both Yolmo and Nepali in everyday conversations, and talk in one language is often interspersed with phrases from the other. Yolmo wa have no standard method of writing Yolmo. When people write out Yolmo words, they usually use Tibetan or Nepali (Devanagari) scripts, each of which poses obstacles to perfect transliteration. English letters are less accommodating still.

Yolmo words cited in this book are spelled phonetically, as they might sound to the English ear; I determined these spellings in consultation with Yolmo colleagues. Since many Yolmo words, especially religious terms, have direct correlates in the Tibetan language, the correlates are often noted, spelled as they are in written Tibetan. They are transcribed according to Wylie's system of Tibetan orthography.[2] The spelling of Nepali words follows the method of R. L. Turner.[3] Foreign words that are set in parentheses and are prefaced by *N.* are words in Nepali. Foreign terms that are not designated as being either Tibetan or Nepali are most often Yolmo words. Key Yolmo, Nepali, and Sanskrit words are listed in the glossary, along with their approximate meanings in translation and, where relevant, their Tibetan counterparts.

Kurāgraphy

"Many years before," Mheme Lama related, "when people would die, the body would vanish along with the soul, and people would cry and get very upset. It was like this a long time before. My father's grandfather and other people from before told about this. Before, before, at the time of dying, the body would vanish like 'phet'! Then the family of the dead man would cry and search for his body in the sky and in the ground. When it was lost, they would ask, 'Where is he?! Where has he gone?!'"

This eighty-five-year-old man was also known as Ghang Lama, or Hill Lama, by other members of his community, many of whom identify themselves as Yolmo wa, or "Yolmo people," an ethnically Tibetan Buddhist people, now several thousand in number, who have lived for generations in hamlets and villages along the upper ridges of the Yolmo, or Helambu, Valley of north-central Nepal.[1] Mheme (pronounced "mhem-mhē") had lived in the village of Thodong, along the southwestern ridge of the Yolmo Valley, until 1975 or so, when, seeking a more comfortable life in the city, he moved with his second wife and youngest daughter into a home in Chabahil, a multiethnic neighborhood about a mile west of the Boudhanath area, in northeast Kathmandu. It was in that home that he spoke of the body's vanishing act, in one of the many lengthy conversations that I had with him in 1998 in an effort to elicit his *jīvan kathā,* or "life story." I was in Nepal then, trying to record and give thought to the life stories of several Yolmo elders.

"Many years before," he continued, after swallowing a sip of tea, "everything would disappear."

I

"Before, the body would disappear as well?" asked Nogapu Sherpa, a Yolmo friend who had accompanied me to Mheme's home that day to help me converse in the Yolmo language.

"Yes," Mheme said. "But then the deities said, 'This is no good,' and they decided that the people must be able to see the body. Now they make the body stay. Now the body remains, and the soul departs. When it leaves the body, the body decays. So the body needs to be cremated or buried. Ah, now they need to cremate the body, compose the ashes, perform the funeral rites. The body can't be kept here forever, so they call the lamas [Buddhist priests, to perform those rites]. And the family feels better, thinking, 'Yes, he has died.' Now the body remains, the body is cremated, the funeral rites are performed, and people can understand that the person is dead. 'It's death' [they say]."

Here vision was as much solace as knowledge. Mheme understood that it was important that a corpse not vanish too quickly or too suddenly. A corpse is an absent presence, the vestige of a person no longer alive. Still, its lingering visual presence provides evidence of the transition from life to death, and so helps people to understand the actuality of any death. If they could not view the corpse, family members would search in despair, bewildered by the person's absence, unsure whether he or she was still alive. Since a lifeless body inevitably decays, it cannot be kept forever. Yet rather than having it vanish "like 'phet,'" as it once did, the gods arranged it so that a corpse would remain as a visible, palpable reminder of a person's death, giving bereaved family members sufficient time and the tangible, ritual means to come to terms with the death.

In Mheme's words I heard themes that often surfaced in my talks with him. He spoke in ways that brought to mind ideas of materiality and immateriality, appearances and disappearances, contact and disconnection, longing and fulfillment, remembrance and forgetting, matter and the decay of matter, the changes that time effects, the fate of sentient bodies, the life and death of things. In most of these conversations vision was the dominant sensory orientation. As was the case with his chronicle of vanishing bodies, motifs of visuality played strongly into how Mheme made sense of the world, how he engaged with others, how he thought of his life, how he envisioned his death.

I first recognized the importance of vision in Mheme's life in the summer of 1997, when I began to work with him to record his life story. Acts and ideas of writing, inscription, visibility, visual engagements, and perceptual clarity often emerged in the matters of which we spoke. But in the winter of 1998 I began to elicit the life narratives of another Yolmo elder, Kisang Omu (pronounced "key-sang o-mu"), an eighty-eight-year-old woman who was living then with her youngest son and his wife in the heart of the Boudhanath area of Kathmandu, about a mile down the road from Mheme's residence. As tape recordings and written transcripts of the two sets of conversations accumulated and I started to compare what the two elders had to say about their lives, I realized that while Mheme's recounting of his life was dominated by motifs of vision and bodiliness, of knowing the world through visual means, and of acting and suffering through the medium of his visible body, Kisang Omu's accounts of her life largely entailed a theater of voices: when narrating significant events in her life, she often invoked, in vivid, morally connotative terms, the voicings of key actors in those events. She also commented frequently on the degree of skillfulness of her own speech and expressed concerns about how others might assess the aesthetic value of that speech.

One saw chiefly, while the other minded most the flow of words. In the pages that follow I want to present a pair of overlapping "sensory biographies" that consider the ways in which certain culturally honed and politically charged sensory modalities have contributed to the making and telling of the two lives.[2] How, for instance, did Kisang's acoustic orientation toward the world tie into the workings of language and memory in her self-narrations? How did Ghang Lama's visualist, text-based orientation play into his take on the presence of death and suffering in his life? How did the sensory regard of both individuals shape their perceptions of my work with them, including the production of this text? How did gender roles and identities play into all of this? How, in short, do a person's ways of sensing the world contribute to how that person lives and recollects her life?

The inquiry builds on recent work in anthropology that investigates how cultural dynamics pattern the senses in different societies. Although a long neglected domain of inquiry, the anthropology of the senses, which can be defined as the interpretive study of the cultural construction and social dimensions of human perception and sensate experience in different societies, is proving to be an increasingly important and generative field within cultural anthropology. Ethnographic research along these lines ranges from accounts of the workings of gender, sensation, and memory in contemporary Greece to studies of sensuous knowledge among the Songhay of West Africa to analyses of the sensor-

ial features of political surveillance and imprisonment in Northern Ireland.[3] Most of this research aims to show how the dominant sensory
orientations of the modern West are historically distinct, and it tends to
focus on culturally pervasive themes and dynamics. My goal here is to
understand how sensory modalities and dispositions play themselves
out in individual lives, how members of a single society live out different sensory biographies.

Yet while a running analytic focus is the place of voice in Kisang's life
and recollections and the role of vision in Mheme's, these are by no
means the only themes or sensory modalities considered. Such considerations serve as guiding threads throughout the chapters that follow,
but they are only two threads among many. For one thing, it was not
the case that Mheme engaged with the world only through vision or
that Kisang lived solely in a world of voices. Sound was an important
sense in Mheme's life, as taste, smell, and touch were, and Kisang saw
and was seen by others. The difference, then, is not one of complete op-
posites but rather one of different emphases, of different patterns,
within two lives. At the same time, to focus on a single sensory modality
or the senses alone within each life would neglect how the senses relate
to other aspects of a life and so would misrepresent the complexity of
the lives in general. It would also fail to show the ways in which sensory
engagements articulate with broader social, personal, and political dynamics. In a recent assessment of anthropological research on the
senses, Michael Herzfeld cautions that the senses "will remain marginal
to ethnographic description unless, in some practical fashion, all of anthropology can be recognized as necessarily shot through with alertness
to the entire gamut of sensory semiosis."[4] A leading aim of the present
inquiry, accordingly, is to help foster such a recognition by showing
how diffuse arenas of life within a Himalayan society are shot through
with diverse forms of "sensory semiosis."

The book is keyed in particular to questions of selfhood and subjectivity. It inquires into the interrelated sensorial, cultural, and political underpinnings of two lives in an effort to help us sharpen our understanding of the relation between culture and human subjectivities—how, that
is, diverse cultural forces contribute to the makings of subjective experience. It adopts, to use an anthropologist's term, a "person-centered" approach to cultural phenomena.[5] A recurring idea here is that, by attending carefully to how a person or two within a specific social setting live
out and make sense of their lives, anthropologists can effectively address
the ways personal and interpersonal concerns of individuals relate to so-

cial and cultural processes and so develop more precise and more integrative understandings of what it means to be a person, to live a life, to
relate to others, to have a body, to be conscious in time. With a few others, I take it that anthropologists should not limit themselves to the
study of social or political formations alone; that culture and history are
grounded in the lives of individuals; that the drift of narratives often
proves to be more illuminating than sweeping statements; and that one
can sometimes learn more by tending to particulars within the folds of
the general. The Israeli poet Yehuda Amichai says as much in "Tourists,"
one of his *Poems of Jerusalem.*

Once I sat on the steps by a gate at David's Tower, I placed my two heavy baskets at my side. A group of tourists was standing around their guide and I became their target marker. "You see that man with the baskets? Just right of his
head there's an arch from the Roman period. Just right of his head." "But he's
moving, he's moving!" I said to myself: redemption will come only if their
guide tells them, "You see that arch from the Roman period? It's not important:
but next to it, left and down a bit, there sits a man who's bought fruit and veg-
etables for his family."[6]

   One could likewise imagine a situation in which Italian or Japanese
tourists visiting the sacred *chhorten,* or *stūpa,* in Boudhanath are told,
"You see the four pairs of eyes painted on the upper facades of the
stūpa? Those are quite important. But don't forget that in a house a few
streets away, to the right and down a bit, there lives a woman..."

...who, in the still days when frail legs limited her to sitting alone in
her room much of the time, reciting mantras with a set of prayer beads
in her hands, happened to be visited now and then by a man from another country, one wealthier and more powerful than her own, who
asked her to relate to him her life story, including her recollections of
deeds and events of times past, through the voicing of words that, he
said, he was going to take and put into a book, one that would be
shown to other people, even though she herself could not read such
words, while all along the man, much younger than she was, younger
than her sons even, was trying, for better or worse, to make sense of her
life, its axes of time and effort and selfhood, by attending, among other
things, to the forms of speech and action that composed it.

   In contrast with many person-centered approaches in anthropology,
which have given priority to psychodynamic perspectives, this study
foregrounds a phenomenological approach.[7] By "phenomenology" I

mean an analytic approach, more a method of inquiry, really, than a theory, that works to understand and describe in words phenomena as they appear to the consciousness of certain peoples. The phenomena most in question here include the workings of time, form, perception, selfhood, bodies, suffering, personal agency, morality, memory, vision, and language as they have taken form, now and then, in several Yolmo lives. As with other phenomenological approaches in philosophy and the human sciences, of particular interest are the ways in which such forces contribute to how humans make sense of and live out significant aspects of their lives, from the ways in which they converse with others to how they recall past events. And as befits an anthropological inquiry, the cultural grounds of such phenomena are always kept in mind.

This is difficult work. You cannot readily tap into the "lived experience" of cultural subjects, be they in Boston or Calcutta. You can only talk with and live among them. So words, really, are the stuff of meaning and evidence here, along with other manifest actions—a look here, a gesture there. In accord with what Yolmo wa themselves hold, that no one can truly know what lies within another's *sem*, or "heartmind," it is important to keep in mind that we are, at best, attending to traces of meaning left in the wake of human action, like echoes resounding in a ravine. All told, the analytic process, this "semology," is interpretive, inferential. As I see it, the phenomenal and the discursive, life as lived and life as talked about, are like the intertwining strands of a braided rope, each complexly involved in the other, in time. The work, accordingly, conjoins a person-centered approach to Yolmo subjectivities with a "discourse-centered" one in detailing how communicative practices, ways of speaking and listening, contribute to how people understand and portray their lives and the lives of others.[8] It attends both to the specifics of the lives in question—she did this, he felt that—and to the flux of cultural, personal, and interpersonal forces that weighed heavily into the dialogic "telling" of those lives.

This is also a book about death and dying. Of the many topics that Kisang and Mheme mulled in my presence, from the best foods to eat to the winter snows that once blanketed the Yolmo region, death and dying were among the more common ones. Both elders understood that, with their life spans coming to an end, they would probably be dying soon. Kisang in particular found herself within the "condition of dying," while Mheme took it that he was on the "verge" of dying. I believe that this had a significant impact on what they told me about their lives as well as on what they thought of my work with them. As spelled out later on, Mheme found in his work with me the possibility of important "echoes" of his life and words remaining after he had passed on, while Kisang was concerned with how her increasing frailty was affecting her ability to "speak well" and, consequently, with how her recorded talk might be perceived by others.

Kisang Omu died, unfortunately, in November 2001. Ghang Lama is alive as of this writing. In their talks with me both elders often voiced their thoughts on death and dying, and they did not mind my asking about them. In general, while it was clear that certain topics, such as sex and childbirth, were best left unexamined, the two were not "shy" in talking about death in general or their deaths in particular. I have found this to be the case with almost all Yolmo elders. (Most are quite reserved, in contrast, when it comes to sentiments of loss and bereavement.) Many Yolmo wa speak openly about death, in part because they find it important to contemplate the fragile, transient, decay-prone nature of human lives. Tibetan Buddhist teachings, in fact, encourage musings on death and dying, for they are thought to generate insights into the impermanence of all composite forms and the delusive nature of human lives, insights that motivate people to transcend such impermanence and delusions through religious practice.[9] And so Kisang's and Mheme's takes on dying are conveyed here, in a multivoiced prose in which traces of their voices coincide with my own. At times, as well, these words seem to involve a work of mourning, my own muted mourning in relation to the losses at hand.

Another potential demise was on the minds of Yolmo people in the late 1990s: that of Yolmo society and culture. This too shaped what people said to me and how and why they said it.

Those who identify as Yolmo wa, until recently known as Helambu Sherpa, understand that their ancestors have lived for three centuries or so along the upper, forested ridges of the Yolmo Valley.[10] At least some of these ancestors were Buddhist priests, known as lamas, who migrated from Kyirong, an area in the southwest of present-day Tibet, to the central upland area of Yolmo after receiving land grants for Buddhist temples bestowed to them by Newar and then Gurkha kings.[11] Much less certain is how many others also migrated from the Kyirong region and, relatedly, to what degree the relocated lama families formed marriage alliances with families already living in the Yolmo region. In any event, in time a class of people known as the Lama People emerged in Yolmo, and it is to these people that today's Yolmo wa trace their heritage.

The Yolmo region ranges some fifteen to thirty miles north of Kathmandu in north-central Nepal, with the southernmost villages a long day's hike from the northeastern perimeter of the Kathmandu Valley (see maps 1 and 2). As yet no roads reach directly to any of the villages, and only a few villages have the use of electricity. The majority of Yolmo villages, which range in size from a few households to some forty-odd houses clustered together, are set along the upper slopes of the mountains that ring the Yolmo Valley in a horseshoelike formation. The villages lie on lands ranging from seven thousand to ten thousand feet above sea level. On the slopes below these lands lie villages inhabited principally by families known today as Tamang. For the most part, Tamang families are poorer than Yolmo ones, and their members often serve as laborers for wealthier Yolmo landowners. At the base of the valley, through which the Malemchi River runs as it drains south into the Indrawati River, lie fertile rice paddies cultivated by Chetri, Brahman, and Tamang communities. In the twentieth century, the successive incarnations of the Kathmandu-based Kingdom of Nepal maintained steadfast political control of the Yolmo region. Only the most recent generations of the region's residents have known themselves to be citizens of an integrated nation-state—as "Nepali," that is. All along, though, families and villages, rich or poor, have been involved in political economies at once regional and international in scope.

For some years now, commerce, land rentals, pastural grazing, and the farming of maize, potatoes, and other high-altitude crops have provided the main sources of food and income for Yolmo families living in the Yolmo region, although recently tourism from trekking expeditions through the region and employment in Kathmandu, India, and elsewhere have brought additional sources of material wealth. In the last three decades an ever-increasing number of Yolmo families have resettled permanently in Kathmandu, primarily in the Tibetan neighborhoods that surround the great chhorten in Boudhanath. While many of their business affairs presently lead them to converse with all sorts of peoples, from Tibetans to "Westerners" to representatives of the Nepali state, Yolmo wa, including those residing in Kathmandu, tend to associate socially mostly with other Yolmo wa, especially members of their extended families. When it comes to kinship, one widely found local preference is for a combination of patrilineal descent and virilocal residence, together with cross-cousin marriage. Yolmo wa live for the most part in households composed of nuclear families, although sometimes parents end up living with their adult sons or daughters. When sons marry, they

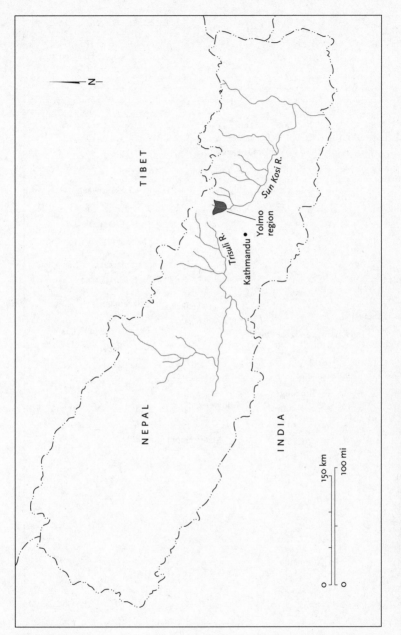

Map 1. Location of the Yolmo region in Nepal.

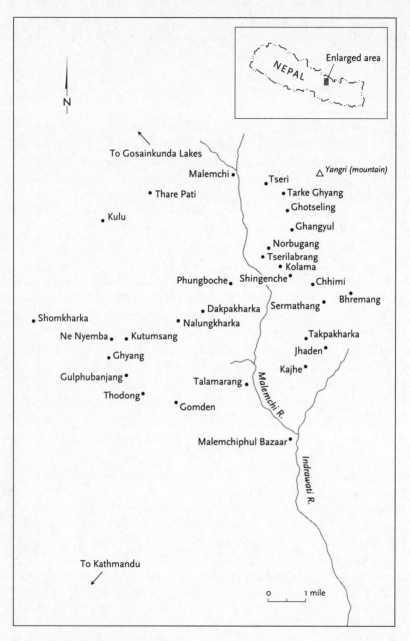

Map 2. Map of the Yolmo region.

usually set up their own households, sometimes on lands adjacent to their parents' homes. When daughters marry, they typically must move into their husbands' homes, wherever they might be. Most Yolmo people are devout practitioners of the Nyingma school of Mahāyāna Buddhism. Religious practices range from solitary meditative practices, to efforts to engage in karmically meritorious deeds, to sincere attempts to live virtuous, beneficial lives, to a family's daily offerings to Buddhist deities, to a community's participation in Buddhist rites. Male religious specialists known as lamas, who maintain village *gompa,* or "temples," inherited through patrilineal descent, conduct most of these rites, which villages and families regularly sponsor. One of their most important responsibilities is to conduct cremation and funeral rites on behalf of recently deceased persons. Hierarchies abound in Yolmo society: lamas, who usually inherit that role patrilineally, call for respectful deference more than laypersons do; wealthy families are generally thought to have better karma than impoverished ones; the young are to pay respect to the elderly; and husbands have higher status than wives.

Those known today as Yolmo wa have always been engaged with other peoples, including various Tamang, Tibetan, and Nepalese peoples, as these groups are known today, with the boundaries drawn between such "ethnic groups" (the term itself speaks to a very recent construct) much less steadfast and much more blurred than they have tended to be since the 1980s. But "Lama" or "Yolmo" communities have also had a sense, especially since the early 1990s, of being a distinct people, with their own customs, traditions, and language. The irony in this social history, however, is that, in the same years when Yolmo wa came to identify themselves effectively as an ethnic group distinct from other communities in Nepal, with a rich cultural heritage of their own, many were also finding that the circumstances of their lives were changing in ways that could, in but a few years, lead to the loss of that heritage and the dissolution of their culture.

I first worked in the Yolmo region in the late 1980s, while I was conducting ethnographic research on patterns of illness and shamanic healing among Yolmo peoples. After concluding my fieldwork in 1989, I returned to the United States, just a few months before the *jan āndolan,* or "people's movement," in Nepal sparked a revolution that led in 1990 to a new constitution predicated on multiparty democracy and the curtailment of the king's once substantial powers. When I returned to Nepal in 1997, after an eight-year absence, I found that much had changed for Yolmo people. Increased engagement with the transcultural

world system had something to do with this; in Yolmo homes in Kathmandu, for instance, cable television linkups had become as common-
place as Buddhist altars. But other factors were at play as well. In tandem with a heightened consciousness of their unique cultural heritage,
made possible by postrevolution laws that now made it permissible
to discuss and promote non-Nepali ethnicities and languages, many
Yolmo peoples were now identifying themselves not as Sherpa, as they
had in the 1980s, but as Yolmo wa.

As with everything else, there was a history to these names. Residents of
the Yolmo region began to identify themselves as Sherpa or Helambu
Sherpa in the late 1960s. Previously, they called themselves Lama People
to distinguish themselves ethnically from Tamang clans, who neighbored them on the southern and western sides of the Yolmo region and
who often served as "sponsors" to Yolmo lamas. But with the increasing
international renown of their cultural cousins, the Solu-Khumbu
Sherpa of the Mount Everest region, families in Yolmo aligned themselves with this prestigious group and began to refer to themselves as
Sherpa to outsiders. By the late 1990s, however, one of the main debates
within the Yolmo community was whether to identify as Sherpa or as
Yolmo people. Many, particularly elders and families residing solely in
the Yolmo region, still subscribed to the former term. But far more, especially educated men and women living in Kathmandu, were now
identifying themselves as Yolmo people. Among other reasons, the latter individuals found it necessary to establish an ethnic identity that signaled that, as a whole, they were distinct from the Sherpa peoples of the
Solu-Khumbu region. All this was in tune with the multifaceted, ever-
shifting "ethnoscapes" of Nepal in the 1990s, in which numerous communities were attempting to establish or reconstruct the collective identities they took and tried to promote to others as their own.[12]
    At the same time, the number of Yolmo people living in the Yolmo
region had decreased in the years following the revolution, in large part
because many Yolmo families and youths had moved to Kathmandu in
search of employment, better education for their children, and more
"comfort" than could be found in any village. People spoke often of the
consequences of these "dispersals": houses in Yolmo were being locked
up; mostly elderly people and impoverished farmers remained in the villages; the forests were growing wild again; children studying in Kathmandu were learning Nepali rather than Yolmo as their first language;
and many youths were leaving Kathmandu to look for better-paying

jobs in places such as New York City. Many I spoke with, young and old, were concerned that traditional Yolmo culture was eroding away, with the histories and lifeways of the "old days" soon to be lost with the passing of the most senior Yolmo wa. And since Yolmo society as a whole was composed of a relatively small number of clans and families, people feared that Yolmo culture as they knew it might soon be a thing of the past.

In response to these concerns, several organizations were created with the aim of cultivating and preserving aspects of Yolmo society.[13] Such projects inevitably led to discussions, arguments at times, of what, precisely, is traditional Yolmo culture as well as who in fact can be considered Yolmo and who cannot. More than a few Yolmo wa, educated youths mostly, also aspired to retain in their society's collective memory aspects of Yolmo culture that they found most significant: folk songs, architectural forms, language idioms, dance steps, styles of dress. "If we don't collect the stories, if we don't know the history, everything will be lost," one member of a Yolmo student association told me in speaking of the work he and other students sought to do in their free time. With such sentiments came the sense, again, of vanishing forms: with the loss of "the old ways," Ghang Lama once observed, "everything will soon be lost."

Given that many Yolmo wa would agree that a death is often "the death of memory,"[14] my plans to record the life histories of elderly Yolmo men and women were well received by acquaintances when I returned to Nepal in 1997. From the start, many Yolmo wa supported my research aims, even though it was never my intention to conduct a "salvage anthropology" of any sort. Some did so in part, I think, because they sensed in my work an opportunity to establish a detailed record of several Yolmo lives and, by implication, the eras they represented, before it proved impossible to do so. Others in Kathmandu seemed to anticipate that any books written about Yolmo people by Westerners could not but help to strengthen their standing and identity within the Hindu-dominated governmental politics of Nepal; ethnicity-based quotas for educational scholarships, for one, were at stake. A few men residing in Thodong, however, expressed doubts that any books I might write about their community would ever benefit them in any tangible ways. At any rate, I soon found myself engaged in a semicollaborative project in which several acquaintances expressed a willingness to help with the research, and I agreed to give copies of all transcripts and taped interviews not only to the subjects of any life stories but also, with their consent, to the archival library of the Yolmo Foundation, a nonprofit organization, based in Boudhanath, whose mandate is to preserve Yolmo culture and language. Beyond giving their permission and support, though, Yolmo colleagues have been quite active in the development of the ideas found within these pages. Well aware of the potential of words to shape or reshape personal and collective histories, they have paid close attention to what I have been writing about them and their neighbors. In the course of things, friends have asked that I identify them and their neighbors as Yolmo people, not as Sherpa; acquaintances have encouraged me to include the word *Yolmo* in this book's title; the most appropriate spellings of Yolmo words and place-names have been proffered; debates among Yolmo intellectuals have swirled around the meanings of several concepts cited; and just about every line of this text has been reviewed by at least one Yolmo reader.

All this weighs heavily into how I have gone about setting pen to paper. Writing has its effects among both authors and readers, as acts of reading, actual or potential, do. "The culture of a people," Clifford Geertz once proposed, "is an ensemble of texts, themselves ensembles, which the anthropologist strains to read over the shoulders of those to whom they properly belong."[15] While the culture-as-text metaphor might be dated, Geertz was, as usual, onto something: ethnographers are forever trying to make sense of how their informants make sense of things. In terms of the present text, however, another spectral relation is in the mix: I very much have the sense that more than a few Yolmo wa are looking over my shoulders as I write these words. Such native readerships will, I suspect, become much more present and forceful in anthropological circles in the coming years, and anthropologists will have to tend to them in ways they think best. As far as my own efforts go, one consequential effect is that, in attempting to write in terms that make solid sense to Yolmo wa or at the least do not disserve them in any way, I find myself trying to conceive of Yolmo lives in ways that do not veer far from Yolmo forms of thought and knowledge or the philosophic suppositions inherent within them. This is not to claim that the book is written from a Yolmo perspective or that it ventriloquizes Yolmo voices. It is to say, simply, that its self-spun musings are acutely mindful of the voices I have heard.

Several of those voices recur in these pages. While Kisang Omu and Ghang Lama offered the most extensive accounts of their lives, I also spoke in depth with six other Yolmo wa about their personal histories. I did so in part to develop a more extensive corpus of Yolmo life stories to gain greater perspective on all the lives related. Since slivers of what these individuals had to say resound in the chapters that follow, it's worth noting a word or two about their authors here.

Phur Gyalmu, a Yolmo woman in her early fifties, related aspects of her life to me in March 1998, while I was visiting the village of Thodong in the southwestern corner of the Yolmo Valley. Phur Gyalmu is Ghang Lama's niece; her mother, now deceased, was his younger sister. When I had lived in the 1980s in Gulphubanjang, a village a few minutes' walk north of Thodong, I came to know Phur Gyalmu and her family a bit. Her husband had since died, however, as had one of her daughters, and she was living then with her remaining three children in the same home. In the course of several days, while I was staying in the home of Mheme's second son, Lhatul, two of Mheme's granddaughters, Tashi and Kunsang, accompanied me in several visits to Phur Gyalmu's home in order to talk with her about her life.[16] While she had always struck me as a quick-thinking, straight-talking person, she expressed discomfort with what we were asking of her. Time and again she said she did not "know how to talk."

Sen Zangbu Sherpa, a Yolmo man in his late sixties, had lived for much of his life in Kutumsang, a village that lies just over the ridge north of Thodong. In 1990 or so, however, he decided to move to Boudhanath to stay with his younger sister, Gom Dolma Sherpa, in a house built on property she had purchased some years before. It was there, in the main room of their home, that Gom Dolma's grandson Dorje Sherpa and I spoke with both elders in the course of an afternoon in May 1998, while several of Dorje's siblings passed in and out. First Sen Zangbu voiced a fast-paced narrative of his and his family's history into the tape recorder; then he answered a number of questions. Then Gom Dolma, "already sixty-one" and bedridden because of a nasty fall she had suffered a few years back, did much the same in speaking of the joys and sorrows of her life. Since I was soon on my way back to the United States, I had to postpone the translation of these tapes until I returned to Kathmandu in 2000. By then Dorje was on to other things, and so I enlisted the help of Temba D. Yolmo, a college student then enrolled in anthropology courses in a local college.

Temba, who speaks Yolmo, Nepali, and English fluently, listened to the tapes to help me to understand Gom Dolma's and Sen Zangbu's words. He also accompanied me during several informal visits with Kisang Omu and Ghang Lama, then arranged it so that I could speak with his own

TABLE I. Yolmo People Noted in This Book

In association with Kisang Omu:	
Wangel Lama, Kisang Omu's first husband	
Rinjin Lama, Kisang Omu's second husband (and Kānchā Lama's father)	
Kānchā Lama, Kisang Omu's youngest son	Neela Lama, Kānchā Lama's wife
Pramod Lama Yolmo, Kisang Omu's nephew (helped the author to talk with Kisang Omu in 1998)	
Temba D. Yolmo (helped the author to talk with Kisang Omu in 2000)	

In association with Ghang Lama:	
Najang Lama, Ghang Lama's father	Pasang Gyalmu, Ghang Lama's mother
Phurbi Lama, Ghang Lama's first wife	
K. B. Lama, Ghang Lama's first son	Hrikchung Lama, K. B. Lama's wife
Karsang Lhamu, Ghang Lama's first daughter	
Lhatul Lama, Ghang Lama's second son	Mingmar Lama, Lhatul Lama's wife
Dawa Lama, Ghang Lama's third son	Norki Lama, Dawa Lama's wife
Rhidu Pema, Ghang Lama's second wife	
Ang Maya, Ghang Lama's second daughter	
Norbu Wangchuk Yolmo, Ghang Lama's grandson (helped the author to talk with Ghang Lama in 1997)	
Nogapu Prakash Sherpa (helped the author to talk with Ghang Lama in 1998)	
Temba D. Yolmo (helped the author to talk with Ghang Lama in 2000)	

Other life history informants:	*Assisting with these interviews and with translations:*
Phur Gyalmu Sherpa	Tashi Lama, Kunsang Lama
Sen Zangbu Sherpa	Dorje Sherpa; Temba D. Yolmo
Gom Dolma Sherpa	Dorje Sherpa; Temba D. Yolmo
Karmu Omu Lama	Temba D. Yolmo
Ghaki Lamani	Chhewang Yolmo, Tashi Lama
Karma Gyaltsen Yolmo	

TABLE I. *(continued)*

General assistance on translations and the writing of this book:

Karma Gyaltsen Yolmo
Binod Lama Yolmo
Temba D. Yolmo

grandmother about her life. Karmu Omu Lama, then eighty, had lived in the village of Sermathang until just a few years back, when she and her husband decided to trek down to Kathmandu to live with their first son and his family. Quiet and soft-spoken, a bit unsure of what she should say, she related to Temba and me significant deeds of her life while her husband, her son, and his wife sat by our sides, now and then offering their own thoughts on the topics at hand. When the cassette we were using clicked to its forty-five-minute end, we agreed that was a good place to stop. When asked what she thought of what we had just done, she said that she was "happy" she had told us about her life but did not elaborate.

Ghaki Lamani, a seventy-three-year-old woman from the village of Ne Nyemba, spoke in less bashful ways about her life around the same time that Karmu Omu did. During several visits to her home in Boudhanath, I listened to her talk, with several prompts on my part, about the hard work she did in life, the "kidnap" marriage to which she had to submit, the death of her husband some thirty years back, her subsequent move to Kathmandu, and the relative comfort she encountered in her later years. Ghaki's grandson Chhewang Yolmo and Ghang Lama's granddaughter Tashi Lama joined me in such visits, then helped me to render their senior's words into English.

The one younger person with whom I discussed his life in detail was Karma Gyaltsen Yolmo, the thirty-six-year-old son of a respected Yolmo lama and political leader who had died when Karma was in his early twenties. I first got to know this artist and thinker in 1989, when he helped me to translate some Yolmo folk songs and shamanic ritual texts. Instrumental to the founding and sustained vitality of the Yolmo Foundation, and knowledgeable about Yolmo religious practices, Karma has since helped me in numerous ways to understand Yolmo lives. On several Saturday mornings in 1998 we sat with a tape recorder between us and talked about the events and aspirations of his life. In the spring of 2001, he traveled to the United States and stayed with me for a month in my home in Massachusetts in order to read through and suggest changes to an earlier version of this text. Karma also discussed with me on many other occasions the ideas and questions raised through my inquiries, as did other Yolmo acquaintances, including Nogapu Sherpa; Ghang Lama's son Lhatul and his wife, Mingmar; several of Ghang Lama's grandchildren; Pramod Lama Yolmo, the man who helped me to converse with Kisang; and Pramod's brother Binod Lama Yolmo, who listened to the recordings of several life story conversations, then read through several draft chapters of this text.

Along with these many offhand and scheduled conversations with Yolmo subjects—"ethnography by appointment," a colleague calls the latter endeavor—came the usual sorts of activities that are beneficial to the "deep hanging out" that field researchers so often rely upon when trying to learn something about ways of life uncommon to them.[17] In addition to being present among Yolmo wa as they went about their lives, I found myself drinking tea with them, shuffling cards, exchanging in wordplay, watching television, bemoaning a loss, attending festivals, noting appearances, talking and listening to the talk of others, thinking about that talk, so much talk, it seems, so many words, so much *kurā*, to use a Nepali word often wielded by Yolmo speakers that can mean, depending on the context and any verb or modifier that accompanies it, either "talk" or "thing" or "matter" or "opinion" or "event" or "problem" or "price." There has, in fact, been so much talk heard, so many matters perceived and transcribed, that my mind is prone to thinking, in its more polyglossic, wordplayful moments, that the present text entails nothing more, but also nothing less, than a "kurāgraphy" of Yolmo lives and deaths, a written account of the sundry talk and items that sometimes matter most in those lives. The book dabbles in "conversations" *(kurā-kahāni)* and "hearsay" *(re-ko kurā)*, "matters of the heart" *(man ko kurā)* and "matters of the past" *(bhūtkālko kurā)*. It deals with the matter of words and the wordiness of matter and so is ensnared within the intricate, Möbius strip–like interweave of the phenomenal and the discursive, life as lived and life as talked about. The materials from which it draws, and its subject matter to some extent, are the often roundabout, often eventful ways that certain moves and arrangements enable people "to converse with others" *(kurā garnu)*, or "to tell stories" *(kurā batāunu)*, or, say, "to brood or daydream" *(kurā khelnu)*, "to reveal a secret" *(kurā kholnu)*, "to catch on to a trick" *(kurā pakranu)*, "to introduce a subject" *(kurā uṭhāunu)*, "to interrupt or 'cut' another's speech" *(kurā kāṭnu)*, "to change a story or distort a meaning" *(kurā badalnu)*, "to talk disparagingly about another" *(kurā lagaunu)*, "to contradict something" *(kurā ulṭāunu)*, "to retract a statement" *(kurā pharkāunu)*, "to engage in 'pricking talk'" *(ghocne kurā)*, "to detect the truth in another's talk" *(kurā samātnu)*, "to heed or mind something said" *(kurā mānnu)*, or "to listen to or be convinced by—to 'eat', literally—someone's talk" *(kurā khānu).*[18] The book offers words on such matters and the issues to which they so often relate. It also includes thoughts on the visible, tangible kurā of its own form.

Hardship, Comfort

One vivid memory I have of Mheme, of a way of looking, to be precise, is from July 1997. I had already been in Nepal several weeks that summer and had hiked up to the Yolmo region to visit the villages I had lived and worked in eight years before. I hoped to meet up with old friends, including Lhatul Lama and Dawa Lama, two adult sons of Mheme who I had come to know well while I was living a few houses down from them in Gulphubanjang in the 1980s. In visiting Lhatul, I learned that his younger brother had traveled with his wife and children to Kathmandu a few weeks before to stay at their father's home in Chabahil. Norki, his wife, was expecting, and they wanted to assure a good birth by staying in the city, a quick taxi ride away from a hospital.

The morning after I returned to Kathmandu I set out to visit Dawa at his father's house. Karma Gyaltsen, another Yolmo friend, gave me directions to the place, which I had never visited before; I had met and talked with Mheme on several occasions during my earlier stay, but only in Gulphubanjang, when he had come to stay with his sons. It took a while to find the house, a modest, three-story structure framed by a courtyard that opened out onto a mound of dirt, apparently the remnants of a house that once neighbored it; the house stood alongside a narrow footpath that ran through a neighborhood of lightly colored brick houses. Mheme's daughter Maya happened to be washing clothes in the courtyard when I arrived. Upon learning who I was, she led me up a creaky set of stairs to the third floor, where Dawa sat with his wife and children in a sparsely furnished room. Surprised to see me again after so many years—"O-ho!" he shouted—Dawa invited me in and offered me

Figure 1. Ghang Lama (Mheme), 1997. Photograph by Robert Desjarlais.

some tea. Soon his son and daughter were playing by my side while their mother prepared a morning's meal of rice and lentils on a kerosene-fueled stove. The sweet scent of fried onions lingered in the air.

A few minutes later Mheme climbed the stairs to the third floor from the second, where he lived with his wife and daughter, and sat down on a stoop close to me, his long legs bent before him. With the contours of his skull evident beneath sun-marked skin, he looked older than he had before, though there was still the same vitality in the quick of his eyes. He did not say much, asking simply when I had arrived in Nepal. But as he sat there, he looked at me in a way unfamiliar to me then. There was kindness and amity in his eyes, a gentle appreciation, it seemed, of the sight before him, and a slight smile curved around his lips. His eyes, a rich, dark brown, seemed to welcome and engage me through a communicative link established with the gaze itself. I have to say that I was a bit unnerved by this. I smiled back, but I did not really know how to respond to the steady gaze sent my way, so I looked away, took a sip of tea, and began to chat with Dawa again. No doubt the look's uncommonness in my life explains why I remember it still.

That evening, as I sat alone in a humid hotel room in Boudhanath, I considered the possibility of working with Mheme in order to elicit and record something of his life story. In the morning Dawa brought me to the home of his oldest brother, K. B. Lama, to ask if I might stay in a vacant flat on the top floor of his family's house in Boudhanath. K. B. said that would be fine, then introduced me to his son Norbu Yolmo, a young man who had learned to speak English fluently while attending a boarding school in India. After we talked a bit and Norbu had expressed an interest in helping me to do some research among Yolmo people, I asked him if he would be willing to join me in some conversations with his grandfather. Norbu agreed to do so, in part because he thought this a good opportunity to learn more about his grandfather, whom he did not know well. When the two of us visited Mheme in his home in Chabahil the next day, the old man immediately agreed to our request. By the time I left Nepal a month later multiauthored, co-constructed traces of a life had begun to take form. When I returned to Nepal again in the winter of 1998, a few months after Norbu himself had traveled to New York City in the hopes of furthering his education and earning some money, I renewed my conversations with Mheme, this time with the help of Nogapu Prakash Sherpa, a Yolmo friend previously mentioned, who hailed from the village of Malemchi at the northern edge of Yolmo.

Although Yolmo wa do have some culturally patterned ideas of biographies and life stories, most of which draw from religious hagiographies and political biographies familiar to them, few, if any, would hold that a person possesses, or could readily relate to others, a single "story" of his or her life. So while Yolmo wa often invoke the Nepali term *jīvan kathā,* or "life story," when speaking of such matters, those words convey, much as the word *biography* does in English, more the idea, simply, of a written or oral recounting of an individual's significant doings, travels, and sayings while alive. I think this is more or less what Mheme had in mind when we started to work with him. It quickly became clear, however, that he would not be talking extemporaneously and at length about his life as though recounting artfully formed narratives without prompting. Rather, and as was the case with most other Yolmo wa who related aspects of their lives to me, he seemed to expect that our conversations would build on a protocol of questions and answers, whereby he would respond, sometimes concisely and sometimes at length, to specific questions posed to him. Perhaps he had gathered from previous observations that this was how I sometimes went about my research, or he had spotted mike-wielding reporters interviewing people on television, or, alternately, a complex set of motives and expectations led us to proceed in this manner. In any event, as his daughter Maya served us cup after cup of salt-butter tea and the tape recorder, set on a rickety chair between us, quietly "picked up" traces of our words, Norbu and I, then later Nogapu and I, asked Mheme a range of questions about his life, from memories of childhood to his thoughts about the fate of Yolmo culture.[1] Mheme, usually relaxing cross-legged in the center of his bed with a cup of tea by his side, tried to answer these queries, sometimes with a simple nod of his head and sometimes with great intensity. There were also occasions, especially when I visited Mheme on my own, that he looked at me in ways that compared with that earlier gaze of his.

I would like to consider that gaze further and explore what it and other ways of looking meant for Mheme in his life. Before we do so, however, it is important to think through a few features of the life itself. We need, in short, to gain a sense of what a *tshe,* or "life," meant for him and other Yolmo wa in those years. To do that, we (non-Yolmo readers, at least) have to try to suspend our own culturally patterned assumptions about what a life can entail and glean from Mheme's words what he took a life, any life, to be about. A great deal was involved here, from the beneficial role of religious practice to an understanding of the ways that times of hardship can lead to stretches of comfort. Inherent in all of this, however, were several orientations to time, different "temporalities," as it were, that shaped how Mheme lived through and understood the actions of his life. To begin to understand these temporalities and their significance in the lama's life, we need to learn about specific events: he did this, he went there. We also need to grasp the implications of those deeds as they emerged in time for him and others and the logics of action that underpinned them. This chapter, then, is about the life of a Yolmo man. It is also about time, action, and the effects of action.

My name, Kalsang Singi, was given to me by a lama. But I didn't continue with that name. I just got the name Kānchā [youngest], although my younger brother was born ten years later. But my name still got stuck as Kānchā. After I was born, there were two daughters only, so they thought I was the youngest son. Ten years later, though, there was a brother younger than I, and then I became Māhīlā [second oldest son/brother].

Born in 1916 or so, Mheme was given the *sangi mhin,* the "purification name" bestowed upon him by the Buddhist priest who cleansed him of the spiritual impurities that came with his birth, of Kalsang Singi. After going by the frequently assigned names of Kānchā Lama (Youngest Lama) and Māhīlā Lama (Second Oldest Lama) early in life, he was later known as Ghang Lama, Hill Lama, and, later still, depending on who was doing the knowing, as Thodong Mheme, "Thodong Grandfather," or Chabahil Mheme, "Chabahil Grandpa." The word that often served as a last name, *Lama,* designated him as being from a "Lama family," which itself implied that his father had been a lama, and his father before that; the word *lama* came from the Tibetan *bla-ma,* a composite term that can mean "the higher," "the superior one," or "spiritual teacher";[2] among Yolmo wa it has usually been used of late in reference to householding priests. The appellation "Mheme," meanwhile, means "grandfather" or "forefather." But it is also used in reference to respected male elders. Like many others, I came to call him Mheme Lama, or simply Mheme when in his presence.

Ghang Lama, as Mheme came to be known in public circles, was the second son of a respected lama from the Ningma, or Tseri, Lama lineage, reputedly the oldest of five lama lineages recognized by Lama or Yolmo peoples.[3] Ningma Lamas trace their heritage back to Nga-chang Shakya Zangpo, a deitylike tantric master of superhuman powers who, as Yolmo history now has it, came from Tibet sometime during the sixteenth century C.E. and established a lamaic gompa, or monastery/temple, in Tseri, a hamlet in northeast Yolmo, after helping to restore the chhorten in Boudhanath.[4] From such divine ancestry, authenticated through Buddhist texts that document Nga-chang Shakya Zangpo's deeds in his life as well as through footprints left by him in stone in Yolmo, Ningma Lamas draw much of their prestige and high status. "Say this name anywhere, and people will pay respect to it," Mheme's son Lhatul told me after spelling out his ancestor's name as we sat in his home in Thodong and looked through the brittle, loose-leaf pages of a lama text he owned.

As is the case with the other lama lineages, any man born into this patriline is considered a "lineage lama" *(lama gyipa),* even if he learns little about the lama's craft during his lifetime. The designation differentiates him from any laypersons as well as all so-called common, nonlineage lamas *(mangba lama):* men, that is, who were not born into the role of lama but who nevertheless learned at least some lamaic skills, such as how to read Buddhist texts, and often accompanied and assisted lineage lamas in the oral recitation of such texts at various rituals.[5] When asked if the respect paid to lamas was the same in his time, Mheme replied,

Yes, but not only in my time. It was also like this from a time very far back, from my grandfather's time on. We are lineage lamas. We are not reading lamas. We're the descendants of a deity. In our case, even if we don't know anything [about the lama work], we're still lamas. We are the family of Nga-chang Shakya Zangpo. Ningma Lamas are from Nga-chang Shakya Zangpo. Other lamas have their own ancestors. When asked, we have to say, "We're Ningma Lama, belonging to Nga-chang Shakya Zangpo," and people know who we are.

"If you would tell us the history of your lineage, it will inspire your disciples," a girl proposes to Milarepa in one of the tales about the great eleventh-century Tibetan mystic. "It will instruct us in how to transform our perceptions."[6] Yolmo men are likewise prone to telling others the history of their lineages, though others sometimes tire of hearing such genealogies. When I told Nogapu about a Yolmo man's recital to me of his patrilineal heritage back to several generations of nobility in Tibet, he replied, "That guy is always talking like that, 'We're from the family of princes!'"

It was not by chance, Mheme understood, that he was born into a lama lineage. He and others took it for granted that the kind of life a person obtained in his or her present life was the result of actions he or she undertook in previous lives. "If we've done *dharma* [spiritually good deeds] in previous lives," he told us, "then we're born into a rich family and have a good life. If we've done bad deeds, we're born into a poor family, and food is hard to come by. If we committed a lot of misdeeds before, then later on we're born into the house of a poor family." In more general terms, this is the principle of karma (or *le,* "work" or "deeds"), as basic and commonsensical to Buddhist peoples as the law of gravity is to others, in which, quite simply, any moral act, good or bad, brings about a correspondingly positive or negative result, either in this or in a future lifetime. The principle, central to Yolmo notions of time and causality, resounded in many aspects of Mheme's life, in his understanding of the moral consequences of actions in a sequence of lives and in his assumption that good comes of good and bad of bad. A person who engaged in acts of merit, he told us, would later reap the benefits of those meritorious acts; crippled or disfigured bodies were the result, he said, of previous sinful actions; a man who did not repay loans in one life would need to work as a servant in the house of his lenders "after being born again."

That logic of consequential action informed Mheme's take on the circumstances of his life. To be born not just a man but into a lama family within the Ningma lineage indicated that Mheme, or, more precisely, the person that Mheme "was" before his present incarnation, had acted in morally good ways and most likely had done "a lot of dharma," in the course of previous lifetimes. In turn, the idea that many lives preceded his present life and that other rebirths would follow it gave a certain spin to the lama's thoughts and shaped the projects of his life. "Our lives are like links in a chain, and we wander from one to the other," a Tibetan author once observed in speaking of the cyclic existences with which sentient beings must contend.[7] Mheme similarly assumed that his present life was but one link in a lengthy chain, with the various deeds undertaken in one link having consequential, ripplelike effects in later segments. When asked how his life would be different if he had been not been born the son of a lineage lama, he replied,

I don't know what would have happened. The gods make the births. Still, I can say that if we do dharma, we'll be in a better position in the next life than the one we have in this one. One will be born a more important man than he is today. If one does dharma, one can be born into the family of kings, one can be very, very rich, one can be a very important lama and live in a rich place. If one sins, one will not be able to wear good clothes. This is what happens if one sins a lot.

Such understandings, shared by other Yolmo wa, gave credence to the high status that came with his position in life. They also underscore a person's need to do dharma and virtuous, merit-producing deeds in his or her present life, for it is only by undertaking such deeds that he or she can assure a good rebirth in any next life. The ultimate goal that Yolmo wa strive for is "to become enlightened" (sang gyegen), much as Sange Shakyamuni, the Buddha Siddhārtha, did, and thereby stop the flow of karmic action in that person's life altogether and so bring an end to the suffering and troublesome desires that such temporalities entail. Once a person attains enlightenment, Yolmo wa understand, he or she can step outside *khorwa,* the continuous *sansāric* cycle of rebirths and re-deaths, and no new rebirths follow. But since such a enlightened state can usually be attained only after several lifetimes of devout spiritual practice, most Yolmo wa aim for the more reasonable goal of a good re-birth in a human body in any next life. That new life is a direct manifes-tation of actions undertaken in the lives preceding it.

Yolmo historical accounts tell us that, after settling in Tseri, Nga-chang Shakya Zangpo did not marry and had no children. After he died, how-ever, there were several successive incarnations of him within the Yolmo region, and these later incarnations married and had children. In time, many of the sons of the sons of the reincarnations of Nga-chang Shakya Zangpo, Ningma Lamas all, left Tseri and its neighboring hamlets, dis-persing to different parts of Yolmo. By the twentieth century lamas who identified themselves as belonging to the Ningma lineage, and hence the "brothers" of other Ningma Lamas, could be found in different parts of Yolmo, especially in the hamlets around Tseri and in the forested foothills in the western and southwestern edges of the region. While tensions within a family sometimes led a son or brother to move on to a new vil-lage and establish a life there, in those years lineage lamas most often moved away from their family's lands when asked by Lama or Tamang peoples to relocate to villages where there had been no "born lamas" be-fore. This was the case with Mheme's father, Najang Lama, who moved, while still quite young, from Norbugang, a hamlet just south of Tseri, to Gomden, a hamlet composed of a set of houses inhabited mostly by Tamang families, along the southwestern edge of the Yolmo region. The residents of Gomden, finding themselves in need of a lama who could conduct rites on their behalf, bought Najang Lama's services by giving him lands in exchange for his services as a lama. He accepted the offer, built a home on fertile lands in Gomden, and engaged in "lama work" on behalf of his newly established *jhinda,* his "sponsors" or "donors," in Gomden and the villages surrounding it while also maintaining ties with sponsors of the Ningma lineage in villages farther north.[8] As was the cus-tom then, the sponsors supported the lama by financing the construction of a gompa, or temple, in Gomden and periodically offering foods and monies to him and his family. The lama, in return, bestowed blessings and performed rites on the sponsors' behalf, including cremation and fu-neral rites when members of their families died.

Najang Lama, Mheme's father, soon married Pasang Gyalmu, a woman from his native village, with that marriage producing three daughters and three sons, the second being Ghang Lama. The first son died around 1954, while the youngest still lives in Gomden, on lands once owned by his father. Of the daughters, Mheme's three sisters, the youngest died in the 1950s ("She got sick, and she died"), and the oldest died at the age of seventy-five, just a few years before the time of our conversations ("She was sick, and she fell down a flight of stairs, and she died"). The middle sister, still alive and well at that time, had at the age of eleven gone to live in a palace inhabited by one of the Rana families that then ruled Nepal. Eventually she married a minister in the Rana government. When the Ranas lost power, she had to flee with her husband to the Terai region of southern Nepal. "I didn't see her for some thirty, thirty-two years," Mheme told us in 1997. "I met her again last year." She came to visit her brother again in the spring of 1998, offering as gifts sacks of rice from the Terai. An elegantly dressed woman who remembered little of the Yolmo language, she spoke, in a refined Nepali, of a son who had become a doctor and of the difficulties of growing old in an inflationary economy.

The home Mheme shared with his brothers and sisters when they were children was a small, one-room structure made of stone and mud walls, a wooden door, and wooden window frames and shutters. Like most houses then, it was roofed with an interweave of thatched grass. Most of the family's activities within it centered around a hearth, where a fire was kept and where Pasang Gyalmu cooked meals that featured foods of different tastes and textures: curried potatoes, corn meal stirred into a paste, lentils, greens, boiled nettles, pan-fried breads, wheat flour mixed with tea, wild mushrooms, ground millet meal, egg soup, buffalo and goat milk, curd, butter, fermented beer, chicken and buffalo meat, and rice on special occasions. While his mother kept busy tending to household duties, his father worked fields of maize, potato, millet, and wheat, traveled on occasion to distant places, and performed lamaic rites on behalf of his sponsors. As Mheme told it, Najang was a respected, hardworking lama-farmer who had little patience for foolish or harmful deeds. "My father was a hard man," Mheme told us when asked what his parents were like.

He was hard [stern, tough]. People said he was a hard man, but his heart was good. People also said that he was a good man, my father. He would advise people, "Don't act like this. Don't talk like this. Don't fight with others. Don't quarrel with others. Don't harm others."

"As far as I was concerned, I never talked back to him, I never shouted at him," said Mheme when asked how his father treated him. "Even when he would scold me, I would just keep quiet and listen, so he wouldn't do anything to me. But others would talk back, and sometimes my father would hit them."

When the lama spoke of his father his tone was quiet and respectful.

I was always going with my father, ah! I was going to the *ghewa* [funeral rites] with him as well. The other two [brothers], they were running away from that. They didn't want to go with our father, so they would run away and hide. I was always going with my father. I didn't want to leave him alone.

I was given the blessing [from him]. He also taught me the lama work, "This is this, this is that," inside the *chhe* [religious writings]. They [my two brothers] didn't stay with us. They didn't learn any religious doctrine. They can maybe only read "ka-kha" [the *abc*'s].

Different sons enacted different projects in life, with different *phal*, or "fruits," resulting from those projects.

Along with accompanying his father at various lamaic rites, Mheme was also put to work looking after his father's herd of water buffaloes, from the age of five on.

They [my parents] did the farming work. My father had a lot of water buffaloes, and I would look after the buffaloes. I used to cut grass [to feed them], and look after the buffaloes. Before, it was like that. It was like that before [in the past].

He said he started to learn to do this work from five or six years of age. "Then I really started working at the age of nine, ten." The increased workload signaled a transition from the first general stage of Mheme's life, that of being a child, to the second, that of being an unmarried youth. Among Yolmo wa these transitions are not sharp ones, nor are they marked by any ceremonial rites of passage, as they are in Hindu communities in South Asia; with time boys and girls simply come to take on increased responsibilities and new roles and identities in life. Asked what his daily routine was then, Mheme answered, "First, I had to read [lamaic texts]. Then I had to go and graze the cattle, then come back and eat a meal, and again I went to graze the cattle, and then, when evening came, I had to get the cattle back home. Then I would eat some food and go to sleep." While he also "worked in the fields, sowed maize, potatoes" when needed, his "duty" was to graze the cattle. He did not mind this work, however, finding that it was "the easiest job," because "one didn't have to work." A boy or girl merely had to guide the animals out to green pastures, keep an eye on them as they chewed on leaves and stems of grass, perhaps lie down in soft grass and whistle a folk song or two, then corral the beasts home by nightfall. The responsibility, he was saying, was one of *kyipu,* of "comfort" and ease. There were no loads to be carried, no steep bluffs to climb.

Mheme, long-legged himself, told his grandson Norbu and me that his father was quite strong, bigger than Mheme even. "The people of those days were very strong. And talking, he was very good at talking, like your uncle Lhatul." Mheme's mother, Pasang Gyalmu, also from the village of Norbugang, was also quite tough: "Ooh, she would carry a heavy sack full of rice from Gomden to Thodong when she was seventy years old."

"What was your mother like?"

"My mother was very skinny. She was Sarma Omu [the daughter of a Sarma Lama]. Sarma [from the Sarma Lama lineage]."

"Was she a hard woman? Would she quarrel with others?"

"No. She wasn't like that. She never fought with others. She didn't know how to quarrel."

Four years older than her husband, Pasang Gyalmu was quite stern, her son recalled. "She was usually stern with the children. Now, I've forgotten many things; it's already been sixty years or more. Now it's almost sixty years since she died." Memories fade in time.

When Mheme was nineteen or so he married Phurbi Lama, a woman seven years his senior from the village of Thodong. The age difference was not unusual, for Yolmo men often married women older than they. Before marrying, Phurbi had worked as a *keṭini,* or "house-girl," in a Rana palace in Kathmandu, as many other young women from Yolmo did at the time. Finding, as Mheme put it, that "it was better than staying in the village," women would journey to Kathmandu, usually accompanied by male relatives, in search of employment in the "palaces" of Rana families, the most powerful of which then dominated Nepal in tyrannical ways. "What the women would do," he explained, "is that, if they heard about women being wanted in certain palaces, then they would go directly to Kathmandu with their men. If the Ranas approved of the girl, she would stay in the palace. If they said no, she would go straight back to the village. In those days they used to keep more girls in the palace, but there are still [Yolmo] women working in the present king's palace.... They used to think the work in the palace was quite easy—it was like looking after the king and queen's children. Just as people now go to America to work as a babysitter, they used to do the

same work in the palaces." To many women these were positions of relative comfort, quite unlike the difficult labors young women could expect to encounter if they remained in the villages.

Phurbi Lama resided in a palace for a year or so, but she "closed" that
work after she married. "She had returned to the village because she got
sick," Mheme explained.

Then we got married, and she never went back. She was sick, and the Ranas
themselves sent her to the village, and after she got well, she could have gone
back to work, but she didn't because she got married.

"It was an arranged marriage," he said when asked. "We had talked
before, and afterward we went in procession to Thodong to get the
girl." His words implied that the marriage was not one of the "capture
marriages" common in that time, in which a group composed of the
groom's family and friends would "pounce on and grab" the woman desired as a wife, then forcibly bring her back to the groom's home.
"Those kind of marriages are nothing but trouble," the lama told us.
"People can get quite angry, and fights can break out. It's much better
when people come with *shalgar* [a ritual offering in the form of a container of liquor] and ask the girl's parents for her."

The couple first lived in Gomden, in a small house next to Mheme's
father's. But because Phurbi Lama's parents had no sons of their own
and spent much of their time tending to livestock, they asked the two to
move to Thodong so that the couple could help farm the lands Phurbi's
parents owned and contribute to the shepherding of livestock in the
woods and pastures north of Thodong. The two agreed to this and soon
had resettled in Thodong, which was composed then, much as it is now,
of a half dozen mud-and-stone homes huddled along the wind-free
sides of a scraggy, knoll-like ridge. The village's position atop that ridge
soon led people to call the lama newly residing there Ghang Lama,
"Hill Lama," the lama who lived on the hill. From when he moved there
to when he left several decades later, Ghang Lama was the senior lama
in Thodong. There has never been a proper gompa built in Thodong,
however, most likely because so few people have lived there.

Threaded along the top of the ridge is a narrow foot road that winds
its way from south to north, and there always seems to be a slow trickle
of farmers, trekkers, porters, schoolteachers, development workers, and
mendicants passing through Thodong to parts elsewhere. The place is
usually quiet, with the most marked sounds being the call of a rooster,

winds rushing past, a farmer's shout to a wayward animal, or the music and news reports transmitted by battery-powered radios. Just to the south lies a forest that people enter daily in search of firewood for household hearths and leaves to feed water buffaloes. To the north are more open fields, with Gulphubanjang down the road a bit, then Kutumsang over the next hill. Along both sides of the road, set below the houses a bit, are steeply terraced patches of land owned and farmed by local residents. The terraces, carved into the hillsides, quickly descend into valleys to the east and west (see figure 2). Hand-led water buffaloes are used to plow coffee-brown soils, which are suited best for crops of potatoes, maize, millet, and radishes.

Along with working on his in-laws' share of these lands, Mheme spent months on end in the mountain forests and pastures north of Thodong, where he stayed in various *ghore*, temporary shelters made of bamboo poles and mats, while looking after the family's herds of sheep, water buffaloes, and *dzomo*, which are female hybrids produced by crossing domesticated yaks *(Bos grunniens)* with a species of cow *(Bos indicus)* common to the lower valleys of Nepal and are valued for the rich butters and cheeses that can be made from their milk.[9] By his count he stayed for eight years in a shelter set up by his father-in-law. "What did I do? I looked after the dzomo, gathered wood, collected grass for the calves. That's it." While the work was straightforward enough, it required a lot of gritty labor with brute and smelly animals while living alone in makeshift huts in muddy, leech-ridden forests.

His efforts were soon rewarded. "I came to Thodong because my wife's parents had no children," he told us. "So I lived there. In this way I lived in the shelters as well. I built some of those shelters. No one else was there. I took care of everything, the house and all the land, so my father- and mother-in-law put the land in my name. Then I got the land." The sentences preceding these words went as follows: "We didn't come to Thodong with my father's property. We left all that land [in Gomden]." He earned what he received from his in-laws, that is, and, unlike his brothers, he did not simply take possession of the lands his father once owned.

The lands transferred to him were some of the most valued in the area of Thodong, for they contained fertile terraces leading up to a flat pitch of land where a house could easily be built. On that land the lama and his family built a succession of houses through the next few decades, breaking down an old one when it became too decrepit, then erecting a new incarnation close to it. Their architecture was similar:

Figure 2. Thodong as seen from the south, 1998. Photograph by Robert Desjarlais.

stone and mud walls, wood doors and wooden window shutters, a loft-like attic, wooden bed frames, a hearth set into a hard, claylike floor, shelves for pots and pans. While the first homes were roofed with thatches of bundled grass, the later structures were covered with aluminum siding purchased and portered up from the Kathmandu Valley. Nogapu recalled to me that, when he was a young boy and traveling through Thodong with his father, he was greatly intrigued by the shiny new roof on Ghang Lama's home, the first he had seen to that day.

Mheme also did a lot of "lama work" in the early years of his marriage. Most of this merit-producing work consisted of religious rites that combined tantric practices, contemplative visualizations, and the oral reading of sacred Tibetan texts. "I began the lama work in Gomden, because my father used to teach me. Slowly, I started to do it on my own, and then that *pūjā* [ritual] work was done in Thodong." He also traveled extensively to other villages to conduct rites on behalf of families who lived there. While many of these families composed the sponsors cultivated by his father and grandfather, in time additional families in Thodong and neighboring hamlets came to identify themselves as sponsors of Mheme's Ningma lineage. The majority of his travels were long journeys on foot to join with other lamas in performing the cremation and funeral rites that needed to be done in order to assure a good rebirth for a recently deceased person. "Eh! I went to many, many places," he told us.

I didn't stay in my house. I needed to go very far away, to Chhubar, to Phading, ah! from far away they called me for the dead person [to perform the cremation and funeral rites on that person's behalf]. At that time I wasn't yet thirty-five or thirty-six. I did the lama [work]. I went there as a lama. Before I married I worked as a lama. We needed to go day after day. There wasn't one free day. I was strong then, so I didn't feel anything. Now, if someone comes to call me, I feel lazy and pained. How can I go up there [to the Yolmo region]? I don't even go to places close to here. When they called during the rainy season, we needed to go in the rain and pass through the leeches. With the ghewa [funeral rites], they had the fixed time [which made it easier, because those rites could be scheduled to be performed after the rainy season ended]. But when there's a dead person [who requires cremation rites], we can't say then, "We're not coming. It's the rainy season."

The seasons set the pace of action and sensation in Thodong. In the summer months, when monsoon rains soaked everything, crops grew quickly, the fields were a rich green, the woods teemed with leeches, illnesses lingered, people traveled less, and dense fogs enveloped the village. In the winter months snows could fall, cold winds chilled exposed flesh, and family members warmed themselves by sitting close to hearth fires with warm cups of tea in their hands. In the fall and spring the air was fresh, trade was brisk, the sun lit up the skies, and the sheer white summits of the Himalayas could be seen to the north and east. When the *shugu mendo,* the flowers of the paper tree, were in bloom, Mheme said, he and others could smell their pleasant aroma. The cries of forest animals could be heard at night. "The deer could be heard shouting, and sometimes the leopards and mountain lions as well."

The lama also traveled outside the Yolmo region on several occasions. Along with numerous trips by foot to and within the Kathmandu Valley, he went to lands that must have been quite new and exciting to him. He went to Calcutta once—"I went with my older sister. She took me there, because her husband was out there. I went there just to roam"—and then, in 1939 or so, when he was close to thirty, he went to "Burma."[10] Sometime just before or during the Second World War, "when India and Japan were at war with each other," he and other Yolmo men were hired by the Indian government to work as civilian laborers on the construction of roads and bridges in Burma. "Our people gathered and did the coolie work," he told us, "and we had lodging, food, all facilities. Japan and India were always fighting with each other. From Malemchi and everywhere else, they went to Burma. Their government gave all the clothes and sandals, they would give us a pair or two. We had to stay in the forests, in tents. Sometimes the work was hard, sometimes it wasn't. We had to construct a road alongside steep mountains. I stayed in Burma for five or six months, then I came back. When the war ended they sent everyone back home. If the war had continued, we wouldn't have been able to return."

"Did you like the work in the military?"

"I don't know if I liked it or not. But we got free food, so I should say I liked it. We had so much food we could throw it [away]. We used to get tin foods—like the ones you people [Americans] eat. Canned buffalo meat, canned fish. Oh, there was so much!"

"Did you have to train?"

"No, there was no training. We just sat and ate, that's all we did."

"What work did you do?"

"We had to unload things, when things were brought in. Trucks used to come with sacks of rice. That was our work, to unload those things."

But the actions of his employers annoyed him. He and other men had to suffer the criticisms and invectives of their handlers, ungracious men by Yolmo standards, most likely lower-ranking members of the Indian army. When asked if he ever considered taking a salaried job, he replied, "No. After my stay in the army, I promised myself that I would never work under salary. We had to bear [obey] what they said, especially when we spoiled the work a little [made minor mistakes]. My mother and father never scolded me. But they [my superiors] scolded me. Since then, I never wanted to stay [in the army] like that."

Farming and grazing cattle, in contrast, were tasks that enabled him to proceed in ways that he thought best, without a commanding voice in his ear. He had also received respect and gratitude for his work as a skilled lama.

In time the lama's wife gave birth to four children: first a son, Karpu Lama, who later adopted the name K. B. Lama; then a daughter, named Karsang Lhamu; and then two more sons: Lhatul Lama, then Dawa Lama, also known as Kānchā Lama. Having married and having become a father, Mheme had entered into the third general stage of his life, that of an adult householder. With those changes came a number of responsibilities and worries that he had not faced as a youth. Before marrying, Yolmo wa say, a man's life is one of lighthearted freedom. After he marries and fathers children, there is nothing but worry. "Before one marries, it's not bad. There are happy moments," Mheme told Norbu and me when asked about a person's worries in life. "One goes with friends, roaming about—that time is pleasant, without any hardships. After one marries, it's hardship upon hardship. After one marries, one has children, one has to give them good food, give them clothes. Isn't that a worry?" Some of the man's concerns centered on his children's futures. When asked what worries a father might have for his sons and daughters, he said, "For a daughter, you have to worry about how you're going to marry her and send her away [to her husband's house]. For a son, you have to worry about whether or not he will be able to do something with his life."

When his two youngest sons were still very small, Mheme's father passed on at the age of sixty-eight. The lama faced another tough loss three years later, when his mother died at the age of seventy-four. His wife's parents died around then as well. Two other departures took place a few years later, when his first son, then the second, "ran away" from home with friends in search of employment in India. It was more or less a custom then for young Yolmo men to leave their parents' homes in search of work when they were around twelve or thirteen, often with the blessing of their elders, so that they could earn some money as well as "see something of the world," as Karma Gyaltsen once put it, much as young men and women from Yolmo now try to seek their fortunes in places like New York City. The Buddha Siddhārtha, after all, fled from his father's palace, and many a Tibetan lama had left his parent's home to undertake a life of merit.[11]

What troubled Mheme about his sons' absence was that in 1964 or so, while two of them were in India, his wife Phurbi, then fifty-four, died after falling seriously ill. Along with the sheer grief felt with this loss—"I felt sorrow for three, four years. When my father died, I also felt sorrow like that"—the lama's hardship was compounded by his two elder sons' absence. With his youngest, Dawa, still quite small, Mheme was left to manage the household and farming work on his own. "Now for two or three years, perhaps, I faced hardships," he said in a raspy voice when asked about this. "Now, there was no one, there was no one in the house. People came to visit, plus I had livestock [to tend to]."

He spoke of this on several occasions, as though probing an old wound to the self: "When your father went to India," he said to Norbu, "and for so many years he didn't return, and his mother died, his [mother] and even your uncle Lhatul weren't there at that time [when his mother died]. Only Dawa and I were there." Then, when Dawa himself was in his teens, he too left for India, joining his oldest brother at a construction site, where they worked as manual laborers. "All my sons went to India. I was alone," he told Nogapu and me.

Nobody was with me then. They had all left. I was living there alone. The two older brothers went quite before then, and Dawa went later on. My wife had died. They came back a year later. At the time I was staying alone. So many Tamang people would come and ask, "Will you come to the Tamang villages [to perform lamaic rites]?" So do I go to the Tamang villages, or do I look after the animals? Sometimes I had to close the doors of my house for a long time. It was a desperate situation then....It was a desperate situation. We had many animals. Grass had to be cut [to feed them]. So many troubles.

He told us on several occasions of the troubles he had had in those days: he had worked terribly hard; he had toiled in the rain and cold; he had traveled long distances barefoot; he had worn tattered clothes; he had carried heavy loads; and then, when his first wife died, he had struggled alone to maintain his lands and household. "I can say that I've had a lot of *dhukpu* in my life." *Dhukpu* is a Yolmo word (*dukha* is its Nepali equivalent) that, depending on the context, can variably mean "suffering," "sorrow," "hardship," "misfortune," "difficulties," or "hard work." The word contrasts sharply with the "happiness," "joy," or "comfort" designated by the word *kyipu* in Yolmo (*sukha* in Nepali). To say he had a lot of dhukpu in life was to hold that he had faced a lot of hardships and had done a great deal of hard work. Whereas other families faced worries over money and sometimes wanted for food, what troubled him and his wife most, he said, were hardships of the body: heavy loads, tired muscles, sore feet. "Money was not a problem for me, at least. Even if we didn't have money, we could eat. What troubled me more was dhukpu of the body.... That's to say, we often had to carry things, to travel in order to buy things. From that there was hardship."[12] Hardships came with other toils as well:

We had to carry the lumber from the forests up above Kutumsang. At that time, where were the shoes and sandals? We had to walk a lot on top of stones. We had to go early in the morning and return home the same day. I faced a lot of hardship then.

I did a lot of hard work. I faced a great deal of hardships. Lhatul's mother died when she was fifty-four. When she was fifty-four.

Carrying heavy loads, building houses by hand, walking barefoot in the forests, wading through rain-swept rivers, shirking leeches and illnesses, bracing against the cold of winter, tending to livestock, farming steeply terraced fields, toiling every day just to eat, collecting firewood and fodder day after day—hardships of this sort, his words implied, were more or less suffered by other members of his generation, and he and his peers often said as much when talking to those younger than they. But these hardships were generally not thought to be encountered by many within his grandchildren's generation, most of whom were able to attend school, eat good food, wear good clothes and shoes, and avoid the gritty physical labors associated with carrying loads. "Today's children haven't done any hardships," he told his grandson and me. "We have seen a lot of hardships. The children of today were in India [in boarding schools], they didn't do anything. We carried loads!"

Other men and women of Norbu's generation told me that they have heard much the same from their parents and grandparents. Such talk is in accord with one of the main tenets of Buddhism, that life is suffering, as the Buddha's First Noble Truth has it. Some elders apparently stress the hardships of their lives, because that is what they understand life to be about and because the means of their lives have in fact been quite onerous. Some also do so with the idea of conveying the principle to others who might not know well what life ultimately has in store for them. Yet another reason for concerns about the absence of suffering among the children of today is the value that many Yolmo wa find in physical hardships, for the world is such that hardships and hard work often lead to good things later on. People also contend that it is especially important for young people to face trying circumstances early on in life, because those hardships can toughen them up and prepare them for the inevitable difficulties of life. A person needs to "know dhukpu," it is said. "If you don't know about dhukpu, it's not good. One needs to know dhukpu," Lhatul once told me when talking about two youths who, as he saw it, knew too little about the ways of the world.

Mheme perhaps came to know sorrow most in the months following his wife's death. His niece Phur Gyalmu told us that, while he used to drink "the most *chhang* [fermented beer]," he stopped drinking soon after his wife died: "She went to heaven, and from then on he quit the chhang, he quit the *raksī* [liquor]." The understanding that emerged from Phur Gyalmu's words was that, once his wife died, Mheme had to contend with a great deal more work than he previously had to and no longer had time for the luxuries of drinking.[13] "At that time," Phur Gyalmu went on to say of Phurbi Lama before her death, "she used to do all the work, everything. She did all the housework—ah, so much!" After Phurbi Lama died, her husband faced the double hardship of bereavement and heavy work.

To lessen the troubles that came with his wife's death, Mheme remarried two years later, when he was fifty, finding a suitable partner in Rhidu Pema, a woman eleven years younger than he, whose first husband had died years before. Such marriages are common among those who have lost a spouse, although it is a bit frowned upon for women to remarry, especially the wives of lineage lamas. From Kulu, a village on the far western side of the Yolmo region, Rhidu Pema had three sons and two daughters from her first marriage, all of whom died, except for one daughter who was living in India. "The daughter that is living is married," explained Rhidu Pema. "She has children, and those children have children now. We heard that she is somewhere in the northern part of India, in Himachal Pradesh."

"Why did you decide to marry her?" Norbu once asked his grandfather.

"Why? All my sons went to India. I was alone. I was alone."

"Were there any other reasons?"

"I was alone. Your father and your father's brothers went to India."

A man could not run a household on his own. When I asked Lhatul about this second marriage, he replied, "My father had to have someone to prepare his food, so he remarried." I later learned that, while Rhidu Pema was attending a funeral in Thodong with several relatives of hers, friends of Mheme's encouraged him to "take" her as a wife.

"How did you come to marry her?" Nogapu and I asked the old man later on.

"How did we marry? We married."

Upon hearing this, Rhidu Pema, seated by Mheme's side, laughed and said in a bashful way, "Why do you have to talk about that?!"

Yolmo wa usually do not talk about such private matters, especially with people younger than they or outside their immediate family. After I mumbled something about the need to know such things, I asked if the marriage was an arranged one.

"She had come to Thodong," Mheme replied, "and I kept her."

"When you took her as a bride, did you go to her place [respectfully], with [a ritual offering of] shalgar?"

"Yes, I went. We have to go."

"Did her family approve of the marriage?"

"Why not? She was already getting old."

Four years after they married—a rebirth, of sorts, for both—Rhidu Pema gave birth to their daughter, Ang Maya, now a quick-thinking, straight-talking woman who, as yet unmarried, lives with and cares for her aged parents.

Mheme continued with the lama work during the first years of Maya's life. When asked if a lama's work caused hardship, he replied, "The work is difficult, for certain. Whatever we lamas are doing in our homes today, people can come and call us. Then we have to go."

"They have to go for nine, ten days," his wife noted.

"We have to go as soon as they call us. Even during the monsoon, or if it's snowing."

"If it's raining, if it's snowing . . ."

"If someone dies during *losar* [the New Year festivities], we have to go even then. In Yolmo, it's difficult. But here [in Kathmandu], it's not."

"Is it troublesome for a lama's family when he goes to do the lama work?"

"Oh-oh! Trouble comes to us, for sure," Rhidu Pema responded.

"Sometimes," Mheme added, "we have to go for a whole month."

"Sometimes we worry about what happens."

"One day there's one man dead in one place. The next day there's another man dead in another place. Sometimes we don't have any free time. We're never free."

As Mheme grew older and entered into the fourth and final stage of his life, that of a grandfatherly elder, a "Mheme," in short, he stopped performing rituals at the homes of sponsors. "I quit it nearly twenty years ago," he said of this work. "Later, I wouldn't go far away or to the Tamang villages. I would only go to places very close to my house. Before, when I was strong, I never felt sore or lazy. Later I lost my strength. The people would come to call me, and I would get a little afraid. I couldn't go. I was getting pained of going. Sometimes I had to go in the rain, and I had to cross rivers." When he left this work, his sons performed rites on behalf of his sponsors. "After me, my children were doing it," he told us. He then added with a laugh, "But they were lazy. They didn't go. Others were sent instead."

Around 1980 the lama gave to his three sons equal shares of the land he owned in Thodong and moved with Rhidu Pema and their daughter, Maya, to a house in a Chabahil, a bustling, polyethnic neighborhood on the northeastern edge of Kathmandu, about a mile west of Boudhanath. Mheme's first daughter, who by then had moved to Kathmandu with her husband, initially bought the house but then registered it in his name as well as hers. "I had to come down [to Kathmandu] in order to sign some papers, and I've been staying here since," he told us. While these and other words of Mheme's suggested that landlordlike duties as well as an inability to work as he once could in Thodong had led him to decide to remain in Kathmandu, as Maya told it the main reason they came to live in the city was that it could offer more comfort than Thodong ever could. "You came here for comfort. For comfort," she said in contradicting what her father had just said.

As such, the move from village to city coincided with, and perhaps even conveyed in tangible, geographic form, a transition from a predominance of hardship in Mheme's first fifty years or so to a predominance of comfort in his later years. Whereas he had to work a great deal in Thodong, he could just "stay like this" while living in Kathmandu, without worrying about where his family's next meal might come from. "What hardships are there to speak of now?" he responded when asked what kind of hardships he faced in Kathmandu. "I don't have to work, just stay and eat." There were sensate qualities to the change; after bracing for heavy loads and working calluses into his skin, he could rest, with a soft pillow to sleep on and plenty to eat. When asked whether it was his *sodi*, or "fortune," to have hardship or comfort in his life, he answered, "It must have been fated that I would have the dhukpu of hard work at first, because I had to do a lot of work. Later on comfort must have been fated, because now there is comfort."

Many Yolmo wa would prefer it this way: if one is to have both hardship and comfort in one's life, many hold that it is better to face hardships in one's early years, then joyful comforts later on. "Which is better, to have hardships first, then comfort, or comfort, then hardships?" I asked Mheme's niece Phur Gyalmu when we spoke about her life in 1998.

"First hardships, then comfort," was her response.

"Why is that better?"

"First, when one is strong, one should suffer hardships. Later, when one is old, one should have comfort."

Along with making practical sense, Phur Gyalmu's line of reasoning would make intuitive sense to many Yolmo wa. The amount of hardship and comfort faced by an individual or a family through the years is the measure of many a Yolmo life, and most lives are understood to bear amalgams of kyipu-dhukpu, "joys and sorrows." A good life is most often one in which hardships bear fruit in some way, such that something is made out of nothing or more out of less. "It's good to have hardships early," Lhatul said when speaking of the two youths who had yet to know dhukpu well. "Then later, things improve." He said the last words—literally, "Then later things get higher"—while looking into my eyes and raising his hand a few inches higher. When one has hardships sooner than later in life, his words and hand gesture implied, one's lot in life has a way of improving. Much the same sentiment can be heard in a proverblike piece of advice that parents like to weigh out to their children. "Dhongle dhukpu bhenaga, tingle kyipu onge" (If at first hardships are encountered, then later comfort comes). Such an orientation to time and matter, a logic of increase, really, informs many different practices enacted within the span of a life for the purposes of improving the conditions of that life or the next, from healing rites that work to augment a person's "luck" in life, to lamaic rites that add to one's store of "merit," to blessings sung at festivals. One song has it,

Auspiciousness, come,
good fortune, come,
good luck, increase only,
do not decrease,
more and more,
do not decrease.

The same expectations apply to those youths who "run away" from their parents' home, since everyone knows they have to come back with more than what they left with or make their lives better in some way. Nogapu and other Yolmo men told me that when they left home in their teens they understood they could not return until they had some money in their pockets. If their pockets were empty, they would feel ashamed upon returning, even fearful at times, since they knew of some parents who had slapped or "beaten" their sons for returning home without anything to show for their efforts. Such themes recurred in the 1990s. When

I suggested to Norbu, on the eve of his departure to the States in 1997, that he could consider returning home in a year or less, he replied, "No. I have to wait until I finish something. I can't return until something good has happened." As of 2001, he was still biding his time. After Norbu had left Nepal, I asked his grandfather what he thought of Norbu's trip to America. "What do I think?" Mheme replied. "I think he should come back having done good, of course, and that he should return before I die. He should also make sure that he doesn't carry blame [for having done something wrong]." He said much the same about his own sons. When asked what time in his life he had the most worries, he answered, "It was always the same. The worries were always the same. When my children were in India, for instance, I used to worry whether they would do well and come back, or not do well."

His sons did do well. After working for several years in India and saving up a substantial amount of capital, Lhatul and Dawa returned to Nepal, married Yolmo women, and built homes for themselves in Gulphubanjang, a well-kept, windswept village, populated by Gurung, Tamang, and Yolmo families, that lay a few minutes' walk north of Thodong, along a foot-road that led to lands higher up. It was in Gulphubanjang, where I conducted fieldwork in the 1980s, that I came to know the two well. Both were respected as wealthy, knowledgeable, kind-hearted lamas. Lhatul struck many as a witty, "smooth-talking" businessman who enjoyed life a great deal. Dawa, a quieter presence than his brother, was said by his father to have become quite skillful in "the lama work." In 1989 Dawa's wife, Norki, gave birth to a daughter named Tshering. When Norki gave birth to a son in 1992, it was decided that Tshering would live with Lhatul and Mingmar, who did not have any children of their own. In 1995 or so Lhatul sold his house in Gulphubanjang, returned to Thodong, and built, on the level lands once farmed by his father, an expansive home and guesthouse. "Thodong Lama Lodge" beamed the sign that welcomed exhausted trekkers on their way to higher vistas. The lodge stood just a few feet away from a smaller, older, and now vacant one-room house previously inhabited by his father and stepmother.

The oldest son, K. B. Lama, remained in India for many years after he left his father's home. In those years he returned to Yolmo only sporadically, once to marry Hrikchung Lama, a Yolmo woman from the village of Shomkharka. He and Hrikchung had two daughters and three sons, the last son being Norbu. After serving in the Indian army for several years, K. B. established a successful business as a building contractor and decided to remain in India while his children attended boarding schools there. The family returned to Nepal in the early 1990s and settled into the second floor of a three-story house built on lands, close to the main road in Boudhanath, that K. B. had the foresight to purchase years before. In 1997 and 1998 and again in 2000, years when K. B. was devoting much of his time to lamaic practices, I stayed in a sun-drenched room on the top floor of this building. At night I tried to sleep to the rhythmic thumping of hand-run looms at work in the single-storied carpet factories owned and managed by Norbu's eldest brother, Arjun, set up on the lots surrounding it.

A logic of increase: When I came to know him in 1997, Mheme lived with his wife and daughter in their undistinguished, three-story house in a crowded but quiet neighborhood in Chabahil, about a mile or two west along the main road that runs through Boudhanath. Nepali families rented the rooms on the first floor, while family and friends often stayed on the top floor when visiting. Their home on the second floor was a modest one, containing but three small rooms, each of which was sparsely furnished and decorated, quite unlike the lavish, wealth-signifying interiors found in the homes of his two eldest sons. In the 1990s the difference in generations assumed a directly visible form in Thodong, where Lhatul's ample home stood adjacent to the much smaller dwelling once occupied by his father.

The old man would be the first to admit that his sons were wealthier than he. Their prosperity spoke well of him, for it suggested that he had acted well in his life. When asked, toward the end of our talks together, what the most important feature of his life was, he replied:

What can I say about this? Until now food was available, until now clothes could be found. Until now there was the hardship of work, as I've said—you've already written about those things. It has been good. One's own [children] have become rich, that has been good. That has been the most important thing. . . . My children have done better than me. That is the most important.

When we then asked if he was proud that his children had done better than he had, he answered:

When one's children have done better than oneself, won't one be happy? Even the villagers, the Tamangs, say I must have done a lot of dharma, since all my children are in a better condition than I was. People also say that my brothers' children are not in such a good condition as my children are. So I feel very happy when people say that.

The success of his children, "one's own," indicated that they bore the fruits of his good dharma.[14] His line of reasoning spoke to the interpersonal, intergenerational potential of karmic action, whereby a man's good deeds not only had consequences in his own life or in a future life of his; they could also benefit the lives of his descendants.

All this also had a comparative edge, his words made clear. When asked if it would be a good thing if his grandchildren became rich, he replied, "Rich. Why wouldn't it be good to be rich?"

If they're all rich, they can eat, they can live well. The Tamang, [Yolmo] Sherpa say this: "All of his children have become rich, so he must have done a lot of dharma." The children of my younger brother haven't [become rich], that's for sure. He's just surviving to eat. But he's the son from the same father [as mine].

People acted in certain ways, and those actions had consequences: in contrast with his younger brother, who, in Mheme's eyes, never did dharma and barely had enough to eat, Mheme did a lot of dharma in his life, and he and his children had benefited from such meritorious deeds. One man's history was compared with another's, and one family's prosperity was measured against the wealth of others. "In our society it's comparative, you see. It really matters," Karma Gyaltsen told me when talking about the various successes and disappointments of Yolmo families. The comparisons range from what different sons working in foreign countries send back home to their parents, to how well women and men have prepared for their deaths, to how much a person earns compared with others. When I asked Mheme's niece Phur Gyalmu what kinds of lives she would like to see her children lead, she replied, "My children, may they have a better life, may they earn money in a good way, may they do extremely well with people—that's what's in my heart." She then added the clincher, "May my sons and daughters not suffer, may they surpass others in earnings."

As for Ghang Lama's earnings, appearances alone would have led many to think that he was a financially unprosperous man, at least by 1990s Kathmandu middle-class standards. This was apparently not the case, however. While it was true that his sons were wealthier than he was, he had not done too badly himself. From the considerable interest accrued on monies lent out to Tamang and Yolmo families in the areas around Thodong, he had managed to accumulate a substantial amount of capital, most of which he had invested in further loans. Even early on during his first marriage, he had enough money to loan out to others. "In those times, we had a little money," he told Norbu when asked where their family's wealth came from. "Even your grandmother had brought some money from the [Rana] palace. At that time, one thousand rupees was like one hundred thousand now, so we had a little money, and we could lend it to people." He lent still more later in life, using monies gained from the sale of food, grains, and livestock, and since he had moved to Kathmandu, almost all of his income came from the interest on money lent out to others. "The interest that I'm getting, that's the only income I have in Kathmandu," he told us. "In the village I worked [as well]. I wasn't just lending money all the time. In the village I was working, growing potatoes, maize, but here in Kathmandu the little bit of money I have I lend to people, with interest."

"Where did the money come from?"

"I worked in the village, grew potatoes, maize, and sold them. That way, I made a little money.... Right now, I don't have anything, everything has been loaned out. In the beginning, I brought around ten, fifteen thousand rupees to Kathmandu. Slowly I lent money to others, and it started to increase. In the village as well, I have money with people right now, twenty, twenty-five thousand rupees."

Some people never paid him back what he lent them, however, having "eaten," so to speak, what he had given them. "They say they will give. When people take the money and don't give it back, it feels as if I shouldn't have given at all."

"Will the people pay it back?"

"People who return the money, return it. People who don't return it, don't return it. But Tamangs are especially good at giving the money back. If people don't pay right now, after they die, they have to pay double [in hell]. If they don't pay, they have to pay double after they die. If someone eats someone else's money, he can't succeed in life. He'll become even poorer. The gods will curse him."

If someone acts in morally "straight" ways, however, people will speak well of him and a good name will result. Such was the case with Ghang Lama. He had developed a reputation for being an honest lama who had never cheated anyone while working hard in his life and completing a great deal of merit-enhancing dharma. "He's the most respected in his [extended] family," Karma told me early on, "because he's the oldest and because people haven't known anything bad about him, I think. He's a simple, honest lama."

"He's a lama, and a proud one at that," Norbu said upon looking at a photograph I took of his grandfather.

"That man is good," said a distant cousin of Mheme's, an elderly woman of marginal status who had spent much of her life in India, after looking at the same photograph. When asked why that was, she replied, "He doesn't talk bad, and even if he is rich, he doesn't brag about it or flaunt it."

"It's also important to note that Mheme never drinks," Binod Yolmo noted after reading an earlier version of this chapter. "A lot of lamas get used to drinking a lot, since they are offered a lot of liquor in the villages. But everyone knows that Ghang Lama is always sober."

People speak good of good people and bad of bad. In all, a dominant temporal orientation was at work in Mheme's life and in how he thought and spoke of his life. Time and again something emerged out of nothing, and more was made out of less: born a lama, a fact that itself suggested good fortune, he had done better than his brothers, he had cultivated the patronage of numerous sponsors, he had received the lands of his in-laws after working hard, his money-lending activities had begotten further monies, he had become wealthier later in life, with comfort and happiness taking the place of hardship and sorrow, and his sons, well-respected in their communities, had done better financially than he had. All of this, and the fact that he had lived a long life, attested to his moral and dharmic worth in this and previous lives. Good fortune came, good luck increased only.

And yet another story might, in time, be told about Mheme and his family, one that he and his sons feared might be the main read on them in years to come: skilled and knowledgeable lamas, simply, were in short supply among his grandsons, and it was quite possible that, in the future, not one of Mheme's descendants would be engaged in the lama work. While Lhatul and his wife had no children of their own, K. B. Lama's sons, Norbu and his brothers, had spent their childhood in India. As a result, they could not speak Yolmo, found themselves to be more "Nepali" than "Yolmo" in makeup, and had little interest in learning to become knowledgeable priests, as Mheme, his sons, and his revered ancestors had done. They were therefore "Lama" in name only.[15] Their disinterest in undertaking any lama work struck me as an understandable, even predictable one, given their upbringing and aspirations in life. But their elders would have preferred it otherwise. "It used to trouble me when I was a young teenager, say twelve or thirteen," Norbu said in 1997 of the pressure he felt by his parents to undertake the lama work. "They would tell me that there needed to be at least one lama in the family. I didn't like that. I thought I should be able to choose [what I wanted to do in my life]." In time, he said, he became less bothered by it all. And since his brothers were of similar minds on this, the family's hopes and expectations fell on Dawa's only son, Surje, who was just a boy in 1997. "That's what everyone is saying. Everyone is putting their hopes in Surje," Norbu said when I mentioned this to him then. A month later Dawa's wife, Norki, gave birth to a second son, Sange Lama.

The family's *ijjat,* its "prestige" or "honor" or "good reputation," was on the line.[16] No matter how wealthy the family might become in successive generations, it could lose much of its prestige and high status within the Yolmo community if no one was doing any lama work or studying the dharma. Some might even say that the family had lost its firm rooting in the lama work precisely because it had become so wealthy. I began to learn more about the significance of all this in the course of a conversation among Mheme, Norbu, and myself. Asked if he was afraid that the lamas in his family might be finished, Mheme replied, "Yes, I'm afraid. But even if I'm afraid, what can be done? It's fated, no doubt."

"Don't you think your descendants should continue the tradition?" Norbu then asked.

"Yes, I want that. I've always said that....If you continue the work done by your forefathers, the people will say you have continued the tradition. If you don't do anything, then ours [our heritage] will be forgotten."

"So, why do people say, 'Some things are good or bad'?"

"Well, they'll say that, won't they? You haven't followed your tradition. So they'll say that....People will talk about the things you all do, about what a family is doing. So it's a case of prestige [ijjat]. If you do lama work, then people will say that our family is doing the lama work—and that work will be dharma as well [and so beneficial in itself]."

I then chimed in on my own. "Will Surje continue the lama work? He's the only one left."

"Yes, he has to do it," responded Mheme, who then looked at Norbu, pointed a finger at him, and said: "If you can, even you all must do it. We mustn't forget what our ancestors did."

"Who do you think will continue the work?" I then asked.

"Well, there's Surje. He can do it, but again it's up to him. And Lhatul Lama doesn't have children, and all of the eldest son's children are Nepali."

"So, who do you think will continue?" Norbu followed.

"I don't know. I'll die, and I won't see who is continuing it. Maybe [my son] Dawa will do it while he is alive."

Figure 3. Surje Lama, 1998. Photograph by Robert Desjarlais.

So much remained uncertain, even though it appeared to be fated in some way.

Yolmo selves are temporal beings through and through; their lives proceed within diverse currents of time. Calendric time, mythic time, astrological time, ritual time, meditative time, environmental time, agricultural time, economic time, diurnal time, the time of sleep and dreams, drunken times, festive times, durations of illness and hardship, narrative time, conversational time, remembered times and forgotten times, these and other temporalities, each with its own rhythm and mood, wind their ways through Yolmo days like an array of differently paced timepieces on show in a busy clock shop. Ghang Lama's life was similarly timed. Of the different temporalities that took hold in his life, from the ticking of a wristwatch to the trajectories of his children's futures, several, it seems, were powerfully at work, in distinct but coinciding ways, in how he thought of his life.

Cosmological time. Like the universes of many of its counterparts in South Asia and Tibet, the Yolmo universe includes substantive processes that expand and subside in time. The moon waxes and wanes; each day the sun gains, then dims, in solar power. In the course of their existence, human bodies first increase, then fade, in size and strength. Government regimes rise and fall. Fundamental to such processes is the idea that the world of forms at large proceeds through eras of relative robustness and weakness, with the present period marked by a gradual diminishment of the sun's brightness, the size of human bodies, the maximum age that humans can live to, the practice of the dharma, the quality of ethics. "With this present period," Binod Yolmo explained to me, "it's like we're now in the evening. During the 'afternoon,' it was quite bright, but now we're in the evening period, where things are dimmer, and less....So in general things are decreasing. But then once it reaches the lowest level, another buddha will appear, and then things will increase again." Mheme understood his current life to be situated within the present, degenerative era. He took himself to be born at a time when things were on the wane. People now did not live as long as their forefathers did, their bodies were not as big and strong, many foods did not taste as good as they once did, and people's morals and values were not as refined as they once were. Many lineage lamas also assumed that what men knew about religious matters had gradually diminished through the years because of the incremental losses that had resulted from the generation-to-generation transfers of such know-how.

Historical time. Ghang Lama understood that the strength of his life occurred in a different era from the times known by his children or his grandchildren, with a series of historical events, from the Second World War to the tragic deaths of the king and queen in 2001, affecting the course and circumstances of Yolmo lives. As he and others knew it, the old days, the days of "before," occasioned everything from a different political system from the one in existence today to different technologies (including new modes of timekeeping, such as wristwatches and alarm clocks) to different possibilities for employment, travel, and happiness in life. In relation to this, a historical consciousness often voiced by him and other Yolmo elders had it that life is easier today than it was in their "time." People can earn money more readily; clothes and shoes are easier to come by; children can go to school; and people do not suffer as much as they once did. While I have not heard Yolmo wa put it directly as such, it was as though the hardships suffered by an earlier generation led to good things often taken for granted by later generations. Alongside such perspectives was the melancholic recognition that the past was irretrievable. "Those days are past," Mheme said of his youthful days and the people he knew then. The past was past, memories faded in time, and ancestors eventually became, at most, names in a family's genealogy.

Consequential action. Ideas of hardship and comfort contributed to another, more personal history in the lama's life: while physical hardships had taken priority earlier in his life, comforts cushioned his later years. Inherent in his assessments of those changes was a recurrent "if-then" logic of consequential action. If one worked hard, then good things would happen. If one performed acts of dharma, one's position in life would improve. For Mheme, that temporal logic played itself out most through the medium of his body. The circumstances of his life were such that, while he faced bodily hardships earlier in life, he found a measure of rest and easy living later on.

Bodily time. And yet that same body grew weaker and smaller as time sped on. His body had a temporality of its own; a child grew into a man whose flesh diminished in old age. In his youth the lama was quite strong, and he did not tire even after working long days, but later in life he was no longer able to travel the long distances he once could. He knew that one day his body would cease to function. In death his body would quickly decay unless it was cremated, and its *nam-she,* or "soul," would find its way into another, newly born body.

A life's course. As his body waxed, then waned, and as he took on different responsibilities in life, the lama found himself to be immersed in different life stages. While the act of marriage was the only overt rite of passage that marked the transitions from one stage to another, the sequence more or less matched those common to other Yolmo lives. First a child, then a youth, he became an adult householder after marrying and fathering children, then took himself to be an old man in his later years. Each of these periods in his life brought different labors and responsibilities, different social roles and identities, and different worries and aspirations.

A dharmic career. In each period of his life, Mheme devoted a lot of time and effort to "the lama work" and dharmic deeds in general. After learning in his youth how to conduct the lama work in knowledgeable, skillful ways, he came to perform a wealth of rites on behalf of sponsors. As he knew it, this dharmic career was a highly consequential one, for it helped to bring about prosperity and comfort in his life and the lives of his sons. Then, when his body's strength started to wane and he began to worry about traveling far from home, he devoted much of his time, as many Yolmo elders do, to Buddhist practices that could increase his chances for a good rebirth in his next life.

Karmic action. The idea that additional rebirths and deaths would follow Ghang Lama's present life, much as other rounds of birth and death had surely preceded it, figured, in substantial ways, in the many actions and perspectives of his long life. Good came of good, bad came of bad. Actions undertaken in one life, he knew well, had consequential effects in future lives.

Patrilineal time. A similar air of continuity was imbued in a different sequence of lives: his family's lineage. Here the divine grace incarnated in Nga-chang Shakya Zangpo continued patrilineally, with at least some force, through the centuries, with the right to work and identify as "born lamas" and claims to the high status that came with that birthright being passed in Ningma Lama families from father to son to grandson. That lineage was supported all along by a network of sponsors that, Mheme made clear, was established not in a single lifetime but through the course of several generations. "The jhinda is not made in a day," he told Norbu and me. "It's made in the course of centuries. In our case, the jhinda we have was not made by me, but by my great-great-grandfather or at least by my father's father." In line with this heritage, much of the old man's identity was founded on what his forefathers had done, what he himself had contributed to the family's name, and what his sons and grandsons might in turn do with their lives. (The actions of daughters were not as important in this regard, since it was understood that, in marrying, they came to belong to another family and lineage.) And yet such an intergenerational, interpersonal take on a life, on a series of lives, really, also rendered of great importance the fact that the continuity of Ningma Lamas within his family was threatened by the scarcity of lamas in Mheme's grandchildren's generation.

A family's legacy. When it came to the history of Ghang Lama's family, several swells and ebbs in time were thus at hand. Throughout his adult life Mheme worried over what would become of his children and grandchildren. He did so because he cared greatly for their well-being. But he also knew that their successes and failures would say something about his own actions in life. Two dominant, overlapping temporalities of consequential action shadowed his life and those of his descendants. The most apparent one, building on a logic of increase, was a tale of success, prosperity, and greater prestige, of having more than before. Yet also seeded within the thoughts of family members and others was a story of decrease, of diminished prestige, of a heritage lost, and worries that the future might bring less than the family had before. One "line," as they say in Nepal, was on a par with images of waxing moons and uphill climbs. Another spoke of waning moons and downhill descents.

Different *dhizi,* different "spans of time," thus streamed through Mheme's life. The timing of his days consisted of several coinciding temporalities that contributed, in highly crucial ways, to how he and others acted in life and to how he thought and spoke of those actions. Some of these temporalities were more cyclical in nature; others were more linear. Some signaled progressions; others indicated degenerations. Some featured a steadfast logic of cause and effect; others were more open-ended. They came into play at various moments in his life, with different temporalities being invoked, thought of, sensed, enacted, shunted, resisted, contested, or anticipated in the course of his engagements with others.

Running through all this was the sense that there was a man, an individual known as Ghang Lama or Chabahil Mheme or Mheme Lama, who had lived a distinct life, one that would end with his death. That person's life could be portrayed in a "life story" inscribed on paper—he did this, he said that. But the subject of that biography would himself hold that it would be a mistake to consider his life as an entity onto itself, of a singular duration that began with his body's birth and ended with its death. For one thing, the lama knew his present life to be but one link in a chain of lives. Consequently, he and others understood his existence in terms of a continuity of lives, with the strands of action that coursed through his present life partly the result of karmic deeds enacted in previous lives of his and partly the cause of action in any future lives of his. Another sequence of action was at work in his family's line, with the deeds of grandfathers and fathers echoing in the lives of sons and grandsons. Viewed in this way, his family's history was more important than any history one might conceive specific to his life. All told, the lama's life, enfolded within diffuse tides of consequential action, was couched within rounds of existence of durations longer than the life itself.

Twenty-Seven Ways
of Looking at Vision

Ideas and motifs of vision, of perceiving, thinking, or acting through the medium of the eyes or the mind's eye in some way, informed much of what Ghang Lama had to say about his life. By no means was he an "idiosensant," living and remembering by means of a single sensory modality. A wealth of varied, interinvolved senses patterned his life. In our talks, elements of taste, sound, touch, smell, and bodily sense were frequently spoken of. When prompted, the lama detailed the kinds of foods he liked and disliked at different times in his life; he appreciated spicy foods and bowls of chhang early in life, salt-butter tea later on. He also spoke of the various smells, good and bad, that he remembered of his herding days in Yolmo: sheep (and shepherds) smelled the worst, but water buffaloes were not too offensive. And it was Mheme who told me that if a man confronts a poisonous snake in Yolmo, he can take a stick, rub it into his armpit, then throw it at the snake. The snake, repulsed by the sweaty smell, will wither up and die.

Yet while Mheme had tasted, smelled, touched, and heard a great deal in his eighty-plus years, vision, I have come to conclude, played an especially important role in how he lived and recalled his life. This is perhaps not surprising. Vision is the dominant sensory mode in many human societies, and scholars have documented the ways in which vision has been a valued means of spiritual knowledge and social engagement in Hindu and Buddhist communities in South Asia for many centuries now.[1] Tibetan Buddhism, which drew early on from ideas central to Buddhist traditions in India, also gives priority to vision. Here, ways of seeing are often held to be highly effective means to assess the truth of things, to envision the forms of deities and bodhisattvas, and to enact ritual transformations. Mheme engaged in religious practices quite like these, and many of his takes on vision were in accord with those found in Tibetan Buddhist settings. At the same time, he also grew up in a Yolmo community, and he sensed the world much as other Yolmo wa did, though there was also something distinct, something of his own, in his sensory engagements. To understand how vision worked in his life, then, we need to understand at once the particulars of vision in his life and the cultural underpinnings of those particulars. All in all, vision for Ghang Lama comprised a way of sensing the world, an instrument to determine the truth, a form of action and interaction, a means to know and communicate with others, a vehicle of judgment and influence, a mechanism of control, a tool for spiritual practice, and an ethics of engagement. "Seeing" or "looking" or "watching" for him, to put it differently, could have metaphoric, pragmatic, political, epistemic, transformative, moral, or intersubjective features. Given this wide array of sensory means, a patchwork of words and observations drawn from his life and the lives of other Yolmo wa can best help to elucidate, in nonreductive, interfocused ways, the importance of vision and vision-based modalities of acting and knowing in his life.

I

How does "vision" work? How does a person "see" or "look at" or "notice" something? One could assume that vision works through a process of optical reception, in which photons of light arrive at the cells of a retina, and then, through the physiology of visual recognition, the retina sends impulses to the brain, which then converts these impulses into images perceived by a conscious mind. Vision in this regard is a rather receptive, interiorizing, noninteractive process. Much as a camera "takes in" patterns of light, which are then transmuted into visual images, the eyes soak up visual data, which are then decoded within the confines of the body and rendered sensible by the brain.

Many, especially those living in contemporary European and American settings, might hold that vision works more or less in this way. Yet such an understanding would not make great intuitive sense to most Yolmo wa. For them, vision operates through a process whose means are decidedly projective in nature: when a person looks at something his or her gaze extends out to the object seen and then and there makes visual sense of it. When speaking of this process, Yolmo wa often invoke the Yolmo expression *mi phoge:* the powers of a *mi,* or "eye," *phoge,* "touch," "befall," "hit," or "strike" an object perceived. Much as a hand extended outward from the body can make tactile contact with an object, a person's gaze can make contact with an object in some way, and through that contact the object is visually recognized by the person looking at it. An appropriate analogy for such a dynamic is much less that of a camera, in which elements of light are received within an enclosed interiority and then assimilated into images, than that of a flashlight, in which an immaterial beam of light reaches out from its source and befalls an object or field of objects, bringing it or them into perceptual recognition. This is, in fact, what people say. "It's like a flashlight," Mheme's son Lhatul said when I asked him about this. "Just as new batteries in a flashlight generate a strong beam of light, so early on in life the eyes possess a strong power, and so one can see well. But later in life the eyes get much weaker."

Lhatul went on to say that, in his estimation, it was not actually a person's eyes that went out in this way but rather his or her sem, or "heart-mind." "It's the sem that goes, not the eyes. It goes here and there. And when thinking of places far away, one has to close one's eyes, and then one can see well." Yolmo wa generally understand a person's sem to be the psychospiritual medium through which acts of thinking, feeling, willing, imagining, and remembering proceed.[2] As Lhatul's words made evident, concluding that it is not really the eyes but the sem that "sees" helps to explain how it is that one can imagine or envision objects and landscapes even when one's eyes are closed. While the sem is usually thought to be centered in the heart, and people often point to their chests when referring to it, many Yolmo wa know that it can readily leave the body and happen upon other scenes imagined or envisioned; when one thinks of or recalls another place, the sem travels to the place thought of. "Is your sem in America?" I was sometimes asked by concerned Yolmo wa when I appeared a bit pensive during my first stint in Yolmo. While younger Yolmo wa tend to speak of such imaginative journeys in metaphoric terms, much as an American might say "my heart is with my mother," older Yolmo wa understand that the sem travels to the place thought of. Just as an immaterial beam of light can quickly flit from place to place, so the sem can swiftly travel near and far. Yolmo minds can reach out to and light upon an object or place envisioned.

When I queried Mheme about how acts of seeing actually work, he apparently did not understand what I was asking at first. I then asked him if he thought the dynamics of vision are more like the workings of a flashlight or like those of a camera. "It seems to me now that it has to be both," he replied. "The sem goes to the object seen, meets it, and then brings back to the person an image of what is seen."

2

Whatever the specifics of their visual perceptions, Yolmo wa are regularly affected by what they see. Two phrases that often pass people's lips when speaking of something they have seen are *semla phosin* ([it] struck the sem) and *semla nesin* ([it was] felt in the sem). "We're affected by the things we see," one man told me. "We see something, and that has an affect on us. It comes back to us." Mheme himself gave the example of seeing someone wearing beautiful clothes or a child crying; the seer's mood is accordingly lightened or darkened in response. Similarly, if a man jealously perceives his wife flirting with another man or spies an old flame with a new partner, that sight can cause his eyes to "hurt" or "be pricked." If the man feels compelled to continue looking on nonetheless, friends of his might say advisedly to him, "Mi su makye" (Don't pain your eyes). This, at least, is how the language puts it; everyone knows the hurt is as much psychological as optical in nature.

If a person does not see something, consequently, chances are that he or she will not be affected by it. Norbu once asked his grandfather if he was worried that the lamas in his family would "finish" with his grandchildren.

"Why should I worry?" his elder responded. "I'll die and won't see anything."

3

People also have an influence on what they see. "Seeing for us is so interactive," Karma Gyaltsen told me. "We're affected by what we see, and we have an affect on what we see."

Those visual affects take several forms. Several scholars working in South Asia have pointed out that in many Hindu and Buddhist communities a person's or a deity's gaze is thought to affect or blend or share with whatever is being gazed upon.[3] A Hindu devotee seeking the *darśan,* or "sight," of a deity at a temple, for instance, can gain that deity's

blessings by visually apprehending its image; since the act also entails being seen by the deity, a divine contact is exchanged through the eyes.[4] A
deity's wrathful gaze can also be dangerous and destructive. By "joining
glances" with a guru, in turn, a devotee can gain access to a benevolent
power that emanates from the guru's eyes.[5] In these situations seeing,
which is sometimes likened to a form of touching, is more than a passive
reception of sensory stimuli. As Lawrence Babb observes, "In the Hindu
world, 'seeing' seems to be an outward-reaching process that in some
sense actually engages (in a flow-like way...) the objects seen."[6]

While such visual engagements, or "engazements," as Jayasinhji Jhala
puts it, do not necessarily work in quite the same way in Yolmo circles,
certain glances can affect others.[7] As in other communities in South
Asia, if someone looks at another's child with envy, an act known in
Nepali as ākhā lagāunu, "to cast eyes on," it can inadvertently fix an evil-
eye-like harm on the child looked upon.[8] For this reason infants are
sometimes shielded from the potentially envious gaze of others, aged
women in particular. Similarly, if a hungry person looks with desire at
the food that another is eating, his or her gaze can "pierce" the food and
later make the other person sick. Mi zuge is the most common Yolmo
phrase used when speaking of this harmful process: a person's eyes
"pierce" or "stick into" or "get rooted in" another person's possessions
or body. As Mheme portrayed it, mi zuge most often occurs when
someone, usually a "witch" or an outsider not well known by the victim, looks with ham, or "envy," at the victim's food or possessions. If it
is food that is desired, the desiring person's envy can then get into the
meal being eaten, causing the other person to get sick or to lose his or
her appetite. If it is an object that is envied, such as a wristwatch, then
the object might not last long or begin to run too fast or too slow. If a
person's life is affected in this way, his or her family needs to summon a
bombo, or shaman, and ask him to "throw" off the envy.

When explaining to me how acts of mi zuge work, Mheme repeatedly
made a stabbing, piercing gesture with his index finger, darting it in a
sharp trajectory from his eyes toward an empty tea cup set on the floor
before us. An eye's daggerlike beam can enter an object or a body and
leave a lasting trace of its presence. Because of this, people prefer not to
eat in open places, and they try to sit and eat in restaurants away from the
entrance, with their backs facing any doors or windows, lest some hungry passerby pierce them with an envious look. In theory, the eyes of
men and women alike can pierce others in this way. In practice, however,
acts of mi zuge are attributed most to women, aged, widowed women in

particular, some of whom are taken to be witches. As in other societies in South Asia, people ascribe malevolent looks and witchy deeds in general to old and marginal women.[9] Something in their presence and cultural status leads people to perceive them as seeing in this way.

4

Much more common, fortunately, are more mundane and more positive moments of visual engagement and copresence in which two people relate to one another in communal, unharmful ways by maintaining continued eye contact. One term for such contact is *mi zinge*, "eye encounter" or "eye meeting," a term that is used to denote any mutual, ongoing rapport of eyes between two or more persons. "It's like you're looking at me, and I'm looking into your eyes," Binod Yolmo explained. Such encounters can take a variety of forms, they can prompt a slew of interpretations, and they can occur between strangers, enemies, friends, family members, or, as Gom Dolma once made clear, between young women and men fond of each other from a distance. "Nowadays girls and boys get engaged after just doing their eyes here and there [mi harta tsurta bheti]," she said in 2000 in comparing the gist of marriage rites then with the "capture marriages" of her day, which she found to be more forceful and less charitable to the bride's interests. By sending amiable, flirtatious glances back and forth, a man and woman can come to know one another without conversing much at all, if at all, and if the man concludes that a union between them would be a good thing, he can suggest to his parents that he would be happy to marry the woman upon whom he has been setting his eyes. Such eye-play is reminiscent of the flirtatious exchange of glances so often seen in Nepali and Hindi films and alluded to in countless love songs and romantic odes in South Asia. "It's like a conversation with the eyes," Karma said to me when we discussed such encounters. "A lot of communication proceeds like this," he went on to say. "There's so much that is said without words, just by looking at one another in one way or another."

Outside of comments like these, people tend not to talk about such meetings of the eyes. They seem largely subliminal processes, operating in the "unconscious optics" of Yolmo lives.[10] An outsider therefore learns of them by noticing certain occurrences.

One day a five-year-old girl named Sonam and her ten-year-old cousin Babu were encouraged by their elders to say the *abc*'s to each other as my video camera recorded the performance. Babu took the lead, enunciating one letter ("*a*…"), and Sonam followed, when she could, with the next letter ("*b*…"), and so on back and forth ("*c*…," "*d*…"). As they exchanged interwoven letters, they sustained a continued interplay of gazes that appeared to me to be at once gleeful and affectionate. When I embarked on a similar recitation with another young girl a few weeks later, the girl acted much as Sonam had, although here she repeated, one by one, the letters I voiced while looking into my eyes. As she mimicked what I said, we engaged in a fusion of word and gaze.

A few months later, while I was staying at Lhatul's home in Thodong, the news of the day was the sudden death of a Yolmo man in a neighboring village. The day after a funeral rite was held for this man, one of his sons arrived at Lhatul's home before walking up to the cremation site above Thodong, where he was being employed by Lhatul to paint the religious images on a *mani* (Buddhist shrine) that Lhatul was constructing there. Lakpa entered into the main room of the house, where Lhatul, his wife, Mingmar, and I and others were sitting, and he sat down without speaking. Both Lhatul and Mingmar immediately exchanged sustained glances with Lakpa, without saying anything and with an absence of levity in their expressions. I was struck by the fact that no words were uttered. Lakpa, in mourning, did not speak, while the couple's visual engagement conveyed their care and compassion.

Encounters like this led me to conclude that, among Yolmo wa, sustained, mutual visual rapport can involve moments of intimacy, affection, and concern. "When talking with friends, our heartminds [sem] should be as one," one man told me once, at a time when there was a lot of concern about a violent feud taking place in a village close to his own. He meant that in order to befriend someone or to maintain a friendship, one needed to develop a shared consciousness or an agreement of minds with that person. Many Yolmo wa work to develop or sustain such a "one-semness" through eye contact in tandem with a host of linguistic practices. Lhatul strikes me as a master of this. When conversing with someone, this "good talker" often sustains eye contact as he works to build a consubstantiality of perspectives. Through such eye contact and skillful use of language, such as repeating what someone has just said and creating goodwill and a sense of playfulness through witty remarks, his actions can work to create a sense of affiliation and bonded mutuality. On several occasions I have been struck by how much sustained visual rapport plays into these engagements. I have also found myself engaging with others through similar means: Just before I left for the States in

1998, a Yolmo friend came to visit and say good-bye. When he went to leave by descending the stairwell outside my room, we maintained eye contact until he turned the corner and passed from sight.

Vision, then, can be a profoundly social medium among Yolmo wa, one that is often practical in nature, rooted in time, and geared to specific embodied perspectives. It can be a harmful force. But it can also be a vehicle of intimacy and friendship. It can be reciprocal, participatory, transactive, responsive, respectful, tender. It can be at once projective and receptive, active and reflective. It can be either compassionate or playful, caring or persuasive, prohibitive or protective. Some ways of looking are more moral than epistemic in nature, more a means of relating to another than a technique for knowing that other.[11] By looking, by inter-viewing with another, one can behold another; one can hold another in one's gaze, either during a forgettable workaday moment or when seeing the face of a dying elder for the last time. If anyone is to make sense of Emmanuel Levinas's inspired but cryptic comment that "ethics is an optics," my guess is that Mheme and other Yolmo wa could do so.[12]

The potential for intimacy and positive regard in these sorts of co-engagements helps me to understand the way Mheme looked at me the day I came to visit his son Dawa after I returned to Nepal in 1997. With a steady gaze he set his eyes upon me, established a connection, and showed an appreciation for my sudden reappearance after an eight-year absence. On later occasions as well, usually when I had visited his home on my own, and then often while I was practicing the Yolmo language with him and his family as we sat in his family's kitchen, he would smile and, without saying a word, look at me with warmth and kindness in his eyes. As I came to do with other Yolmo wa close to me, I soon learned to return his gaze with one I took to be similar to it; I would visually engage his eyes with a sustained, unshifting look that, to me, was at once calm, appreciative, and welcoming. At other times, though, I felt overwhelmed by his benevolent regard. After I met his gaze with one of my own, I sometimes found myself looking away after a few seconds.

5

My displaced looks were probably not too foreign to Mheme, however, for if Yolmo wa can engage others by maintaining eye contact, they can just as readily evade or disconnect from others by avoiding such contact. There is a telling passage in *The Life of Milarepa,* the biography of the beloved Tibetan yogi and poet, in which the young Milarepa returns to the home of his master, Marpa, after previously leaving Marpa to seek teachings from another sage. Once Milarepa arrives, Marpa's wife tells him to greet Marpa in his room. This is no easy task, since Marpa was greatly angered by Milarepa's departure. "I went," Milarepa tells his readers. "The lama was on his terrace making his devotions, his face turned toward the east. I prostrated myself and offered him the silk and the turquoise. He turned his head away and looked toward the west. I went to this side and prostrated myself again. He looked toward the south."[13]

Yolmo wa turn in similar ways. "And if a person is angry at someone else, he probably wouldn't look at him so much," I said to Karma one day, hoping to confirm my nascent understanding of this. "Yeah, he'll just do this," he said, turning his head to the side, as if avoiding his potential interlocutor. "He would just look somewhere else."

Many other visual disengagements, which do not imply anger or dislike at all, proceed through parallel means. One day I visited Norbu's parents in their home below where I was staying. As K. B. Lama sat beside me and his wife, Hrikchung, sat on the floor, uttering mantras with the use of a *mālā* (set of prayer beads), I took out a recent ethnography of a Yolmo village and showed it first to K. B. He looked through the book with enthusiasm for some time, scanning the photographs closely, identifying people he knew, then held it up to show to his wife. Hrikchung apparently did not want to look at the book right then, occupied as she was with her prayers, and while she acknowledged his signals with a few words, she did not look up from the rosary. A few seconds later, her husband gestured again with the book, but she turned her head away so that it faced away from us, as though at once to cut off any exchanges with us and to signal that she was not to be engaged.

We might think of Hrikchung's effort as a culturally meaningful "action-form" of sorts, one of many known to and utilized by Yolmo peoples. The effort entailed an action in the sense that a bodily act was undertaken by an individual. But the action also had a formed quality to it; there was a gestural shape to it, head turned to the side, eyes looking away, which meant, among other things, that the gist of the action could be enacted in different ways by different persons in a number of situations.

One afternoon I was introduced to a woman whose teenage daughter I had previously met and spoken with. I found this girl to be unlike many other young Yolmo women, for she was unbashful and inquisitive around me. "This is my daughter," the mother said, nodding toward her daughter who stood between us.

"Yes, I know," I said. "We've met before. She's not shy."

Immediately after saying this, I realized that I had used a Nepali expression, "lāj lāgdaina," that can also be heard as "she is shameless." The girl, perhaps embarrassed or put on the spot by my last comment, looked toward the ground and did not say anything—again, as if to disengage from the interaction by altering the visual field.

Once, while Nogapu Sherpa and I were visiting some friends of his, our hosts asked him if he wanted to drink more chhang. Nogapu turned his head away, then moved it broadly from side to side, as though to disconnect visually from the request while also making clear the finality of his disconnection.

Those suddenly faced with some kind of sadness or pain will often avert their eyes or block them from the possible regard of others in some way in order to alter the geometry of gaze and voice particular to a situation, and so make their sorrow less public. When a boy once stumbled and fell down while running along a path in Thodong, he lay for a minute or two flat against the ground, face down, with his face buried within his hands. When Ghaki Lamani spoke to us about her life, tears welled up in her eyes when she related to us the early hardships of her marriage. When this happened, she looked down toward her side and fiddled with a knitted cap that she held in her hand, thereby supplanting a predominantly visual and verbal engagement with her surroundings with a more tactile one. The action led her interlocutors to mute their visual regard of her; we looked away, drank some tea. After a few seconds, she picked up the cap, put it on her head, and began to speak and look at us again. Two days before, she had told us that she was once peeved at someone because he had taken a photograph of her at a moment when she did not want her image to be recorded. It was during the New Year festivities a few years back, while she was seated amid a group of women who had gathered at a family's house. "I was talking about my daughter's death, and there were tears in my eyes, and I put my head down [when it became clear that a photograph was going to be taken]. But he took the photo anyway."

When in the villages of Yolmo, I often found that children would watch me while around me, while I was eating, for instance. When I would return the gaze and look at them with a bit of a smile, they would look away. At other times, children, especially girls who did not know me well, would hide behind the bodies of friends and family members if I looked at or spoke to them. Soon they would reappear to look at me again, only to hide anew if I returned their regard.[14]

Mheme would also avert his eyes now and then. During some of my informal visits, especially when they coincided with social calls by relatives of his, I found that he tended to keep quiet at times, as though he did not want to say too much in the presence of these others, and although he would settle his eyes on his visitors time and again, he would quickly look away if any of us returned his gaze. Other situations induced disengazements of a different sort. When the lama was offering his thoughts to Norbu and me on the demise of Yolmo language and identities, he maintained eye contact with Norbu, as he usually had during his earlier conversations with us. Yet all this changed at a significant moment. "If a person knows the language," he said, looking at Norbu, "people will recognize him as somebody's son, somebody's grandson. Until your time, maybe young people can speak [Yolmo]. But after that, no. They won't know our language."

He then shifted his eyes from Norbu to me and kept his eyes locked on mine as he continued: "Now our relatives' children, they don't speak our language. When we talk to them, they talk to us in Nepali. After they go up there [to the Yolmo region], others will say, 'This person is not Yolmo.'"

I was struck by Mheme's transfer of vision, because this was one of the first times that he had steadied his eyes on me during our formal conversations together. Norbu later told me that he had also taken notice of it. Asked about any possible reasons for it, he said that he thought that his grandfather might not have wanted to embarrass him by looking directly at him while voicing his disapproval of descendants who could not speak Yolmo.

6

Looking into another's eyes implies a distinct way of seeing. Yolmo wa know there to be two main kinds of vision. Each is conveyed through a different verb form. *Thonge* is the verb that denotes acts of vision in general, of having the power of vision, of seeing or viewing in the broad sense of perceiving something in the world—a bird flitting by, a taxi pulling up— through optical means. It refers to the faculty of seeing more generally. To be blind is to be bereft of this faculty. Such seeing is not necessarily active, intentional, or willful; to notice something, to have something within the horizon of one's vision, or to see something out of the corner of one's eye is an action that falls within the verbal arena of *thonge. Tage,* in contrast, is to look at something intentionally, to set one's eyes upon something, to view something willfully, be it a book, a child, or another pair of eyes. Its processes thus imply active, intentional, and selective efforts. To examine, to stare at, to reflect on, to ponder, to study, to pay attention to, to take notice of—these are all gestures that fall within the semantic domain of the verb *tage.*[15] The distinction between the two visual acts points to a person's ability to perceive through both intentional and unintentional means. It also suggests that the tandem of eyes-and-sem constantly fields a range of visual data, through acts of *thonge,* "seeing." But it can also focus in on a chosen object or image, through acts of *tage,* "looking."

Both kinds of vision can lead to knowledge. By letting one's eyes fall upon something, either by noticing it unintentionally or by looking at it directly, one can come to know something about it. Indeed, among Yolmo wa, seeing often entails a primary medium of knowledge and understanding. To see something with one's own eyes is often to confirm its existence. This is often the case in instances of wrongdoing. When one man in Gulphubanjang complained to another that money for a local school was being "eaten" by members of that village, the second said that he had not "seen anything" and so could not do or say anything about it. Without direct, visible evidence of the theft, he was unable and unwilling to take action.

"He has a bit of a drinking problem," one man told me of another whom we both knew. "They say this?" I asked. "No," the man replied. "I myself have seen him, walking drunk with his friends."

To see someone actually drunk is usually much more confirming than to hear about drunkenness, especially since gossipy words, for Yolmo wa, can be rife with untruthfulness. To see something with one's own eyes, in turn, can make for a powerful form of witnessing. "I saw it with my own eyes," said Sen Zangbu Sherpa, while pointing a finger toward his eyes, of the Rana regime's hanging of four martyrs that he had witnessed in Kathmandu several decades before: "It was a terrible thing that I saw."

"It seems to me," I once suggested to a Yolmo friend, "that if people hear something, they're not sure it's true or not. But if they see it for themselves, they know it's true." The man replied, "Oh yeah, that's true. To find the evidence for yourself, that's the important part."

Mheme's various takes on knowledge often heeded a similar rule of vision. When the subject of *swarga,* or "heaven," came up once during one of our conversations, he observed, "Well, nobody has actually seen heaven, nobody has actually seen hell. It's just that people say we go to heaven or hell after we die. But who has seen it?" Norbu and I later asked him if it is true that deities enter a shaman's body when he is healing. "They say such a thing," he quickly replied. "We haven't seen, we cannot say." What remained unseen could not be spoken of definitively.

7

To see something is often to know it, to be familiar with it. People "saw hardship" in their lifetime, and youths left home "to see something of the world." Mheme told us that his first son had seen his grandparents before they died, and that he himself had seen Rhidu Pema before she came to the funeral in Thodong, where he decided to take her as a second wife: "I saw her many times before. People from [her village of] Kashir used to use the route through Thodong, so I saw her while she was walking through." Rhidu Pema, in turn, recalled seeing Mheme only once before in the days leading up to their marriage. To "see" a potential bride in this way was not just to scan her visual features; it was also, and perhaps more important, to come to know something about her style of acting, her way of talking and being among others.

We once asked the lama if any injustices were ever enacted against him or his family. "Before, when I was young, it happened," he said. "But I never had to go to court. I've never seen a court up to today. This unfair thing was done by my own relative."

"Which relative?"

"Up there, a man on my father's side. He couldn't see that we were living a better life." This relative could not "see," or tolerate, the relative prosperity of Ghang Lama's family, and Mheme had never "seen" a court in his life.

Other Yolmo wa drew on similar wording. "I had thought that I would never again see the face of a man in my life," Ghaki Lamani said of her contented state of mind while staying in a cloistered Rana palace when she was a young woman, yet to marry. "Seeing our struggles in life, a deity gave us a blessing," Gom Dolma recounted a crucial time in her life. Lhatul once told me of how, when he ran away from his father's home to seek work in India, he left late at night and traveled with a group of youths, including his older brother, through the forests south of Thodong. When I asked if his parents were angry at him then, he replied, "No. They couldn't see [me]."

8

When it came to knowing things definitively, vision for Mheme typically assumed priority over hearing or any other sensory faculties. Speech for him was largely a matter of breath and wind. A person's voice was "like the wind," moving about, fleeting, quick to die out. Certain comments of his hinted that, for him, human speech was closely linked to human vitality. On one occasion he noted, "If our bodies did not have enough fire and water, we could not talk. There's fire and water in our bodies. The water is our blood. Because of the flame, we can speak. Otherwise, how could we speak? We would be as dead." Life for him apparently came with breath and voice, all of which were ephemeral in their makings and easily extinguished.

Print, in contrast, tends to connote something lasting and permanent for many Yolmo wa, especially those involved in lamaic practices. Written texts as well as other kinds of physical inscriptions in the world, such as the footprints of great saints cast in stone, can serve as powerful bits of evidence of someone's existence or actions in the world. Whereas speech is of breath and wind and so is fleeting and unreliable, words printed on a page are commonly invested with connotations of truth and permanence.

Lamas base almost all of their religious practice on the oral, and often communal, recitation of Tibetan texts. These texts, said to be the inscribed talk of various buddhas, bodhisattvas, saints, and learned lamas, are understood to be eminently sacred and truthful. "Chhela bhridi yheba" (It's written in the sacred texts), Yolmo lamas can be heard saying when defending their grasp of how the world works. A well-intentioned reading of these same texts brings great benefits to those who read them as well as to anyone in close proximity to those readers. All this amounts to a kind of "grapholatry," in that texts and written marks of various sorts are in themselves valued as sacred objects.[16] Graham Clarke, a British anthropologist who conducted fieldwork in Yolmo in the 1970s and 1980s, wrote well of the hallowed nature of the religious writings so revered by Yolmo lamas.

The word itself is sacred. Books must not be placed on the floor but stored above in special shelves, and the touch of a book on the head is itself beneficial. One cannot sit on chests that contain books, and when a book is so worn that it can no longer be used, it cannot just be thrown away but must be buried in a sacred site.... Tibetan characters, whether inscribed on paper and made manifest by the turning of a prayer-wheel, or on a prayer-flag made manifest by the action of the wind, or on the paddles of a wheel turned by water, or just read from a book, are always sacred.[17]

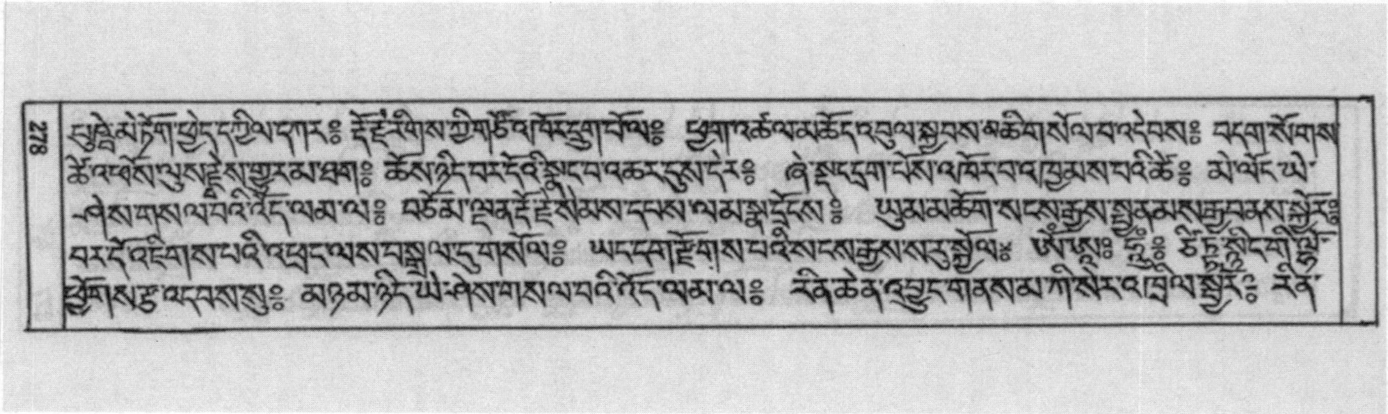

Figure 4. A page of a Tibetan religious text, the Bardo Thedol.

"Sins will come if we step on them with our feet," Mheme said of religious writings, often referred to as chhe. "We should not step over the chhe," Rhidu Pema reiterated. "Sins come."

I soon had the occasion to talk about such matters with Karma Gyaltsen, who, himself from a lama family, had studied with a Tibetan lama in his early years. "We're brought up to look at the lama books as being more precious and more sacred," Karma told me. "We can't step over them. If I had a page of Tibetan writing—if, for example, my brother wrote a letter to me [in Tibetan]—then I wouldn't just throw it into a trash bin."

"Why wouldn't you?"

"I think it's because of the writing. I don't know. It's just the feeling we get. We prefer to burn it."

"And what if it was written in Nepali?"

"If it's in Nepali, then it's nothing. It's how we're...how it's just etched into our mind. It's like that. Anyone from Yolmo would say, 'It's the lama writing.' If it's on the floor, 'Oh, it's lama writing' [and so it is inappropriate for it to be on the floor]. So you just put it aside, or put it someplace where people won't step over it. I think it's the way inside [us], the way we have linked ourselves with the writing. It just comes spontaneously. I feel bad if I happen to step over a piece of lama writing. From inside I feel that I'm doing something wrong. I don't know the reason behind it."

Karma reintroduced the subject a week later. He said he had been thinking about what he had said and why the writing itself was so sacred to him. "It's the whole context of where I learned it," he explained. "It goes together with the teachings and the prayers. When the lama taught us, he told us that one couldn't just study it and learn it like the abc's. One needed to practice it, experience it, and have it become part of one's life."

When Karma happens upon such writing, then, the whole atmosphere of his religious training is spontaneously brought to mind, and the writing cannot be separated from the atmosphere. For him and other Yolmo lamas the writing is always already associated with the sacred.

No other kind of script in the Yolmo universe carries the aura of sacredness and authenticity that Tibetan religious writing does. But many writings of various sorts, be they in Nepali, Hindi, or English, nevertheless convey for many Yolmo wa an air of truthfulness that few mediums of speech do. Certain kinds of writings authored by Western scholars have, in particular, recently acquired a certain presumed veracity to some. When I traveled to Nepal in the winter of 1998, I took with me several of Clarke's published writings to include in the archival library of the Yolmo Foundation. When I gave copies of these writings to Karma, he said, "Ah, this will be really good." He immediately read through several passages with great interest and located discussions of his family's lama lineage. Later he said, "This will be really good. Now, when we talk to people about 'Yolmo' [as the name of our society], we can say that even the Westerners have written this, and we can show them this. When people see something written, they believe it to be true. That's the way they think. Especially with things written in the West—or in the lama scripts."

The differences presumed by many Yolmo wa to hold between speech and writing are evident in tensions between lamaic and shamanic forms of knowledge among Yolmo wa. Many contend that the lama scripts convey a brand of knowledge and meaning superior to a shaman's speech-based divinations. "He can't read. How can he know what is right, what is the truth?" one lineage lama said caustically of a bombo's defense of the ritual sacrifice of animals, such as chickens and goats. He then defended his own Buddhist-based aversion to such sacrifices by noting, "It's the deity's word. It's written in the holy books. So it's true, isn't it?"

Many Yolmo wa, lamas in particular, also contend that the oracular divinations of a bombo, in which tutelary deities, when properly summoned, "descend" into the bombo's body and speak through his form in order to "reveal" vocally the causes and nature of any afflictions troubling a person or a family,[18] are "like the wind," fleeting, unstable, and quick to die out. In contrast, a lama's knowledge is, because it is written down, less prone to being lost or distorted than the bombo's knowledge, all of which must be remembered "by sem." As one Yolmo lama explained to me, it is better to have ritual knowledge recorded in texts. There is always the risk, he said, that if a bombo dies, all of his wisdom and experience will also perish. Lamaic texts, in turn, endure beyond the lives and bodies of their authors and readers. At the same time, if one tries to retain matters in the sem, some memories can be lost, while others can be "incomplete" and not fully correct. In working with texts, in contrast, there is less chance of forgetting or rendering imperfect religious truths. "The bombo's is not the perfect word," he concluded. "But with the lamas, there is a perfect record."

As might be imagined, bombo do not necessarily agree with either the conclusions or the criteria of truth and perfection advanced by these and other lamas. Many Yolmo wa do in fact find more value in the bombo's ritual practices than in the lama's, especially when they or family members of theirs are trying to recover from illnesses. Nogapu Sherpa, for one, expressed skepticism toward the hallowed nature of Tibetan writing. "Tibetan people see a small piece of paper with just a bit of lama writing on it," he told me, "and they say, 't-t' [what a shame] and pick it up and put it [above] in a pure place. The writing in English, people use that even when going to the toilet. But still they [Westerners] have built bridges and traveled to the moon in spaceships." What good came of the lamas' grapholatry, in other words?

9

Nogapu grew up in Malemchi, a village in a forested area of northern Yolmo that is populated by shepherds and farmers and straddles the divide between the eastern and western ridges of the Yolmo Valley. Although he never went to school, he learned to speak English while working first as a porter, then as a guide, on trekking expeditions into the Nepal highlands; reading and writing came to him less easily. He then parlayed the money he earned into a successful construction business. There were no lamas in Nogapu's extended family. There were several bombo, however, and he himself had studied a bit with one. On a few occasions, he felt the force of their gods course through his body. It was for these reasons, perhaps, that he sided more with the "knowledge" (N., *bidyā*) of shamans than that of lamas. "I don't think the lamas can do without books like the bombo can," he told me.

Ghang Lama's life and optics, in contrast, were founded on lamaic forms of knowledge and practice. He had undertaken a distinct education in seeing, he had lived a life of reading (but not writing), he inhabited a world of liturgies and letter-waving prayer flags, and, by all appearances, he had "linked himself" with lamaic inscriptions in the ways that Karma detailed. Perhaps more than most other Yolmo wa, he abided by many of the perspectives on speech and writing just noted.[19] "Looking" into sacred texts, as he might say, had been an integral part of his life for some seventy years. He said he learned to read Tibetan letters at an early age, when he was around six or seven. He used to read religious texts each morning as a child, before he led his family's cattle out to pasture. In helping his father to perform religious rites he gradually learned about the contents and meanings of several texts. Later on he participated in a series of retreats and esoteric trainings, many of which entailed reading particular texts and enacting the spiritual practices that accompanied them.

In time this lama mastered many texts, especially those concerned with funeral rites for the deceased, and he came to know many passages by heart. Much of the religious practice in which he engaged in his life entailed the oral reading of sacred texts, whether when performing funeral or exorcism rites or when reading merit-enhancing texts at the homes of sponsors. Most often these texts, which laypersons usually do not understand, are read collectively by a set of lamas, who chant the texts in a cadenced singsong that is accompanied by sacred hand gestures and forceful music rung from bells, drums, and horns. Mheme "left" much of this work a few years back, though, finding that he was getting too old to travel to the homes of sponsors. When I came to know him, he attended only the funeral rites of close friends and important rites sponsored by friends. In attempting to increase his chances for an auspicious rebirth after he died, he was devoting much of his time then to reading texts that worked to "cut," or reduce, the karmic import of any sins he might have committed. He read several texts daily, most of them upon waking in the morning. "One reads as much as one can," he once told us. "If one reads more, one reaches heaven." Yet when I visited him in 2000 he told me that, with his eyesight growing increasingly poor, he could no longer read as he once did. "Up to last year I could read the books. Now I can't." He then began to rely primarily on the utterance of mantras and prayers, without the aid of any texts. "Now, I just pray in the sem [without reading any books]. Even when I go to sleep at night I perform mani [prayers]."

In line with other Yolmo lamas, who usually brought their own texts with them when they participated in Buddhist rites in different homes and temples, Mheme owned more than a dozen texts. He kept these texts, each wrapped carefully in silk cloth, in a windowed cabinet set within the wall above his bed. When I mentioned a certain text during a visit in 1998, he said "ah" in knowing recognition, turned around and opened the cabinet, found the text in question, unwrapped it from its protective cloth, and, while delicately leafing through a few pages, proceeded to tell me about its contents and meanings. When talking with Nogapu and me, he would often have in his hands a well-used text that he would look at whenever he had a chance, and we would sometimes have to draw his attention back to the conversation at hand. On numerous occasions he made reference to certain texts, perhaps to justify or authenticate something he was saying: "That's inside the book they have as well." "This comes in the book. This means 'bodhisattva.'" Once, while discussing the history of Nga-chang Shakya Zangpo, he noted that this divine saint left a footprint in a place just below the village of Tarke Ghyang in northeastern Yolmo. "It's a little below Tarke Ghyang. In the stone. Nga-chang Shakya Zangpo stepped on a big stone. The footprint's there. You can see that inside the temple." He then went on to say that Nga-chang Shakya Zangpo's *nam-thar,* or "spiritual biography," was inscribed in a text. "You can also see [about him] inside the book," he said. "We have it inside there. If you look there, you can see there." To read was to see. To see was to know for certain. To know for certain was to authenticate the origins of a lama lineage and so legitimate the high status of men born within it.

Considerable prestige came with his ability to read and understand sacred texts and to tell others about the meanings inscribed there. To quote Clarke again:

And the priest who can select a suitable text and manifest it through reading has the power of control over this sacred order: hence the significance of reading as a public sign of religious competence. No such reverent attitude attaches to literacy in Nepalese, which in the village is regarded as a useful skill, but one independent of the religious order and status.[20]

Mheme's ability to read the letters in those texts set him apart from women and men who could not, while his facility in understanding what was written there gave him more authority than those lamas who could only pronounce the sounds of letters and syllables without understanding their significance. "If someone doesn't know the meaning, just how to pronounce the 'ka-kha' [the *abc*'s] and some letters, it's useless," he told us. "There's no meaning there." In his world, certain acts of reading privileged some humans over others. He was clear on the elevated status that came with knowing the chhe, the religious knowledge contained in lamaic texts and practices. "It's good if people know the chhe," he told Nogapu and me. "If a person doesn't know the chhe, he needs to sit below, not above."

When performing rites, lamas customarily sit in a row, with the most senior lamas in a lineage seated "above," close to the head lama and the altar, and the most junior and unskilled lineage lamas seated "below," followed by "common lamas," then laypersons; women tend to cluster in groups beside and below the men participating in the rite. Mheme was saying, then, that if a person did not have the appropriate religious expertise, even if he was a "lineage lama," he would have to sit below, among those also known to be unskilled. He then continued,

If someone is an expert in chhe, then everyone respectfully asks them, "Come sit above." If somebody doesn't know the chhe, then no one calls them to sit higher up. They have to stay below. The "skilled ones" means those who are learned in the dharma-chhe. They can earn more dharma [earn more merit]. If someone just knows about talk, he's a worthless trifle [N., *jāba*].

These words came in response to our asking what he would like to see his grandchildren do in their lives.

10

There are, however, limits to what one can know through acts of seeing or reading. Yolmo wa often advance the idea that "one can never know what's in another's sem." The running idea here is that, since the sem, or heartmind, usually lies within the body and so cannot be seen by humans, and since life is such that people are usually either unwilling or unable to voice their thoughts and feelings to others, much about friends or neighbors remains hidden.[21] "If I were a god, I could see inside your sem," one man once said in conveying this idea to me. "But since I'm not, how can I know what lies within your sem?" A Yolmo pain song rues,

> When a forest catches fire,
> everyone sees it
> [but] when one's heart catches fire,
> only one's own self knows.

In other songs authored and sung by Yolmo men, women are held to be particularly opaque in contrast with the presumed clarity of men's hearts and actions.

> The sons are diamond and pearl,
> they are crystal clear
> the daughters are coral and turquoise,
> what is within?

Hidden within the folds of a body, many thoughts and feelings go unseen, and so unknown, by others.

II

A person's fate or luck or fortune, meanwhile, usually referred to in Yolmo as one's sodi, is inscribed indelibly on one's forehead. Some say that such words are written on the skull, beneath the skin covering the forehead. "It's already written on our cranium [*kapli*]," Mheme said on one occasion. "Inside. Inside, on the cranium there are letters. Everything is written on these letters: this person will die at this time, this person will become a rich man, this person will be poor, this person will have comfort or sorrow. Some die with sorrow, some die with happiness.... Some live carrying very heavy loads, some live without even carrying loads. All that is [inscribed] on the forehead." The phrase "already written" hinted at the abiding quality of the fateful letters. The lama also understood that the individual fortunes of his family members, including whether or not the lama work would be continued through generations, were written on the forehead of each.

Several proverbs speak to the nature of such writings. "Thala-la yhinna, tu-lu-lu onge" (If it is [etched] on the forehead, it will definitely come), goes one phrase in Yolmo. Another, in Nepali, comments on the kind of spouse a person is destined for: "Lekheko mātra paincha, dekheko painna" (You get only the one that has been written; not the one that has been seen). We get the person we are fated to marry, that is, not the one we might have lovingly beheld with our eyes.

Yet despite the profound, set-in-bone importance of such inscriptions, humans can never access or read what is written there. A Nepali proverb sometimes voiced in Yolmo speaks to the limits of legibility:

Bhābīle lekheko
chālāle ḍhākeko
kasari nadekheko?

Written by fate,
covered by skin,
how can it be seen?

12

While the vision of humans is limited at best, the contemplative gaze of buddhas is "equal to a perfect vision," as a Yolmo lama once put it. Deities can see "everything everywhere." "The god is watching. He sees everything," Mheme told us.

Humans cannot return that gaze, however. They cannot see any deities but are able to witness only artistic imaginings and fleeting traces of their presence. That was not always the case, however. Mheme told us that in an earlier era people used to be able to speak to and see deities. "But people started to do more bad deeds, that's why God [N., *bhagvān*] hid himself from us.... Now we can't see him. He can see us, we can't see him. He is looking at everything, who is doing what, he knows everybody's deeds. We don't see God, that's why people say there's no God. God is there! He's with us. Wherever you go, he's there."

Everyone, everywhere. On each of the four sides of the stūpa in Boudhanath, known in Yolmo as *jahrung khashor* or *chhorten chhenpo,* the "Great Chhorten," are a luminous, incisive pair of eyes that can be seen from miles away (see figure 5). Asked about the meaning of these "eyes of wisdom" *(yishi gi chen),* Mheme replied:

That means the buddha [represented] sees east, he sees south, he sees west, he sees north. He can see everywhere, for sure!...The chhorten has four faces: east, south, west, north. Everywhere can be seen. We have two eyes, and how much can we see? So he has four sets of eyes. Some deities have a thousand eyes, a thousand arms. Phagpa Chen Rezig has a thousand eyes, a thousand arms.

When I posed the same question to another lama, Kisang Omu's son Kānchā, he said, "The meaning of this is very important. The deity sees everything. We can only see in front. But the deity can see behind, to the side, in the past, in the present, in the future. These eyes are extraordinary; they can see all the different worlds and locations, from the heavens to the underworld, as well as the events and sorrows that occur in those worlds. He can also see inside us, what's in our sem. There is nothing in the universe that is invisible to these eyes. They are the eyes of the buddha, the eyes of compassion." The eyes, significantly, are the last element that an artist paints when completing the construction of a chhorten.

A deity's transcendent vision, unconstrained by the usual limits of time, corporeality, and interiority, made for an all-seeing, all-knowing presence. "He could see everything with his big eyes," Lhatul once said of his heroic ancestor, Nga-chang Shakya Zangpo. "He knew a great deal."

13

Humans, restricted to singular perspectives in space and time, can see much less than deities and buddhas do. While deities possess absolute

Figure 5. The chhorten in Boudhanath. Photograph by Robert Desjarlais.

gazes, humans can muster, at best, tempered looks. In contrast with other animals, however, the capacity of humans for rational thought and morally purposeful action makes it possible for them to strive toward greater knowledge and clarity of vision. A central aim of Buddhist practice, in fact, is to obtain a more truthful understanding of the world—to develop, that is, clarity of sight in removing any hindrances that cloud one's perceptions.

> Whenever your life example is heard,
> Darkness in the mind of this little one, Chökyi Gyatso,
> Is always dispelled.

Or so writes Chökyi Gyatso, the translator of *The Life of Marpa the Translator,* in a colophon that ends Marpa's biography.[22]

Analogous tropes of light and darkness, clarity and obscurity, illumine a great many Tibetan Buddhist texts. Among Yolmo wa, spiritual "defilements" or "impurities" are known as *dhip,* a word related to the term *dhipsa,* "shadow," "shade," "stain," "obscurity"; defilements darken, stain, obscure the person defiled. Darkness is on a par with ignorance, confusion, evil, ghostly forms. Light, in contrast, is a symbol of wisdom in Tibetan Buddhism, and vision is a privileged medium of perception and understanding. In accord with this, Yolmo wa talk of having their "eyes cleared" *(mi salge)* or their "eyes opened" *(mi khaphege)* when speaking of the impact of important moral lessons taught to them by lamas or elders in their lives.

Acts of *mo,* or "divination," usually conducted by either bombo or lamas, also enable humans to know more than they might otherwise. There is a strong visual dimension to such acts, especially when conducted by lamas. People customarily speak of "showing" themselves to a bombo, lama, or doctor when they are sick, and lamaic divination is often spoken of as a kind of "seeing."

Mheme was known as a skilled diviner, and people used to come to his home in Chabahil to have their fortunes "read." His usual method of *tsi,* of "calculating" or "counting," was to consult several astrological texts that bore information on the astrologically patterned destinies of individuals, as predetermined by the years in which they were born—mouse, ox, sheep, and so forth. This information, when collated, could foretell good or bad days to undertake such activities as holding a wedding ceremony, starting off on a trip, or launching a new business venture. "I read the different books," he explained, and I find out what ailments will occur, the bad days and the good days, the good and bad dates, all of this. With the good and bad, what there is, we try to find out. What is bad, what is good, after reading, conclusions emerge.... You have to match many books. It's not just one book.

As Karma Gyaltsen explained it to me, such calculations are not really divinations in the way that a shaman's oracles are. "Everything is already written down," he noted. "So it's a question of finding things out, not one of predicting them." This meant that, for him and others, the lama's method was more certain than the shaman's, since everything was predetermined, inscribed in texts. Mheme put it well when he explained to us why he and others found his text-based divinatory practices to be more reliable than a shaman's oracles. "There are so many bombo," he said. "People don't believe in their predictions. They only come to me. The bombo just say it with guessing. But this thing [a divinatory text] has been written by a deity many, many years ago." A powerful ideology of speech, writing, and religious practice was being asserted here: whereas a lama reads texts "written by a deity" years before, a bombo "just says it," guessing without conclusive knowledge.

Mheme said he learned how to read the astrological texts on his own early in life and was soon "seeing" for others what might be afflicting them or what might happen in their future. His skills as a calculating "seer" apparently put him in great demand, particularly when he was living in Thodong and often visited the villages that neighbored it. "Before, while I was seeing mo, many people would trouble me [to perform calculations for them]. The people of the valley [below Thodong] would come one day, the next day, and the day after that! A-pa!...When I went to other villages, people would come to me, and everyone would say, 'See for me,' and usually then I would be late in getting home. Sometimes I wouldn't have time to eat. They would come early in the morning, before I had a chance to eat breakfast....Everybody was asking me to look into their future."

"Do you feel happy that people come to you [for this reason], or do you feel irritated?"

"Sometimes I get irritated. Sometimes I'm happy that people come because I know [how to do this]."

By 2000 he said he was declining any requests to perform calculations. With his eyesight weakened, he could no longer read the astrological texts.

14

One of my first memories of Mheme, one of the first times that I saw him before I knew him at all really, is of him sitting on a blanket in the sun along the main path in Gulphubanjang, back in the summer of 1988, a day or two after he had hiked up from Kathmandu to visit his sons and check on his old home in Thodong. A set of lama's texts lay next to him or in his lap. Throughout the morning several men approached and asked him to divine their astrological fates. "Please see for me, Mheme," they asked. He saw for each of them, patiently, methodically. I sat a while and watched him sift through the texts and mumble calculations. Someone brought him a glass of tea.

15

A second memory from that week is of him sitting atop the roof of Lhatul's home. The roof, made of interleaving aluminum sidings, reflected the sun's warmth well. Newly washed clothes were often laid flat on the sidings to dry, but I had never seen a person seated there before, and it took me a few minutes before I noticed him. Mheme was sitting on the roof, his long legs stretched out before him, observing the happenings on the street without being observed much himself. I remember thinking then that the roof, along with being a good place to gather some warmth from the monsoon sun, offered an effective way for the lama to distance himself from anyone who might "trouble" him for a calculation.

Ten years later, as Nogapu and I approached his home in Chabahil one morning, I spotted Mheme standing with a cane on the top of the terrace of the building's third floor, looking out at some children playing in the dust below.

16

I found that many others in Kathmandu also made of habit of standing or sitting on the open terraces that roofed many multistoried households, often alone but sometimes in the company of others, while quietly observing what they could see of any goings-on in the courtyards and public fairways below. I took notice of this evidently pleasurable pastime by doing much the same when I lived on the third floor of the building owned by Norbu's parents, and I was quickly reminded of its complex slants when I returned in 2000. Sitting in my room the morning after I arrived, nursing a dose of *jet lagyo* with a cup of salt-butter tea, I noticed, while gazing wearily out a window, that a woman was standing on the roof of the building just to the north of my own, drying her newly washed hair in the sun. Since that rooftop was a bit higher in space than the room I was in, I could see only the top of her head as she bent over and disentangled the wet strands of her hair. Before I looked away, not wanting to spy, I also observed, in the direct line of my vision, another man, standing on the rooftop of a building, higher still than the one the woman was on. Looking our way, he appeared to be watching either the woman drying her hair, or me watching her, or both. A few seconds later I was surprised to see that yet another man, standing on the rooftop of a building beyond and just above the second man's, was gazing as well in our direction. A bit later I closed the window's curtains. Unhurried scopofilia.

I also found that people did a lot of patient watching in general. Anything of interest going on in a public setting could attract the visual attention of bystanders. When any fights or disputes broke out on a street, people would quickly crowd around and quietly observe the altercation. Parents are said to "watch over" their children as they mature. Day in, day out, people eyed others, and they were eyed in turn.

Such observations often assume a gendered form. Young women in particular must live amid the steady visual regard of other Yolmo wa. The reasons for such gazes vary. Parents want to ensure that their daughters are acting in socially proper ways; neighbors are often on the lookout for potential wives for their sons and grandsons; boys watch girls when they happen to be present together at the same social gatherings; men can sometimes be seen scanning the physical forms of women; and relatives often observe their "nieces" in order to see how skillful and dutiful they are in terms of household work and social relations. While young men's actions are also noticed, the collective gazes fall much more constantly on women. "The people watch you," Norbu's sisters Tashi and Kunsang once told me. "If you go somewhere, they'll be watching you. Mostly it's the girls [who are watched]. So the girls become very careful, very aware." In the course of time, an attentive vigilance becomes ingrained within a woman's sense of self, and women learn to conduct themselves as though they are presently being observed by others or might soon be again. They are thus always in some way within the judging sight of others. Culturally established forms of visuality thus contribute in substantial ways to the subjectivities of women.

One consequence of all this watching is that men and women alike are quite aware that others might be observing them. They therefore tend to become "very careful, very aware" of how their appearances or actions might be regarded by others, since anything from the clothes a person wears to whom she or he associates with can be noticed and later talked about. When I brought a video camera to Thodong in the spring of 1998 with the idea of filming something of everyday life there, Lhatul made sure that he would be able to "see all of the video" at the end of my stay. In part he wanted to enjoy the opportunity to see what was recorded. But he also wanted to make sure that all the images and scenes depicted were appropriate ones. He was particularly concerned about what would be "seen down there," in Kathmandu, or in the United States. One morning he asked that I record over a few minutes of tape that had been recorded in his house and appeared somewhat dark and opaque. "If they see this down there, they'll think we're like ghosts. We look very dark."

Being embarrassed or disgraced often assumes a visual cast. Yolmo wa often speak figuratively of being shamed or dishonored as an act of having one's nose "cut" *(naasum tupke)* or "thrown" *(naasum kyurke)*. Drinking too much, sleeping around, or having been caught stealing can lead one's nose as well as the noses of other family members to be "cut." Mheme told us:

The "nose is cut" means that if children have done bad things and their parents go someplace, then people will tell them about this, and their noses are cut. "The nose is cut" is said, and "the nose is thrown" is said. If their children have done bad things, like stealing something, or they have gone to jail, then people say to the parents, "Oh, look, your children have been in jail," and then the parent's nose is thrown.

When asked what he could do if someone in his family were to do a bad thing, he replied:

What can I do, now? We have to tolerate it, for sure. If someone does something bad, I become very ashamed. If people from around here know, I'll be ashamed, certainly. It becomes difficult to show my face. So I have to stay quiet. I can't talk to others. It's not only if my children do bad things. It's also the case if it's my cousins or anyone in my family.

Given these concerns, parents often implore their sons and daughters to act in morally good ways and so "hold their noses" *(naasum zunge)*.

Along with bursts of language, a strong visual component belongs to these sentiments: it becomes difficult to "show one's face" when one is morally disfigured. Indeed, those reported to have been strongly shamed are often said to be quite shy about showing themselves in public. "Since then, nobody has seen him around much anymore...." Acts of seeing and speaking thus often work together, like the two blades of a scissors, in collective perceptions of people's actions and identities.

Since Yolmo communities seem to possess a thousand eyes at times, and since so much can be seen in daylight, people sometimes try to do things under the cover of darkness. When a young man's parents wish to propose a marriage between him and the daughter in another family, they usually do so by formally presenting a shalgar, an offering or blessing in the form of a container of liquor, to the daughter's father. If the man accepts the shalgar, it means that he has agreed to the marriage proposal. Drinks of liquor are then offered to the gods, then consumed by those present. An instructive feature of this process is that the groom's representatives almost always visit the potential bride's family at night, with the shalgar carried in a bag, so that they will not be unduly embarrassed if their proposition is turned down. Karma, for instance, told me that it was customary that people go at night. "First," he said in explaining how the practice usually proceeds, "they don't come with a big shalgar, they hide it in bags. They don't want anyone to know this at first, because they're not sure the proposal is going to work. So they hide it. And they come in the evenings, you see."

"Why is that important?"

"For two reasons, I think. First, because not everyone will see you coming and going in the evening."

"Because it's dark?"

"Yes. People especially look to go when it's dark. So sometimes it's very late night, this thing."

"And they go quietly."

"They go quietly. And second, the evening is also when everyone is free, and so people can drink and have a good time. It's customary. Everyone goes at night. Never in the morning or the afternoon."

The potentialities of vision, in short, are deeply implicated in Yolmo social engagements, moral sensibilities, and aesthetics of personhood. In living their lives, people have to contend with a multitude of visualities. Mheme, who "saw" a great deal, was subject to the views of others. His life was framed by the determining mutuality of seeing and being seen, of facing and being faced by others. Glances, double takes, watchful eyes: these acts imply moral judgments, the possibility of kindness, the threat of violence. Yolmo optics is an ethics.

17

Many knew Mheme as a quiet person who tended not to talk much at social gatherings. "He doesn't talk," Phur Gyalmu said of her uncle. She then added, "Before, before, he drank a lot of chhang, though." When I asked Norbu's sisters what values they thought their grandfather was trying to teach them, Tashi replied, "He doesn't say much." Kunsang then followed, "Yeah, he doesn't say much. He doesn't teach us any-thing....He's a very quiet person, he doesn't talk much. We've heard from our father, our mother, they say that our grandfather has always been quiet, quite shy, and even you can see that."

I could see that. Most often he struck me as a "watcher" of sorts, in that he usually seemed to prefer observing what was going on around him, glancing surreptitiously at others now and then, without verbally participating much in ongoing conversations.

He learned a lot by watching, he said. Toward the end of our conver-sations in 1998, Nogapu and I inquired into Mheme's moral education. "Mheme," we asked, "you know the dharma, you know how to be straight, how to treat people well. How did you come to know these things? Did you come to know them on your own, or did your father and mother teach you?"

"I came to know on my own, certainly," he answered. "My father and mother didn't teach me. It just came to my sem to do this thing, to act this way, to treat people like this. It just came." He then continued:

By watching people, I understand. People do this, this happens. They do that, that happens. I learn these things by watching. If we don't treat others well, we gain enemies, and it's difficult to go outside. If everyone says, "Please come here" [if they invite us into their homes], it's good. If enemies are made, then we're afraid to walk on the roads outside.

By watching people, by observing well the consequences of their ac-tions, the lama learned how to act in morally skillful ways: sons who talked back to a father were hit in return; if people treated others poorly, they risked being harmed or shamed if they showed themselves in public. Implied in the second precept is the idea that acts of violence can follow the act of being seen in public. Being seen by others carries the threat, however slight, of being harmed.

Others also spoke about learning skills or habits through watching others and then imitating what they did. When I asked one woman how it is that children acquire the same tastes for foods as their parents, she said it was because children "watch their mother and father, and so they have the same [tastes]." Lhatul said he learned how to do things by "looking at how people do things, then doing it." And when speaking of the skills required in farming work, Nogapu explained, "If we watch the people doing these things [farming work], if we watch them, then we can learn how to do it." He also noted that he and others learned how to pay *she-sa,* or "respect," to others through observation and imitation. "When people are paying respect to others, we can watch, we can hear, so we can do those kind of things."

To learn well is often to see well. Lhatul once spoke proudly of his nephew Surje's ability to learn quickly by taking in a great deal at once. "He sees here and there!" he said with a back and forth wave of his hand.

18

To remember well often entailed seeing well, at least for Ghang Lama, who spoke of remembering as being predominantly an optical endeavor. When asked if memories come more by seeing or by hearing, he replied, "When we have seen, we can get the memories. If we have heard, we can't remember. Without seeing, we cannot remember. If we see, the memories come. How well I remember the great earthquake.... "

Others similarly said that they remembered better through seeing than through hearing. "How can I remember things by hearing?" Ghaki Lamani asked when I checked with her on this. "The things heard cannot be remembered. Things that are seen can be remembered." When I asked Norbu's mother, Hrikchung, about this, she replied, "The things seen are remembered most. The things that are heard—the people just tell you about them, and then you forget them." Indeed, the recollections of many who concluded much the same often toted a crisp visuality. "The people who went to Gosainkunda used to get sick and die," Gom Dolma said, for instance, when recounting the pilgrimages that she undertook as a child with her family to Gosainkunda, a sacred lake set atop an arid mountain that crests more than fourteen thousand feet above sea level. "They used to leave the dead bodies along the sides of the trail. I could see the dead bodies, just the skeletons."

For Mheme and others, many memories resulted from the sem's imaginative, speed-of-sight travels to places once visited and then recol-

lected. When I wanted to ask the lama what he remembered of Thodong when he brought it to mind, Nogapu posed the question as follows: "When your sem goes to Thodong, Mheme, what do you remember, what do you see?"

"How well I see by the sem—Ama Jomo Yangri [a sacred mountain
of Yolmo people], and Sermathang! I see all this for sure.... Everything
is there. Ama Jomo Yangri, everything, I can see with the sem. The hills
on this side [to the northwest] can also be seen very clearly. I can see very
clearly with the sem. That place I've seen before. Otherwise, where,
where? [How could it be seen?] Because I've reached the [Gosainkunda]
lake several times, I can see it very clearly."

"You can see clearly?"

"Yes, I've been there before, so it comes clearly, that kind of water in
that place. If one hasn't reached there before, then where, where? [What
can be remembered of it?] Just that."

Memory for Mheme proceeded primarily through optical means. A
person tended to remember what he saw, not what he heard, and one
could remember only sights seen previously.

19

That Mheme could see so well when he imagined being in Thodong is
not all that surprising, given that the village nicely saddles a ridge that
divides two steep valleys, such that substantial lands to the east and west
and the Himalayas to the north can readily be seen. Throughout the
year's clear months, the sun rises in dark blue over the Himalayas to the
east and sets in red skies in the west. Such a panoramic layout was in fact
one of the reasons that Mheme appreciated living in Thodong when he
could, for "everything could be seen" from there:

Up there [in Thodong], the Yolmo Valley can be seen, the lands over there can
be seen. The Gosainkunda area can be seen. North, east can be seen, west can be
seen. Here [in Chabahil], we can't see anywhere. Up there, everything can be
seen.... Our village up there, how nice it is. Up there, everything can be seen.
One can see east, west, north, south. Here one can't see everywhere. Up there,
how nice it is.

Other men sometimes expressed a similar appreciation of clear vistas.
Mheme's son Lhatul once told me about a village "where life is not very
good." "The work is very difficult," he said, "and one can't see well." A

few days later, on a crisp and clear March morning, Lhatul and I hiked up to the cremation grounds situated on a hilltop just to the south of Thodong to attend to a small shrine that he was building there in honor of his mother: "Everything can be seen!" he joyfully announced soon after we arrived. When I asked Karma Gyaltsen if evaluations of this sort made sense to him, he said, "They do. People prefer where they can have a really good view. Even here when people are looking for a piece of land to build a house, they usually prefer the high places."

Thodong fits that bill well. Mheme and others held that the name of the place came from a union of two words, *to*, which means "above" or "on top," and *thong*, from the verb "to see." Everything can be seen from up above. Some doubted this etymology, however.

20

That a great deal can be eyed from Thodong was one of several important reasons Mheme wished to die there, even though he had moved to Chabahil years before in order to find more "comfort" in life and had not visited Thodong for some time. Often in those days Yolmo wa living in Kathmandu, elders in particular, preferred to return to the Yolmo region when on the verge of dying in order to die in the villages they thought of as home. Sometimes such elders walked on their own; sometimes they were carried; quite rarely still, those from wealthy families would be taken by helicopters hired for that purpose. If such a journey before death proved impossible, many wanted their corpses to be carried up to the Yolmo region in order to be cremated there, in part because the cremation grounds in Kathmandu were thought by some to be spiritually polluted by the "burnings" of low-caste Hindu people.[23] Bereaved family members could then be seen transporting deceased parents and children wrapped in white cloths up into the foothills north of Kathmandu, by taxi or bus until the road ran out, then bodily along winding footpaths.

When talking with Norbu and me in the summer of 1997, Mheme said that he also intended to return to Yolmo before dying: "Now, at the time of dying, I can't stay here. I have to go up there. Up there, Yolmo can be seen—"

"Once you go there, will you stay or will you return?"

"I'm not going to come back after going up there. At the time of dying, it's good there. The place, how nice. The people of the village—"

Figure 6. The view from Thodong, 1998: Lhatul Lama, the author, and Surje Lama. Photograph by Robert Desjarlais.

"So, after going up there, you won't return?"
"Nope."
"What will you do with this house?"
"I'm going to sell this house, now. Sell this house."
"Why do we have to die in the village?"

"If you die in the village, it's good. Everyone is there, all your people are there."

"Why shouldn't we die out here?"

"Well, here, the name itself is Nepal [it's like a foreign country to us]."

"Well, isn't our village in Nepal?"

"Yes, it is. But it's different. You can't compare our village to here. Around here you have bad people as well as good. Our place up there, how nice! One can see everywhere. Here, what can be seen?"

"What does it mean to die up there?"

"The place where one is born, one should die there."

"Why is that?"

"Because then one reaches heaven, it's said. If one dies in between, one will be in between. If one dies in one's village, one's parents have also died there; one has to keep that in mind. Here in Kathmandu, who has died, who has died? [Haven't so many unknown, impure people died here?] Here is a place in which all sorts of people die."

Several months later Nogapu and I asked again about his plans. "Mheme, you said before that you didn't want to die here, that you wanted to go up to Thodong."

"That's right."

"Why is that?"

"If I stay down here, I'll never become enlightened. Our village is where we're born. In the dreams it's seen [I see it in my dreams]. Kathmandu isn't seen in the dreams—it's always up there. Because our lands are very clean, and every place is seen from Thodong. It's a good place. Here, the dogs are dying. The *kāmi* [blacksmiths] are also cremated here."[24]

"Good dreams are seen."

"Yes. Good dreams are seen."

"What does it mean that dreams of Thodong are seen?"

"We lived there, we were born there, we worked there—that's why we see the dreams of that place."

Kathmandu for him was a foreign, defiled, dog-dying place, unsuitable for a lama's cremation. Holding no clear views, it was visually tainted. The Yolmo region, in contrast, was where he was born and where his mother and father had died. Far "above" the impurities of Kathmandu, it is also a good, "clean," "pure" place, where one can see "everywhere." He therefore wanted to die there and so increase his chances of a good rebirth. It was not by chance that he grouped purity with clear vistas and spiritual pollution with limited views.[25] Purity meant lucidity. Defilements were obscurities.

21

Ghang Lama also wanted to die in such a way that his children would be able to "see his face" *(dhongba tage)* before his corpse was cremated. Many Yolmo wa talk of the importance of viewing a person in this way, especially when one's father or mother is on the verge of dying. The phrase figuratively denotes the act of viewing or being present with the dying person one last time, with visual rather than verbal engagements taking precedence. While the act is not strictly a visual one, since words often do get passed around, the phrase does point to the importance of vision and face-to-face encounters in Yolmo social relations, moral sensibilities, and acts of remembrance. In many respects the face is the most important visual feature of a person's body. Children who wish to avoid the looks of others often cover their faces in some way. Those who claim they are unattractive will say that they have "no facial appearance" *(chhenda mhindu)*. To be shamed or embarrassed by something is, literally, to be "face-heated" *(ngo tshasin)*. To recognize someone is to "know the face" *(ngo she)* of that person. The face and its elements—mouth, nose, eyes, eyebrows, forehead—are the body's most prominent means of communication. The face of something can indicate its true nature, a point attested to linguistically by the presence of *ngo*, a formal term for "face," in such terms as *ngoma*, "real, authentic, original," and *ngo te*, "explanation that shows the nature of a thing."[26] A face "shows" a lot about a person's nature and ongoing thoughts. A face is also responsive to others; it both sees and is seen. To behold another's face is to know something significant about that person; to engage with others face-to-face, eye-to-eye, is to render oneself knowable, to expose oneself to their potential gazes and actions, to relate to others in situations rich in proximity and possibility. So, in looking upon the face of a dying person, a family member can work to retain valued understandings and memories of that person.

If family members cannot be present before the person dies, they often wish to view the face and body of a family member before it is cremated. Mheme himself worried then that, since two of his sons lived in Thodong, a long day's walk from Kathmandu, they might not be able to be present when he died or to view his body before it was cremated. When Norbu and I were ending our conversations with him in the summer of 1997, we asked if there was anything else that he would like to say. "What to say, now?" he replied.

When I die, will everyone [in the family] be together or not? I worry about that. If my sons had stayed in one place, then it wouldn't be a problem. But now that they've all dispersed to different places, they're all bound to worry, [saying,] "If he dies, I won't be able to see him." Isn't that something to worry about? Now, my sons have gone, my daughter has gone, one's own have gone. When a man dies he's cremated. If his children cannot see his face before he's burned, [they ask,] "Where has he gone?! Where has he gone?!"

I later asked Nogapu what he made of Mheme's concern. "Some people do ask to see the body," he said. "If the sons have not arrived, they might wait three or four days [before cremating the body]."

"Why is that important?"

"Because some want to see the father's face."

"Why?"

"It keeps the memory."

In making moments of intimacy and recognition possible at the most crucial of times, the visible presence of a dead body, soon to be incinerated, can help people to remember deceased loved ones. In much the same way that Yolmo wa try to retain the memory of something by gazing intently at it for a while or scan the face of a loved one about to set out on a journey in order to remember her well after she is gone, so studying the face of a dying or recently expired loved one can help to secure a lasting visual impression of that person. When Binod Yolmo read through an earlier version of this chapter, he wrote in the margins of the present paragraph, "A strong visual capacity is needed for the permanent imprint of a visual object."

Yet Mheme's words also pointed to the idea that gazing at a deceased person can help family members come to terms with the death. If family members do not have an opportunity to see the face before it is cremated, they can remain unsure of its presence or absence or whereabouts, asking, "Where has he gone?! Where has he gone?!" When a lifeless body is in evidence, however, people can quickly understand what has happened. They can begin to comprehend that the death of a loved one has taken place, they can brace themselves for the imminent destruction, through cremation, of the body, and they can begin to grieve the loss of that person. As Mheme told it, it was such efforts that the gods made possible, or at least less difficult to undertake, many years before by arranging it so that a body did not vanish at the moment of death.

22

Another concern of Mheme's was that a person can see only poorly after dying, in part because everything is seen as it is in a dream. "It won't be like when one is awake," he told us. "It will be completely like dreams. In dreams, sometimes we reach different, different places. It's like that." At the same time, the sun cannot be seen by the deceased. "We don't see the sun after we die."

Because of the absence of a clear light after one dies, Mheme and others proffered that it is important to burn a kind of "offering lamp" known as *chemi* while one is alive.[27] As understood by Yolmo and Tibetan lamas, the main reason for lighting these small candles, which draw from a source of liquid butter, is that the lamps are a light of wisdom; by lighting them in a devout and mindful way, spiritual knowledge can be increased among sentient beings. Yet Yolmo lamas also say, especially when trying to explain the practice to others in concrete terms, that the semiritualized lighting of these small candles has the effect of later lighting one's route to a good rebirth after dying. Mheme's explanation to us followed suit, although it was difficult to know whether his explanation was intended simply for our benefit or whether he himself understood this to be the case. "When we're alive," he told us, "we should burn a lot of butter lamps. Then we can see our path very well."

"Why do people burn chemi?" I asked.

"Chemi is to light the road, for sure. If we do the chemi, then the road can be seen after dying. If one doesn't burn the butter lamp, we'll go to a place where it's all dark. If we burn the butter lamp, we go to the clear place. The sun isn't seen. If we burn the butter lamp, we can see. It's enough to burn just one lamp a day."

People also light chemi on behalf of persons already deceased with the idea that the lighted lamps might enable the deceased to see better in any subsequent lives into which they have been reborn. Different people possess different ideas about what such vision entails, however. For many, "to see better" is to eye things more clearly. For others, lamas especially, the act increases one's measure of enlightenment in the world.

23

It made sense that Mheme compared the visual perceptions of a deceased man after dying to those common in dreams, for Yolmo wa find that death and dreaming have a lot in common. Both are occasioned when a life force departs from the body. Dreams occur when a person's sem leaves the body and travels about, reaching different places; the scenes encountered during such travels are what a person sees while dreaming. As such, the dream state is sometimes referred to as a small death, in contrast with the "big death" occasioned by the departure of a person's nam-she, or "soul," at the moment of death. The difference between the two lies in the sem's ability to return readily to the body and the nam-she's inability ever to return once it has left the body.

Both "deaths" ride on visual perceptions. When speaking of what humans can expect to encounter after they die, Mheme concentrated on what he and others would "see" then. Similarly, when Yolmo wa speak of their dreams they usually focus on what is "seen" in them. Mheme saw good dreams of Thodong, for instance. People also tend to report just a few images, a rising sun, a burning house, which can carry symbolic, foreboding meanings, for good or bad. "At that time, the bad dreams were seen, for sure," Phur Gyalmu said when asked if she saw bad dreams when her *la*, or "spirit," was spooked from her body once. "Where, where?— walking lost in the forest. A ditch was reached. Below, a bad place was reached. Going up and down was seen, at night, in the dreams. After seeing this, 'It looks like my spirit has gone.' One thinks this, in the sem."

In speaking of the image-by-image progressions common to Yolmo dreams, Karma Gyaltsen favored the English word *snapshots*, a word that I had once used in writing about Yolmo dreams.[28] "I think that's true," he said after rereading what I had written. "When people talk about their dreams or tell stories even, it's not a long narrative, as you say. It's just the snapshots, with one image following another."

Snapshots: "Yes, I see," Mheme said when asked if he saw dreams that had great meaning. "If good things are seen, good things happen. If bad dreams are seen, bad things happen. Going uphill means one is going to heaven. Going downhill means one is going to hell."

"Have you seen any dreams like that?"

"I have, I'm telling you. Once I saw the Dalai Lama in my dream. I was receiving a blessing from him. It was the time when people were going to visit the Dalai Lama, when he was performing a pūjā [ritual offering]. [My son] Dawa was saying, 'Come quickly, you have to get his blessing,' and then I woke up."

"Do you see dreams these days as well?"

"I do, but it's not like it was before."

"What dreams did you see as a child?"

"Ah, what is, what is?—many sorts of dreams were seen. Falling from trees was seen, falling from a cliff was seen, seeing a tiger scaring me, snakes scaring me."

"Did you not see any good dreams?"

"Sometimes I saw. These days, falling from trees, falling from a cliff, I don't see those dreams. Before I used to fly like birds, like an eagle as well, in the dream."

He then laughed a bit and said, "Before I would see [myself] flying. His father's corpse!"[29]

"Have you seen Thodong in the dreams?"

"Why not? It comes. I can see all the lands of Thodong. I can see the lands, even though I'm not there."

"Are the people seen, Mheme?"

"I can see the people as well, the people who have died. The dead and the living as well."[30]

24

Thought itself is quite often understood to proceed through images. Yolmo heartminds often appear busy with visual activities, as though mental activities themselves are a form of seeing, and Yolmo wa value the sem's ability to construct visual images through imaginative means. Karma's mind, for one, tended to be deeply visualist in its habits and doings. When asked if he had a dominant sensory orientation toward the world, he said it was his experience that he thought, imagined, and remembered primarily through images. "I think it's the images," he said. "It's the images. Seeing things. Seeing patterns, images, I think it's that. Even today, while reading something, if something comes as an image, then it remains with me." He found that it was like this since he was a child. "When someone said something about something I hadn't seen or I hadn't known [before then], then I would start to see something. It could be different from what it actually was, but then it was easier for me to remember through my own images as well."

This artist has a knack for envisioning his paintings, colors and details and all, completely in his mind, constructing them bit by bit, sometimes for days at time, before setting paintbrush to canvas. "I paint in my mind, and then my paintings are the equivalent of the [mental] picture I have." He therefore thinks a great deal through images. "For me, maybe because I'm an artist, it's easy for me to think in terms of colors and forms and images. I can just put them together, I can collage them, just in my mind, without needing to sketch anything on paper."

25

Karma found that the visualization practices he undertook while on meditative retreat contributed to his ability to think in images. As is the case among many Tibetan and other Buddhist peoples, Yolmo religious specialists engage in tantric practices that involve the imaginative construal of deities, visualizations that include details of the deities' appearances and accoutrement.[31] A key word here is *gom,* a verb which variably means "to fancy, imagine, meditate, contemplate, consider."[32] When performing healing rites, bombo imagine a detailed image of the deity that is helping them at the time. They imagine the deity in this way in order to summon it or embody its qualities. Lamas rely on a similar kind of visualization in the course of their own ritual and contemplative practices. In many rites, they effect certain realities and transformations, such as a deity's invocation or a ghost's exorcism, through the vivid construal of imagined scenarios. They also enact such imagined realities during collective or solitary retreats. In such settings, practitioners imagine a deity's features, then acquire something of that deity's knowledge or power or purity or divine grace by identifying with the form imagined.

Karma told me once of a contemplative meditation retreat that he and several other young men undertook in Yolmo under the guidance of their lamaic guru, an elderly Tibetan man who lived on a forested ridge just above Karma's village of Takpakharka. At the heart of this retreat was a tantric practice, commonly known as Vajrasattva meditation, in which the meditators mentally imagined the enlightened body of Dorje Semba, a buddha associated with mental purification, in order to purify themselves "of the different levels of obscuration and confusion in the mind and the negativity and negative karmic patterns that develop as a result of that confusion and obscuration," as one Tibetan exegesis puts it.[33]

Karma's own account (in English) of this practice pinpointed the ways in which certain visualizations work to purify a meditator's body, thoughts, and perceptions.

Here, the main objective was to cleanse myself of all the sins and all the shortcomings or whatever, all the bad things, in a larger sense.

We start of course in the morning, and we make an offering to the deities. And then later on, when you come to the meditation part, you sit in the position that you're required to, and then you're just imagining, contemplating in the space above you, Dorje Semba, this particular deity of purification. And then you see this deity not really in a solid form, but still in the form of rays, energy. So it's like something which doesn't have solid shape, but it's there, and you realize it. And you have to follow all the details in your mind, and then you imagine the different ornaments, the different attributes. These are actually guided imageries, strict guided contemplation, taught by our guru.

And then inside this deity, you see this mantra also, the mantra that we have to chant while we're meditating. And then it's like [we're seeing] inside the deity itself, it's rotating, revolving. So it just goes around—you see this deity filled with nectar, the blessings, the essence of being a purified god. And you imagine the drops of this nectar slowly falling on the crown of your head, and then this nectar slowly dissolves into your body. Slowly this nectar fills your body, and you slowly feel completely transformed into this same deity, so that the deity comes into you. Afterward you feel yourself like the deity. You see everything similar to this deity [similar to the way it sees]. And all the sins are really dissolved into this white nectar. And then after, you are completely filled with this white nectar. We have a metaphor: "Like the crystal bottle filled with the white curd... crystal clear within and without." So you have the image of that. And so you just contemplate like that—it's a continuous process. And at the end of your session, now this washed solution within you leaves through your anal orifice and goes into the ground. It goes into the ninth level of the ground, there's all this distance, and there's all these underworld creatures to consume all these impurities and things.

And in that way you feel completely purified. It's meditation after meditation, meditation after meditation. It's just like the hundred thousand times, the same recitation; you're always counting on the [prayer] beads. And so this is a long process of this retreat. And by the end, as it develops, as it develops, you feel as if you're cleansed. I could really feel the drips really coming through, and I could really feel it going through my body. It was developing more and more. And, of course, we had assignments in between. I had to go to our guru, and explain what I was contemplating, and [find out] whether the contemplation was right, according to his guidance and what I was feeling and what the developments were.

After completing this process, I really found myself—it was really something I can't explain, but then I found something very different in myself, the way I looked at the world, the way I saw things. It has changed.

Karma was apparently greatly affected by this experience, for on several occasions he spoke of how it changed his perception of the world.[34] "I had a completely different outlook when I came out; I really found myself changed," he noted. "I thought the way I looked at things was more the Buddhist way, a more peaceful way, I should say, of looking at things." A new subjectivity, a new personal vision, was taking form. He also said that he could not but wonder whether what he had learned about "visualizing certain figures" during this retreat gradually contributed, in time, to the imagination skills he employed while painting, or whether his skills as a painter had enabled him to visualize the deities with ease then, or both. He also ventured that the success of many Yolmo artists, who were "trotting around the globe" then in accepting commissions to paint the intricate, symbolically rich interiors of Buddhist temples, was due in part to their ability to visualize in their minds, in great detail, complex forms and figures.

Mheme never drew or painted at all. His life was founded much more on "reading" than on "writing"—on perceiving already received marks, that is, than on producing new ones. Yet in mastering numerous meditative retreats he had also developed a similar talent for visualization. Norbu and I once asked him what one needed to do during one retreat, whose purpose, he told us, was "to meditate on the deity."

"One has to make the deity's body like one's own and think of it as such," he replied. "On that we have to meditate."

"One sees with one's sem [one imagines it]?"

"With one's sem, yes. How is it that one could [actually] see [the deity]? With one's sem, yes? Our guru teaches us that this is the way to do it, to meditate that way."

"Now, when we are meditating, the deity's face comes here," he said later on, pointing to his chest. "We have to meditate, making the images of the deities."

"When you call these deities into your body, do you feel more like yourself then or more like the deity?"

"We have to feel more like the deity."

"At that time, is your sem like the deity's sem?"

"Our sem is like the deity's sem, yes. One has to think that whatever thoughts one has in one's mind are what the deity is saying."

While Mheme did not say it in so many words, one of the main purposes of such practices is to "transfer" the imagined qualities of a deity, such as qualities of kindness or compassion, into one's own body and sem. By feeling "more like the deity," one can acquire new attitudes and perceptions that later influence how one acts in life. Often these visualizations are accompanied by prostrations and mantras, such that all three aspects of a person's existence—body, speech, mind—work to simulate the qualities of the deity imagined.

Several months later Nogapu and I asked Mheme how the deities "appeared" to him when he sat in retreat. "We have the lightrays [*heser*] of the deities," he told us.

Those lights hit upon our body. Our body should think about the deities. So the lightrays are just like the sunlight—yellow, red, all mixed together. That kind of thing is building up. In the morning, we have to do this much pūjā [ritual devotions]; in the evening, this much; at night, this much pūjā. We don't think about our bodies then. We think about the deity's body, not ours. At that time, we have to construct the deity's body.

At that time, we should contemplate the buddha's body. We should think that we have the bodies like Chen Rezig. We should imagine that our bodies are like Phagpa Chen Rezig. That's why lightrays appear. White and red lightrays appear. The white sunbeam is good; it's very peaceful, not wrathful. The white rays are soft, and the red rays are hard.

Phagpa Chen Rezig never talks rough. He's always telling us, "Don't talk hard to people, don't trouble others, don't treat others badly." That's why he doesn't appear hard. He acts with compassion. Phagpa Chen Rezig never says, "I want to fight, I want to cut people, I want to kill people." He always talks gently to people, with compassion. He's like that.

When we sit in meditation, we should make our bodies like that. We should make our bodies like the buddha's body. Whichever deity we're sitting with in meditation, we have to think our bodies are like that deity's body. If we get very good lightrays, then it will prevent hindrances happening to us. Then we'll be blessed.

An active, photonic self-fashioning was in effect here. By visualizing the body of a buddha like Phagpa Chen Rezig and letting that buddha's divine lightrays hit upon his own imperfect form, a meditator can "make" his body like the buddha's and so incorporate something of his perfect virtues. By taking on the qualities of another subject, former modes of thought and action can be transcended, and new subjectivities and new, more enlightened means of perception can be cultivated. Beneficial blessings can also be had.

26

Vision among Yolmo wa, then, does not entail simply a subject's detached, observing, receptive gaze of an object or perceptual field, which is what one might surmise vision to be about if one were to read through many contemporary scientific and philosophical treatises in North America. Vision can be constitutive, constructive. The mind's eye can create certain imaginative realities, which can in turn affect one's life. A person can soak up the qualities of a form imagined and so transform how he looks at the world.

In fact, one of the fundamental tenets of Tibetan Buddhism is that vision, along with the other senses, can be highly fabricative in that it can entail illusory, miragelike fabrications of a reality. While a person might take this lived "reality" to be truly real, it might, in actuality, be highly illusory and subjective, with the truth obscured by that person's habitual thought patterns, worldly attachments, and karmic heritage. Some apply this precept to the world in general. More than a few Yolmo lamas, Mheme included, echo Buddhist teachings in asserting that the phenomenal world is nothing more than an "illusion" (*gyuma*) woven out of faulty thoughts and perceptions. When asked about this, Mheme told us flatly, "Everything is like an illusion. Everything in this life is unreal." A main aim of Buddhist practice, accordingly, is to see the world for what it really is.

Everything therefore depends on how one sees things. I once asked Karma if he would agree that seeing is a very important means of perception among Yolmo wa. "Yes," he said. "But instead of *seeing*, I would rather use the word *realize*." His reason for this preference, he went on to say, was that acts of seeing are actually acts of realization, of mediated perception, wherein one draws upon what one knows, either directly or indirectly, as well as what one has done before, in recognizing something. To recognize something, then, is to perceive it in the terms that one knows it or can know it. "It's more a mental thing," he observed, apparently in stressing what he took to be the subjective, psychological basis of perception. A person sees what he thinks he sees—a rope in the road is a snake in the road, a swirl of karmic energies is a flesh and bone person—until he learns differently.

A person's sem, or heartmind, is known to play an active role in the construction of any perception, thus accounting for the fact that people perceive differently. When speaking of how people can see an object in different ways or remember events differently or have contrary perspectives on a subject, Yolmo wa often voice the phrase "sem gi zokyo" (the sem made it; the sem constructed it). Integral to such a statement, which can be expressed, for instance, when a friend's take on something is different from one's own, is the idea that the sem is involved in all acts of perception and hence all acts of knowing; that all perceptions, sensations, and memories are patterned by the sem; that a person's knowledge and experience is subjective and individual in nature; that there is no ultimate truth to be had.

In many cases, what a person (thinks he) sees determines the effect it can have on his life. In the course of a conversation about the chhorten in Boudhanath, I asked Mheme if people could be blessed simply by looking at the eyes painted on the top of the structure. "It depends," he promptly replied. "If we think it's the eyes of the god, then it will reflect well on us. But if we think it's just something that someone has painted, then it does nothing."

The lama's perspective here brings to mind a Yolmo proverb that stems from a Buddhist parable: "If one acts in true faith, even the dog's tooth begins to radiate" (Mheba bhena, khyi so la h'e thung).[35] The frame of mind that a person engages in while looking at something can pattern both what she sees and the effect that the perception has on her. The world is what one sees it as.

27

There is a plurality of visions, to be sure. If anything can be deduced from this freeze-frame tour of Yolmo visualities, it is that Ghang Lama's life was patterned by a multitude of visual modalities that enabled him to know and relate to the world in diverse ways. Vision was a mode of sensation; by "seeing" or "looking" Mheme could apprehend the world. It was a means of knowledge; through certain uses of his eyes he could witness events, learn through watching, or see into the future. It entailed processes that contributed to the makings of a person; in seeing others and in being seen by them, certain forms of subjectivity were established. It was a tool for effective memory; with his mind's eye he could remember an earthquake or envision the lands around Thodong. Vision was an aid to religious knowledge and transcendence; through various contemplative and visual practices, the lama could read a sacred text, imagine the divine, purify his form, or forge more enlightened ways of being. Vision also offered a means of engagement and contact with others; by exchanging glances, by eyeing others just as they were eyeing him, he could know, judge, reproach, silence, or bond with others or be known, judged, persuaded, or valued by them. Many around him engaged in similar practices by way of their own takes on vision, making for a complex, politically charged, thousand-eyed scene of interfocused glances and observations.

By no means was this polyoptic world a seamless, harmonious one. There was no single, fully agreed upon visual order, no singularly pervasive scopic regime. Yolmo ways of seeing resist closure. They cannot be held within any one speculation. Still, certain themes recurred. Acts of seeing usually transpire in fields of intercorporeal, reciprocating glances. More often than not, vision is participatory, active, communicative, and constructive in means. It is sited in particular times and places. It also carries certain themes and possibilities. Yolmo acts of seeing and being seen are seeded with thoughts of presence and absence, of contact and disconnection, of fulfillment and longing, of reality, appearance, and illusion, of clarity and opacity, of purity and taint, of comfort and violence, of the life and death of things. If someone wants to learn something fundamental about Yolmo lives, she could do worse than center her musings on the features and practical force of thoughts such as these.

And yet there are other ways of being, other ways of sensing the world.

Startled into Alertness

Very present in my mind are the dominant tones of Kisang Omu's speech: crisp, sharp, lucid, with a clarity of sound and expression, at turns reflective or grievous or joyful. Her voice is foremost in my memories of her.

We first met in the winter of 1998, a few days after the Yolmo losar, or New Year, activities ended for that year and shortly after I had returned to Nepal for a four-month stay after being away for nine months. She was living then in Boudhanath, a few twisted streets north of the chhorten, with her youngest son, Kānchā, and his wife, Neela.

Karma Gyaltsen had suggested that this elder, known to many as Ibi Kisang, "Grandma Kisang," might make a good subject for a life history, given her longevity, certain particulars of her life, and her knowledge of past events. When I related this to Pramod Lama Yolmo, another Yolmo acquaintance who had just then agreed to help me with my research, he pointed out that he was related to her; his father, a respected Ningma Lama, was her first husband's cousin and her second husband's youngest brother. Since this meant, among other things, that Pramod knew her family well and she would feel comfortable in his presence, I asked if he could help me to record her life story if she herself was willing. He agreed and phoned to see if we could pay a visit soon.

When we arrived at their home the following morning, we learned that Kisang's son Kānchā, a knowledgeable, dedicated lama, was away for the day. Neela Lama, a woman of Tamang descent who had married Kānchā a few years after he had separated from his first wife, greeted us and took us to her mother-in-law's room, a few steps from the entrance to their home. Kisang was sitting upright in her bed, reciting a set of prayers

Figure 7. Kisang Omu, 2001. Photograph by Robert Desjarlais.

with a mālā in her hands. Her back was hunched over, as though centered upon the task before her. She was wearing a red sweater, and a red knitted cap covered her closely cropped hair. Heavy gold earrings hung from ears that framed a lively, intelligent face. With only her head and torso apparent to the eye, it looked as though her body was a faint echo of the taller, stronger body she had possessed earlier in life. I was struck by how old she appeared and by the stillness of the room, so different from the noisy bustle of Boudhanath's roads and alleyways. Photographs and *thangka* (scroll-paintings) hung from the walls, while dark cloths were suspended over the room's two windows, permitting slivers of sunlight to fall onto the bed, which occupied much of the room, its large size dwarfing its tiny occupant. At the head of the bed stood a large cabinet made of polished wood, which, I later learned, contained all of Kisang's cherished possessions. Besides this, across a small narrow table used for the placement of tea and meals, were two chairs. Pramod sat in one of the chairs and asked me to sit in the other. Since his aunt could not see or hear very well, she did not immediately recognize Pramod, and he told her who he was. After Kisang expressed pleasure in his visit, he introduced his "American friend." "Please drink some tea," Kisang said warmly.

After her daughter-in-law Neela served us tea, we explained why we wanted to come and talk with her. Kisang demurred at first, saying that she could not remember much of the past and could not speak very well. "Everything is like a dream," she said of her memories of the past and, later, of her perceptions of the present. We, in turn, found her to effect a dreamy presence in the world. At first her utterances were difficult to follow. She seemed to be talking as much to herself as to us, and Pramod and I were not sure how well we would be able to follow her, or she us. There was a moment early on, while Neela was in the kitchen brewing more tea and Kisang sat before us, that Pramod and I mumbled quietly to each other in English that it might not make much sense to work with her. But with her consent we decided to try a few questions to see how her words might proceed. The more we spoke with her, and the more we adjusted to the quiet pace of the room, the more we found her to be a remarkably animated, quick-witted speaker who had a great deal to say, often in striking poetic terms, about her life and death. "The problem with being old," she said at one point, "is that one can only sit in bed. A person can't do things or go outside to attend social events. I've done everything before, and now I want to die. But Yama Raj [the Lord of Death] won't let me, it seems."

I am not all that sure why Kisang agreed to work with us. Either she was simply being polite, or she felt compelled to do so, or, as appeared to be the case with other Yolmo women and men I worked with, she appreciated the idea of having her words and stories recorded in a lasting way. In any event, she accepted our requests, and for several months after that first visit, through the winter and spring when Nogapu and I were engaged in conversations with Ghang Lama and Kisang's son Kānchā was away days attending a Tibetan lama's teachings, Pramod and I returned regularly to Kisang's room to talk with her further. Our talks together, recorded on tape, tended to involve a mix of Yolmo, Nepali, and English. I would often consult with Pramod in English about topics I wished to discuss with Kisang, and he would then introduce these topics to his aunt in the Yolmo language. Kisang would usually respond in Yolmo but often salted her utterances with Nepali words and phrases. There was no steadfast order to these switches in language; while Kisang usually spoke in Yolmo, it appeared that Nepali sometimes struck her as the best language in which to say something. On other occasions, stock Nepali phrases passed her lips. On yet others, it sounded as though she sought to convey her thoughts in Nepali in order to make sure I understood clearly. When necessary, Pramod and I would talk to each other in English, usually for less than a minute or so, in order to clarify the gist of what his aunt was saying.[1] At such times Kisang would wait as her nephew and I spoke in a language unknown to her. At times she would intersperse stretches of silence on her part with words quietly spoken to herself. At others it appeared that she had enough of our strange, exclusive chatter, or she was eager to tell us something else, and she would try to get our full attention again by introducing a new line of words. Quite often as well Kisang and I would converse directly, either in Nepali, which I speak fairly well, or in Yolmo, which I had a moderate understanding of then. In the days that followed a conversation, I would visit Pramod at his own home, and we would proceed to play back the tapes in order to transcribe and convert into English all of the voices heard. Karma and Pramod's brother Binod also helped me to refine the translations in the months that followed; with hefty dictionaries by our sides, we tried to hammer out the best ways to say in English what Kisang was saying. The translations are therefore multiauthored, having been forged in a space between languages and cultures.

As the case was with Ghang Lama, most of our conversations together took the form of questions and answers, with Pramod and me asking questions, and our elder responding as best she could, usually with a few quick utterances before her pauses led us to ask further questions. On several occasions, however, Kisang entered into a storytelling mode and began to talk in animated detail about significant happenings in her life. We soon learned to keep quiet when the talk came like this and let the tape recorder pick up her words until it seemed she had said all that she wanted to say.

What follows is one such story. The tale emerged during an early visit with Kisang, when we asked about her first marriage, and she responded with zigzagging words that said a lot about the means and ends of a marriage ceremony that had taken place some sixty years before, in "horse year," when she was twenty years old and living with her father and brother in the village of Sermathang, along the eastern ridge of the Yolmo Valley. Sermathang then was a relatively new, but rapidly expanding, village. A cluster of houses and shops set just below the ridge, its importance drew from its location, which was central for trade and nearby several other prominent villages, and from its housing of several lama families renowned for their artistic skills. Kisang's father and brother belonged to one of those families of *kheba,* or "skilled ones." Above all, Kisang's marriage was a union of two high-status families from two different lama lineages. Wishing to form an alliance through marriage with a Sarma Lama family, members of a Ningma Lama family from Shomkharka, a village on a sloping mountainside at the western edge of the Yolmo region, undertook the two days' walk to Sermathang with the intent of asking Kisang's father if he would be willing to have his daughter marry a member of their family, a sixteen-year-old youth named Wangel Lama. After her father agreed to the marriage, Kisang was reluctantly brought to her new husband's home in Shomkharka. "My father arranged the marriage," Kisang recalled one morning when Pramod and I asked about this.

They [the groom's party] sweet-talked my father, they presented the shalgar to him, then they asked for me. My brother was angry at my father. "Why did you give my sister to an unknown place?!" [he asked]. "We had the marriage circle, so what could be done?" [my father replied].

Because of the "marriage circle" in place then, in which Yolmo lama lineages exchanged women in marriage, her father felt compelled, when asked, to give his daughter "to Shomkharka." To do otherwise would have signaled disrespect to the residents of that place and lessened the prestige of his family. Kisang, the woman "transferred" from one family to another, found herself in a flow of ritual acts that transformed the circumstances of her life.

In talking with Pramod and me, Kisang spoke of both the course of events that led up to her exchange in marriage and the ritual actions that constituted her passage to her husband's home in Shomkharka. It's worth attending to the words she generated, both during the marriage procession and when talking with us sixty years later. As I hear it, her narration of the events of her wedding deftly illustrates, simulates even, the ways in which a complex set of voices, ritual protocols, cultural discourses, and speech genres contributed to a woman's subjectivity—her thoughts and perceptions, her feelings, what she knew or wanted to know, her ways of acting in the world, her means of engaging with others, her sense of self and the situations she faced—as it took form within the course of a few rather memorable days. Her narrative modeled something of the grounds and features of her life then. By attending closely to it, we can begin to grasp how certain dynamics of language, time, and political agency operated within her life.

All this is in the words themselves. More often than not, though, it's in the words as Yolmo listeners might hear them. If non-Yolmo readers were presented with Kisang's utterances alone, they would, I think, miss a great deal—the intonations of her voice, what her words implied, how they related to other words and situations in Yolmo lives. Given this, I have found it worthwhile to rely on a double-voiced narrative strategy: interwoven with a running transcript (in italics) of our discussion that day, involving exchanges among Kisang, Pramod, and me, is a commentary on those exchanges that includes a crosscut assortment of asides, explanations, other statements of Kisang's, kurā culled from a number of days and persons, and remarks on both the "narrated event," the wedding that took place, and the "narrative event," Kisang's talk about it some sixty years later.[2] The commentary is greatly informed by conversations I have had with Yolmo friends about the meanings of Kisang's words. It is keyed in particular, as I find the narrative to be, to the narrator's subjective concerns during the events related and the political, cultural, and communicative underpinnings of those concerns. In time, these perspectives build to a greater sense of Kisang's lifeworld and narrative style, several dimensions of which are explored in more integrative ways in the next chapter.

Our discussion that day about her marriage, which came after words on her childhood years in Sermathang, began with a question raised by me in English and then converted into Yolmo by Pramod:

When you married, did your father and brother arrange it, or were you captured? Before, when marrying.

Was her marriage the result, that is, of arrangements made between her male elders and her husband's family, or was it in the form of the "capture marriages" common in those days, in which the bride was "grabbed" by members of the groom's family, often without the previous knowledge or consent of the girl's parents, and forcibly brought back to the groom's household?[3]

To which Kisang quickly replied:

My father and brother gave me away!

Her words carried a strong moral sense. They marked a wound that stayed with her still. Her father and brother, who she usually spoke of with pride and compassion, surprised and betrayed her through this action. She had no choice or agency in the matter, she was saying; her father was the one who acted.

These words worked in contrast with how she usually spoke of her father, for she often expressed pride in his life's work and sorrow in his death. "Hetta!" she exclaimed when early on I asked, innocently enough, if he was a "born lama." "Hey! He was Sarma Lama! We don't belong to a low caste. There's no caste above us, right?" Sitar Lama, as her father was known, was from the Sarma Lama lineage, one of the five lama lineages recognized by Yolmo people. He was an artist, or "skilled one" (kheba), she said, mostly of woodcarvings, although he constructed several gompa as well. Not having remarried after his wife died when Kisang was but a child, he raised his daughter by himself, with the help of her elder brother, until she moved away in marriage. "My father raised me, then he gave me to [the village of] Shomkharka." The good man died, from sickness and a "swollen" body, several years after his daughter married. "My mother died. My father stayed, then later he died."

After hearing that Kisang's father and brother gave her away, Pramod followed, on his own, with a second query:

You weren't captured, while in the forest?

Often the unsuspecting bride would be "seized" *(zungyo)* while she was collecting firewood or fodder with friends in the forested "jungle" neighboring her village and then brought bodily to the groom's household, despite any resistance on her part. In answering Pramod's question, Kisang spoke of actions that were just as sudden and surprising to her then.

No. My father gave me to them. To the house itself they [my husband's family] came with the marriage procession, from Shomkharka. When I first married, my husband brought the marriage procession, eh? [On the way back to Shomkharka] it passed through Chhimi and Shingenche, and they presented the shalgar. They also put the shalgar in my mother's village, in Kolama. Then we stayed in Phungboche gompa for the night.

... Ah, they put the shalgar in different places.

With such words Kisang entered into a storytelling mode of sorts, in which a "narrating I," the eighty-six-year-old Ibi Kisang spoke of events encountered by a "narrated I," the twenty-year-old Kisang Omu.[4] As such, her account bore affinities with other accounts of marriages related by Yolmo women as well as to those of women in Nepal and South Asia more generally.[5] In particular, her words invoked an unnamed narrative genre among Yolmo people, one that we might call the reluctant bride, in which a young woman at first resists a marriage designed for her, but then eventually submits to the marriage in order to preserve her family's honor, and, in time, comes to love her husband in raising children with him. It was an old story, one that structured Kisang's actions and her voice and thoughts in crucial ways. But it was also a story that the narrator made her own.

Another script at work here is the set of ritual procedures that made up an arranged wedding among Yolmo wa. In the villages in those and later years, events usually occurred in this way: Once the father had accepted the formal offering of shalgar from the groom's party, a procession composed of friends and relatives of the groom arrived at the bride's home on an auspicious day. After a brief set of wedding rites performed by a senior lama, the procession took the new bride, sometimes by carrying her, sometimes by pulling her, along a route that led back to the groom's village and household. The bride usually made a show of her resistance to the marriage by trying now and then to wrestle free of the hands set upon her. In villages along the way, the procession stopped in front of offerings of shalgar placed on the path. These offerings primarily served as ritual acts to invoke good fortune among all those involved. At the same time, by offering shalgar to the groom's party, members of the bride's extended family signaled their acceptance of the marriage. If any of the bride's close relatives did not place shalgar in this way, the slight implied their disapproval of her parents' choice of a groom. At each stop the bride and groom were seated on a mat placed in the middle of the path. The young woman usually hid her face beneath a brightly colored shawl and twisted her body away from the man, seated to her right, his own body shying away from hers, the shalgar set on a low table placed before them. Others standing around the two gave blessings to the deities, drank to the new union, then took the woman by the arm and got her to stand, then escorted her, pulling her farther along the road until the party reached another shalgar offering presented neatly on the trail before them, and so on until the procession reached the groom's home.

Kisang spoke of such recurring events—"the system we have," she once described it—in noting that members of the marriage procession (N., *janti*) came from Shomkharka, where the groom lived, and arrived at her home in Sermathang. Then, after the formalities of the wedding, the procession took Kisang with them when they began the journey back to the groom's home, along a zigzagging footpath that descended west through cultivated lands into the valley, through a succession of villages, including Chhimi, Shingenche, and Kolama, where her mother had lived before she married.

Of her mother, Kolama's Dawa Bhuti, Kisang remembered only a little, mostly partings and separations. "My mother I remember, certainly. I would follow my mother when she went somewhere. When my mother was going to her mother's house, I would tag along. Sometimes my mother would hit me, sometimes I felt sad. My mother's parents' house was in Kolama....I don't remember much about my mother. I was an infant. She died when I was an infant, my mother. When my mother died, I took the food and walked in front of my mother's corpse [to the cremation site]. I don't remember. I was a year old when my mother died...how old was I?"

"How did your mother die?" we then asked.

"She got sick, and then she died. I was maybe a year old at that time. It's a very vague memory. I was just a girl, walking ahead of my mother's corpse. Everybody told me later on that I was walking in front of the corpse and crying. I was small when she left me. I was small when she left me....I don't remember."

Another rite of departure took place some eighteen years after her mother's cremation. As the marriage procession moved from Sermathang toward Shomkharka, residents from several villages presented ceremonial shalgar to the bride and groom, who, as custom had it, drank from the containers that held the offerings of liquor. So, an account of Kisang's first marriage entailed a series of actions that led her away from the life she knew in Sermathang.

P: *When married, were you shy?*

K: *Yes, I was shy. [Yet] if I was to act shy, nothing would come of it. It was impressed here [on my forehead]. They brought me, and we stayed in Phungboche*

Figure 8. A wedding in Malemchi, 1989. Photograph by Naomi Bishop, MEDIA GENERATION.

one night. The next morning they brought me to Shomkharka. Everyone put the shalgar along the way, and everyone was performing the wedding songs and dances [si lu] *along the way, where, where?! [so many places] Then they brought me to Shomkharka.*

To say that something was "impressed" *(kosin)* on her forehead was to draw on the idea that her fate or fortune, which determined the course of her life, was inscribed on her forehead. Since the actuality of marriage was imprinted on her skull and so destined to occur, it would not have mattered much if she felt shy. "Nothing would come" of such a sentiment; there would have been no *phāidā,* or "benefit," resulting from it. And yet Kisang's reasoning simultaneously pointed to a power-ful consequential force in her life: her karmic heritage fated her to be born as a woman, then to enter a "foreign land" in marriage. "This time, I was born a woman. I can't be a man. Maybe in the next life, maybe I can be born a man," she replied when asked what her life would have been like if she had been born a boy.

One reason that most Yolmo wa conclude that it is better to be born a man than a woman is that, according to Tibetan and Yolmo lamas in particular, if one is born a man, he has a much better chance than any woman does of obtaining enlightenment during or at the end of that life. The best that women can hope for is to be born as men in their next lives.

Another, more prosaic reason is that, on a whole, Yolmo women live more difficult, less favored lives than those of Yolmo men. Many Yolmo women are encouraged to be competent, self-willed actors, and many adult women participate in influential ways in family decisions and a family's business affairs. Women are treated with respect by men in both public and private settings, and they can leave or divorce their husbands if they feel that they have been treated poorly. There are also few cultural principles or ritual practices that designate women as an inferior, polluting, or dangerous sex. At the same time, a number of cultural precepts and practices suggest that women are not the equals of Yolmo men. Deference is paid to men in a number of telling ways. When gathered together in a room, women usually sit on the floor, "below" any men present, who will be offered cots or chairs to sit on; women are also advised not to walk in front of their husbands. The travels and movements of women are more curtailed than those of men, and women have fewer opportunities to engage in business or social activities outside their homes. Whereas married men are expected to support their families by engaging in "outside" business activities, their wives are expected to attend to the "inside" duties that come with running a household: cooking, cleaning, nurturing children. Quite often these chores, along with any farming or field work that women in Yolmo might need to engage in, lead women to work in more arduous and time-consuming ways than the men in their families. Women are understood to possess weaker bodies and sem than men, and so are more susceptible to illness than men if they exert themselves too much. They are also thought to be more emotional, less rational thinkers than men. Since the establishment of the first schools in the Yolmo region, many parents have encouraged their sons to attend school more than they have their daughters. When parents pass their wealth and property on to their children, the bulk of the inheritance usually goes to their sons, not to their daughters. Whereas men can have more than one spouse, women cannot. Even though domestic violence appears to occur seldom, women do risk being beaten by their husbands. Women, elderly widows in particular, are also more prone to being identified as *boksi,* or witches. So, while a woman's situation varies depending on her station in life, and while gender is only one of many intersecting factors that contribute to a Yolmo wa's lot in life, by and large women face more trying circumstances.[6]

Yet another reason a Yolmo woman might express a desire to be reborn a man is that Yolmo femaleness also brings a fate of relocation in marriage. "By my no-good forehead I came to Shomkharka," Kisang once noted, echoing an idea voiced in a Yolmo "pain song" *(tsher lu)* that speaks to the generic sorrows of the reluctant bride:

> Our mother and father had told us:
> "Do not enter the foreign lands,"
> but due to the fate of their daughter
> she arrived at the door of others.

The transitional *but* in these lyrics underscores the twist of fate as well as a contradiction between the protective teachings of parents and their subsequent actions. The jolting dissonance between these two realities helps to explain, I think, the shock and sense of betrayal that Kisang felt. While her father lovingly provided and cared for her in her youth, he was now consigning her to the lands of others unknown to her.

The carefree tenor of her early childhood years no doubt contributed to the sense of a jarring change. While Kisang said, when asked, that she could no longer remember much about her early childhood, what she did recall to us of this time in her life centered largely on memories of playing with friends "in the dust" and of being provided for by her elders. "It was nice," she told us. "Everything for us was done by our parents. They fed us, everything.... What to say? When a child, we just played with the dust. The memories don't come." In general, however, Kisang's recollections fit with a common pattern of early childhood among Yolmo wa. While young children are responsible for some minor household chores, much of their time is spent playing with siblings or friends, with few hardships to speak of. "When I was a child, it was a happy life," Kisang noted on another occasion. "We would go to the houses of our family elders and dance and eat. Then if we didn't do the work, they would scold and hit us. Even then we weren't afraid of them. We just stayed and ate." When asked, she said, "Sure, there was happiness. My father and brother gave me food, and I could play. It was pleasant. Then 'Eat, come, eat!' After eating, I would play in the dust [*thalbi*] with friends. That was it when I was a child."

The Yolmo words for "playing in the dust" convey much the same as "playing in the dirt" does in English, though I cannot but sense something faintly Buddhist in the first phrasing, what with dust consisting of wispy, almost insubstantial remnants of something once intact but long since decayed and dispersed. In any event, to Yolmo ears the kind of dust-play that Kisang spoke of would be rather inconsequential and insubstantial. To "just stay and eat" as a child would be play pure and simple, without the labor or worries that adults need to endure.

Only later, when she was a bit older and began to do household chores and work in the fields, did Kisang appreciate life's inevitable slide from "comfort" to "sorrow." "Me? What work was there to do as a child?" she said when asked what she did when she was a young girl. "Dancing, eating. Everything was given to me by my father. What to do, then? After I grew up, we needed to eat, so I needed to tend to the potatoes. I needed to do the work. Without work, we cannot eat. So I needed to work. What to do? Sorrow means that, it turns out."

Sorrow can also mean being brought to the doorstep of others in marriage. While the marriage was an arranged one, the customary way in which the groom's party escorted her on the road back to Shomkharka embodied, as many such processions do, themes of forced capture; she was physically "brought" to her new home, despite any protests on her part.

These actions were quite consequential. A new life lay before her. Her marriage was a rite of passage.

P: *You came to Shomkharka?*

K: *To Shomkharka, first. I came to your elder uncle. They brought me there. What to do? My brother wrote [painted] the temple.*

Her brother, nine years her senior, took good care of his only sibling after their mother had died. Like his father, Tenzin Lama was skilled as an artist, having "written," or painted, the deities inside many gompa in Yolmo. "My brother was an artist, of writing the deities [*lha bhri*]. Inside the gompa."

One of the gompa within which her brother wrote the deities was a newly built one in Shomkharka. His genial residence in this village while working on the temple led, in time, to the union of two families in marriage and his sister's transfer to a lama's home. In this whorl of cause and effect, almost all agentive actions were carried out by others, and while it is true that Kisang "came" to her husband, it is more accu rate to say, again, that his family "brought" her. Consigned to her social fate, she had little ability to act and little choice in the matter. What, then, could she have done about this arrangement?[7]

> P: *After you married, did you stay with your husband?*
> K: *I stayed. What to do? They gave me away. My father, brother, everyone gave me to him. So I needed to stay. What to do? I needed to keep [the word of my father and brother]. My elders gave me to him, and my elders made the gompa there, so I needed to stay.*

Her elders, namely, her father and brother, acted in ways that compelled her to move to her husband's village: their work on the gompa in Shomkharka contributed to affable interchanges with her husband's family, which in turn led to a beneficial alliance, by marriage, between the two families. Since they had promised to give Kisang in marriage to this village, she needed to keep their word, even if she disliked the transfer. I wanted to know more about what she thought about these and other arrangements. "Your father, brother, husband," we once asked, "they forced you to marry, to do this, to do that, yes? They advised you to do these things, yes? What do you think about this?"

"What do I think?" she shot back. "They don't let the women stay!"

> P: *Was there love when you married?*
> K: *I didn't know him, before [we married]. My father and brother gave [me] to him. I didn't know about the Shomkharka lama. When I arrived in Shomkharka, then I came to know such things. Then I joined [with him].*

I had asked if Kisang had loved her husband when she married. Pramod translated my question as such, which led to Kisang's affirmation that she had "known" neither her husband nor his village.

This was not the first time that Kisang had left home. Much as Ghang Lama's first wife, Phurbi Lama, and other Yolmo women were doing at the time, she had traveled at least twice to Kathmandu with friends in search of employment within the palaces of the Rana families that then ruled Nepal. When she was twelve, she and several other girls from Sermathang undertook the three-day walk to Kathmandu to live and work within the luxurious confines of a Rana palace, where Newari teachers trained her and other girls to perform songs and dances for the reigning elite. She stayed there for nearly one year, she told us. "Once we went inside the palace, we weren't permitted to go outside, so I never came to know about the outside of Kathmandu." Of the work there, she said, "It was good, for sure! We could eat, we could dance.

Singing, dancing—I was twelve then.... At that time, it [the performing hall] was a pleasant place, like a cinema, with chairs put around [a stage], and all the kings were watching. It was pleasant to live in the palace and to sing and dance.... But there's no memory now. Worthless memories."

She left the palace a year or so later and trekked back to Sermathang, only to return with friends to the palace in Kathmandu shortly after, in search of work. She and several other girls were selected to work in a royal priest's house in Naxal—in a royal zoo, to be precise, where it soon became her job to teach parrots to talk. "Before, they kept the tiger and bear there," she said of this zoo. "Villagers and others visited there to see the animals. I stayed there continuously. I stayed very nicely. Early in the morning I had to work, to sweep the floor. The parrots' cages were kept in a straight row. Their noses were bent. Then, they gave me the duty to teach them. I needed to teach the parrots one by one. Maybe there were four or five cages. Still, they could actually learn, and I could teach them."

"How many years did you live there?"

"Me? Two and a half, maybe. I needed to talk to the parrot, but they also spoke. 'Gopī Kṛṣṇa koho! Śrī Hari Kṛṣṇa koho!' [Cowherdess, just say Kṛṣṇa! Lord Viṣṇu, just say Kṛṣṇa!] One needed to say this. Once I taught them, they would talk."

"They would talk?"

"They would talk, for sure. 'O-a-o,' they would say. Then after, they were doing well."

"Was this work good?"

"I thought that the owners' work was good. Then after, I didn't stay. I ran away. Later I returned [to Sermathang], running away." She then added with a laugh, "I felt sad. I felt homesick."

After returning to Sermathang again she had thoughts of seeking further employment in a Rana palace. But less desired travels were in store. When we asked what work she found best in her life, she replied, "When I stayed in the palace. The work of the palace was good.... If I had had a chance to stay in the palace, it would have been nice, certainly. But my forehead did not allow that to happen, then. We need to marry with our [Yolmo] people."

P: *Before you married your husband, did you give your love to him?*

K: *No. No. My father gave me to him and sent me nicely.*

P: *Was your husband nice to you?*

K: He did well. He did well. The bride was from far away. I hadn't seen him, and he hadn't seen me [before we married]. After we married, then we saw each other.

Kisang then added, while Pramod and I were speaking a bit in English:

To an unknown person he gave [me], our father.

These words were said gravely in Nepali (Pāta nabhaeko mānchelāi dieko, hāmro bāule), possibly so that I would be certain to understand, in the tone of a whispered moral censure: her father gave her to an unknown man from an unfamiliar place situated on the far, western, forested ridge of the Yolmo region.

My brother scolded my father for that. "You're giving to an unknown person?!" he asked. From the other side [of the Yolmo Valley] they came, the procession.

Kisang herself could not scold then. As she told it, voice and agency still remained largely with men.

Then later, what to do? My brother, "Our father already gave to them, and so if you would like to go, you can go. Go well," my brother said. My brother coaxed me, my brother.

The flow of time was steadfast, consequential.

P: Who gave you [away], your brother or your father?
K: My father gave me! They presented the shalgar to him in the gompa. My brother was away then. The gompa was [recently] finished. Before the marriage, two men came to our house and put the shalgar and asked my father to make a thangka for them. First they put the procession in another place, then two people came. One was Ashang Wongda, and I forget the other man's name. What was it?...I called him Uncle. They put the procession in Kami's house in Sermathang—he has a house here now—and Ashang Wongda and Ashang Dawa Sitar came to our house.

This is to say that the groom's wedding procession entered Sermathang in secret and hid in a house nearby. Then, while her brother was away, by chance, having recently completed the gompa in Sermathang, two representatives of the groom's family came to the gompa under the pretense of asking her father to craft a sacred thangka for them. They carried with them a shalgar offering, which is typically offered to another person or family when requesting something important of them.

It turned out, however, that they had in fact come to ask for Kisang in marriage, first concealing their true purpose, then later putting the shalgar in front of her father in formally establishing their request.

> P: *When did they put the shalgar?*
> K: *First they put the shalgar, asking to make the thangka! Later it became clear that they had asked for me. I didn't know, my brother didn't know. [Then he realized,] "Eh, what did he do? Eh, little sister! Our father has done well. You need to escape. Little sister, our father has done well. What to do? You need to escape. Don't stay. Our father isn't good." My brother said this.*

"Later it became clear": Yolmo knowings are often predicated on images of appearance and opacity, clarity and obscurities, purity and taintedness. Here first one thing was thought, then another. Her brother told her to make herself obscure, by leaving the house, without anyone knowing of her departure, and so temporarily displacing herself before others displaced her for good. He also had harsh words for their father, declaring sarcastically that he had "done well" in sending her so far away and saying, in effect, that, in the world of this particular moment, he was morally tainted.

"Why did you come with the shalgar?" my brother asked them. My brother didn't know about this. This deed was done by my father. My father arranged to have me taken.
   Before, they came with the shalgar. Then my brother said, "Sister, come here."
   "Why?" I asked.
   At that time we were dancing, at that time my father was doing the tsog-ya.

Her father was performing a religious rite known as tsog-ya, and some of the people who had gathered in support of this rite, including Kisang, were participating in folk dances. "Everyone was present."

Then my brother told me, "Come in."
   Then he told me, "They've come with the shalgar to take you. This is our father's work. Not my work."
   I was startled into alertness [tanga tonge ghalsin].

Tanga tonge ghalsin is a phrase difficult to translate, but one that is used to describe, for example, a rabbit busily feeding in a field, then alerted by a sudden sound, such that it freezes in midchew and with vigilant ears and eyes scans its surroundings. Kisang's depiction of how a brother's words alarmed his previously unsuspecting sister deftly pointed, in stream-of-sem terms, to changes of consciousness, to how she came to know of the marriage and the ways of men who arrange such marriages. In this way, her turns of mind marked a sudden end to her childhood and the start of her adult life.

P: *When they came for the bride, after they put the shalgar, then, Auntie, what [thoughts] came to your sem?*

K: *In the sem, [I thought,] "Why did my father give me to the unknown person and the unknown place?" My brother also said, "Our father is not good. I'm not sure whether you would like to stay there or not. If one looks at the sky, one sees only the sky. If one looks at the ground, one sees only the ground." My brother said that. I had never been to Shomkharka. My brother told me that. "I don't want to go to such a place." I said that.*

She questioned, to herself, her father's actions. Her brother, in contrast, spoke his mind, and his words perhaps confirmed to her and to later hearers several worrisome aspects of the father's actions. Although she had yet to visit Shomkharka, her brother had stayed there for several months while constructing a gompa. He commented on the fact that the village was built on a sloping, sparsely inhabited hillside surrounded by high mountains on both sides, such that when a person looked around he or she saw either sky or ground but not much else. His description was a fitting one: as seen from Thodong, the houses of Shomkharka cling to the southern face of a sloping mountainside. "He said that to frighten me," Kisang said when later asked about her brother's words. What frightened and angered her, to be clear, was not that her father had arranged her marriage; she knew all along that he would do so, and that in itself could be a good thing. It was that he had chosen a husband whose family lived in a remote and distant village set on uneven lands.

The unwanted sorrows of strange lands. "This is the [Yolmo] Sherpa woman's life story: you have to marry and move to a new place, and you have to stay there," Lhatul's wife, Mingmar, instructed me upon hearing that I was interested in recording such histories. "You can't leave. You have to stay. You have to leave your mother and father and come to a new place, where you don't know the area, where you don't know what is what or where is where." A woman's life is founded on displacements.

Kisang was similarly faced with a displacement from the world she knew:

I had one friend, Ro Namdo. She and I were at the [Rana] palace together. I used to need one friend with me. If the two of us wanted to sleep, we would go above, to the top of the house [attic]. Even she said, "Run away."

In those days she and her much-needed friend Namdo, whom Kisang had befriended when they stayed together in the Rana palace, would sleep in the attic of their fathers' houses, away from others, knowing what was what, until Kisang left for Shomkharka. "We separated from each other then, when they took me," she said later when asked what became of Ro Namdo. "Then I left her. Then, I don't remember anything else [about her]. I left her when I went." Other friends were lost as well. "Yes, I had my friends," she said when asked if she had good friends when she was "small." "But everything is lost. All my friends died before me. No friends. Now there's not. I alone have stayed. A person without luck." The presence of friends and family in stories of times past can underscore their absence in later years.

With her friendship with Ro Namdo stitched into her account, Kisang's words shifted back to her brother's refrains:

My brother said to me, "You need to go, go. That's not a good place. If one looks at the sky, one can only see the sky. If one looks at the ground, one can only see the ground. That village is maybe like Langdep." I hadn't reached Langdep either.

She knew so little of these "foreign" places. When asked once, "What in the human life is the best thing above all?" she replied, "Where one is born."

"Of the places that you have lived, which have you liked the best?" we continued.

"I feel that the best was where I was born, of course. Sermathang."

"Why is that?"

"I don't know. I was a child then. I lived with my mother. That's where I was born."

And yet she knew from an early age that she would probably not be able to remain there. "This is not your home [N., *ghar*]. This is not your home. Your home is where you have to go to when you marry," Phur Gyalmu told Norbu's as-yet-unmarried sisters Tashi and Kunsang in my presence when they were visiting their father's lands in Thodong for the first time and casually informed their father's cousin that they were glad to visit their native "home" in person. When I later asked the two what they thought of Phur's remarks, they said they weren't bothered by them, in part because their parents had been telling them as much since they were young girls. "Daughters leave. Everybody knows that. The daughters become part of another family," Nogapu told me in explaining once why no one expects daughters to care for their parents when they get older. What often remains in question for girls as they mature, however, is where, precisely, their parents will send them in marriage and whether or not that "home" will be within walking distance of their parents' house (N., *māita*), much as elderly Yolmo wa worry over where they might be reborn upon dying.

Later I asked my father, "Why did you give me to that type of place?"

Different voices, different *ke,* sounded through the narrative. The narrating Kisang, Ibi Kisang, portrayed family and friends as mouthing words that were at turns cautionary, or coaxing, or authoritative. The narrated Kisang, the lama's daughter, likewise adopted several voices, speaking here in frightful whispers, there in sharp questions. The present utterance was voiced to Pramod and me in a plaintive, accusing tone, as though she could not fathom why her father would have acted in this way. It is unclear at what "later" point she asked her father this question; it could have been hours, days, or years after her father had given his word. While one might have expected her father to respond, he remained silent in Kisang's recounting, and it was her brother who spoke again in the narrative at hand, on the day of her betrothal.

"Go, go! Don't say anything. They didn't put the shalgar for the thangka. It's for your betrothal. It seems they've put the procession in another place," my brother said to me. "You need to run away. Run away."

Leave, without speaking, her brother was telling her, as though in response to her query to her father; do not get tied to a conversation that will carry you into the ritual moment.

On this advice she acted:

Then we escaped. My friend and I both ran away! Ro Namdo's grandmother's house was below my house. We ran away. To Ibi Gorgen, in the nighttime. We ran away, then we stayed that night.

Her late-night "escape" from her father's house, often attempted by Yolmo girls when faced with a marriage, was an act of evasion. In an attempt to avoid the consequences of the actions of others, she moved from a domain of men to one of women, to one of shared interiority and more egalitarian engagements, where she became soundless and invisible to the men.

"Ibi, Ibi, open the door. It's your little sister. Please open the door. Today we need to stay here for a while."
"Why, why, in the nighttime?"
"Today we have some work to do, so please open the door quickly" [laughs].

Now teamed with Ro Namdo, within the realm of women, she was acting in more direct terms than before.

After she opened the door we went inside, and with Ibi Gorgen we stayed.

Huddled inside, they spoke of the situation. In a hushed voice Grandma Gorgen offered sympathetic words:

"You two girls have come, escaping. Friend, they've come to take you." She was worried. Ro Namdo I had, and Ibi Gorgen.
"What can I do, friend?" We talked back and forth to each other. We stayed there, we stayed there.

These phrasings conveyed a supportive, mutual talking back and forth that involved uses of words unlike so many of the power-laden commands and questions that preceded this time of waiting. Still, there was little she or her friend could do.

Then, a long time after, they came to call [for me].

Time moved on. A potent "they" summoned her back.

"I'm not going," I said. "I'm not going. Before you told me to run away." Saying this, I was angry.

She was angry at her brother for first telling her to flee, then later calling her back. "Some anger I keep inside," she once said with a laugh when we asked her what happened when she got angry. "If I'm not able to keep the anger, then I show it, certainly. What to do?" She chuckled again, then added, "As much as I can."

Then later, "Come, come," they said.
Then I thought, "If I don't go, Brother will be angry." So I went back.

Kisang's words now channeled something of her thoughts then: since her brother's potential anger overrode her own discontent and, quite possibly, a sense of betrayal by her brother, his actions won out and compelled her to return to a space of male elders. When Temba D.

Yolmo and I later asked Kisang, in the presence of her son and daughter-in-law, if a woman could in fact escape for good and so deny her parents' decision, she gave this answer: "In our society, there is a tradition of hiding the bride when somebody comes to take her, and I did the same. When my brother frightened me, and when I heard from my friend Namdo that a group of people had come to take me, I went to her grandmother's house as a way to deny my father's decision. But later they forced me, and I had to go and get married. Also, my brother came and convinced me later on."

Kisang's daughter-in-law Neela then added, "She was, I think, playing a traditional role by escaping to her friend's house."

"If she had wanted to escape and not go at all," her son Kānchā then said, "she could have stayed away, and anyone else [in the same situation] could have done so as well. Nobody can force [the potential bride to stay] too much if she isn't interested at all."

It was not always as simple as that, however. While a woman ultimately has the right to refuse any such marriage, and some do return to their parents' home, many women told me that, when they themselves married, they felt great pressure to stay with their new husbands. Gom Dolma said that her parents "compelled" her to marry the man who had "captured" her when she was sixteen. "They said that, once I was taken to his house, I had no chance to return, and I could not marry anyone else. . . . My parents would scold me and sometimes beat me when I refused to go back to my husband's house." Ghaki Lamani said that her mother and father scolded and beat her when she refused to stay with the man who had recently "captured" her. Temba's grandmother Karmu Omu, for her share, told Temba and me that, while her father was not quite satisfied with a certain family's request for his daughter in marriage, her mother insisted that Karmu agree to the marriage: "My mother threatened that, if I didn't go there, there would no longer exist any relation between mother and daughter."

Kisang continued:

When I returned, the two men were still waiting. "Why are they still there?" I thought. I slept in the attic of the house. O-ho! The house was full of so many people. It was nearly morning. There were many, many, many people. My brother had told me earlier that people had come to take me. So maybe it was true. I went to the attic and stayed there; then after, they said, "Come down, come down."

As the hours flitted by, Kisang further realized what was taking place.[8] The fact that so many unknown people waited in her father's house through the entire night gave additional credence to the idea that she would be taken away. Her invocation of "many, many, many people" would have also underscored to a Yolmo audience the social force of the situation and the need for a stunned and hesitant girl to go along with what was planned, lest she bring shame to her father and brother. To evade the crowd's watchful presence she slept in the loft, perhaps accompanied by Ro Namdo, until she was again summoned.

My brother came up the stairs to the attic, and said, "Don't be angry. Your father gave you. We'll send you with blessings. Now don't show that you're angry. Don't wear a black face."

Though she might have been angry, she could not ruin the occasion by looking gloomy and so showing her anger visually. A play of interiors and exteriors, feelings and facades.

There was then a pause in her recounting, which we disturbed with another question.

P: *During the time of being married, was it pleasant?*
K: *It was pleasant for others! They were having a good time, performing the wedding songs and dances, and playing the cymbals.*
P: *And Auntie?*
K: *Me?*
P: *Yes.*
K: *"Where is it, where is it?" [I wondered]. The place where my mother hadn't even reached, to that place I had to go. My brother told me, "If one looks at the sky, one can only see the sky. If one looks at the land, one can only see the land. That place looks curved [like the inside surface of a bowl]." My spirit was taken. How could I go to such a place? I didn't want to go. Everyone had already come [to take me], dancing and singing. It was compulsory that I go.*

Many Yolmo wa understand that a person's la, or spirit, can be "lost" or "taken" *(kherti)* from the body if that person is startled by a sudden noise or event, such as birds rustling in a woods or a slippery fall into a river; the absence of the la can result in illness or death. In noting that her brother's words spooked her spirit, Kisang was most likely speaking figuratively, much as an American might say that she was "scared out of her wits." Kisang was perhaps increasingly disheartened, resigned to her fate. Yet she seemed less spirit-startled by the person she was to marry than by thoughts of the distant, unvisited, unsightly place to which she was being forced to go. That displacement became "compulsory" [N., *kargi*] in part because "everyone" had already arrived and had begun to celebrate her marriage. If she tried to escape then, her actions would publicly disgrace her family. Ritual as compulsion.

My brother said [quietly] to me, "Little sister, you need to keep our nose." Mheme of Thalo, who had a conch-mark on his bare foot, was also there then. All the Mhemes were there. At that time, my father was sponsoring a tsog-ya, so my male relatives, everyone, had gathered. At that time, I took the blessing from Mheme and other relatives and I went to Phungboche. I was sad. My father had done this. My brother said, "If one looks at the sky, one can only see the sky. If one looks at the ground, one can only see the ground."

Mheme of Thalo is remembered as being a powerful, high-status lama from the village of Thalo, below Takpakharka, who bore a birthmark in the shape of a conch; as with many such signs, the mark designated sacredness. To receive a blessing from this spiritually advanced man, as well as from other male elders who were attending the tsog-ya rite incidental to the marriage, was a highly auspicious act. And yet Kisang noted, in a matter-of-fact tone, that she was saddened by her imminent departure, which her father had brought about.

"If one looks at the sky..." Her brother's refrain, when reiterated in tandem with invocations of elders, blessings, and sadness, seemed to impart well the complex vectors of her consciousness in this moment. And yet the clustering of these many themes in her account, themes that did not necessarily occur in the world at the same time but perhaps combined simultaneously in her mind later on, led her again to get ahead of herself in her storytelling, and she had to backtrack anew.

Then they said, "Come down from above."
    I came down [from the attic]. So I went [to them]. At that time, my father, brother, all my uncles were there. "Come down," they said.

Did she go to them, or feel compelled to go, precisely because everyone was there?

He told me directly. "Don't throw our nose. Father already gave you, to Shomkharka. Don't be angry. Don't throw the nose. Our father already gave [you]." My brother coaxed me.
    I went down. At that time too many people were gathered. I didn't recognize all of them.
    They were from far away. I went down.

And so she returned to the domain of male elders.

"Come, come," they said.

There was nothing for me to do but cry, surely! I wanted to cry because they gave me to a place far away.

"For a flask full of wine, don't give your daughters to others," advises a Yolmo pain song, as though punctuating a betrayal,

But if you must give us away
Don't send us beyond the mountain [to a place far away].

Those attending the marriage ceremony offered different advice.

What to do? "Don't throw your father's nose and your brother's nose." Then later everyone said, "Don't throw the nose. Hold your father's nose. Your father and grandfather are also here."

The presence of these elders was an auspicious, appreciated one, for Yolmo wa often find it fortunate when one's family is present when events of importance occur.

The next words quoted were voiced in a tone that somehow conveyed the sense that Kisang was not so sure at first of their veracity:

"You're very fortunate," everyone said. "Your grandfather and your father are here. You're very fortunate," everyone said.

She was fortunate for two reasons, Yolmo friends have told me: the groom's side came respectfully; and her elders, among others, were able to attend and witness this marriage between a lama and a "lamini," as a daughter of a lineage lama is often titled. And yet fortune and compulsion coincided here.

Maybe it's true. So I agreed.

The doubt in her voice fell away here, and she spoke a bit more quietly.

I agreed, then. Then, morning came. Morning came, and they offered food. So, acting so—I don't remember what time it was—they offered food. "Please eat, please eat." What time was it? My family elders were there.

She lost track of time, was a bit bewildered, in a subjective moment. Others were more sure of what was to happen.

P: How long does it take to go from Sermathang to Shomkharka?

> K: *Two days. They performed the marriage one night, right? Then they took me*
> *the next day. They took me, and we needed to stay overnight in Phungboche.*
> *We arrived in Shomkharka the day after that.*

"In this way," acting so, the procession moved through terrain that grew more unfamiliar to the bride as the marriage party proceeded west. A Yolmo pain song comments on similar displacements from loved ones:

> One mountain crossed, no pain
> two mountains crossed, no pain
> [but] when crossing the third mountain
> I remembered father and mother clearly.

The couplets speak to the linkages among partings, absence, pain, and memory: only after remembering her absent parents, as she steps farther and farther away from them, is the speaker pained.

Two other significant ritual moments known to Yolmo wa involve movements across a landscape. Both are associated with the transformations of death: the procession that carries the body of a newly deceased person to a nearby cremation grounds, and the later procession that carries the deceased's effigy from its former home to the lama's gompa during the ghewa, or funeral ceremony. Both movements denote changes in a person's social identity, as the marriage process does. Death is indeed like another movement, wherein one travels to a new place, and marriage for women parallels the process of dying in a few ways, since one life is left behind and a new one begins. Ritual as movement.

> K: *After passing Kyeldong we came to Chhimi. In Chhimi was the house of my pa-*
> *ternal male relatives. Chhimi is the village of [the] Sarma Lama [lineage],*
> *Chhimi is. Then they [my husband's family] put the shalgar. Then they said,*
> *"Oh, you've stolen our cousin!" [laughs a bit]*
> P: *"We didn't steal your cousin!"*
> K: *"We didn't steal your cousin. We requested her." Like this they were joking well*
> *with each other.*

They came to the village of Chhimi, where members of her father's family and lama lineage lived. Here the groom's party offered shalgar to these men in paying respect to them. In response the men deftly joked about the "theft" of their cousin Kisang. The response elicited, and quickly anticipated by Pramod, signaled well the semiritualized agency involved and the sense of goodwill conveyed by supporters of the two families.

The groom's family and friends carried her bodily, which is often the case when a groom's party first sets off with a new bride. Also present during this journey, Kisang later related, was a "bride's friend," a cousin of hers named Sonam, an age-mate who was there, Kisang explained, "just to take me there. I took her with me as a friend." A friend often accompanies a Yolmo bride like this, then returns home shortly after they reach the groom's home. "I didn't go there alone," she told us on another occasion. "My husband's family came with the wedding procession, and they took me back to the husband's house. On the way the people in different villages offered us shalgar." There was little mention, here or elsewhere, of the groom himself, who was apparently not yet a significant part of the agentive field.

In there they put the shalgar. They did the chepa *[blessing]. Then my relatives said, "Come inside. Come inside, then."*

They replied, "We don't have time. We need to go early." Then we left.

Then later at Shingenche they put [shalgar]. They also did the shalgar at Shingenche. The time was going down, down. Then later on the procession arrived in Norbugang. We arrived at Tashi Ghyang, below Norbugang. They did the shalgar there as well.

"Stay, stay for the night," they said then. They were the cousins [of my husband]. The time was going down, down. "We're not staying. We can make it as far as Phungboche." They said that. They knew the people from Phungboche.

As the time of day steadily descended and the procession moved farther west, the groom's party entered into lands more familiar to them but unknown to Kisang. Despite gracious offers to put them up for the night, they aimed to stay with family in the village of Phungboche.

Then after we came to Tserilabrang we received the shalgar. We reached Phungboche. We reached Chyanjagang, and up from there to Phungboche. Then that night we stayed in Phungboche. Then, after we stayed that night. The dawn came. We took tea in the morning. Then they took [me]. They took [me], then.

Though it went unsaid in a series of events recounted in a rhythmic cadence, they had crossed the Malemchi River and begun to climb the western ridge of the Yolmo Valley. She was being "taken" still.

Then after they took me, we arrived in Dakpakharka, where a nephew lived. We arrived in Kānchā's cousin Mendo's house. They put the shalgar. It was put like this along the entire route, until we reached Shomkharka.

The number of places where shalgar was offered spoke to the considerable respect paid to the marriage and to the two, newly linked families.

> K: *Then we passed Dakpakharka, Nalungkharka, then Laing came. Then Takhor, these days there's a shrine there—you know that, don't you, Nephew? From there the open field is seen?*
>
> P: *Yes.*
>
> K: *Earlier my brother had said, "Father already gave you. If one looks at the sky, one can only see the sky. If one looks at the ground, one can only see the ground. In such a place, how can one stay?"*

Her brother's words echoed in her thoughts as she anticipated lands new to her: would she be able to live in such a place?

Later, we arrived at Kashingdap's pass. Then after that there was a clearing. It was called Laing, it turned out. Then I thought, "It's true, there's just one or two houses, like my father said." I saw just two, three houses, and one or two herding shelters [ghore] when walking. Eh! One person came and said to me, "You see that shelter for the rainy season? Our brother's place [the land of her husband], it's this. This is the place."

"It's true." What she saw now matched with what she had heard of, but had never seen, before. Her companions then told her that a tiny, insignificant, woods-bound hamlet, composed of but a few houses and temporary shelters, contained her husband's cowshed of a home, where they expected her to remain.

Then I remembered my brother's words. "I'm going to stay in such a place?" [I asked myself]. Ah, I struggled, and I didn't agree.

"Why did he give me to this place, my brother?! Why did he give me to this place, my father?! What kind of brother are you? You mentioned the land." I thought about that kind of place.

While her father's description of Laing matched her perception of it, her brother's assessment of Shomkharka as a place with open land did not fit with the obscure woods she saw before her, and she was pained by the possibility of a further betrayal.

"Spit! [Thuk!] I won't stay in this kind of place. Tomorrow I'm going back," I said.

"Spit!" Among Yolmo wa this utterance usually carries an import similar to English swearwords like *shit!* or *damn!* especially when they are uttered by someone confronted with a highly unwelcome or distasteful situation. And so Kisang's utterance of "spit!" was directed at the situation she found herself in, not at the people responsible for it.

"It was something she couldn't even imagine," Karma Gyaltsen said upon hearing Kisang's words.

I stayed then. Everyone was coaxing me, then I was trying to walk.

The phrase "trying to walk" suggested her body still could not proceed willingly or that she could not quite act on her own, of her own volition, but she tried to proceed nonetheless.

Then, everyone was laughing.

They were joking, teasing, it turns out.

Then I thought, "This is not the place."
Then one person in the group pointed out for me, "Way over there, where it's bright and clear, that's Shomkharka."

Finally they showed her Shomkharka, standing "bright and clear" in the distance. Obscurities of place and knowledge fell away.

"Eh. Why did you show me such a nasty place before?!"

She reproached her escorts for telling her that the wooded hamlet was her husband's village, when in fact that dark, vile place was quite the opposite of Shomkharka.

Then the marriage procession took me. They were taking me joyfully. After we passed that place, even the group of people from there came to the Laing shelter to receive us. There the people came to receive the procession. They came there, and we came there.

An honor, it was, to be met on the road like this. It was a "big wedding" all around, chiefly because two lama lineages were involved.

While singing, we arrived in Shomkharka. In Shomkharka, everyone came near the spring to welcome and receive us. They came with shalgar.

The presence of "everyone" was double-edged, for in Yolmo social consciousness, such spirited amity could imply, at once, respectful well-wishing and a subtle pressure to stay.

Then, in the house we arrived, certainly. We arrived in the house.

Her voice shifted here from a narrational one to a more assertive, assessing one.

What to do, then? My elders sent me. Such is the forehead of the daughters. [To be] in
Shomkharka, it was written, it turned out. The gompa was written by my brother.
  In that way, I became like this. Nevertheless, it became nice. It all became nice, yes?

Her words molded a summation of sorts. What could have been done
with such certainties, how could she have acted differently, especially when
residing in Shomkharka was inscribed on her forehead? "What to do? My
own fate...where, where I had to arrive," she once mused. Another kind
of writing, she noted, was also of consequence here: as we have learned,
before her betrothal, her brother was commissioned to paint, or "write,"
the sacred images inside the newly built gompa in Shomkharka, and
through this work her husband's family came to know of her family and
her unmarried status. So two kinds of writerly determinations, one karmic
in means, the other social, led her to arrive in this way and to become who
she was, "like this." Nevertheless, the consequential fruits of such writs
turned out to be good ones—didn't they?—and her father and brother
were perhaps forgiven for sending her away in marriage. "They were both
good. Loved ones," she said of her now deceased father and brother.

I stayed. What to do? I stayed. The noses of my elders I haven't thrown. We arrived
there. What to do? Everyone treated me well. Like this, I stayed here.

She stayed in her husband's house, and did not "throw" or "cut her family's nose" by returning to her father's house.
  She then said quietly in Yolmo:

I was twenty. Your uncle was four years younger. He was [born in] ox year. Ox year.
That's when I arrived. He didn't live a long time [after we married]. Twelve or thir-
teen years [from when we married]? He left. He left me behind.

The last words were voiced in a quietly emotional tone. The sad
irony was that, leaving her family and home, Kisang came to and stayed
with him only to have him "leave her behind" when he died a few years
later. Hers was a life told, and perhaps lived, through movements, stay-
ings, and departures, all of which could have informed her next assertion, uttered moments later, as though again to herself:

...Eh-he, I didn't know sorrow, happiness.

"Eh-he, nga dukha sukha mha she." What to make of this striking utterance? It could be that it was voiced self-deprecatingly, much as Yolmo
women often say they do not know about something asked of them.
During a visit three days before I had in fact asked, among related ques-

tions, who had more sorrow in life, women or men. "To say happiness, sorrow, I don't know," Kisang answered then. Other overly general or abstract questions of mine usually met with similar responses, as though she was hesitant to speak beyond the specifics of her life. Perhaps, then, her account of her passage to Shomkharka was a way for her "to say happiness, sorrow" through means familiar to her. One elderly Yolmo man said as much when I asked him why he thought Kisang might have said what she had. "Whatever she came across she could speak of," he said, after thinking it over a bit. "But she couldn't talk about things in an abstract way." With this in mind, I also hear in her words a subtle, cutting comment on how she first came to "know dhukpu," for in many ways her account is a story of emergent knowledge, of how she came to know something about sorrow and happiness.

Karma offered another, perhaps more plausible, interpretation upon reading through this chapter while staying in my home in Massachusetts in 2001. As he saw it, Kisang's words carried the idea that "she didn't know sorrow *from* happiness, she couldn't tell them apart, because it was all mixed together, in a confusing way, because sorrow became happiness, and then when she was expecting sorrow, there was happiness, then sorrow again, and so on."

Yet another possibility, suggested by the words that immediately preceded the statement "He left me behind," is that Kisang had in mind the idea that it was only with the death of her husband that she came to know the full range of sorrow and joy in life.

Whatever Kisang's words meant to her, they seemed to bring her tale to a close. Then, impressed with her vivid rendering of events that took place sixty years earlier, I asked her how it was that she could recall so much.

> R: *How is it that you can remember all of this talk [kurā]?*
> K: *It has stayed [laughs a bit].*

A physics of staying, of remainders and reminders.

> R: *In the sem…*
> K: *…in the sem, doing this, doing that, it comes. Nobody teaches it. It just comes. The time of arriving [in Shomkharka] has stayed in the sem. When I try to delve into the past, it comes.*

A Theater of Voices

Think of a fabric—a piece of cloth, say, or a carpet, or a shawl. Consider the ways in which different threads are woven together in forming a texture of interlacing strands.

Karma asked me to do just that, one afternoon as we sat at a cluttered table in my home in Massachusetts and discussed Kisang's narrative of her first wedding. In speaking of Kisang's decision to abide by what her father arranged, he wanted me to understand the profound importance of family and social ties in Yolmo communities, especially when it comes to important decisions that people make in their lives. "Everything is interrelated," he said in English. "Everyone is connected to everyone else. It's like a fabric, a very extensive fabric." Within that intricate, multithreaded fabric of relations, he went on to say, everything and everyone is interconnected in time and space; actions shape later actions in time, words relate to other words, bodies to other bodies; what one person does affects other members of his or her family, such that people give a lot of thought to how their plans in life will affect their relatives. The social bond itself compels people to act in certain ways, and yet that bond is a welcome, valued texture in Yolmo lives, for it gives reason and relatedness to them. "The fabric is a necessity. It's a must," he told me. "Without it, we're not ourselves. So even though I'm now in the States, not all of me is here." Karma's point, I came to understand, was that Kisang's share of that fabric was such that, whatever she might have preferred for herself, she had to act in ways that preserved her family's honor.

While Karma was speaking then of how the relations among persons within Yolmo communities are fundamentally interinfluential in nature, one can also apply the simile to the constitution of persons in themselves. As Yolmo wa know it, a life or a person is, like a fabric, woven out of many different features. The vitalities of body, spirit, mind; voices heard and sounded; delicate ties with others; sensate engagements with the world; moral and aesthetic sensibilities; the churnings of time and karmic action; the markings of pain and comfort within a body; the rounds of remembrance and forgetting that course through a sem—these and other forces contribute, in interthreaded ways, to the constitution and reconstitution of persons.

Such a take on personhood, in which an involved aggregate runs the show, is in accord with the spirit of many Buddhist understandings, from the idea that a person is composed of a conditioned, nonessential, transitory, ever-changing "heap" of "aggregates, fields, senses," to the conviction that all things are mutually relative and interdependent, to the Buddha's insight that all conditioned experience is founded on a principle of "dependent arising."[1] While most Yolmo wa would not talk precisely in such refined ways, they do understand persons to be composed of karmically and socially patterned bundles of interworking psycho-physio-spiritual faculties. In general, the form and tenor of Buddhist perspectives resonate with the makings of Yolmo personhood in ways that Western theories of the self do not. There is a close fit between Buddhist conceptions of the various groupings, disbandings, and regroupings of sentient beings and Yolmo takes on the interfabricating, interaffecting formations of a life. And an individual life, in turn, is connected to the other lives close to it.

With such thoughts at hand we return to Kisang's narrative of her wedding. We need to spell out further the ways in which the narrative conveys the grounds and features of her life then. It seems best to do so, however, with the design of fabrics and bundles in mind, for it is only by maintaining an idea of dynamic, interwoven multiplicities, both within and among different subjectivities, that we can make effective sense of such things. Of particular interest are the ways that certain processes of action, time, language, pain, and memory contributed to how she spoke of her life.

It is fitting that Kisang said that memories of "doing this, doing that" came to her when she delved into the past, for her recollections of times past focused largely on specific deeds undertaken by others or herself. Other Yolmo wa speak in similar ways. The focus in Tibetan Buddhism on the karmic import of personal action probably has something to do with this. And yet there is an intensity and fullness to Kisang's representations of specific deeds that stands out. Her words alone intimate that, for her, life was composed of a series of significant actions, from acts of staying and going to ones of betrayal, kindness, and coercion. This can be heard in the sentences she uttered when speaking of her "transfer" to Shomkharka in marriage. Almost every sentence depicts a specific action. Many of her utterances, which are usually quite brief and compact, have a similar structure: there is a doer and a deed done by that doer: "My father gave me to them." "We ran away." "I stayed." Depictions of nonhuman events also tend to be rendered in active terms: "The sky was opening." "The time was going down, down." Much the same goes for memories, feelings, and states of mind: "I was startled into alertness." "The time of arriving has stayed in the sem."[2] In accord with this act-based narrative style, which is common to many Yolmo stories, a string of phrases or sentences can depict, to use a Yolmo expression, a *"pat-pat-pat"* series of actions in a stretch of time, enacted by a person or a group, as when Kisang recounted how the wedding party passed through a series of villages on its way to Shomkharka:

> O tingle Tserilabrangla lepsin.
> Shalgar chusin.
> Phungbochela lepsin.
> Chyanjagangla lepsin, olegi Phungbochela.
> O ghungmu Phungbochela dhesin.

Then after we came to Tserilabrang we received the shalgar. We reached Phungboche. We reached Chyanjagang, and up from there to Phungboche. Then that night we stayed in Phungboche.

The "then, then" tenor evident in many of Kisang's utterances is underscored by the structure of the Yolmo language, in which the verb almost always comes at the end of a sentence and pronouns often remain implicit, such that a more literal, word-for-word translation of the above lines would read:

> Then after in Tserilabrang [we] came.
> Shalgar [we] received.
> Phungboche [we] reached.
> Chyanjagang [we] reached, and up from there to Phungboche.
> Then that night in Phungboche [we] stayed.

When spoken and when heard, the stress usually fell on the action entailed in the verb, and what often resulted in narrative time was an act-by-act litany of specific happenings: we reached, stayed, took, passed, left, met. Yet each sentence in a narrative could also have a particularistic quality to it, as though it along with all that it implied stood by itself, with a gap of time apparent between the acts chronicled in a string of sentences:

> He did well. He did well.
> The bride was from far away.
> I hadn't seen him, and he hadn't seen me.
> After we married, then we saw each other.

"Our lives are like links in a chain": for Kisang, happenings within a single life, as well as events within a particular story, were themselves like links in a chain: separate and distinct, yet also interconnected and interaffecting.

Actions she described were interconnected in part because they almost always bore consequences. In many of Kisang's accounts of deeds done, usually implied but sometimes made explicit were the consequences of any actions depicted. These consequences could be actual or potential, and they could be either immediate to the situation or realized much later on. As such, Kisang's take on the effects of action paralleled what Ghang Lama had to say about consequential actions in his life. Like Mheme, Kisang understood that her karmic heritage contributed to her station in life as well as to significant arrangements during that life; her "no-good forehead" led her to be born a woman and to marry with the village of Shomkharka. But just as significant in her recollections of her life, and, we may suppose, in that life itself, was her attentiveness to various everyday actions, which, while not necessarily of the heavy-duty karmic sort, were quite consequential nonetheless. Whereas Ghang Lama usually spoke of the effects of action in terms of the general circumstances of a life, Kisang's narratives often highlighted the social and pragmatic effects of actions within the course of a day or two.

The narratives are characterized by a hyperconsequentiality of means, for almost all actions prompted effects. Kisang's words make it clear that she was acutely conscious of the matter-of-fact implications of specific actions. Her father's efforts, for one, brought sadness: "I was sad. My father had done this." In the long run, however, "it all became nice," apparently. At the same time, her mindfulness of the consequentiality effected by, and sometimes seemingly inherent in, many actions linked up with her ways of talking about past events. In speaking of the events that led her to move to Shomkharka, for instance, she would often end a phrase with either a rising or a decreasing inflection while slowing down her rhythm of speech ("We stayed there, we stayed there") and then pause for a second or two while her words tarried in the air. Such a narrative pacing has the effect of underscoring the ways in which the actions she had just spoken of continued to maintain an active, effective presence in any next instance of action that she then put forward ("Then, a long time after, they came to call"). This new utterance would, in turn, maintain its own presence in the shadows of any next words uttered ("'I'm not going,' I said"). The meanings and sounds invested in utterances B and C thus contributed to the import of utterance D, which in turn helped to shape the semiotic gist of utterances E and F, and so on. Each utterance had its own life, within the moment of its utterance, and death, in the silence that followed. But each utterance also carried a rebirth of sorts, within the semiotic force of subsequent utterances. With different strands of cause and effect coursing through the same narrative moments, Kisang's words held a sustained and overlapping temporal richness. Every utterance, every action, took place within a complex weave of time.

An indication of Kisang's orientation to the force of time during the days of her wedding can be found in the linguistic markers of temporality evident in her narrative. There are frequent references to the time of day, and the progression of night into day, then into night again: "The dawn came." "The time was going down, down." These notations on the passing of time are coupled with a host of adverbs like *then* and *before,* which initiate many of her sentences: "Then we passed Dakpakharka, Nalungkharka, then Laing came." These phrasings sometimes contribute, particularly in the account of the journey on foot to Shomkharka, to a fast-paced recounting of events, with village after village quickly being passed as the wedding procession made its way through the valley. Through all this one gets the sense of a rush of time, the inevitability of its passing, and the ways in which Kisang was being swept into a new time and place in her life by a hurried progression through time and space. That progression often had an air of causality to it, with one deed leading to another and one chain of events setting the stage for the next sequence of action.

In some instances, the air of causality that streams through her narratives can be heard within the syntax of sentences: "My elders gave me to him, and my elders made the gompa there, so I needed to stay." The use of the conjunction *so* in this and other statements of hers says a lot, for it speaks to the ways in which certain deeds created situations in which she found herself compelled to act in particular ways: "Then I thought, 'If I don't go, Brother will be angry.' *So* I went back. Then they said, 'Come down from above.'...*So* I went."

Other, implicit *so*'s thread other scenes: "There were many, many, many people [so I could not leave]." "At that time, my father, brother, all my uncles were there [so I had to obey them]." "'Father already gave you, to Shomkharka [so you must marry].'" Her actions, what she did or did not do, what she said or did not say, were greatly shaped by the real or possible actions of others and by the fabric of relations that made up her life.

To be a good daughter for Kisang and other women of her time was to know well what *so*'s were implied by certain actions and to know as well the importance of following through on what was expected of her. Yolmo girls and young women then did not live under terribly confining conditions, nor were they especially cowed by the adults in their lives. But they did need to mind what they did or said, as well as what others told them to do. Staunchly under the authority of the senior members of their families, they knew from an early age the benefits of submitting quietly to authority, of responding to provocation with silence, of avoiding confrontations with authority figures, and of getting things done through indirect means.[3] So it was with the twenty-year-old Kisang. Often, when speaking of her passage to Shomkharka, she was clear about what she needed to do then, what she could or could not do, and why. Power in the Yolmo world is the ability to effect significant consequences through one's actions. "The lama is the one who affects, not the one who is affected by," Karma once told me in speaking of Yolmo lamas, senior men who, if they are learned and respected enough, possess a substantial degree of power and authority. When she was about to marry, Kisang was the one affected by, seldom the one who affected. She was carried along in a stream of actions.

There were several dimensions to this. For one thing, people acted in ways that compelled her to act in certain ways: her brother summoned her, they brought her, they carried her. Although she sometimes acted on her own then and would in fact come to possess a stronger agency after she married and bore children, more often than not at this time in her life she had to go along with the wishes of others, and so she was taken along by her elders' actions, with little choice or ability to act otherwise: "It was compulsory that I go." There was also subtle social pressure to submit to the wedding. That "everyone" was present to celebrate and honor the wedding foretold an auspicious, highly respected union. But it also spoke to a ritualized coercion that compelled her to join in the procession. Coinciding with this were the constraints of ritual time: once the wedding rites were underway, and the groom's party began to make their way, shalgar by shalgar, back to Shomkharka, the rites took on a temporality of their own, and there was then a certain inevitability in how events proceeded. Once ritual actions of this sort get underway, they are almost always carried on until their completion. It would have been very difficult for Kisang to have broken from those ritualized actions, to have removed herself from the flow of ritual time, without bringing everything to a dead stop. If she had done that, she would have created a rupture in the social fabric and brought dishonor to her family. The social drama in which she found herself also framed her actions. The narrative genre of the reluctant bride, the sentiments conveyed in a brood of folk songs, and the "traditional role" she adopted in fleeing her father's house had the effect of shaping how she and others spoke, thought, and acted. Kisang herself spoke of how her karmic fate destined her to part for a foreign land in marriage. Other, more human-authored scripts were also at work.

Several forces thus fixed what she could do then. If the situation had been different, if Kisang had been older, or if she had had more political clout at the time, things might have proceeded differently. As it was, she seemed stunned by it all, immobilized even: "I was trying to walk." Her body could come to a standstill. She knew well that there was little she could do at times: "There was nothing for me to do but cry, surely!" "If I was to act shy, nothing would come of it." "'What can I do, friend?'"

One thing that she could do then was to ask questions of this sort. Language offered her a means to act in the world, to generate signs, to comment on the actions of others. Talk was very much a kind of action. An utterance was a le, a work or karmic deed. To her, speaking was much more than a way to refer to the world, to state something, or to name or represent an object. It was a kind of doing, and a politically and morally charged one at that. In her world a great deal of action took place through talk and the various intonations, silences, looks, and facial expressions that accompanied it. Time and again people engaged dialogically with others through such veritable speech-acts as praising, sweet-talking, coaxing, advising, warning, scolding, commanding, instructing, asserting, imploring, frightening, questioning, summoning, blessing, beseeching, joking, deceiving, teasing, laughing.

These verbal acts had consequences; they did certain things in the world, in diverse ways, whether their speakers knew it or not. People were silenced, or scolded, or respected. The effects of many utterances were quite clear in her narration. Her brother's description of Shom-kharka spooked her "spirit"; she was startled when he alerted her to what their father was arranging; and she grew angry when her brother tried to call her back home from Ibi Gorgen's. Her brother also "coaxed" her into agreeing to the marriage, and only after everyone coaxed her on the way to Shomkharka did she try to walk again. In turn, the comments by everyone that she was "very fortunate" led her to agree to the marriage. Words also helped to seal her fate, as when her father agreed to give her "to Shomkharka" in marriage.

Some acts of speech are life-enhancing and world-affecting. Blessings from elders, for instance, are known to bestow long lives among those so blessed. Kisang said that she herself blessed her own children and grandchildren later in life. "In my sem I think about my children, 'May they eat well in doing well.' I bless them," she once explained. "'Live well, eat well,' these things I said. Whatever they aspire to, I bless them, for sure."

"What do you wish for them?" I asked on another occasion.

"'Long life come. Prosperity come. Happiness come.' I just say this."

She also prayed that misfortune did not touch her own life. "I pray to the deities, 'May good come, may hardship not come,'" she said when asked to explain how she prayed. "To the gods and goddesses I prostrate, 'May hardship not come in another life as well.' Wishing this, I prostrate to the gods." Other kinds of prayers enhanced her "merit" and that of others.[4]

The logic was pervasive. For her, as for other Yolmo wa, talk could have a tangible, palpable effect on someone's sem, body, or life. People often say in the course of everyday conversations, through words direct or indirect, that hearing certain statements can make them feel happy or sad.[5] Many understand that saying the name of a deceased person can cause harm among the living. People also often refrain from pronouncing the names of family members who are of higher status than they are—husbands, parents, elder brothers—for fear that such utterances will diminish the life spans of those spoken of. Kisang, for instance, never referred to her former husbands by their names; when talking with us, she spoke of her first spouse as "my husband" or "the lama," and the second as "Kānchā's father." Insulting talk spoken by low-status people to any high-status neighbors of theirs can cause the life spans of the latter to be shortened. Curses injure in much the same way. Talk about a family or an individual can form into *mhi kha,* or "people's talk," a malevolent force that can cause people to fall ill and businesses to go bad. Ritual speech can also effect transformations. "If they say the cure, then it can be cured," Kisang once said of the ritual healings of bombo. The sacred prayers known and used by lamas can likewise bring into being certain realities. Words wound, words heal. Words, simply, were a very real and transformative force in Kisang's world.

Other statements, from words shared with a friend, to calling someone uncle, to the songs sung along the road to Shomkharka, also affected aspects of her life, if in more oblique ways. A good example of how Kisang recalled words having a significant effect in her life lay in her explanation for having refrained a few years back from returning to a health clinic to receive medical care on cataracts that were clouding her eyes, as doctors in Kathmandu had advised her to do. "They said to me, 'Come back to the hospital after six months to have your eyes examined.' But they [my children] didn't take me. I took advice from others. I myself did not go. I just remained still."

"Why didn't you go to the hospital?"

"Why didn't I? What was it? Either others didn't take me, or I said, 'I'm not going.' Everyone said, 'Don't go to the hospital. If you go, you'll become blind.' Someone's daughter said, 'Don't go. Don't go. I've seen a lot of people who have become blind.' I listened to her talk, so I didn't go. A person did that, so it [my vision] was ruined."

Because a person "did that," and because Kisang "listened" to that woman's talk and refused to go to the hospital, she was now nearly blinded by cataracts. Listening to another's words could alter one's life.

Early in her life Kisang listened a great deal, and necessarily so. This was the case when she was about to marry, for she so often abided by, and perhaps had to abide by, the assertions and commands of others. She also seemed not to have spoken much herself, at least in ways worth mentioning later on. By my count, in the account of her transfer to Shomkharka the twenty-year-old Kisang spoke out loud to others ten times in all, compared with some forty instances of quoted speech attributed to others. Most of what she said was in response to the direct assertions and summons of others, while other thoughts were voiced only to herself. In being carried along by the forceful actions of others, she found it necessary to listen well to what others said and to take care in what she herself said. All this would have been in line, both then and now, with the political and communicative situations of young Yolmo women, who often find it difficult to speak their minds directly to more powerful elders and who, if they want to convey their wishes to them, usually must rely on intermediaries to do so.

Yet Yolmo women do talk about the conditions of their lives with others, particularly with other women of the same general age. Kisang herself spoke of how, after she had fled her father's home, she huddled together with friend Namdo and Ibi Gorgen in the latter's home and "talked back and forth" with them through the night. The scene was not an uncommon one, for Yolmo women, young or old, often visit one another in their homes, sometimes with young children in tow, sometimes within the earshot of men. Among other topics bandied about, they often discuss any hardships they or others face in their lives. In other situations in everyday life, including those where men are present, women, married women with children especially, talk more generally about the actions of others. With talk of this sort, women can comment on those actions, and they can listen to, and either support or confirm or counter, the commentaries of others. Their words or responses can also speak to the moral import of the actions, as they understand it or wish others to know it. They can talk about others as well as learn what others are saying about them. Through such commentaries a certain degree of "social power" is wielded.[6] While Yolmo women do not hold public positions of power, and they customarily pay deference to the views and declarations of men, they do have a considerable say in what people do or think they should do. In talking with others, they can be told to shut up, or they can be silenced indirectly, or their words can fall on deaf ears; but they can also interrogate relations of power, they can praise or deride the actions of others, they can subtly encourage others to act in certain ways, they can, in the course of words, shape how events unfold or are told or retold.

Kisang's wedding narrative worked along similar lines, even though its most immediate hearers were two men. In narrating to Pramod and me the terms of her marriage, Kisang depicted the effects of certain deeds and utterances on her own person and life and so situated what happened in a vital moral and political landscape. Although, according to her own reckoning, she did not say all that much to others at the time of her marriage, given her youthful status and the demands imposed on her then, she could tell others about such demands and impositions later on. This was storytelling as moral commentary, voiced at least once but perhaps more than once. Much of her narrative had a slightly rehearsed, ritualistic feel to it. Some of this could be due to the effect of

the rites and "traditions" enacted in those days, which structured
Kisang's recollections in such a way that her words carried a preset architecture; she could recite what happened, deed by deed, much as she
might proceed, mantra by mantra, through a round of prayer beads.
But it also sounded as though this was not the first time that she had
told this story, in one version or another. I therefore had to wonder, but
could wonder only, whether, and in what situations and among what
kinds of audiences, she had told this story before, how the different versions varied, and what kinds of effects or responses, if any, those narrations provoked.

Ghang Lama also minded the flow of words. Yet motifs of vision were
more central to how he made sense of life. What accounts for the differences between the two elders? It would make little sense to say, simply,
that Yolmo men are essentially visual creatures, while Yolmo women are
aural or vocal ones. There is nothing in being a woman or man per se in
this context that would lead a woman to attend to the world primarily
through verbal means or a man to attend to it through visual ones. Many
Yolmo men are, in fact, rather word focused, and women must engage
visually with others when interacting with them (consider, for instance,
how many watchful eyes observed Kisang during the course of her marriage rites). But it would also be a mistake to hold that gender dynamics
played no role at all here. Gender was a factor in the sense that certain
identities, roles, and practices associated with the two sexes in Yolmo society contributed, in combination with a slew of other factors, to the
ways in which Kisang and Ghang Lama sensed the world. While it's best
not to couch things in overly determined lines of analysis, it's fair to say
that Ghang Lama often approached the world through visual means in
part because he was born the son of a lama, because he devoted many of
his waking hours to acts of reading, because the world appeared to him
as a series of signs to be "read," because he took himself to be a knowledgeable lama, because the status of lineage lamas rested on visually perceived forms of knowledge and evidence, because lamaic practices gave
priority to visual modes of perception and knowledge, because he was
trained to imagine deities through contemplative visualizations, because
he divined people's futures through textual assessments, and because vision somehow became prominent in his life. Kisang Omu, in contrast,
related to the world primarily through verbal means, because she so often had to heed the words of others, because the actions that often
counted the most in her life were vocal ones, because her social identity

was greatly defined by what others said about her, because spoken words had greater relevance in her life than written ones, because she knew well the power of words, because she could see but poorly in her later years, and because, quite simply, that's how she engaged with others.

As the case was with most Yolmo women of her generation, acts of speaking and listening occupied Kisang more than ones of writing or reading did. Since an early age she had been aware of certain techniques of writing, of how writing worked in Yolmo and Nepalese circles, having once learned how to read Tibetan letters. But there were no schools in her day—"Where would the school have come?"—and what she did learn at home she had forgotten long ago.

"No, I don't know," she said when asked if she knew how to write and read Nepali script. "I didn't study the Nepali script. I didn't have the opportunity to read. I'm illiterate. Illiterate."

"Do you know the lama script?"

"I did a little bit. But now the memories are lost. Before my brother taught me. Then I swallowed the memories with food. It's forgotten. It's not of the present, it was a very long time ago. Now, the knowledge is swallowed. It's not, now."

"Previously, I knew a little," she said on another occasion. "First I studied the 'ka-kha' [the *abc*'s]. I read, then I learned how to spell in my mind. First I read, then I picked it up. Now the memory is lost—it's not. Before, I could read. I taught my children [to spell] as well, very easily. Now, I'm unable. Now, I've forgotten."

Acts of writing were a significant force in her life nevertheless. Her brother's "writing" of the temple in Shomkharka, for instance, led to her transfer to that village in marriage, while the words inscribed on her forehead fated her, among other fortunes and misfortunes, to be born a woman and later to leave her father's home. Yet as it was, the writing on her forehead kept her from learning another kind of writing: because she was born a woman she could not engage in any lama work or in any of the acts of text reading so crucial to this work, nor could she undertake in full any of the painterly "writing" in which her father or brother excelled. "If I was a boy, I would also have learned these [artists'] skills," she once noted. My brother taught me. I helped my brother when he was painting the thangka. I prepared the cloth and frame. My brother said, 'Make this. Apply the white primer.' . . . I was doing everything. My brother said to me, 'If you were my brother, then you could have been my assistant. But you're a girl, alas.' My brother said that."

"Women cannot learn [this craft]?"

"They cannot. How is it that I could have learned [these things]?"

Cut off from the possibilities of reading and writing, the inscriptions she encountered came to her from the outside, they took form in the realms of men or the divine, and they stood out in their uncommonness. While she was affected by them, as she was by many actions rendered by men, she never had a direct hand in their authorship. Like the invisible and indelible words marked on her forehead, the writings of men were something with which she had to contend but never took in fully.

Much more elemental in her life and present in her memories were the workaday utterances voiced by others and herself. From her early work as a song-and-dance girl and a teacher of bent-nosed parrots to her conversations with us some sixty years later, she lived in richly speech-oriented surroundings, where even the act of spitting was rendered as a word sputtered: "Spit!" In contrast with Ghang Lama, who seldom told stories and whose words tended to involve mostly an array of observations, pronouncements, and general "tellings," Kisang's words often had a narrative, dialogic cast to them. That narrative language was participatory, performative, socially attuned, emotionally engaged, subjectively rendered, multiply determined, acoustically mimetic, responsive, tense, rooted in time. Recollections of her life comprised a theater of voices. When depicting significant events in her life, she often invoked, in vivid, morally connotative terms, the utterances of key actors in those events. Speech and voice were directly phenomenal here; they were the primary substance of a life. In her narratives, significantly, her thoughts were usually recounted not as thoughts per se but as words spoken to herself: "'Why are they still there?' I thought." "Then I thought, 'It's true, there's just one or two houses, like my father said.'" Her thoughts were word-lively. Perhaps this was even more the case when I knew her, when she was half-blind and bedridden and could act only through speech. When alone in her room, it seemed, she would talk to herself much of the time, often while reciting mantras with the use of a mālā, and when talking to us she would also talk to herself, maintaining a running commentary, a stream of consciousness in words, in the pauses between our exchanges. And yet this monologue itself had a strong social tone to it, with all the intonations and flows of everyday conversations, as if there were always an audience or at least a potential audience, as though her words were always already intersubjective.

Speech was integral to her life. Her life had been one of listening and speaking, of attending to the effects and implications of words. She was concerned about her own speech and action, and she was acutely conscious of the effects of words and other deeds. It is no wonder, then, that her memories appeared to be founded primarily on various utterances, in connection with the actions that accompanied them. In contrast with Ghang Lama and others, who said, when asked, that memories of past times proceeded primarily through visual imaginings, Kisang said it was mostly the talk that remained, that "stayed" with her still. "The words come just like that," she once said of her ability to recall certain events well. If Ghang Lama posited what might be called an optic-graphic memory, Kisang's narrative suggested that her memories tended to be phono-graphic in substance; they consisted of lingering traces of sounds and voices that continued to resound. Her brother's "If one looks at the sky..." refrain about Shomkharka, which recurred repeatedly in her account of her transfer to that village, seemed to model well how memories often took form for her. While her brother could have voiced his observations in her presence several times, his words were just as likely to have been uttered once, and then they reverberated in his sister's thoughts after that. In any event, they continued to echo later on, in his absence, as she approached Shomkharka—"Then I remembered my brother's words"—much as they resounded some sixty years later when she related these events to her nephew and me. When she searched the past, talk emerged in her sem.

It is quite possible, in turn, that Kisang remembered "the time of arriving" so well because of the frights and worries she endured then. The gist of her narratives was often cued to how certain events affected her, whether, to put it most fundamentally, they made for moments of comfort or hardship. Of such events she appeared to remember most times of pain and hardship, as well as various cuts, nicks, and tears to the self, inflicted by others. She said as much herself. When Pramod and I asked her if she felt that anyone had treated her poorly in her life, she said, "Yes. I remember these things, if someone treats me with contempt. The people who treated me with contempt, it's very present in my sem."

"And if they do well?"

"If they do well, then it's lost," she said with a laugh, "If sorrowful deeds are done, it stays. If good happens, it's lost, in the sem."

Such was the impress of others. If people treated her poorly, or if painful deeds were enacted, then memories stayed with her—a point well attested by the stories she told. "It's true. She's right," an elderly man said when I related to him Kisang's discourse on memory. "We have a very good memory of the times when others treat us poorly, and we recall them time and again. But when good things happen, or people treat us well, all that is forgotten."[7] Others I spoke with likewise agreed that moments of sorrow and hardship are much more easily retained by the sem, while times of happiness are readily forgotten. "That's because when the things of sorrow occur, they leave an imprint on the heart," Binod replied point-blank when I posed the question to him. Others held that people tend to remember whatever has a strong impact on their lives, for good or bad. Any intense pains or joys can leave an indelible mark, much as a wound to the flesh can result in a scar. While less incisive memories never impress themselves in this way, or they are later "lost," the gist of certain happenings can, as Yolmo wa commonly put it, "strike" (phoge), "touch" (dege), or "affect" (nege) the heart, and particularly memorable events can "remain" in (lige) or be "held" by the sem or "get inside" a person.[8]

Or memories can be "etched" into one's mind. Men in particular spoke in ways that suggested that, metaphorically at least, memories can be "inscribed in" or "impressed into" a person's sem, as when Karma spoke of how a high regard of lamaic texts came to be "etched" into his and others' minds, or when Binod suggested that memories can be permanently imprinted. "That was printed here," another man said, while pointing to his skull, of the moral education he received as a small boy from his grandmother, who explained to him the meanings of painted scrolls that detailed how sinful acts led to fitting punishments in the lower realms. The graphic force of the grandmother's depictions created indelible imprints in the grandson's moral imagination. Among Yolmo wa, actions can be a kind of writing on a mind.

An analogy might help to illuminate the affinities between memory and inscription. In Yolmo villages boys interested in learning how to draw or paint often first learn how to sketch figures with the use of a "practice tablet" (jhang shing) composed of a wooden slab coated first with a sticky black soot, then white ash. "What we have is a board," Karma explained the process, "and then black soot is put on it. Then, because it's oily, sticky, you can throw white ash over it and make a white surface. Now you can use something small, something like a stick or a pencil, just to mark it.... It's like you're writing in a layer of grease. Just very soft, very soft.... If we made a mistake, we would have a cloth pouch with ash inside, and we would just [say,] 'tsk-tsk,' then just cover the mistake over with ash."

When I later mentioned to Karma that I was struck by the apparent commonalities between the process of "marking" such tablets and the ways that Yolmo wa speak of the workings of memory, he said the analogy made a lot of sense to him. Only certain incidents pass beyond the surface facades of the self and, in getting "inside" a person, leave a lasting mark on the adhesive contours of the sem; other events never impress themselves in this way. Among Yolmo wa significant events, hurtful ones especially, can leave a mark, a trace, at times a *maja,* or "scar" (literally, an "after-wound," a nick in time), within a person's sem, much as words can be carved into stone or sounds engraved within a phonographic record. And this, Yolmo wa say, is partly why people, elders especially, when gathered together and talking about times past, usually speak of scenes of hardship and sadness, for those are what they remember most. "If the sorrows and hardships of the past are recalled, they are innumerable," Gom Dolma said in speaking of the fissures of her life. Personal histories among Yolmo wa can be composed of a series of wounds or marks to the sem.

But there is still something illusory, something phantomlike, in such marks. Memories are imagined, ghostly realities. A memory can be likened to a *shul,* a Tibetan and Yolmo word that can mean either "trace, track, remainder" or "empty place, a place that is no longer occupied."[9] The word is often used when speaking of something left behind by a person departed or of a thing removed or expired; in Tibetan *mar-shul* refers, for example, to the butter that adheres to a container emptied but not yet washed, and *mhe-shul* designates the extinguished cinders left by a fire. A memory, likewise, is a trace or vestige of something once there but no longer there. It is an empty presence, an absence that is still present. Memories are immaterial residues of the past that remain within the holdings of the present.

Perhaps, then, this is how Kisang, mnemonist of decisive voicings and consequential actions, was able to relate to us so sharply events that took place sixty years before. When she delved into the past, her phonographic memory would kick in, and doings that had once "struck" or "touched" her sem came to mind. Her words would then follow the thread of a story much as her fingers might trace the ridges of a scar. Friedrich Nietzsche once posited that the main clause of the "oldest psychology on earth" is, "If something is to stay in the memory it must be burned in: Only that which never ceases to *hurt* stays in the memory."[10] Kisang would likely have agreed with this observation as she might have heard it: the impressions left by certain sorrows can last a very long time. Some hardships were specific to women. In his conversations with his grandson and me, Ghang Lama often proclaimed that men face more hardship in their lives than women do because of the many worldly labors and travels they have to endure.

"But grandfather," Norbu once suggested, "hardship also comes to women. When marrying they have to leave their homes and go to another home. That's dhukpu, isn't it?"

"Yes, that's dhukpu," the old man conceded. "In leaving, women have to carry [bear] the dhukpu."

For Kisang, to bear the sorrow of a painful departure was to carry memories of it. Her recollections engaged a tracework of wounds to the sem.

"The daughters are coral and turquoise, what is within?" asks a Yolmo folk song sung by men. "A great deal," Yolmo women could very well respond. In Kisang's case, a close regard of her wedding narrative and her talk in general reveals several features of her subjective life. Hers was a world and a life founded on action. A sustained awareness of the consequential force of karmic and everyday actions shaped what she knew of her life's circumstances. A rich temporality of interconnected actions coursed through the strands of her life and the sentences of her narrations. A mix of social constraints, ritual protocols, and narrative designs structured her thoughts and actions. The words she herself spoke offered her a means to act in the world, to question or alter its contours. Acts of speaking and listening, which almost always carry moral weight, engaged her much more than acts of writing and reading did. She inhabited a world of talk, and a world of talk remained with her. The import of significant actions could "strike" or "touch" her heart. Recollections of the past often traced the marks left by such wounds. All in all, the makings of time, causality, personhood, consciousness, gender identities, speech, moral sensibilities, pain, and memory figured in her life in complexly interthreaded ways.

Her words seemed to speak to such matters. In recounting the events of her wedding, Kisang was both depicting and reflecting on how they contributed to her lifeworld then. Her narratives are highly subjective in nature in that they depict events as their narrator perceived and knew them as they occurred in time. To couch it in Yolmo terms, she spoke of what she had "undergone" or "experienced" (nhyungsin) in life. As Norbu's mother put it upon hearing several of Kisang's stories as recorded on tape, "She has spoken well. Whatever sorrow has come to her heartmind, she has spoken of it." What Hrikchung was saying, I think, was that the content of Kisang's stories tend to embrace, in a fairly inclusive manner, a specific dimension of her life: they speak not of the histories of lineages or general social processes but of deeds and hardships that had "struck" Kisang's sem in some way.

They speak of such things in rather illustrative, simulative ways. A common word for "story" among Yolmo wa is *pe-tam*. Ghang Lama used the word, for example, in describing the nature of a spiritual biography of Nga-chang Shakya Zangpo's life and deeds: "It's like the pe-tam we tell to our children, of things that happened many years before: the people did this, they did that, they built that. It's like that kind of pe-tam." Most literally, the word means something like "model-talk." While *tam* by itself means "talk," "speech," "discourse," *pe* can be translated as "model," "pattern," "example," "copy." *Pe* is also found in words like *pe-zjha*, a colloquial term for the lama's sacred texts. Invested in uses of the word *pe-tam* is the idea that religious stories and texts can offer narratives and discourses that stand as exemplary models or examples of spiritually enlightened ways to live and think. Yolmo men with whom I spoke about pe-tam surmised that the word probably signaled religious narratives alone at some point in time, then later came to denote stories more generally. In any event, the idea that stories are models in some sense is now built into Yolmo thoughts about storytelling. A pe-tam can be doubly mimetic. In chronicling a story to be emulated, such as a yogi's spiritual accomplishments, it can be a "model for" something. It can inform others, through the power of example, how to undertake a life of spiritual devotion. But in order to do so effectively, it has to be a "model of" those accomplishments.[11] It has to depict, in active, illustrative terms—he did this, he did that—what that yogi achieved.

Considered in these terms, Kisang's account of her wedding is more a model of than a model for. It is unlikely that she or other Yolmo wa would hold that her narrative is a pe-tam in the formal sense of the word; there were no obvious spiritual accomplishments to speak of, and her tale does not fit within the genre of spiritual biographies as Yolmo wa know it. Still, her words do offer an effective pe, a pattern or model, of a woman's subjectivity at a critical juncture in her life, one that other women could emulate. In hearing her narrative, one is given the sense of a young and startled woman who, subject to the words and actions of others and reluctantly transferred from one family to another in marriage, was carried along through a flow of ritual events that led her to a new life in a distant village, though in the end spoken words offered her a means to comment on those events and model the effects they had on her life and self then. This model of action could, in turn, give other

Yolmo women a sense of how to face such hardships. Instructive here is Kisang's response to a question posed by Pramod and me one morning.

"Auntie," we asked, "what advice would you give to Yolmo girls who face weddings of their own?"

"What advice do I give?" she answered. She then said after a pause, "'Go well, stay well. Hold the family's nose.' What else is there to say, is there something else?" She laughed a bit and added, "What to say? It doesn't come well. *Ayo!* [Ouch!]"

"To all Yolmo [women, what would you say]?"

"To all Yolmo [I would say], 'I myself came from far away. So go well yourselves.'"

She had traveled to a distant, unknown place in marriage. Despite the hardships she endured, she went in a good way, then stayed in a good way, and so preserved her family's honor. Other Yolmo women, she was suggesting, could follow, should follow, the example she set. Her narrative models a woman's subjectivity at a crucial time in her life.

"I've Gotten Old"

As Yolmo men and women age, they inevitably grow weaker and frailer. A person's age "decreases" or "becomes less" (N., *umer ghaṭnu*) in the sense that his or her life span decreases as the years wear on. To have become "old" among Yolmo wa situates a person in a particular bracket of time and in a social grouping that is distinct from being young or "recent." Some of these changes are for the better. A person can find a degree of wealth or comfort in his or her later years that was hard to come by in earlier ones, and a lifetime of actions can effect respect and a good name for oneself and one's family. An elder's children and grandchildren, in turn, can offer pleasurable affection and companionship.

When it comes to the faculties and look of a body, however, getting old among Yolmo wa is decidedly a process of waning forces. "I've gotten old" is a common lament voiced by people over fifty or so. Heard as "Nga ghapu ghalsin" in Yolmo or "Ma buṛo bhayo" in Nepali, the phrase is usually offered to others in a matter-of-fact tone or with an air of bemused dismay, as though people are baffled by the onrush of time. The words imply a temporal process; they speak to an action that already has happened, one that has been completed and cannot be undone. In such contexts, no one ever says, "I am old," but rather voices words that convey the idea that "oldness has happened to me." When speaking such words, people sometimes gesture toward or look down at their bodies, as if to note the evidential grounds of their aging. Among Yolmo wa, in fact, aging is very much a bodily process: a body tends to diminish much more than the faculties of will and spirit housed within it. This helps to explain the bewilderment that some people express, for a discrepancy is sometimes sensed between a continued youthfulness of spirit and a diminishment of bodily features and abilities. Old age seems to sneak up on people, since they still feel young at heart, so elderly people can feel betrayed by their bodies. Time has its effects. As a person ages he or she regretfully grows weaker, more decrepit, less handsome.

Concerns for one's appearance are significant here, for, as with other material substances that exhibit decay on the surface of their forms, a person's body can come to *look* old. The cultural dynamics of vision play an important role here: eyes that can find fault with a girl's demeanor or the facades of a family's house can also be used to evaluate the gradual erosion of a body, including one's own. While Yolmo are far from narcissistic mirror-gazers, some elders are nonetheless concerned with their aging appearances. When we were preparing to take Phur Gyalmu's photograph inside her house the last day we came to talk with her about her life story, she said that the photo would not come out well because she was old. "It's better to take pictures when one is young," she then noted.

Sentiments like this recall a stanza in a poem penned by Gyalwa Kalzang Gyatso, the Seventh Dalai Lama, in the eighteenth century:

I remember this body when it was a child's,
As it gradually took the form of a youth.
Now its every limb is twisted and worn.
It is my own body, yet it delights not even my own eyes.[1]

A body's wrinkles and fatigued skin can signify a person's age and inevitable demise. Tibetan Buddhist sages have seized on this fact to teach others about the impermanence of human forms. "If you look at a youthful photograph of an old friend," Khetsun Sangpo Rinbochay, a revered Tibetan lama, tells us, "you feel immediately how good-looking he was, but now his flesh is wrinkling, there are old age spots on his face and he is beginning to look ugly."[2] The lama's observation supports this Buddhist principle: "Everything that is made, everything that depends on causes, is affected by impermanence."[3]

With impermanence come change and loss. When talking with Phur Gyalmu in Thodong, I asked her if she thought that a person's way of thinking changes upon getting older.

"It changes, for sure," she replied. "How could it be like it was at first?"

"How does it change?"

"Well, one might think, 'I've become old, and there's nothing that can be done about it.' This is felt, for sure."

"Compared to before, what is thought?"

"At first, at first, 'Now, there's strength now,' I said. 'I can walk with friends. I can also dance.' I thought this, for sure. Now, I can't walk with friends. I can't dance. Nor can I sing songs. The songs from the past I've forgotten. I've eaten them with rice. Now, there isn't. It's that, for sure. After getting old, one can't remember like before. One can't [remember] like before."

"Now, there isn't": In the many swells and ebbs of time, more can become less. A person can find that certain elements of her life, from friends to songs once remembered, are now absent or quickly on their way to becoming absent.

Ghang Lama configured the losses that he associated with getting old in several ways. He found, for one, that he had come to look old. "Ṭhikkai chha?" I asked him once upon giving him a framed enlargement of a photograph I had taken of him several months before: "It's okay?"

"It's okay," he said while looking at the image in his hands. "I've gotten old."

Memories of the past were forgotten. "No, there isn't anything," he said in response to inquiries about regrets he might have had in life. "I can't remember anything now. Now, I'm starting to forget things. Now I've become old, I've already crossed eighty. Now when one thinks back to the old things, slowly one forgets many things. And similarly for me now, what is comfort, what is hardship, I can't distinguish."

Lost as well were recent memories. "You can put down anything," he said when asked what should be included in his life story. "Because I've already forgotten everything. I've already forgotten the words from before. These days, I forget what I've just talked about. I can't remember the kurā of before. What to say? I've forgotten everything. Now I'm thinking only of enlightenment."

Friends that he once knew were now dead. When Norbu and I asked if he ever thought of good times he once had with friends, he replied, "Well, those times are not here, and the people are also not here. All the people [I once knew] in Thodong have gone."

He said he no longer "saw dreams" as he did when he was younger. "Before, I saw many different dreams," he told us. "I saw many different dreams before. Now, I don't see dreams—only a few are seen. It's because I'm getting old. . . . These days, I don't remember dreams so much. Sometimes they come. Otherwise, when one becomes old, dreams don't come as well. When one is young, a lot of dreams come. Now, in old age, dreams are forgotten."

Lost was the robust appetite of his youth. "Before I could eat a lot," he told Norbu and me. "I used to eat so much before. Now I can't. Until last year I could eat a lot. These days I don't get hungry so much, that's to say." Nine months later he related this to Nogapu and me: "Now, I don't like foods so much. No taste comes to my mouth. Now I'm getting old.... These days I don't feel like eating. If I eat a good-tasting food, there's no taste. Before, the food without much taste tasted good to me. I didn't need curry before [to add taste]. I could eat the foods in themselves." When we asked if the loss of appetite was because his body had become weak, he replied, "Why is this, now? I'm getting old, perhaps. I don't know why this is. Now I don't feel like eating anything. Any food I eat doesn't have any taste."

He was unable to sleep as well as he once did. "It's not just me," he said one afternoon of changes perceived by the aged. "Everyone says they don't sleep well. Everyone. Even those who aren't yet forty." Then he added with a laugh, "Now I can never get to sleep. Before, if I put my head on the bed, I could sleep very well."

Along with the effacement of sleep, hunger, friends, and memories, he felt that his body's strength and its visible presence in the world were diminishing as his life became "less." For him and other Yolmo men, the size of one's body, in tandem with one's physical strength and stamina, was a measure of aging. "Up to the age of forty our bodies grow," he told us. "After forty, one gets fat. Then, after eighty, we become thin and get crushed down. Up to forty years, we're plenty strong. This lasts up to fifty-five. Then after, if we get close to eighty, the strength doesn't come anymore."

After sipping a bit of tea, he continued. "Before, I could come here [to Kathmandu] directly in one day and return to Thodong in one day. But now I can't go. I need to be carried. Before, if I left in the morning, I could reach there by nighttime."

These last words invoked a common theme. Many Yolmo wa surmise that they are getting older because they cannot walk as far in a day's time as they once could. Mheme spoke in much the same way. Because of a pained back and stiff legs, he could not travel on foot as he could in his youth. "In my case," he once said, "I'm already eighty. I don't know when I'm going to die.... From last year, I haven't been able to walk around, because my back hurts. I can't move my legs so much. Before I could reach up there [to Thodong] in one day, on time. Now, where can I go?"

Before, before. He often compared the current status of his body with its status in an earlier time in his life, when he was young and strong, could eat and drink a great deal, could walk far and quickly, and did not tire easily. "I didn't feel much, because I was strong then," he said on several occasions, implying that he was relatively impervious to pain or hardships then.

Later, though, he lost his strength, he lost his resilience, and he could not walk as he once could. One reason that the inability to walk troubled him was that he desired to return to Thodong to enter into a sustained meditative retreat. Unable to walk well, however, and finding uphill stretches most difficult, he could not readily make the journey on foot and would likely have had to be carried in a basket by a porter. When Norbu and I met with him in the summer of 1997, he spoke often of his plans to return to Thodong to enter into retreat.

"How will you go?" we asked. "By walking, or...?"

"How can I walk? Somebody will have to carry me, and I'll go. A few months back I went to the village and stayed there a month."

A man who carried loads in his youth was later carried by others.

When I returned to Boudhanath the following winter I found that Mheme had still not traveled to Thodong.

"I said I would go for sure," he said when asked about this. "[But now] my body is unable."

"His back is hurting," his wife added.

His waning ability to work or travel as he once did led him to consider that people might not have the same confidence in him as they once had. When Norbu and I once asked if he ever thought about what it was like when he was young, he replied:

What to do, now [even if those thoughts come]? The time is already past. When I was young everyone had confidence in me. I was like a military man who was in the service. Everyone said that I was a man who had a job in the service, even though I didn't actually have such a job. At that time, people implored me to stay in the service. Now who will have confidence in me? I'm an old man. Who will count on me?

Earlier in his life, his body was one of those that deserved to be in the military. He could carry heavy loads, he could walk long distances in a day's time, and he could work long hours without tiring. The truth now was that, with his diminishing strength and size, friends and family members might not rely on him to get things done.

"Mheme, thinking [of the past] does not come?" we continued.

"It comes, but what can be done if it comes? If those thoughts come, sleep doesn't come. If there's a lot of thinking, one can't sleep. Then a man is finished, and madness comes."

"Why is it that when you think of the old days sleep does not come?"

"If one thinks of how it was in the old days, will one be able to sleep, then? In one day I could walk to so many places in those days. These days, it's a burden to go to Boudhanath even."

"Is it that when you think of the past things, it's like, 'I'm still young, like before'?"

"Yes, it's like that, but what can one do? While I can't do much with my body these days, my mind still feels like it's going around, doing things, like the things that I did when I was young."

"Do you feel sorrow if you think of those days?"

"Yes, sorrow is felt. Also, I can't sleep well."

His words immediately brought to my mind phrases from a Yolmo pain-song that I had recorded once.

> My body grows older and older,
> [but] my sem feels younger and younger.
> One only gets older,
> growing younger cannot be.

Though Mheme might still have wished to act and work as he once did, a lack of strength deterred him. "These days," he told us, "I feel that if I were strong enough, if I had any animals I could look after them. But I don't have the strength to do that now. Before, we had to cut the grass and make the grass covering [for the animals]. Now I'm old. I can't do that." Others have said much the same. "Although I'm seventy-one years old, my desires have not died," explained Sen Zangbu Sherpa when relating his life story. "I want to do the things I wished to do in my youth," he continued. "But now I have less strength, less energy."

At work here was a sense of absence, of feeling betrayed by the body, and a mournful longing for its youthful form. Unnerved by this, Mheme knew that madness could come if he dwelled too much on any of it.

There was an optical dimension to his ever-vanishing form. In the past few years his body had, to him, become increasingly small and less visible. Norbu and I once asked him if he had any photographs that were taken of him when he was younger. He said one of his sons had taken pictures many years before, but he did not know where those photos might be. Thoughts of those photographs apparently then led him to recollect the size of his body at that time, because he continued to talk. "Before, before," he said, "among my brothers, I was the one with the big body. The rest of them had small bodies. Nobody's clothes matched me, not even my sons' clothes. Only my youngest's [Dawa's] matched me—he's also big. Now, then, I'm already eighty-one years old. Where has it gone?! Where, where?!" He spoke the last words while gesturing toward his torso.

Like a waning moon, his physical form was becoming absent to the eye. In ways reminiscent of how the bodies of the deceased would once vanish at the moment of death, his body was disappearing on him. Others also "lost" their bodies and, in a sense, mourned that loss. "When some people are young," Nogapu told me, "they eat lots of food, and they have very healthy bodies. When they get older, they lose their bodies, they become very weak, and they get very worried." One reason for worry relates to people's fear that, when their bodies grow weaker, others might not hire them to perform jobs, from cutting wood to building houses, that they were previously asked to do.

Regrets over the loss of his youth and body came across in several conversations in which Mheme introduced considerations of aging. "Now, when you look back on your life," Norbu and I asked, "what do you think—have you been a man with comfort or a man with sorrow?"

"What has it been?" he answered. "Well, it's all on one's forehead. If one has hardship written, there's hardship. If one has happiness written, there's happiness. But even if one thinks happiness is written on the forehead, and one just sits [without doing anything], it won't happen. One has to work for it." He then added,

When a man is still strong, when he is young, he has to earn money, he has to cut grass [to feed his family's cattle]. When he grows old, he can't do anything, he can't earn money, he can't cut grass. Isn't that a hardship?

A like-minded shift to the topic of being old and the differences in abilities between young and old occurred on another occasion, when Mheme was explaining to his grandson why it is better to live today than during his "time."

Because business can be done, it's easier to earn money than in those days. It's good for all of you now. You all have strength, you can go to different places to do business. As for me, I'm old. I can't do that.

Along with longing nostalgically for the body of his youth, the lama sometimes appeared to envy the physical abilities of people younger than he, including the interlocutors sitting across the room from him.

On a few occasions the lama attributed the diminishment of bodily strength to the dimming of a burning flame lodged in a person's forehead, a flame that humans are unable to see.

We have a burning flame [N., *batti*] here, in our forehead. Once this goes out, we die. We can't see this fire. There's a flame in our forehead. If one makes a fire, after the firewood finishes, the fire also becomes dimmer and dimmer. After growing old, in our bodies there's no more fire. After the fire is finished, we can't talk, we can't go here and there. Don't people say, "When the fire is first lit, the fire is strong"? How much fire is in our bodies.[4]

When we later asked if he felt that his fire was "finishing," he replied, "Yes, now I feel like the fire is finishing. Now, it can't be increased."

"Since when has this been?"

"Now it's been two years."

"As though the fire is decreasing?"

"As though there's no fire. When the fire is gone, there won't be any heat left."

"And how does one feel when this fire is finishing?"

"The whole body becomes very heavy. If someone has fire and water in his body, he feels very light. Now, there is not so much time left, though I do feel that there's a little left in me, there's a little strength."

In his youth he had much fire in his body, making his form feel light and energetic. In the past few years, however, the fire had dimmed, weighting his body and slowing his pace. A law of entropic decrease was at work. The thermal force could not be restored to its earlier intensity. A man could not grow younger.

The metaphysics of vision, as Mheme knew it, played a role in all this. Motifs of vision were a central aspect of the lama's life. Yet these motifs shaped not only how he perceived the world, or engaged with others, or spoke and thought about acts of seeing per se. They also gave form to how he made sense of his life and the world in general. The metaphysics of his life often tied into a metaphysics of vision, of tangents of clarity, visible presences, and vanishing forms, such that the elements of his life, from his youth to his old age, had a kind of seeable, apparitional quality to them. More than a few aspects of the lama's life, for instance, were founded on themes of presence and visibility. Among other things, he invested a great deal of time in reading the legible marks in sacred texts, he took knowledge to be best achieved through visual means, he valued undistracted states of mind, he sought clarity in his waking thoughts and visions, he relished times of companionship and fullness, and he took pride in the visibly robust presence of his body in his adult years.

As the years wore on, however, his life was increasingly galled by themes of absence and disappearance. "Whether you are attending to an object of meditation, of thinking, or of hearing," a Tibetan teacher advises his readers in a discourse on how to avoid distractions, "do not think about what you did in the past, for it has already disappeared like words written on water."[5] The same could be said of certain elements of Mheme's past. Memories, dreams, his appetite, his body, his physical strength and abilities, the faces of friends, the confidence of others, the times of his youth, all these had disappeared like words written on water. While the analogy is overtly of my own making, there is something to the idea that Ghang Lama, in so often approaching the world through visual means, sought out the legible presence of things in the world, and then, when oldness happened to him, he found that certain things were no longer present in his life. And the ways those things either became absent or disappeared had, despite their many different forms, an air of expunged visibility to them, either in quite literal terms ("Where has it gone?!") or in highly metaphoric ones ("Well, those times are not here"). The strands of visuality that patterned so many of his thoughts and actions contributed to the ways in which he configured the act of growing old. Much as something once seen, letters, bodies, faces, could suddenly cease to be seen, so certain aspects of his life had vanished before him.

Essays on Dying

Some of Kisang's words told of acts of dying. They spoke of the decease of loved ones, of the ways that harmful actions could cause someone's end, and so carve out a "chapter of sorrows" within a woman's life.[1]

After her marriage to Wangel Lama, Kisang stayed with him in Shomkharka, in a house adjacent to the gompa, or temple, that her brother had just finished painting. "I arrived there, I stayed there, and I needed to do the work," she told us. "I didn't feel anything," she said when asked what she felt about getting married. "What to do? My brother and father gave me by procession [respectfully] to my husband. After I married, I came to my husband's house, I didn't feel anything. I just needed to work in my husband's house. My sem wasn't here or there [my mind wasn't in two places at once]. My father and brother bade farewell to me. I lived in Shomkharka. What to do, then? I needed to stay....Ah, then, I had a lot of hardship."

The work she did was much like what most Yolmo wives undertake, and, by many of their reckonings as well as mine, of a mulitvarious, physically laborious sort that is more than what most Yolmo men do or need to do in their lives. Tilling fields of potatoes, planting corn, carrying firewood and other loads, tending to the family's livestock, distributing manure in the fields, spinning yarn, knitting clothes, caring for her children, washing clothes, cooking meals and scouring pots and pans, hosting any relatives or "sponsors" who might visit, taking care of her household and the gompa associated with it—Kisang spoke often of the hard work she had to undertake in the years following her marriage: "With work I faced hardship." While some tasks are undertaken by men

Figure 9. Women working in the fields below Thodong, 1989. Photograph by Robert Desjarlais.

and women alike, there is a general division of labor common in Yolmo families, in which men usually engage in "outside" work and business, and women attend to "inside" household duties and agricultural work. As women know it, their spouses have it easier than they do. When asked whether a man's life or a woman's life was better, Kisang promptly replied, "The man's life is better. How can a woman's life be better? The man's life is good. The man's life is good. The man's life is good."

"Why? Why is the man's life good?"

"The man's life is good. His work is one-sided [N., *ekohoro*]. Women have to do many things—cooking, household work."

"Auntie, did you carry loads?" we said in asking about a common form of labor in Nepal, wherein a person carries anything from rocks to potatoes in a wicker basket supported by a strap worn across the forehead.

"I carried a lot, I carried," Kisang answered. "I carried....I didn't take things to Kathmandu [for sale in the markets there]. I would carry firewood and leaves, near the house. We collected the wood for the rainy season, a-ma. A-ma, did this head carry just a little?! These days I don't do it. I wore the strap on my forehead. If you look, you'll see an indentation there. Now, it doesn't happen. I have a pleasant life nowadays. Nobody carried loads like me. Before, I carried the loads of two people. I had that kind of strength."

"Was that work very hard?"

"Sure it was hard work. If I didn't do it, who would do it for me? We needed those things. We needed to collect the leaves, then we needed to layer the firewood atop the basket. We needed to use the spade [for digging soil]. No one worked harder than I did."

In speaking of such hardships to Pramod and me, she spoke proudly of the amount of work she could undertake when she was younger. She also compared her abilities then with the little she was able to do later in life.

"Were you very strong then?"

"I was very strong, for sure. A-ma-ma! Even though my body is like this." Of her ability to walk long distances, she said, "When I had the strength I didn't feel any pain. I could dig uncultivated land very easily, I could carry heavy loads. So much work was done—I'm that kind of woman. Now I'm suffering. Before I did the hard work. Now I'm suffering, I'm staying while suffering."

At times she spoke as though she was suffering then because of the hard work she undertook earlier in life. At others, her words seemed to imply that the hardships of earlier times helped to bring about the comforts of life in Kathmandu. When asked when she had comfort in her life, she replied, "Since I've come to Kathmandu, comfort has come. When I was in the village, I was able to eat because I worked hard. Even the children have had to work hard."

Some had more than others. Kisang mentioned a girl who was employed in her household as a servant, which suggested that she and her husband were relatively well off then. But there was still a lot for her to do. One important responsibility of hers after she married was to help invite her husband's sponsors to their gompa, prepare well for their visits, and host them well once they had arrived at her and Wangel Lama's home. "After getting married, there was no playing games, just work. I needed to invite the sponsors. Sponsors. Without food, I couldn't host well. Without offering food, we couldn't reciprocate with the sponsors. We needed to give [drinks of] *balu* to the sponsors, we needed to serve raksī. If we had run out, it wouldn't have worked."

At first, while they were still living in Shomkharka, her husband shared the same sponsors with his father and other lamas in their family. But as she and her son Kānchā recalled, her husband did not get along with his father, and the two would quarrel even when they went to perform rites together:

Our grandfather [my father-in-law] and my husband were both going to the sponsors' houses to do the lama work. Fighting, fighting, fighting. They hadn't any fear [of each other]. They didn't get along with each other. If they had stayed in the same place, then they might have gotten along.... They were always fighting each other. They would even fight when they went to the sponsors' homes to perform rituals.

It is possible, as the case often is today as well, that some of the tension related to competition among local lamas for the patronage of various sponsors. In any event, because of conflicts between Kisang's husband and father-in-law, the former separated from the main line of his lineage several years after marrying Kisang and moved from Shomkharka to Ne Nyemba, a village an hour's walk east of Shomkharka. His brother joined them on neighboring lands in Ne Nyemba a bit later.

Her husband, having been promised control of a newly built gompa in Ne Nyemba, moved to lands offered to him by sponsors who lived in and around this village. "The sponsor took us to Ne Nyemba," Kisang told us. "They gave us the land. We needed to watch over the construction of the gompa." Around this time Kisang's father died. "Then, father, later, when we were thinking of building the Ne Nyemba gompa, at that time, my father died. What to do?" Later, Kisang explained further: "Father had gotten old by then. We were planning to build the gompa, so I was preparing the wood. Then after, he went over there, and then he died. His stomach was sick.... He left me alone. I'm alone."

Her brother, by then the father of seven, was commissioned to "write" the sacred paintings and idols inside the newly built temple in Ne Nyemba. But he also passed on, his stomach similarly "swollen," while attempting to complete this project. "While writing, writing the gompa, my brother passed his life. My brother died while making the twenty-third gompa.... After completing [the structure of] the Ne Nyemba gompa, my brother's wish went unfulfilled, because he wanted to write the pictures of the deities on the inner walls of the gompa. That was his strong, strong desire. But his life ended."

Later on, several elders from Sermathang told me that Kisang's brother was known to do magic tricks, creating optical illusions of sorts, such as conjuring a snake out of a long strand of grass or making a gompa appear as though it was shaking from the ground up. But since such practices worked contrary to the values of Buddhist dharma, these same people said, the magic tricks were thought to have led to a powerful *barchad,* or "hindrance," in his life that ultimately resulted in his early death, at the age of thirty-four.

Once the work on the gompa in Ne Nyemba was completed, Kisang's husband began to undertake in full the kind of work expected of him. This work, which he performed well for more than a few years, chiefly consisted of conducting lamaic rites, both in the gompa itself and at the homes of sponsors who lived in Ne Nyemba and neighboring villages. "What work did he do, now?" Kisang said when asked this question of her first husband:

He did the lama work, he had a lot of sponsors, he needed to go outside [the village] as well. He had a lot of work. We were managing the household, and we ate, for sure. He didn't stay in the house. Not even during losar [the New Year festivities]. He had to go the sponsors' places. There was a lot of work. The work of the past was difficult work.... The lamas needed to go to the sponsors' houses. Every day the lamas needed to go to the sponsors' houses. Where, where? Every day someone was dying, at the sponsors' places.

Along with the grief they brought to those homes, the deaths meant that at least one lama, usually the senior lama in charge of a gompa, had to travel to the villages of his sponsors to perform the cremation and funeral rites for any recently deceased members of those sponsors' families: "The gompa lama needs to go the sponsors' houses, and to the ghewa [funeral rites]." It was during one such occasion that her husband fell gravely ill and died a few weeks later, as Pramod and I learned in speaking with Kisang one afternoon.

P: *How did Uncle [Wangel Lama] die?*
K: *In the place, in Ghangyul, where some of our sponsors lived, a lot of children were affected by dysentery, and a lot of children died then. Then, he was called there to cremate those children.*
    He went alone. One assistant went with him.
P: *To Ghangyul?*
K: *To Ghangyul. He went to cremate the children. After that, my husband caught the disease. Then he also suffered from dysentery—there was blood as well. They*

were doing the last rites for the children at that time. He couldn't return [home] after that.

When children in the Tamang village of Ghangyul died from dysentery, their parents summoned Kisang's husband to perform the necessary cremation and funeral rites. Wangel Lama, then thirty-one, traveled to the village with a single assistant and helped to cremate the bodies. In the weeks that followed, while he was enacting the "last rites" for the children, he also fell ill. The severity of the ailment kept him from reaching home. One funeral led to another. Ritual as contagion.

"A lot of children died then." The infant mortality rate was quite high in those days, as it is today among the more impoverished families in the Yolmo region. By this time Kisang had herself given birth to five children. Her first child, a daughter, died in her first year, she told us in a quiet, mournful voice.

"I married in horse year. One year later I had a daughter, but she was lost."

"Did she die after being born?"

"Yes, after. When she was small. She was [born in] sheep year. She died no later than one year. She died just like that. Then after that I had Lama Mingmar's father."

That was in "monkey year," a year after her first child died, she explained on another occasion. She gave birth to another daughter five years later, in "mouse year," then a second son in "tiger year," and finally a third son in "snake year."

"What diseases affected her?"

"Was it a disease? I don't know what it was. My daughter was lost in the cradle.... I took her [from my stomach]. She lived two nights. I put her in the cradle, but she went. My daughter. After that I had a son."

"Auntie, is the woman's life difficult?"

"It's difficult, for sure. What can be done? [Chi bheche?]"

"When your first baby died, did sorrow come to your heartmind then?"

"It came, when I lost my daughter. It came and grew in the sem. My first daughter, after being born, died. She didn't live long. After that, I gave birth to Lama Mingmar's father [my first son]."

This is a chapter of sorrows.

At that time shamanic medicine was the main recourse when someone fell ill. "We need shamans when we are alive. Lamas, when we die," Yolmo wa often say in speaking of the bombo's ability to cure illnesses and the lama's complementary skill in performing the funeral rites for the recently deceased. Yet that logic was jumbled when a shaman's medicine led to a lama's death.

Uncle Tashi Bombo—Tashi Bombo, from Shomkharka, yes?—he said to him, "You need to eat dhang men."

The power, and consequential force, of authoritative speech: Tashi Bombo, a shamanic healer related to her husband, advised her husband to consume the leaves of the dhang men plant, a medicine used then as a purgative.

Dhang men looks like the radish leaf, yes? He brought two bundles.
 To Tashi Bombo, to say, what to say?

"Tashi Bombola, mazjhe mana, chi mazjhe?" (roughly: If I did say something to Tashi Bombo, what could or would I say to him?)—as though in response to the shaman's words and actions. Or, as Yolmo interpreters glossed this phrase: Kisang had many things to say to and about Tashi Bombo, given what resulted from his intervention, but she could not say them directly to a man who was closely related to her husband. "If he was not her cousin, she could blame him [for the death]," one man explained. "But since they were related, she couldn't say anything.... She wanted to scold him, but she couldn't say anything." How, in effect, could she speak of the harmful wrongdoings of others when she could not really say anything? And yet she did say something later on, at least to us, but perhaps also earlier on, through a rather cryptic question. When I asked Temba D. Yolmo's parents if Kisang's question was an indirect way of saying that Tashi Bombo was responsible for her husband's death, his father replied, "Yes, that's right. It's the roundabout speech [*kor tam*], because Tashi Bombo was her close relative, and she could not have said directly to him that he was responsible for her husband's death."

Roundabout though it was, Kisang's question carried a lot of weight in the present retelling. It set up the moral tenor of the narrative, anticipated consequential events to come, and configured responsibility for the death.

Then, by the hill above our house, "Make me a ghore [a shelter]," he [Wangel Lama] said. "Make me a shelter." His mother was there, his sister was there, I was there. Lama Mingmar's father [my first son] was just thirteen then. He was thirteen then. So we made the shelter for him. He wanted to have us make the planks of wood and to put the mattress and pillows and everything on it. Then everything was arranged.

Another crucial utterance: Her husband told members of his family to build a comfortable shelter for him, away from the village, where he could rest and, with luck, recover from his ailment. Such makeshift shelters, the kinds of structures that Kisang's escorts in marriage feigned that she would have to inhabit, were typically inhabited by shepherds tending to livestock in high-altitude forested areas, as Ghang Lama and his in-laws did for several years. Wangel Lama's uncommon decision to have one built for himself pointed to the urgency of the situation.

"Go. Leave me alone. You need to go back to the house. I'll stay alone."

This was a striking statement, given that it is so unusual for a person to remain alone in this way, on the outskirts of a village. The one exception to this is when lamas enter into meditative retreat. Usually a lama going on retreat will try to dwell in *tsham,* or a "demarcated place," by detaching himself from any contacts or exchanges with others. Kisang's husband wanted to isolate himself in a similar way, but not for the purpose of going on meditative retreat, and Kisang remained perplexed as to the reasons he wanted to stay alone. "He told us to make a small hut like that of the shepherd's shelter," Kisang later said when asked about this. "'Why do you need that?' I asked. 'I want to have fresh air here,' he said. Then I asked, 'Why do you want fresh air? There's some at home as well.' I didn't know that his cousin [Tashi Bombo] had brought some medicine and had given it to him. He had asked us to build the hut so that he could take that medicine, but we didn't know about that. He told us that it was so he could have some fresh air and stay in a cool place, but his intention was to have the medicine."

Others who heard Kisang's account pointed out that Wangel Lama had probably wanted to stay in such a hut because he likely anticipated that it would be better to take the purgative outside his home, away from others, since it would quickly lead to a further outflow of diarrhea that would soil everything around him.

Through his mother's side, Tashi Bombo was a relative. On this side, the sister [my husband's mother]. On the other side, her elder sister [Tashi Bombo's mother].

Kisang spoke of the shaman again and noted how he was her husband's cousin, as though, in order to explain how her husband died, she could not simply chronicle the events that occurred; she also needed to depict the binding social relations that shaped the actions producing those events. Implicit in this linkage was the idea that a certain respect had to be accorded to Tashi Bombo, who was her husband's elder cousin. Her words also helped to explain why it would have been difficult to ignore the man's instructions or to criticize or condemn him directly later on.

He [my husband] said, "Go back." To Shomkharka. At that time, we were removing the husks from the rice.

Another statement and another duty that helped to seal her husband's fate. Unaware that he was planning to consume a medicinal plant, the women and his son needed to return to their homes in order to complete the work required of them. He was left alone to care for himself.

After a while, Lama Mingmar's father [my first son] called. "Father is calling! Mother come! Grandmother come! Sister come! Auntie come!"

So much of the action detailed in Kisang's narrative rested on words voiced in emotionally pitched terms. Her son, who must have visited his father, returned home to relay his father's summons. The tone of the boy's utterances, as voiced by Kisang in our presence, was one of desperation, alarm, and terrified concern. Her questions in response were uttered in an achingly high-pitched voice:

"Why?!" I said. "What is it?"
"I don't know," he said. "Father is, eh—Father is hurting, so he's struggling in pain!"

Something significant had happened, though Kisang's son was unsure what was causing his father's painful state. His physical struggle indicated that his would be a bad death. (Kisang drew from the same verb stem, *bol,* in describing her attempts to wrestle free of the marriage party when they were "taking" her to Shomkharka; "Ah, I struggled.") Her husband's words resounded through an intermediary here, as though in his tormented state he had lost some of his voice, consciousness, and agency. Perhaps in relation to this collapse of language, vision now took priority over voice, and any potential words of his were replaced by descriptions of his physical state.

Then, all of our family went there to look after him. When we reached there, the intestines were damaged. There was nothing left. He ate one bunch of dhang men, and the other was under the pillow. Under his pillow.

Wangel Lama had eaten too much of the medicine. As a result, the medicine was not only purging the ailment from his stomach and intestines. It was also destroying his digestive organs. What his family saw was portrayed compellingly and economically, with precise details later envisioned: "under his pillow."

"What did you do?!" Everyone—Mother, Auntie, everyone—scolded him.

Uttered in a terribly worried, uncomprehending voice: What did you do to bring about this misfortune? What actions induced these effects? Her husband, silent still, did not respond to this question, though Kisang's next words drafted a response of sorts.

Because of his own actions, he died. Not by the disease.

A powerful statement: He died, not from the disease, but from his misguided attempts to annihilate it. Yolmo lives can be understood as consisting of a series of actions, of le, or deeds, that can be executed through skillful or unskillful means. Such actions can be morally good or bad in nature, they can have great benefits or negative or insignificant effects, and they can affect others in consequential ways, for good or bad. Much the same economy of action held for her husband's death, a profoundly consequential, nonbeneficial act that, for Kisang at least, issued from the effects of certain inept actions and the persons responsible for them. Of the many ways to die in Yolmo, from falling off the edge of a cliff to "passing" from one's body in sleep, this was truly a horrific death.

When we went there, his intestines were discharged. The ringworms were also discharged. Worms! The mother worm, the mother worm was there. It was alive. Twisting, slithering.

The last utterance, "khyug-khyug," was accompanied by a disturbing tick-tock of Kisang's index finger.

Lo. Everyone was bewildered.

"Bewildered" as in astonished, perplexed, at a loss for action.

"What did you do?! What did you do?!" we asked.
There was too much dhang men. The dhang men ruined it, no doubt!

His body, his life, and any chance of recovery were ruined, destroyed, soiled, rendered incomplete, by too much medicine, too many worms, too much discharge. The purgative also destroyed the couple's time together. "I wasn't able to stay with him for the whole life," she once noted. "Pointless. We stayed together thirteen years."

Then, everyone carried him to the house. Again and again, oh, they [the discharges] happened, oh!

If he was to die, better that he be brought home to die.

Kāñchā's father and your [Pramod's] father were there, then. The two arrived playing the flute very nicely. He [my husband] used to love both of them. He treated them so well, a-ma-ma-ma! The one who died.
Loved one.

Another social bond detailed: Oblivious to the tragedy at hand, his two beloved cousins arrived at his home, playing sweet flute music that contrasted harshly with the worried voicings and twisting worms. Kisang often spoke of the first cousin, Rinjin Lama, as "Kāñchā's father," because, several years later, he married Kisang, then fathered Kāñchā; to say his name outright would have been disrespectful.

Then my husband said to me, "Make tea for them."

Even in his dying, ruined state, Wangel Lama acted gracefully, caring to honor his guests well. With these words, his last noted in Kisang's account, his love for his cousins became clear. He was a good man.

Loved one.
He was treating his brother very well.

Speaking of relatives in a manner quite common to Yolmo wa, she again referred to Rinjin Lama as her husband's brother, though in fact he was his cousin. Her husband did have two brothers, including one who lived next to him in Ne Nyemba. Wangel was not all that close to them, however, and preferred to spend time with his cousins. So as he lay dying, he asked to die in his cousin's arms rather than in his brother's, as might usually happen in Yolmo families. "Your father [Rinjin Lama] had to be there with him," Kisang told her son Kāñchā when we spoke together about the death later on. "He would say, 'My dear brother, stay close to me, I can't stay without you.' Your father was with him until he died."

"I heard," Kānchā then said, "that uncle [your first husband] died in my father's lap. Is that so?"

"Yes, he died in your father's lap, because he loved your father so much, more than his own brother even. Until his death, he never let your father go away from him."

"Why didn't his younger brother come there?"

"I don't know. They weren't so fond of each other, I think, and they had some misunderstandings. He never called for his brother but treated your father as his own brother."

The strength of Wangel Lama's affection for his cousin and his cousin's presence at his death proved crucial to later developments in Kisang's life, for it is with his "last words" while dying that her husband asked Rinjin Lama, "Kānchā's father," to look after Kisang and their children after he died. Rinjin promised to do so. He later married her and fathered two sons with her, including her youngest, Kānchā Lama, with whom she later lived. One set of actions led to a subsequent chain of actions.

So often now the breath was trying to go out.
"A-ma! What can be done?! What can be done?!"

Though he was still alive, his last breath was trying to part from the body, and they were helpless to save him. The only recourse to action was to wait, to bide the flow of time. The only voicings then were unattributed ones of desperation and compassion, which nevertheless characterized sharply the moral tenor that settled around this waiting game. At the same time, what those involved knew then, what they did not know, what would happen, whether the lama would live or die—the spoken sense of knowing and not knowing here situated the narration not only in a lived place and time but within the passing of time itself.

His breath hadn't gone. He stayed alive. How many days did it stay like this? Maybe twenty or so, so many.

So many days, so much hardship; truly a bad death, dominated by a quiescent, liminal stasis before the actual death.

On another occasion Kisang said that her husband "survived for two, three days even" after being carried to the house.

Then, he died. He died.

His death, marked with the honorific form of the past tense of the verb *to die (thongsin),* was couched, grammatically at least, as another action undertaken. As it was, Kisang spoke on occasion of her husband's death as an act of taking leave, an abandonment even, in that he "left" her. "Like that, he left. Five children," she told us. Some sixty years later she was still pained by his absence. "What did I see? I saw very blurry," she said in response to questions about what she did or did not dream about then, shortly after we had spoken about her husband's death. "Sometimes I could see good things. I could see one or two things—not a whole lot. I didn't see. What to do? I didn't see. My will is broken." She then added, somehow reminded again of her husband, "He obtained enlightenment [*sang gyekyo*]. Where, where did he reach, now? He left me. Now I don't see. I don't see anything. Now my will is broken."

As Pramod began to explain to me in English how her husband died, Kisang continued to speak in Yolmo.

What to do?

No other actions, then or now, could have countered the slow doing of his death. "Jīvan estai chha," they say in the foothills (Life is like this only).

He died. What to do?

"Chi bheche?" The repetition of this phrase seems to underscore the sorrow and bewilderment she and others felt.

Then, after getting our attention while Pramod and I spoke a bit in English, Kisang spoke slowly in Nepali, as though to communicate directly to me.

K: *By his own hand, his own life/person went.*
P: *Yes.*
K: *What to do?*

"By his own hand …" (āphnai hātle, āphno jan gayo): The echoic economy of her syntax features a self-effecting, self-affecting economy of action: the lama's actions resulted in the loss of his life.

And again in Nepali:

The man who gave it [was] also bad.

Her words speak to Tashi Bombo's actions in more direct terms than before. "He should not have brought such a large amount of medicine," she said when asked about this later. "He should have said that taking too much would be dangerous. And he should have told him [my husband] how much to take."

P: *Who gave it?*
K: *Who gave it? The elder sister was Tashi Bombo's mother, and the younger sister was my husband's mother.*

Kisang identified the giver, Tashi Bombo, through his relation to the receiver, Wangel Lama, as though this was all one needed to know in order to understand what was at stake and why her husband could not have readily ignored or distrusted his cousin's instructions.

A stab of harmful actions led to a death. Complex webs of action course through the circumstances of Yolmo lives. Implicit, culturally pervasive takes on time, action, and moral responsibility are inherent in the textures of a story. When I discussed Kisang's narrative of these events with several Yolmo friends while visiting Nepal in 2000, it became clear that, for them, an individual's actions almost always have consequences in the world. Actions therefore tend to carry strong moral, interpersonal edges to them. Actions bring consequences, and people are constantly judged by the deeds they undertake, particularly in terms of how those deeds affect others, with any such judgments conveyed through words direct or roundabout. It was this idea of moral action that friends found most directly expressed in Kisang's words. As she told it, Tashi Bombo's advice and Wangel Lama's efforts to follow that advice led to the latter's death. That death meant sorrow and hardship for others.

And yet there's another perspective to note, one that stresses the more distant karmic aspects of suffering. When Karma Gyaltsen was staying with me in the States in 2001, he read through a version of this chapter, one that ended with the two paragraphs just above. In discussing these paragraphs with me, he said that, while they were fine as they stood, he also thought it important to include an additional line of thought: that Yolmo wa also understand that any misfortune they face in life, either at their own hands or the hands of others, is also a consequence of their karmic heritage. A person who is harmed by another or who bears witness to a loved one's suffering at the hands of others knows that his own karma determined that he would encounter such harm—that he and others "fit into the situation" of the actions undertaken, as Karma put it. One implication of this, Karma went on to say, is that people tend not to blame others too much for any wounds inflicted by them. Significant events in a life, from an abrupt death to a lasting grief, are the net result of previous actions undertaken by an individual, and any hardships suffered are, at least in part, a reflection of one's own deeds.

Kisang's narrative put the blame for her husband's death squarely on actions immediate to the situation. Karma, in turn, wanted to balance Kisang's assessment with another perspective. He wanted to make it clear to me, and to any readers of this text, that Yolmo wa also know there to be other, more anterior actions that lead to suffering in life. "It's how we think about our lives," he said. "It's how we think about what we do, about what happens to us or to people close to us." Since Karma felt certain that Kisang would have thought along similar lines, there remains the question of why she did not mention the force of her husband's karma in his death or the weight of her own karma in suffering that loss, when talking with Pramod and me. Was it simply that such thoughts did not come up, or was it that they went without saying, or was it too painful for her to think or narrate them? It's difficult to say for sure. What is clear, however, is that some lines of thought stood like shadows alongside other, more apparent ones.

"Dying Is This"

Kisang's account of her first husband's death involved a different narrative voice from the one expressed in her tale of her marriage to the lama. The tone was somehow more direct, more mature, even a bit world-weary. It was the voice of a worried wife, one who had already mourned the death of several loved ones. The narrated *I*, Kisang, was also more assertive in her pronouncements. Now the mother of several children and settled within her husband's household, she was more able and willing to voice her own judgments, to mouth critical words in response to the actions of others. Kisang's words again modeled significant features of her subjective life at a particular, crucial time.

One feature common to both narrations, however, was a keenly descriptive narrative style. Kisang's narrations tended to be phenomenalist in spirit, in that her words so often and so graphically evoked a swirl of sounds, sights, thoughts, and matters remembered and re-presented: "leave me alone"; "twisting, slithering"; "under his pillow." In fact, in thinking about Kisang's account of her husband's death, one could say that it entailed a loose phenomenology of dying in the sense that it depicted, in specific and concrete terms, the strands of awareness, perception, and sensate consciousness that formed around one person's dying. To an extent, the narration bore affinities with another unnamed genre sounded among Yolmo wa, for on occasion Yolmo wa tell stories that chronicle, deed by somber deed, the events leading up to someone's death. Kisang's narrative of dying spoke in particular to the causes of a death. In attending to her words on Wangel Lama's death, we learn something about how certain orientations to time, action, language, and power and authority common to Yolmo lives shaped how some made sense of one man's undoing.

Another meditation on dying was inherent in her words. But this mediation leaned more toward an account of dying per se, of her own passing, in fact. Our conversations with Kisang in 1998 led to the makings of a "death story" of sorts, one that spoke to a woman's subjectivity in the face of death. Embedded within her various remarks were asides on her aging state, her imminent death, and the force of her demise in general. "Now, in the time of dying, I need to stay like this..." (Marne yahi ho, ahile...); "Dying is this, now...." When speaking about such matters, her tone was at times playful and defiant. At others, her words conveyed an air of sadness and frustration. In general, though, her words seemed to figure the "thisness" of dying, as though she had been trying to detail, either to herself or to others, what dying is and what it entails. While she did not put it so, these various observations amount to a phenomenology of dying in which her words conveyed, in first-person terms, what she perceived to be the decaying phenomena of her body, speech, and mind.[1]

What seemed to pattern a lot of these concerns were particular casts of mind and language, ways of thinking and talking that gave certain form to her demise. Her dying took form within a sea of words.[2] For one, there was at times an intensity or allness to her thoughts about dying, as though only thoughts of dying filled her days then. "What can be done by living?" she once remarked. "It's better if I die. I think only of dying. What can be done by staying? I can't walk, I can't eat well. Now, dying comes to my thoughts, certainly. What to do?" Relying on a language in which thoughts and feelings "strike" or "come" to a person's sem, she spoke as if death blanketed her thoughts. "Nothing comes to my sem, for sure. Only death comes to my sem. It has decayed."

The force of this presence in those days seemed to overwhelm at times. Death, perhaps the true agent here, had come to her sem, unwilled by her, and her lifeworld then was one of dying. Yet while she did indeed speak often and incisively about death, on other occasions her words also displayed a similar intensive totality. In many of her accounts of her earlier years, for instance, there were glimmers of an intensity of thought in general, as well as an occasional totality or allness to something. In speaking of her marriage, she noted that there were "many, many, many people," that shalgar offerings were "put through the whole way" to Shomkharka, and that all her uncles were there. In recounting the manner of her husband's death, she spoke of how "a lot of children" were dying, then of how "nothing was left" of her husband's intestines, which were ruined by "too much dhang men." For "so many days" it stayed like this; "so often, so often the discharges happened." When we asked in 1998 if many people came to visit her, she quickly replied, "Iii-iih!! Everyone, everyone, everyone from around the chhorten comes!" Such phrasings named a repletion of thought or action, in which there was an allness or fullness to something going on in her life. ("Kisang," by the way, derives from the Tibetan phrase *kun tu bzan po*, "all good.")[3]

Elsewhere I have written about an "aesthetics of repletion" among Yolmo wa, wherein people value things that are full or replete in some way. "A successful festival is one in which many people come"; the walls and cupboards of a prosperous house are lined with photos, kitchen utensils, and bottles filled with colored waters; and a guest, on leaving a home, should not empty a teacup served to him for this would suggest that his hosts are either stingy or unprosperous."[4] Thangka, similarly, are replete with richly symbolic images and colors, as the painted icons and interiors of a gompa are. If a person dreams that she is swimming in a vast ocean, buoyed by waves, it is a sign that wealth will come to her soon. Hosts often serve food after food to any visiting guests in the hope that the latter will leave with full stomachs and sated minds. Women, in turn, speak of the need to assure that their children do not want for food. "Although I had such a hard life, I fed my children's stomachs full," Gom Dolma told us. "If we had plates full of rice for our children, and we could feed our children's stomachs full, it was regarded as the richest deed." Some worry that they might not have enough to eat in their final years. Fullness can signify wealth, prosperity, well-being, goodwill, perfection of form, or a richness of spiritual devotion.

Yet lately I have come to realize that one can also speak of a "rhetoric of repletion" in Yolmo communities as well, for Yolmo wa often invoke the allness or muchness of something when trying to make a point or when trying to relate an event to others in persuasively compelling terms. This is often the case when people speak of significant hardships faced in their lives: the flow of sentences during such moments has a way of marking an excessive abundance of suffering. "Dhukpu nhyungdia, nhyungdia, nhyungdia, nhyungdia, nhyungdia, bhiza chingi ghalsin" (Facing, facing, facing, facing, facing that hard life, I had twelve children), Gom Dolma recalled of the first years of her marriage. "It was a lot of trouble. Trouble upon trouble," Ghaki Lamani said of the physical labor required in order to clear her family's fields for farming. "Me? I don't know how old I was," Ghaki later avowed when I asked her how old she was when her parents died. "How could I know the dates? There was only work upon work and lots of children who had to be looked after."

It's not just occasions of suffering that receive such treatment, however. Other communicative acts can also call for a crowd of nouns and adjectives that attest to the muchness of something encountered in life. Kisang, for instance, had a knack for stressing the ubiquity or plenitude of certain matters, as is evident in her use of charged words like *so many, too much, so often,* and *everyone:* "Then *everyone* put the shalgar along the way, and *everyone* was singing along the way—where, where?! [*so many* places]—then they brought me to Shomkharka." Persuasion by totality.

My sense is that this way of putting things also played into how Kisang spoke of dying then. There were two sides to her rhetoric of dying. Dying was an entirety for her; she thought only of dying. Only death came to her sem. But this also meant that her mind was depleted of everything else. Other thoughts were stilled: "Everything is lost." No other actions could be undertaken: "I don't have any thoughts here now. Now I'm gone. I'm contemplating Phagpa Chen Rezig."[5] Her memories as well were depleted, with many recollections having been forgotten, or "swallowed with rice," as they say: "But now the memories are lost.... By now I've swallowed the memories with food. Now the mind is swallowed. It's not, now." In accord with this occasional repletion of depletion, there was a quality of "justness" in talk of this sort. If she was "just playing in the dust" when she was a child, then later in life she was just dying, or just living, or not really living fully anymore.

Here and elsewhere her words conveyed an aura of nothingness, of a dead time between one life and the next, of smarts and willful thoughts lost—"Aba chaina," in Nepali (Now, there's not). "What comes now?" she said when asked what wishes she had for the future. "'I have this to do, I have that to do'—that feeling is lost. There's nothing. Everything is lost. Now I'm on the verge of dying. It will be today, or it will be tomorrow. Tomorrow, or today. The intelligence is lost. I don't have any smarts. There's nothing, now. What to do? When am I going? When Yama Raj [the Lord of Death] will come to take me, this is all I think about. Aba chaina."

There was no movement, no urgency to action, she was saying. Nothing but the anticipation of her death. Death was allowing little but its own force to be thought.

So much was involved here. Thoughts of dying had overtaken her sem, much as certain spells of "love magic" in Nepal make the enchanted one think only of the person he or she presumes to love, or the loss of a Yolmo wa's la, or spirit, depletes that person of will and volition. There was also a oneness to her thoughts here that compared to certain singularities of speech and action evident in her accounts. Her brother's constant refrain about Shomkharka's layout, for instance, spoke of a singular vision: "If one looks at the sky, one sees only the sky." As she approached death, correspondingly, she thought only of death. The singularity of thought here helps to explain, I think, why her comments on her situation lent themselves much more to a phenomenology of dying than, say, to a sociology or a political economy of dying: while increasingly detached from others, she was regularly engaged in an almost meditative focus on the phenomena of her own demise.

Some would say that such a point-blank minding of death was the mark of a spiritually devout Buddhist preparing well for death. As noted at this book's outset, Tibetan and Yolmo sages encourage meditations on the features of death and dying. "My mind turns to thoughts of my death," drones Gyalwa Kalzang Gyatso, the Seventh Dalai Lama, in an eighteenth-century poem of his, composed of twenty-seven stanzas, twelve of which end with that observation.[6] The poem, entitled "Meditations on the Ways of Impermanence," concludes with a colophon that sums up the lyrics' intent: "Verses for meditation on the ways of death and impermanence; to inspire the minds of myself and others."[7] It is likely that perspectives similar to these infused Kisang's concentrated musings on death. Indeed, if she had failed to convey that her own mind had turned to thoughts of her death, others might think less of her for it. Any Yolmo wa who is getting on in years but who has apparently not given serious thought to his or her death risks being considered a bit foolish and ill-prepared by others. "We say, 'He's such an old man now, but he doesn't think of dying, he doesn't think of death,'" said Karma on the subject. A skillful death is, in part, one in which a person has seriously considered his death and devoted his final years to accumulating karmic merit, merit that can help him to gain a good rebirth in any next life. And since others always seem to be looking on, ready to deride unskillful acts, elders are often inclined to say that they are, in fact, preparing well for death. "I don't have any wishes or thoughts," Gom Dolma told her grandson and me when we asked what hopes she had for her remaining years. "Now I think only of dying. I think about how I might die, and what will become of me after I die."

When thinking of death, Kisang's occasionally single-minded focus had a lot in common with the "one-pointed" meditative practices that many Buddhist treatises expound, in which an adept is encouraged to cultivate a mind that can "naturally abide with its chosen object...without wavering," or words to that effect.[8] Such efforts themselves bear affinities with ideas submitted by early Hindu and Indian Buddhist philosophies. According to J. N. Mohanty, for example, early Buddhist philosophers spoke of three in-composite dharmas, or "point-instances": *ākāśa*, or empty space, *nirvāṇa*, and "a temporary cessation of attention to other objects when the mind is exclusively attending to one."[9] Elsewhere Mohanty notes that Ānandavard-hana, an influential ninth-century Indian philosopher, held that the enjoy-ment of *rasa*, the generalized "mood" or "flavor" cultivated by classical San-skrit dramas, unfolded through several stages: "Other objects disappear from consciousness until rasa alone is left, the particular feeling is universal-ized into an essence, then finally there is a state of restfulness. Aesthetic en-joyment then becomes somewhat like the contemplation of the *brah-man*."[10]

While any linkages between such philosophies and Kisang's lines of thought were distant and indirect at best, her words pointed to a similar intensive singularity of purpose at times in her life, especially now that she was approaching death. At times her thoughts were stilled and pure, like an adept's one-pointed concentration in meditation on a single mental notion. As other matters faded from her consciousness, her mind attended exclusively, without wavering, to thoughts of dying. Those thoughts were cultivating, restlessly, a rasa of dying.

In all, her take on dying involved a direct undoing of her world and her means of engaging with that world: her body was dissolving, the quality of her speech was eroding, and her senses were deteriorating, leading to a disengagement from others. At the same time, the words and images she used in depicting the dissolution of her self tended to echo ways of thinking and talking specific to her life. They also in-volved, as will soon become clear, certain sensibilities of form, time, and action common to a range of cultural happenings. Cultural themes and imageries patterned how a woman subject to dying spoke of elements of her demise.

The Painful Between

Cultural forces shaped how Ghang Lama spoke of dying similarly to their shaping of Kisang Omu's words. But the means were different. Mheme approached death in ways distinct from Kisang Omu's approach, and the tenor of his last years was unlike that of Kisang's. For him, being on the "verge" of death meant mostly a liminal time of fear, uncertainty, and longing.

He told us, for instance, that his heartmind was "disturbed" as of late. The disturbances were in line with his understanding of what happens to people when they come close to dying. "The sem gets disturbed," he told us.

The sem gets disturbed. Then, the time of dying comes. Then, it's like a dream. One wonders, "Is it a dream or is it reality?" That's the between-state of dying. The between-state of dying arrives, for sure.

The word translated as "between-state" here is *bardo,* a Yolmo and Tibetan term that draws from the word *bar,* which means "between" in either a temporal or a spatial sense. The word *bardo,* in turn, which means literally "between two,"[1] can designate any intermediate period between two actions or two stretches of time. The moments between sleep and waking can be said to be a bardo, as a pause between utterances can be, or the waiting period that many youths inhabit after they have finished their studies but before they have married or secured lasting work. "*Bardo* means 'between,'" Mheme told me right off when I checked with him on this. Most often, though, Yolmo wa speak of the bardo when referring to the liminal, transitional period between death and re-birth. During this stretch of betweenness, which is commonly thought to last up to forty-nine days, a recently deceased person travels about in a disembodied, dreamlike state until she or he achieves liberation from the cycle of rebirths or obtains another rebirth.

While most Yolmo wa speak of the bardo as a single intermediate pe-riod between the end of one life and the beginning of another, Yolmo lamas, like their Tibetan counterparts, often profess that there are, in fact, six between-states that humans commonly pass through in living out their lives and entering into new ones. The first three pertain to the intervals understood to transpire between birth and death, between sleep and waking, and between waking and meditation. The last three occur during the processes of dying, death, and rebirth. *Chhi khai bardo,* or *"the between of dying,"* is realized when a person is dying and so is hov-ering between life and death. At this time, a profound state of con-sciousness called the clear light occurs. If the dying person recognizes the clear light as the true reality, then he or she is immediately liberated from rebirth. If reality is not perceived, then *chhe nyi ki bardo,* or "the be-tween of *dharmata,"* occurs. This bardo, which begins after a person dies, consists of a prolonged conscious state, in which the sounds, col-ors, and lights of dharmata, a person's innate nature, are perceived as "pure phenomena." If the deceased person does not perceive the nature of reality in these phenomena, which include the appearance of "peace-ful" and "wrathful" deities, then the *si pai bardo,* "the between of becom-ing," dawns. In this final intermediate period, the person emerges in a mental body and encounters various birthplaces; a liminal time of seek-ing a new rebirth in one of the six worldly realms, it concludes when one enters the womb from which one will be born again.[2]

In speaking to us in 1998 about the psychological implications of "the time of dying," Mheme, who had been reading up on such matters, ap-peared to have most in mind the chhi khai bardo, or the "bardo of dy-ing," literally, the bardo of being on the "mouth" or "verge" of death. In Tibetan texts, this between-state refers specifically to the moment of death, when a person's consciousness separates from the body. As one text defines the term, "For a certain period the consciousness undergoes a separation from the embodied state and enters a state totally without solid grounding. That is the second intermediate state, the painful bardo of dying."[3] While some Tibetan authors suggest that this state lasts but a moment, others hold that it can entail a lengthy illness or moribund state that eventually ends in death.[4]

Mheme appeared to be using the term more in the latter sense, as a general, transitional period between life and death. Although he was not mortally ill, he understood himself to be at the edge of death, hovering between a full life and a full death and so swayed by the bardo of dying. "The chhi khai bardo arrives, for sure." As with any bardo interval, flux, unfixed changes, and dreamy uncertainties soon became the mean for him. Between life and death, a liminal period, without solid grounding, as "unstable, fluid" as other "between" moments, encroached.[5] Sleep was difficult to come by. His thoughts had become fickle and uncertain. The abilities and sense-faculties of his body were beginning to dissolve. At times life had become "like a dream."

Mheme, in turn, had become a bit like a child. As he saw it, the minds of old people in their final days resembled the minds of children. Intrigued by comments made by Yolmo friends that likened old people to children, I asked him about this one afternoon in the spring of 1998.[6] "It's true," he said in response.

They become like children. Children and old men are the same. The old people think like children, first wanting to do one thing, then wanting to do something else. Their sem are just like the sem of children. Many years before, when I was a child, my mother told us, "The old men are just like infants." Now I've also become like that.

He went on to say, "People think about so many different things when they get old—sometimes they're crying. . . . It's not just me."

For Mheme, old people are like children in that both evince a fickleness of sem.

One's thoughts become more irresolute, vacillating from desire to desire. Such a disposition was at odds with the "straightness," clarity, and undistracted focus of sem that the lama valued throughout his life. One can resort to Western ideas of senility or dementia to explain these "disturbances." Yet Mheme's own words suggested that he took an elder's flighty, childlike thoughts not to be a result of oldness per se. Rather, they are a matter of transition and uncertainty as those forces arise when a person hovers between life and death in the final stages of a life. Given the logic of rebirth, this made a lot of sense to him, since, like others, he might soon become a child again. Childlike actions among the elderly can presage a new life to come. As with the turnings of the moon, the flow of developmental time is cyclical in nature; a child becomes a man, then an old man, than a child again. Ultimately

Mheme seemed to be suggesting that old people can enter into a liminal period between life and death, between one life and the next. He found that he himself was now living in a kind of limbo, with his present life fairly over with, and a new one now encroaching.

The transition brought sorrow. In their discussions of "the bardo of dying," discussions which are often replete with fine-grained exegeses on the deathly dissolution of human faculties of sense and thought, Tibetan authors speak of this between as a "painful" one. "The bardo of dying is said to be painful," notes one teacher, "because the process of passing away usually involves pain and suffering."[7] Along with the pain and suffering that can come with a life-ending illness, such authors have in mind the idea that the moment of death itself, when the life force is "interrupted," can be a painful one.[8]

For many Yolmo wa, the end of a life can also be painful because it entails sentiments of sorrow, fear, and longing. Many say that the most fretful aspects of dying are the separations entailed. Lhatul's wife, Mingmar, spoke about such concerns in her home in Thodong one March afternoon. As she prepared tea and I warmed myself by the fire, she spoke about the death of a youth's mother and that boy's subsequent orphan status, then ended her commentary with the statement, "Life is like that. There's sorrow."

"In your life?"

"No. In our lives. It's good when we're young. But when we get older, we have to worry, we have to go here and there, and then we die. There's sorrow, sorrow of the sem."

She later spoke of the activities she most enjoyed doing, including planting potatoes and making trips to the forest to graze animals. "I like to do a lot of things, like going to the forest to collect wood and working in the fields. I like to do these things very much," she said, then added, "In life we like these things, then we must die. This is our life: we like things, we like to do certain things, and then we die. There's sorrow."

Sorrow is felt in the years and days before dying, because one longs for, and foresees the annihilation of, the pleasures and companions that make up a life. Mheme never spoke directly with me about any sorrow he might have felt in conjunction with the end of his life, perhaps because it would have been in bad form for a knowledgeable lama to express or to heed any attachments felt to this world, and my few attempts to broach the subject directly soon trailed off into different discussions. Nevertheless, I do think he was saddened and dismayed by the inevitability that he would soon have to part from the bonds and pleasures of his present life. I have only empathy to draw on here, a kind of indirect knowing that is flimsy at best when it comes to understanding someone from another society, but something in the shadings of his voice suggested that he enjoyed being alive, in the way that he knew it, and that he did not wish to die.

A life's end implies a rupture of the everyday. It forces a disruption of the familiar and the known, of a life and the relations it held. It spawns confusion and uncertainty. It means the demise of clarity and self-presence. It brings partings, separations.

The old man did not like the prospect of dying. Remaining alive had its virtues. "Dying is not good," he told Norbu and me. "It's good to live as long as one can." He seemed to be particularly concerned about what would happen to him (and others) after dying. What kind of life would he get? Into what kind of place would he be reborn? What kind of judgment would the gods make? Questions like these worried him and made him fear what the consequences of his actions in life would be after he died.

"Mheme, are you afraid of dying?" Norbu and I asked.

"Yes, I'm afraid. But being afraid doesn't help at all. . . . "

"Why are you afraid of dying?"

"After dying, now, the god is seen. Now, what kind of place is reached? Will we reach a good place? Or, sometimes we reach on the cliff, sometimes we reach in the water. One is afraid of the deity."

He and others feared a deity's ability to judge a person's life and then determine the nature of that person's next life. At work here was what anthropologist Gananath Obeyesekere once called the "psychologically indeterminate" nature of the Buddhist principle of karma: while "the past determines the present which (combined with the past) determines the future," Buddhists cannot know what the future holds in store, because they do not know what their past sins and good actions have been: "Although the individual knows that the good which he does in his present lifetime will be rewarded in a future lifetime, he has no idea *how* his future will be related to his present existence."[9]

Obeyesekere had most in mind here the idea that, in Buddhist circles, humans cannot fathom the ways in which the moral tenor of past lives influences present or future lives. Also in question for Ghang Lama was the moral import of his present life. After he told us one day of the consequences of human actions after dying, we asked what he thought the deities would conclude with him.

"If one has done sin or not, they will show these things clearly," was his response.

"Do you think it's as if you have sinned or as if you have done more dharma in your life?"

"How can I know that, whether I have done more sins or dharma in my life? If one has sinned in life, there is a dharma book in which there are ways of reducing sins." He then reached around to the cabinet set within the wall behind him, took out a Tibetan text, and showed it to us. "One has to read this day after day." In that way the text, known as *dhig-shyag*, or "sin-removing," is understood to be effective at "cutting" the reader's sins and so improving his or her chances for a good rebirth.[10] "One reads as much as one can," he said when asked what the purpose of his daily reading was.

If one reads more, one reaches heaven. This is work for later, not for now. This is work for the time of dying, this reading, that's to say. One gets the route [to a good rebirth] when one dies. Everything is written in the books. After one reads and reads, won't one get the route?

But certain doubts lingered. "I myself feel," the lama continued after a pause, "that I have sinned in life, and also that I have done dharma in life. The Hindu astrologers tell me that I haven't done sin, or dharma, in my life. Neither sin nor dharma has been done."

There is no way to be sure of any of this. In contrast with the all-seeing omniscience of the gods in these matters, humans cannot know with any certainty what their karmic heritage is or what lies in store for them. Although a person's everyday life is, like a text, often quite visible and knowable, death cannot be foreseen and so always entails uncertainties. As Binod's father, Palsang Lama, once conveyed it to me, "I'm telling you, [according to] our Buddhist dharma, if we're born, we have to die. If we're born, we have to die. From when we're born until when we die, we know about the things that happen. But after dying, what happens, how it is, nobody sees, nobody knows."

Nobody sees, nobody knows. Unlike the intense visibilities he employed in other aspects of his life, Ghang Lama could not foresee what would happen after he died.

Nor could he see when he would die. "We can't know when we'll die, not even the scientists," Lhatul once explained to me. Although Mheme thought he would be dying soon, he could not know precisely when or how his death would occur. He could die after a long illness or he could die suddenly, as his father had years before and at a younger age than

Mheme himself had already reached. The rapidity of his father's demise seemed to give him pause, for he noted it on two occasions, without prompting on our part. In the course of one conversation he interjected, "Now, *one moment,* our father, one—he came from the upper part of Yolmo, he slept at night, he wasn't sick, and he died."

"Who was this man?" Norbu asked.

"Our father."

"Whose father?"

"My father."

"Eh. Grandfather's father?"

"Hmmm."

"At what age did he die?"

"At sixty-eight."

"He had gone to another part of Yolmo," Mheme told us on another occasion. "He came back home, he was very healthy, and while sleeping that night he died. He had gone to a village higher up, for his aunt's funeral, to do the lama work."

"He wasn't sick at all?"

"No. He participated in the funeral dances."

I took it that Mheme was concerned that, within the echoic folds of a "like father, like son" logic, he could very well duplicate the manner of his father's passing. His own death, at any rate, could come at any time.

All this spoke to the ways in which the between-state of dying was, for Mheme, a time of uncertainty and ungrounded thought and being. His death, while certain and imminent, was unforeseeable. His thoughts were disturbed. Meanings were growing uncertain and unstable. Because life had become a vague dream to him, he was left to wonder what was real and what was not.

Desperation

Desperate times can lead to desperate actions. Within the fabric of Yolmo lives, it can be said of one woman that she felt compelled to remarry; of another, that she died of jealousy.

The consequences of Wangel Lama's death in Kisang Omu's life were several. In the days that followed his passing, she had to make arrangements for the funeral rites that needed to be conducted on his behalf. "What could be done?" she said to Pramod and me. "When having the ghewa performed and everything else, I needed to do everything by my own hand. I needed to pay [for the rites] myself. Like that, he left. Five children [we had together]."

The funeral rites performed were elaborate, well-attended ones, with the members of two different lama lineages, Sarma and Ningma, conducting the ghewa that took place some seven weeks after the death. All of this was an indication of the great respect accorded the deceased lama and his wife's virtuous actions at this time. When asked if the ghewa was done well, Kisang replied, "I did! For the ghewa, a-ma-ma! We invited a lot of Ningma Lamas from the four directions. Ah, they gathered here. I did well. Ningma Lamas came there, and Sarma Lamas as well. They made two altars."[1] To say that she "did well" was to assert that she had skillfully arranged for the funeral rites to be conducted properly and with appropriate respect for her husband and his family.

Among Yolmo wa, being a widow does not entail a precise social identity in itself. In contrast with high-caste Hindu communities in Nepal and India, few ritual restrictions apply to widows only, and the circumstances of widows' lives vary greatly.[2] In Kisang's case, her husband's death brought hardships of a specific kind. Her husband had "left" her, she mourned his departure, she was still responsible for the care of the gompa in Ne Nyemba, and she was left to raise four children on her own, with one still "very small." "Chi mazjhe? Chi mazjhe?" (What to say? What to say?), she said when asked what were the best and worst times of her life. "When we did well, we did well. Good things happened, and we hosted the sponsors well. We established the gompa. We had a fine life. The lama [my husband] also passed away, so I faced hardships.... The hardship was the hardship. The lama also left me. We did well while we were together. When he left me, I did all the hard work. In this way, what to do? During the good times we did well."

A repletion of suffering troubled her in those years. "Hard work I did, did, did, did," she told us.

"When your first husband died, did you stop feeling happiness?" we once asked.

"Where would happiness have come?"

"Was there sadness in your sem?"

"A-ma-ma-ma! For me, the sorrow, where has it not come? No one else has sorrow like me. I've dealt with so much hardship. What to do? I needed to care for the children. Father, none. Children—"

Yolmo wa often say, when speaking of children who have lost one parent or both, that they risk *ala khyamge*, "wandering aimlessly about in life."[3] The phrase speaks to a sense of aimless, even hopeless, wandering, of being without proper direction or guidance and bereft of any secure financial support in their lives. "This is the main worry we have about children when a parent dies," one man told me.

Kisang's concerns about her children and Rinjin Lama's promise to their father that he would look after them after the latter died led in time, and in connection with a series of other deeds, to a second marriage for Kisang, some twelve years after her first husband had died. The new groom was this same Rinjin Lama, the cousin in whose arms Wangel Lama had expired, a man, nineteen years younger than Kisang, who had previously been married to another woman.

> P: *After Uncle [your first husband] died, then you went to his brother [you married his cousin Rinjin Lama]?*
> K: *Then, indeed.*
> P: *When did you do this?*
> K: *Ah, it was after many years. I stayed a long time.*

   While Yolmo cultural precepts do not prohibit a woman from remarrying after her husband dies, such remarriages are not especially approved of, particularly if the deceased was a lineage lama. Many widows do remarry nevertheless, in large part because the potential benefits of a remarriage, namely, increased financial and residential security, outweigh any critical gossip that might result from the new union. In speaking of her second marriage, Kisang seemed attentive to the possibility of gossip, particularly as it might apply to the means of the marriage itself. She was making clear that she had remarried only after staying for "many years" in the home she once shared with Wangel Lama.

   Yet it was only after Rinjin Lama's first wife had left his household for a village at the southern edge of the Yolmo Valley that Rinjin and Kisang married. Kisang said:

After the birth of her son, she was jealously angry at me. Now I have to talk about it. She was jealous of me. She was jealously angry at Kānchā's father [Rinjin Lama], so she took some goods, she took everything. She took everything.

   Our talks with Kisang led to a situation where she could no longer avoid discussing what had happened then, and she now had "to talk about it."

   While *mi ser,* which means literally "yellow-eye" to some, "eye-prick" to others, is the Yolmo word for "jealousy" here, it is a specific kind of jealousy, one that pertains to the sentiments of jealousy and resentment enacted by one person because of an apparently flirtatious or romantic involvement of that person's spouse with another. The woman, literally, "did mi ser" or "did jealousy" to Kisang; she acted in a jealously angry manner toward her. The verbal structure said a lot about how Yolmo emotions can be intensely active and interpersonal. The woman, who was herself from another region of Yolmo, was peeved at her husband, Rinjin Lama, for the attentions he paid to Kisang and her children in the wake of Wangel Lama's death. Acting so, the woman renounced her life with him and vacated Ne Nyemba, taking with her everything but the kitchen pot. This left Rinjin Lama in need of a wife to manage his household. That role was soon filled, but not too soon, by Kisang, who married Rinjin Lama and later gave birth to two sons, the younger being Kānchā.

Then, later, I remained a long time, eh? I didn't go anywhere. "I'm not going," I said.

   That she remained a long time in her own home after her husband's death before moving into the home of Rinjin Lama, even after Rinjin's wife had vacated the scene, bolstered her contention that she was morally "straight" in these matters, and the woman had no right to act jealously toward her. The timing was crucial. Her declaration that she was going to stay put in her first husband's home, "I'm not going," stood as a voicing alone here, but it sounded as though it was in response to persistent coaxings along the way. Every voicing implied other voicings.

Later, everyone said to me, "You need to marry him because his first wife left the meal for you. So you should eat it."

Others in her family were then unanimous in their assertion that she should take up the challenge enacted by the woman who had left. This challenge could prove beneficial to Kisang, because an opportunity for marriage stood like an abandoned, uneaten meal that she herself could consume. Since it is important for a widow to find a domestic "meal" to subsist on, and given that "everyone" was telling her to respond to the woman's actions by marrying Rinjin Lama, Kisang felt obliged to go along with her in-laws' wishes.

With this said, I went by procession, with the wedding songs and dances! I didn't go without doing anything!

"With this said," with the coaxings of her in-laws in full force—once something is said, it defines a field of action in the flow of time and so justifies how someone acts—Kisang went to Rinjin's house by means of a formal marriage procession, with all the requisite rituals celebrations. She did not go "without doing anything," that is, in shacking up with the man, as some Yolmo women might have done. "They didn't just live together. They married," Kānchā Lama asserted later on. His mother therefore maintained the honor of her husbands' families. Ritual as legitimation.

P: Later?
K: *Well? Later. Oh, what's with that woman? I was straight. I'm still alive. Later on, she died before me. But I'm still alive. Perhaps she died earlier because she spoke untruths.*

The word *later* can imply different trajectories of time and action; the afterward Kisang apparently had in mind here involved the subsequent karmic consequences of the woman's actions. Kisang was morally innocent, or "straight" [*dhangbo*], in these and other engagements and so had lived a long life. The other woman, in contrast, was already dead, perhaps because she had spoken untruthfully. In this Buddhist world good comes of good and bad of bad. Kisang skimmed from this logic to position the morality of her actions and those of "that woman."

His wife took her son also, she took everything, even the ash. She acted jealously toward me.

The woman's evacuation from the household was a remarkable, insolent gesture, for it entailed the removal of herself, her son, and all worldly possessions from her husband's domain, in a complete cessation of co-presence and exchange with him and his family.

Everyone made me enter. Then everyone said to me, "His first wife gave you the food. You need to take hold [of it]."

Literally, "everyone entered me," as though those active others were the true actors then. Grammar can say so much about a logic of agency and desire.

"So, it wasn't my desire to go [to marry again]," she told us. "What to do during a time of hardship? With this said, I married."

With this said, before I married, I didn't stay in just one place. I went back and forth, back and forth.

She trekked back and forth between Ne Nyemba, the home of her now deceased first husband, and Shomkharka, the home of her second husband, an hour's walk away, in order to take care of both households and the temples associated with them. A life of movement, karmically so.

What to do? The woman's forehead. I didn't go without any procession.

To be clear on that most significant point, especially since her words were being recorded: the marriage was a proper, honorable one.

She then said to herself, with a bit of a laugh, as Pramod and I spoke to each other in English:

I need to say everything.

"But she's saying the zigzag," Pramod noted in exasperation two days later when we sat in his home and hammered out a translation of his aunt's words.

In continuing her narrative, Kisang said quietly, to herself, as though she shared in Pramod's later observation or at least anticipated such comments and relistenings:

They've recorded everything . . . even though I don't know how to talk.

Perhaps she did need to say everything. After Pramod and I listened to and translated Kisang's account of her second marriage, I wanted to learn more about why her second husband's first wife was so angry at her. We therefore reintroduced the subject the next time we visited her.

> P: *Auntie, my uncle [Rinjin Lama] had a wife before [he married you]. Why was she jealous of you?*
> K: *Who?*
> P: *The wife, the one who left Ne Nyemba.*
> K: *Eh! Ibi?*
> P: *Yes. Why was she jealous of you?*
> K: *It happened like this. Sometimes he used to come to me. At that time, before he died, my husband arranged for his brother to live there. Your father and uncle would go to Ne Nyemba [to visit].*

"It happened like this": To tell this story well, to convey how it really happened, to justify her actions, Kisang had to begin with the death of her first husband, Wangel Lama, and the close bond between him and his "brotherly" cousin, Rinjin Lama, who often came to visit Wangel in his home in Ne Nyemba, often accompanied by his younger brother, Palsang Lama, who years later fathered Pramod. The strength of their affection for each other prompted Rinjin Lama to visit Kisang and her children occasionally, in ways that soon became clear.

> P: *Whose father?*
> K: *Your father. The two brothers. The two brothers would come there [to our home in Ne Nyemba]. Then, their brother [my first husband] would arrive. Loved one. He would tell me to offer them tea and food. "Auntie is not staying here." Your father and his brother would come while playing the flute. To Ne Nyemba they would come. They brought us food.*

In friendship and mutuality Rinjin Lama, his younger brother, and their cousin Wangel Lama partook, before the latter died, of flutes, tea, and food. The quoted reference to "Auntie" is unclear, but cotranslators told me it probably implies that Rinjin Lama's wife was not staying in the area, and so Wangel Lama wanted to make sure his "brothers" were well cared for nonetheless. The statement could also imply that this woman was not around much and so was perhaps not providing well for her husband.

That woman was very hostile and dying of jealousy. She was jealous of me. It's the shameful thing, she acted jealously toward me. I didn't think about this thing. At that time, he [my first husband] hadn't yet died.

She had no thoughts of going with the woman's husband, she was saying, especially since her first husband was still alive. So perhaps even before her first husband's death there were tensions between the two women.

Then, later, he died in the lap of Kānchā Lama's father. With his last words, my husband gave the responsibility to his brother [cousin] to take care of my children. "If you travel here or there, please take good care of my children." He promised that he would do so.

With these words Kisang referred to a conversation that had occurred a few years before, one that functioned as an important "shadow conversation" that shaded the grounds of later conversations.[4] As her first husband lay dying and voiced an "oral will" *(kha jhem)* to family members gathered around him, as Yolmo men and women often do before they expire if they have the strength and opportunity to do so, he asked his cousin Rinjin Lama to care for his and Kisang's children after his death. Rinjin Lama promised that he would do so. "My first husband died in the lap of Kānchā's father," Kisang told us on another occasion. "Then my husband said to his brother, 'Take care of the children, brother. Your sister-in-law manages the money [for the children]. Please feed the children. Your sister-in-law cannot get about easily [to collect food and so forth].' My husband asked Kānchā's father to do these things. In that way, I went to Kānchā's father."

When her son Kānchā later heard a taped recording of these words, he exchanged glances with me and said, "This is not a lie. She's not the only one who says this. Other people have said the same thing, like my cousin, for instance. It's not a lie. He did say this." Kānchā relayed what Wangel Lama had said in dying: "'My children are young. Please look after my children. Treat them with compassion. They have hardships.'"

Given that it was not always thought appropriate that widows remarry, what Kisang, her son, and others said about such requests and promises served to justify why she remarried later on. It also helped to explain and legitimate the reasons for Rinjin Lama's frequent visits to Kisang's house, despite his wife's protests to the contrary.

Then, that woman became very jealous. She was very angry with them. She was saying, "She seized my husband." [But] It's not the shameful things that I am talking about.

The collective "them," presumably Kisang's in-laws, continued to be assigned agency here. And while Kisang averred that there was nothing shameful in her actions, the voicings of unrelated others were also at work, as Yolmo women often fear might be the case when they arrive as strangers in an unfamiliar village in marriage. A Yolmo pain song submits:

> If we walk in the fields of summer,
> we fear that we might slip.
> When a daughter parts for a foreign land,
> she fears gossip might fall upon her.

Alluding to just this sort of gossip, Kānchā Lama later told us that, when his father did look after Kisang's children, there was "cutting talk" (N., *kurā kātyo*) in the village concerning the relationship between her and this man, talk along the lines of "She's going to another person."

"But it was a fact," he noted in passing. "They weren't just staying together."

She was doing so much mi ser to me, so much, so much. I went there to quarrel with her. "He didn't go just like that. His brother became very ill, so he asked him to stay with him [when he was sick]. He didn't come for my sake." Like that, I went there to curse.

Enraged by the woman's slanderous accusations, Kisang approached the woman's home in Shomkharka to confront her accuser and argue her case. Rinjin Lama visited her home for a good reason, she insisted. He first stayed by his cousin's side when the latter was dying, and he later frequented Kisang's home for her children's sake, not by choice, but because he had promised he would do so.

Any fighting that was to take place would be with words. "We fight with our mouths, we don't fight with our hands," Kisang explained once when discussing disputes among Yolmo women. "Women can't fight with their hands. People restrain us."

"Auntie, with whom have been really angry?" we then asked.

"With whom have I been very angry? With the woman who acted jealously toward me, the one who became my enemy."

I went inside the temple [in Shomkharka]. "In regard to your husband, don't hold me in contempt [N., helā]." Like this I went there to struggle. "Eh, your husband is yours. Your husband is yours. There's not one thing between us. Why are you treating me with contempt?"

Another contemptuous act, another struggle. How different, how much stronger was Kisang's voice here, compared with how she por-

trayed herself as speaking, or not speaking really, when she was younger
and on the verge of marrying for the first time.

On that side [of the family], he had died, he had died before I had said this.

Her first husband had died before she had said any of this, her words
made clear. This meant that, whatever else might be said, there was no
question of her having been involved with another man while her husband was alive.

*I challenged her. "Come outside!" She couldn't come outside, though. She didn't come
outside. She didn't say a single word in response. I was twisting and turning outside
the house. "Come outside. Eh! You should say only the necessary [truthful] things, not
the unnecessary things!"*

Attempting to engage her enemy, with her "name" on the line, Kisang
swirled in a rage outside the woman's house. One spoke truthfully; the
other, "unnecessarily" or "unusefully." Kisang once said of the anger of
women in general, "Anger comes, but it won't amount to anything. To
other women [anger comes]. If someone is angry, acting scornfully,
then she circles about. . . . What does it amount to?"

   "Women gossip, and a village is aflame," a Yolmo woman once offered up this proverblike adage after hearing about an ongoing feud in a
neighboring village. Sometimes such gossip forms into harmful mhi
kha, or "people's talk." "*Mhi kha* means that someone is saying that this
woman is doing this thing, she's doing that thing, she's doing this
thing. That's mhi kha, surely," Kisang said when asked what the word
means.

*At that time, my husband was dead, he was dead when these words were spoken. Then
later [I said], "You need to take care of your husband [Rinjin Lama]. Don't say whatever you feel like saying. You shouldn't talk like this. You need to take your husband in
your hand. . . . Come outside!" I went to Shomkharka to quarrel.*

   She spoke of another's thoughtless, harmful talk and advised the
woman to control and attend to her husband. She also reaffirmed her
marital status at that time, as though the moral and existential circumstances of her life then were closely interwoven with her thoughts and
words, both then and when talking with Pramod and me. She might
also have wanted those circumstances to be clear to anyone who might
happen to hear her narration as recorded on tape.

Then, she didn't come outside. She didn't.

Though the woman had been "back-talking" about Kisang, she declined to meet her challenge and hid in silence.

Then I said, "Don't talk like this! If you talk like this, it's not good!" I was so furious then. She was scorning me. She was scorning me.

"If men are angry, they can hit someone," she told us. "Women just talk worthlessly." While men can fight if they are angry, women can only talk. Seldom does anything "good" come of such talk, however.

I went to Shomkharka. I swore to her [that there was nothing going on]. But after I had left, she took everything with her, her son as well. Ibi [my mother-in-law] came to inform me that she had left the house.

The woman's departure bore affinities with the "vanishing" of a body at death, with but a few articles and some ash remaining, though the dead can never take possessions with them. And so the intensity of the woman's voidance and the allness of the depletion signified, however faintly, a self-willed social death in the vicinity of Shomkharka and a new life and new social ties in another village.

Ah, she swept up everything! With her son also. There was one copper water container [remaining], and the ash, and some of the old wooden goods.
That was after the death. Later. She left the house then. My husband had already died by then. She vacated the house. She didn't take her husband in her hand.

The woman was at fault for not caring for or keeping an eye on her husband, Kisang was saying. She failed to act in the right ways.

Then later, my mother-in-law, [your] father's mother, and others, four in all, they set the way. They coaxed me. In coaxing me, they said, "She has put the black face on you [she has made you look shameful]. So don't leave either temple. She has done this to you; [so] you should eat the food she's left for you. So you need to take care of everything. You need to look after this temple, and the other one as well."

Kisang's in-laws were quick to act, perhaps because it was in their interests that their daughter-in-law assume responsibility for the care of both households and temples. They would also be concerned, as Kisang would have been, that any "black face" infixed on her would bring shame to everyone in the family. Setting another "way," invoking a causal logic of "so" and a world of needs, they coaxed her into saving face by responding to the woman's challenge. All told, it was a matter of voice, face, agency, need, and responsibility.

One was your father's [and Rinjin Lama's] mother. Then along with her was my mother-in-law [Wangel Lama's mother]. She [the woman who left] was my cousin. Then, she left me everything.

While identifying who was who, Kisang also noted how she was related to this cousin of hers, who may in fact have had less true agency in the matter than her two mothers-in-law. But since Kisang was in fact distantly related to this woman, the question arose then as to whether it was legal for her to marry the same man that her cousin had just left. A trip to the district center of Nuwakot was therefore necessary.

Then, because she was my cousin, they went to Nuwakot to inquire about the marriage. Then Nuwakot gave the permission. "You can marry." They said that we could not have married if we were mother and daughter in relation.

Since the two women were only cousins, however, the marriage could proceed. The final, written words, which came from the government court itself, legitimated her place in her new husband's household and ruled out any effective return by the woman who had left it.

My two mothers went there, my mother-in-law, and your grandmother [Rinjin Lama's mother]. In this way, I needed to look after each temple. On this side and on that side.

The upshot was that she then needed to manage two households and temples, one set in Ne Nyemba, the other in Shomkharka. Such were the binding effects of local voicings.

Before, my husband said to his brother, "Take care of my children after I die. I have given the money, everything, to your sister-in-law. She will buy everything for the children." From then on I was bound to look after the temple on this side as well as the one on that side. In this roundabout way, here and there, they put the responsibility on my head.

A roundabout but binding course of action led to a life lived here and there, a narrative aesthetics of zigzag, and a heavy burden. "She then had two temples to look after," her son told us once. "She had two responsibilities, like a person who has to carry two loads."

After she [Rinjin Lama's first wife] left Ne Nyemba she had one more son. She didn't die easily. She died by the stinging nettles. She treated me with contempt. I heard this, and it's true. If she hadn't talked, it wouldn't have happened. Thoughts about your uncle would not have come.

Bad came of bad. The woman's troublesome talk produced two particular consequences among others. Early on it triggered ideas, in the minds of Kisang and her mothers-in-law, of Kisang staying with and marrying Rinjin Lama. Later the woman died a terrible death, wherein someone, apparently her second husband, hit her repeatedly with branches of stinging nettles. To Kisang, however, who was alive and talking still, the woman brought all this on herself. She died of jealousy, it could be said.

It was because she acted so jealously. It happened out of desperation.

What, precisely, happened out of desperation? Either the woman's jealous anger or Kisang's response to it were desperate acts, or the woman had died in despair. Whatever Kisang's specific intent in this instance, the word *desperation* applies to each of these happenings, since there were few other options in each situation.

Other themes repeated as well.

P: *Did she marry after she left Ne Nyemba?*
K: *She married, yes. She died before the lama [her second husband] did. I forget when it was, before or after. I don't remember.*
   Yes, she died first, she died first. Her husband beat her and burned her with nettles. From our Pema I heard this.

The word from a niece was that the woman had died at the hands of her spouse. In this chronicle of voicings-as-actions and the moral implications of those actions, a woman who harmed others was harmed in turn. Stinging words begat scalding nettles. Yet Kisang's words also spoke to the extent to which the lives of women are swayed and sometimes brought to an end by the actions of men.

The Time of Dying

So the woman who left Ne Nyemba suffered an uneasy death years before, whereas Kisang herself was still alive.

All the same, an abiding question for Kisang and others was why she had come to live for so long, and, consonantly, whether her "staying" was the karmic fruit of either good or bad deeds that she previously undertook. During our numerous visits to her, she often mused on the possible reasons for living so long. "Why am I staying? Heh!" she once interjected.

"People usually die before they reach your age, but you're staying a long time. Why is that?" we asked in the course of an early visit.

"I think about that," she replied.

"Why do you think that is?"

"The grand age, I don't know. Everyone dies younger than my age. Who blocks me in dying, who blocks me in dying?! I wonder about that.... Everyone has gone to die. Why am I staying? I don't think I've done any bad deeds. When I was digging soil in the field, maybe I killed a few insects by my hand, just one or two were killed, perhaps. 'Please forgive [me].' To Phagpa Chen Rezig I'm doing *mani-padme.*[1] 'Please forgive.' I didn't do a single wrong thing. I made the ritual offerings, I did dharma. So why am I still alive? I wonder about this."

In touching on the unanswerable question of why she had stayed alive for so long, Kisang's words alluded to several possible reasons for her longevity. In asking who was "blocking" her in dying, she was suggesting that a supernatural force might be hindering her passage into death. The sentiment is a sensible one. Since she was so often forced to move from place to place in life, why not suspect that someone or something was now forcing her to stay put?[2] It was also possible, she noted, that the discomfort she faced was the karmic result of any sins she had committed, such as inadvertently killing a few insects while farming.

Still, she did not think she had done any "bad deeds" of any serious import. While she had lived a good life, she could not die well. "What to do, eh?" she asked on another occasion. "I don't think I'm suffering from any illnesses [that might lead to my death]. What to do? Bad [luck] is written on my forehead. Unlucky. Without fortune. I have to stay alive. I'm tired."

To say that "bad" was "written" on her forehead was to say that aspects of her karmic fate or fortune, including the timing of her death, were inscribed there. Yolmo wa commonly understand that a person's karma determines the manner of his or her death. "Every person's death is due to his karma, what he has done before," Ghang Lama once told me. He went on to explain that, if someone is sick or in pain while dying, especially for a lengthy period, then that kind of death is a punishment from the gods. Karma put it differently: "If someone has a bad death, we say, 'His karma must have been really bad before, because he couldn't even have a good death.'" Being beaten to death by one's husband or dying after taking a purgative that liquidates one's stomach would fit the criteria of a bad death, as would a painful erosion of one's body. That Kisang "had to stay alive," though tired of living, suggested to her and perhaps others that she was "without fortune" in this matter, much as she had had the misfortune to be born a woman and to be widowed at an early age.

On other occasions she offered more positive reasons for such a long life, proposing that she was still alive perhaps because she had received a blessing from the Dalai Lama while visiting his residence in Dharamsala, India ("I was in the attending audience, so I'm alive now"), because she was "straight," or innocent, throughout her life, or because she had accumulated karmic merit in maintaining the two temples in Shomkharka and Ne Nyemba. "I took care of two gompa. So I've stayed a little bit longer, it seems to me."

Different days, different conclusions, perhaps. Yet it also appears that Kisang could not come to any easy conclusion about her dying because two different narrative scenarios were at work. Yolmo wa generally consider a long life to be a very good thing and the result of good karma. Yet they also understand that any illness or suffering a person encounters at the end of her life is the result of bad deeds enacted in previous lives or during her present life. Both scenarios applied to Kisang's dying: she had lived a very long life, longer than almost all of her peers, but she was also suffering in her final days. Her dying thus appeared to be the result of a mix of good and bad karma. And while she might have wanted to know what was in store for her, she could never know for sure what her "fortune" was. "What is written? What is written?" she replied when asked if good fortune was written on her forehead. "The Three Precious Ones [know].³ I don't know. [Whether] the Precious Ones wrote, 'You will live ninety years or over ninety years,' I don't know. When the time for dying comes, the words will have come. I don't know what they are." Any words written on her forehead would become known only in death.

That death would occur within time and at a certain time. The Yolmo language offers a verb form not directly available in the English language: *renba*, "to be the time (for something)." In the course of their days, people talk of how "it's time to eat" (to sa rengyo; more concretely, "the time for eating food has occurred"), or of how "it's time to go" (do rengyo), or of how "it's time to work" (le bhe rengyo). Some also say, especially if they feel their lives are soon to end, that "it's time to die" or "it's the time of dying" (shyi rengyo). Kisang often voiced such words. In much the same terms as those used by other Yolmo elders, she announced on different occasions: "I'm dying, it's the time of dying." "The time of dying has already happened." "The human life is finished."

As such, Kisang was living and dying within several, culturally recurrent engagements with time. Death is a temporal process; it proceeds in time. Perhaps because of this, the presence of death within the lives of the living often brings into sharp relief the passage of time and the effects of time. It can also give emphasis to the different temporalities that course through those lives. In Kisang's case several temporalities contributed to the timing of her death. *The effects of time:* For one, the sheer force of time contributed to the erosion and imminent end of her body. *A person in time:* Well aware of this, she was waiting for, anticipating, the act of death to occur. *The time of dying:* She and others knew that dying could entail a specific and sometimes lengthy stretch of time. *Fated time:* Her karma destined her to die at a certain time. *An unknown time:* Yet she could not know when that time would happen. *An unforeseeable time:* Nor could she know, really, what would become of her after she died. *Cyclical time:* But still it was likely that she would be reborn into a new life, and another one after that, unless she was able to escape from the churnings of karmic actions altogether. *Acts in time:* The actions of the past and present could, in accord with the principles of karma, have a significant, echoic effect on her future. *Moral chronologies:* She and others would understand, consequently, that the manner of her death would signify the ethics of her actions, with a long, prosperous life indicating a life (or lives) rich with virtuous actions, but a prolonged, painful death attesting to a life (or lives) of sinful transgressions. *The timing of a death:* Moral presumptions thus swirled about the timing and mode of her dying. *The timekeeping of others:* Others, she knew well, would take notice of her way of dying and so mull her way of living. *Dying, among others, in time:* Despite the dreamy isolation of her life then, her consciousness of her passing was acutely temporal, and interpersonal, in scope.

Her son Kānchā, for one, seemed to be mindful of the manner of his mother's dying. During one of several conversations I had with this learned lama, we got around to talking about good and bad ways to die. When asked what was the best way for people to die, he replied,

In my opinion, dying due to illness or having a lot of pain is not good. But when compared to the death by accident or suicide, dying at an old age or dying as a result of a minor illness is the best way, I think. No one can die without there being a cause [N., *niu*]. So getting a little sick as the cause, and then dying, is a good way to die.

In stating that no one can die without there being a *niu,* a "cause" or "reason," for that death, Kānchā was proposing that, even if a person's destined time to die has arrived, that person will die only if some kind of event or action, such as an accident, an illness, or a suicide, triggers the death.[4] Given this, it is clearly better to die after having lived a long life and as a result of a "cause" that involves relatively little pain. When I relayed these words to Binod a few days later, proposing that Kānchā had perhaps had his mother in mind when voicing them, Binod agreed with me. Kisang's way of dying was a good one, her son's musings suggested. They also implied an explanation for why she was taking so long to die, for even if "the time of dying" had already arrived, she could not die unless some sort of cause, minor or major, resulted in her death.

She had almost died two weeks before Pramod and I first came to talk with her, during the losar (New Year activities) in 1998, when first one abscess then another wounded her mouth, and she could no longer eat. "I was gravely ill then. During losar I was gravely ill," she later told us. Her family wanted to take her to a hospital, Neela told us, but she refused to go, maintaining that that was where people went to die. She therefore remained at home, unable to eat or speak much, surrounded by visiting family members. "Eh, saying, 'Ibi,' they came to give respect," Kisang told us after she had recovered from the ailment. "They all came. 'How is it?' they asked. I just gestured now and then. I gestured, then said, 'I'm not here. I'm going.'"

Her health slowly improved, but only after she lost consciousness for a spell and was close to death. "Maresakyo, tyo belāmā!" (She was already dead, at that time!), a concerned relative of hers told me a few weeks after he had visited her then. Kisang herself related: "Before, it was like I had died. At that time, I didn't feel any pain in my body. How pleasant a place I arrived in, apparently. A-ma-ma! I felt I had arrived in a very beautiful place, but here everyone was crying, crying. It seems I had died. But then my breath returned. It turns out that my flour is not finished. My ration is not finished. After dying, I returned. It was pleasant, the life on the other side."[5]

Kisang's uncommon, metaphoric allusions to stores of flour and rations not yet depleted evidently ties into the idea, common to many Tibetan peoples, that each person has a finite life or life span (tshe) that slowly becomes less or lower as that person's years wear on. Barring misfortunes or impediments to that destined span of life, a person can live out its full length but not much longer than that. As one Tibetan master tells it:

There are two primary causes of death: either our time has run out or temporary circumstances result in death. When our life span has reached its end, nothing more can be done; death is unavoidable.[6]

Or as Ghang Lama put it once, "When it's time to die, it's the deity's time.... If our life is going to end, nobody can save us."

That Kisang had yet to die suggests, then, that her supply of life might not have been finished. Still, she sometimes said that it would be good to die, even if she was kept from dying, because the "time of dying" had arrived. "What can I say?" she said in response to one of our questions. "It's time to die. Now my sem is of a person who is growing old. I feel I haven't hope to live. Now, this life is gone. This life is changing [altering into death]. Now, I have no hope to do this work or that. There isn't, now."

There was no longer any phāidā, or benefit, to living, she was saying. "Why keep me alive? There's no benefit like this." At one point she explained, "Now, my sem is dying out. It has already died. What can I do? I wonder why my body is alive. It's better to die now....There's no benefit like this." No advantageous consequences, for her or others, could result from such an action or inaction. Nothing would come of it.

Death Envisioned

"A bugbear." "The sleeping partner of life." "Pale priest of the mute people." "A black camel, which kneels at the gates of all." These are but a few of the ways that humans have given image to death in different lands and centuries. Death has been designated as a transfer, as annihilation, as "the ultimate horror of life," as an "ugly fact." In poetry it has been portrayed as "the mother of beauty," as a "spongy wall," as "but a name." In philosophical discourses it has been defined as "nothing," as "that possibility which is one's ownmost, which is non-relational, and which is not to be outstripped," and, contrarily, as "the impossibility of having a project."[1] While death so often proves itself to be beyond the reach of what the living can know directly, its very unknownness and its towering, inescapable importance in life somehow lead people to try to name it and anticipate its features.

Ghang Lama had his own take on death, one that he was willing to share with Nogapu and me. As such, it remains unclear to me how much of what he related to us was a direct manifestation of what he thought himself and how much was offered up for the benefit of his interlocutors, two younger men who, as he saw it, could apply his observations to good effect in their own lives. Were his words out of conviction, or was he trying to warn us that death inevitably follows life? While my guess is that there was always a little of both going on at once, it's difficult to say for sure. We have but his words on death. Be that as it may, the substance of those words suggests something quite unified: death, according to Mheme, is a "between," a transitional time between one life and the next, a time in which a disembodied, disoriented soul has to navigate a slew of

dreamlike perceptions in trying to achieve a good rebirth or to absent itself from the sansāric world altogether.

What is also clear is that the workings of vision play an important
role both in Mheme's depictions of death and in how he himself appre-
hended and prepared for his own passing. The old man understood the
"death between" to be a stretch of confusion and perceptual vagueness.
He was preparing for his death by reading up on what would happen
then. He had come to think single-mindedly of death. He perceived
that it was now "time" for him to die.

Several observations, several things he "saw," led him to reach the latter
conclusion. Along with the sheer number of years he had lived, the fact
that his body was growing smaller, his limbs were growing heavier, and
his physical strength and abilities were waning indicated to him that little time remained for him. "For Yolmo people," Nogapu and I asked, "if
they get old, what is seen in the body? What things happen?"

"Ah, what happens?" was his response.

Some people feel, "The time of dying has come." Some come to know that, but
others don't know. We don't know if we'll die today or if we'll die tomorrow.
When we get very old, we think only about dying. Now it [my body] is getting
smaller, smaller, smaller. Earlier on, a person gets taller, taller. Now I'm getting
shorter. We become old and feel that the time has come. I'm eighty-two years
old. Can I live longer? Maybe not.

"We become old and feel that the time has come." As the case was
with Kisang Omu, Mheme's long life indicated that he was bearing the
fruit of good karma. But given his considerable age and increasing bodily frailty, he had concluded that he did not have much time left. In 1998
he told us: "The time is already past." "After two years I'll die, then that's
all." "Now, I won't last very long." In responding to various queries from
Nogapu and me, he said point-blank that it was time for him to die.

"Do you still worry about money?" Nogapu asked.

"No, what's the use?" Mheme replied. "Now it's time to die."

"What wishes do you have for the next few years?"

"What do I wish for? Nothing. Maybe that I could stay one or two
years more. But now I don't think I can stay that long."

"These days, what thoughts come most to your sem?"

"What thoughts come? No thoughts come to mind. Only that I'm
going to die. Now it's already time. What else is there? Thoughts like 'I
won't be able to eat' don't come. I've already grown old."

"Mheme, have you ever gotten angry in your life?"

"No, I haven't. It's time to die. Why would I get angry? Now it's time to die. Now where, where is the anger?"

At the level of utterances, although our questions opened up the possibilities of a life, his responses, mindful of death, closed them down. Statements like his hinted at a disinvestment from the exigencies of life, as though his impending death rendered pointless any worldly thoughts or feelings or engagements with others. Anger was as absent as the body and friends of his youth.

The time of dying thus brought thoughts of death for Mheme. "For me, there's no worries," he said when asked about the common worries of elderly Yolmo wa. "The only thing I think of now is death. That is the only worry." Difficulties in sleeping well compounded such thoughts. "When I was young, I would sleep for a long time. These days, I sleep just a little. So I have all this time to think. All the time I'm thinking a lot. I'm thinking about dying."

Mheme's mind had turned to thoughts of his death, much as Kisang Omu's had. Though the fact of dying unnerved him, his "straight" character, his "one-sided" thoughts, and his Buddhist creed led him to maintain a contemplative focus on dying. The exclusive, single-minded temper of his thoughts led to a fearful (and, I think, admirable) consciousness from which he felt he should not turn away. It also recalled the penchants of devoted lamas to "wait" for death in a solitary locale, away from the disturbances of everyday life. Lama Merit Intellect, the sixteenth-century Tibetan sage, included these verses in a "mental vow" that he tacked up outside his meditation cell after growing weary of the many beneficial works he had to perform at the request of others:

> Now I won't last for long. I shall certainly die.
> Thus I yearn to perform some religion for my death.
> Noise and disturbance are the devil's interruptions.
> So that attachment and hatred in their various forms may not be my
>   companions,
> I stay to await death in this solitary spot.[2]

Ghang Lama's pledge that he was thinking only of dying obliquely echoes the desires of lamas to await and contemplate death in isolation. His expressed yearning to do much the same was one of the reasons that he wanted to travel to Thodong and enter into solitary retreat there, for in doing so he could perform dharma and think mindfully of death with few disturbances interrupting his practice. All told, such an excluding practice would assist him in an effort to "renounce the affairs of the perishable world," as a common Yolmo phrase, *jigten gi jhawa pange*, puts it. Many Yolmo wa express an interest in quitting the "doings" (jhawa) of *jigten*, a word that can mean "the external world," "the secular world," or, more literally, "the receptacle of all that is perishable."[3] People can be heard saying, especially when work and family responsibilities make life less than easy, that they want to leave the sansāric world of everyday life and adopt the life of a renunciant. Few, however, find it feasible to do so.

Mheme nevertheless had similar plans in mind. "I'm going to make a shelter [N., guphā] for the retreat and stay there," he told Norbu and me in 1997.

"Why would you stay in a shelter [instead of in a house there]?" we then asked.

"If I stay in the shelter, I can read alone, with no one disturbing me. If I stayed in a home, people would come to visit."

"Where will the shelter be?"

"It will be below the field, on the northern side [of our property there]."

"What will your wife and daughter do?"

"If they want to go [to Thodong], they can go. If they don't want to go, they can stay here [in Chabahil]."

As for what the lama's thoughts of death actually consisted of, his musings were geared mostly to what could happen to a person after dying. This, at least, is what he spoke of to us. In our varied discussions of what happens to humans in death, the lama related little about the funeral rites that have to be undertaken if a person is to attain a good rebirth. Instead, he offered thoughts more on the plight of the deceased's soul in the death between and on the practices that a person can undertake in life in order to be better prepared for what happens when it comes to an end. All in all, he understood that the themes of confusion, opacity, and loss that so often "arrive" at the end of a life will carry on into death.

Much of this tied into his sensory take on the world. Whether it be reading Tibetan letters or appreciating clear vistas, Mheme had a bias for lucidity over opacity, visibility over obscurities, purity over defilements, and singularity of purpose over disruptive actions. Such inclinations correlated with how he regarded forms of human consciousness. From what I have gathered, he thought that waking consciousness should be clear and focused, with a strong self-presence of mind, and free of distractions, vagueness, confusions, and clouded thoughts. In general, a healthy waking consciousness for him implied clarity, visibility, and perceptual distinctiveness. Unconscious states of mind entailed much the opposite. To be *behos,* or "unconscious" (to use a Nepali word), was to be "insensible," to be bereft of the perceptual faculties that normally characterize states of *hos,* or "consciousness."

One day we asked him if he had ever been seriously ill as a child. "Yes," he said. "Once a bombo said I was going to die. I was nine or ten then. I was...I didn't talk for one whole day, and they said I was going to die. And then a Brahman came along and said it was food poisoning. He made up some medicines, and gave me some, and from the next day on I was better."

"What happened?"

"First I got a fever, then slowly I became unconscious. It was like dying. For one day I had died. I was completely unconscious. I didn't see anything, not even dreams."

To be completely unconscious in that way was not to see or say anything. It was like being dead; "Behos is like dying for a moment," Lhatul once told me. Such an equation implies that being conscious, being alive, can be first and foremost to see, to perceive and engage with the world through visual means. For Mheme, to be fully conscious meant, ideally but also usually, to see with clarity, with distinctiveness, not at all like the seeing associated with states of dreaming, which tend to entail murky perceptions and inchoate, tough-to-remember images. "Dreams are full of confusion," one man told me. "A dream is like the wind," said another, "just coming and going, and so it's difficult to remember so well. The dream is not part of our body. It's like a guest who doesn't stay long."

Mheme spoke of dreams in similar ways, spotting them as something vague and illusive. Yet he did so less by talking about dreams per se than by comparing the features of turbulent moments in his life to features common to dreaming. When Norbu and I asked how he felt when his first wife died, he gave this response. "[It was like] 'Where, where?' Now I was as if blind. It was like a dream, or the daytime I couldn't make out."

Andho, the Nepali word for "blind" here, also carries connotations of "unaware, oblivious." "Confusion. That's what he meant to say, I think," Karma said when I asked what he thought Mheme meant by the word *andho* here. "I think he meant, 'I was a mess, I was confused.'" When his wife died, the lama was rendered unaware, confused, oblivious to the world around him, unable to perceive daytime images, as though sifting through a dreamlike fugue: "It was like a dream."

Mheme used the same expression when talking about the love that develops in arranged marriages. When Norbu and I asked him whether a person begins to feel love for his or her spouse before or after marrying, he replied, "It's after the marriage, usually two to three years after they marry."

"And for one or two years, you don't feel anything?" Norbu asked.

"Well, I can't say what that feeling is. Whether it is love or not, it's like a dream. After two or three years, after one has children, then that's when one usually begins to love."

"So, before one falls in love, what is that feeling?"

"To us it's nothing. We just know that she's our wife. The love that we have then is a strange love. I can't explain."

The initial bond of affection between man and wife was a "strange" love for Mheme, one that cannot be described or explained, much as the elements of a dream cannot be clearly distinguished or easily recalled. In love, as in dreams, vagueness reigns.

Much the same holds for death. Death is "like a dream," he told us. He spoke often of the understanding that a dead person's state of mind and body during the death between is similar to a human's consciousness during the "little death" of dreaming, with the windy visions and opaque, unsteady perceptions characteristic of dreams vexing most of what a dead person thinks or sees. "At one point, after dying, we can't even see dreams," he explained. "We're just unconscious. Then slowly one sees like dreams. Then after it comes like dreams."

For Mheme, the dreamlike qualities of the death between entail confusion and opacity and an inability to think or see clearly or converse well with others. Many other Yolmo men I spoke with held that the perceptiveness and intelligence of humans increase significantly during the bardo state and that humans oscillate between moments of clairvoyance and confusion. Mheme, in contrast, spoke of the ways in which disembodied souls are frightened, confused, and occasionally "shocked" while traveling through the between.

Such confusion and discombobulation relate, in part, to the person's loss of the body after dying. Mheme and other Yolmo wa understood death to coincide with the departure of the nam-she, or soul, from the houselike abode of the body. "Our soul doesn't go outside easily. It's very difficult to die," he told us. A day or two after death, the body is cremated in a rite that accords with Tibetan Buddhist practices. The lama told us often about the consequences of these events.

Our soul goes outside, it goes everywhere, but our body remains. It doesn't go. Our body's here, in this way.

At the time of dying, the soul separates from the body. Soul and body separate. Our soul is like the wind, it flies out of the body. Without the sem and the nam-she in the body, the body decays. It's like a house: if there's no one living in the house, then what happens to it? It decays.

The disappearance of a body, which for Mheme was a process that began when his own physical form and strength began to diminish, continues, in an amplified form, in death. A common euphemism for death among Yolmo wa is that it is a "passing from the body." What is thought to take leave from the body are a person's soul and consciousness; as the body begins to decay and then is cremated, these spiritual forces become disembodied, making for a handless, touchless existence. As the lama saw it:

Only one's soul goes up. Everything is burned, even your body is burned.

This body won't be there, these hands won't be there. It's only the mind that goes away.

We have ears now. If we die, then the ears will burn. After we die, they burn everything, everything but the soul.

Other materialities must also be left behind, including any wealth or possessions accumulated. "Even if we're very wealthy," Mheme noted, "we have to leave those things after dying. We leave our work also.... When we die, we have to leave everything and go. One can't say, 'But I have so much wealth.' One can't take any of that wealth. One has to leave behind even a needle and thread."

A body of sorts does emerge for the traveler in the between after death, but it is an illusory, very subtle one, similar to one's body as seen or sensed while dreaming. One Tibetan text refers to this body as a "mental body made of instincts; even if it is killed or dismembered, it cannot die!"[4] Mheme apparently had much the same in mind when he told us that, in death,

only the soul is there. There's no body. The body and soul separate. When the soul separates from the body, it's like the wind. It's like a dream.... After dying, it happens like this. There's no body. We travel to the cliff, and we're afraid of falling from the cliff. We think, "Oh, I have a body. If I fall from the cliff, I'll die." [But actually] there's no flesh, no bone, no blood. If we fall down, we don't get hurt. But we're afraid in the sem. If we had flesh, bones, and blood, our body would get hurt. But in the sem, it's just like dreaming.

When the deceased's soul goes away, it wanders about the countryside in a dreamlike fugue. Without a stable body to anchor it, its kinesthetic grounds are altered, and the aggregate of soul and sem now moves about quickly, unsteadily. "The soul wanders to many places. Sometimes here, sometimes there."[5] Such a journey usually occurs in twilight, in a sunless kind of darkness. "We don't see the sun after we die," the lama explained. "It's like a dream, but we can't see the sun after we die."

As Ghang Lama knew it, friends were as absent as sunlight in death, for after dying a person is alone and largely without the help of others. "After, when one dies...one can't ask for help from anyone. One can ask for help only from the deities. One can't ask help from other people. If one goes up [in achieving a good rebirth], it's the deity's decision. If one is sent down, it's the deity's decision." In this respect, Mheme probably would have agreed with Pascal's remark that one dies alone.[6] This perception was underscored by the understanding that, although a deceased person might try to talk with loved ones following his or her death, the living cannot see or hear the disembodied soul. Mutual visual and acoustic contact cannot be maintained. Face-to-face copresence is no longer possible.

"When he's dead, he's confused," said Mheme of any recently deceased person. "He doesn't know what's happening to him then." At first unaware of the death, the deceased person gradually realizes that he no longer has a flesh-and-blood body. A common narrative image among Yolmo wa is of a deceased man roaming the countryside in the days after his death, unaware that he has died. Each day at dusk he returns to his home to eat and be with family members, but since the dead lack corporeal form, he goes unseen and unnoticed by loved ones. "He talks to us," Mheme explained. "But we don't hear him." Horrified by such negligence, the dead person leaves in despair and slowly learns that he no longer remains with the living. "At that particular time he realizes, 'I'm a dead person.'"

Given the deceased's aloneness and the fuguelike confusions that cloud his or her mind, lamas are needed to summon and then advise and guide the itinerant soul.

At that time, the lama is the voice of the Buddha. So during the *nebar* [a funeral rite], the lama calls to the dead person, "Wherever you are, come here." The lama says by meditating inside [his sem], "You are such and such." The soul of the dead person is not like that of the living person. It's like he's dreaming. He can come and go in a moment. We do the funeral rites for him, and the lama calls to him, "Wherever you are, come here!"

While vision deceives and confuses in this situation, hearing attends to a guiding source. Yet despite the useful instructions of lamas, the deceased's soul continues to encounter a frightening array of apparitions, including the visitations of peaceful and wrathful deities.

> The between of becoming [si pai bardo] means something very bad. We're already dead when we arrive there. We get very frightened from all the gods. This deity comes, that deity comes. All the deities are inside our own mind. Inside the mind are the peaceful and wrathful deities. And these deities are what cause much of our fear.

In noting that "all the deities are inside our own mind," Mheme was advancing the Buddhist idea that the visions encountered and perceived in the between states after death are, in fact, emanations of one's mind. As Robert Thurman notes, many Tibetan peoples understand that a person's consciousness and body in the death between are "structured by the imagery" that results from that person's karmic heritage, which is to say that the shadowy images a deceased person encounters in the death between are manifestations of his or her psychic and karmic disposition.[7] Or, to quote Mheme, "The bardo [between] means one goes there, one meets this thing, that thing. They try to frighten us. They're trying to frighten us. Then, the frightening things are within our bodies. The peaceful and wrathful deities are within our mind. The frightening things, the scary things, appear." If a recently deceased person can keep in mind such an understanding when mired in the bardo state, then he or she has a better chance of identifying and grasping the subjective nature of fearful emanations. "Before we die," said Mheme, "we need to develop a memory of this, so that afterward we can recall it, and we can recognize what we see."

To prepare for the phantasmagoric journey through the death between, Mheme often read a text that helped him to anticipate what he could expect at that time. This was the Bardo Thedol (*bar do thos grol,* in written Tibetan), a set of mortuary texts, with different versions organized by various editors, famously and somewhat inappropriately known in the West as the Tibetan Book of the Dead.[8] Usually pronounced as "Bar-do Thay-dol" in Yolmo, thought to be authored by the great master Padmasambhava in the eighth or ninth century, used primarily by adherents of the Nyingma school of Tibetan Buddhism, and more accurately translated as "liberation through hearing/understanding in the between," the Bardo Thedol explains in great detail what a person can expect to occur in the hours and days after dying. If a reader or listener understands the texts' teachings well, it is held, he or she can achieve liberation from the sansāric world of khorwa—hence the use of the Tibetan words *thos grol,* which might be best translated as "liberation through hearing/understanding." As Thurman notes, "The words *thos grol* mean that this book's teaching 'liberates' just by being 'learned' or 'understood,' giving the person facing the between an understanding so naturally clear and deep that it does not require prolonged reflection or contemplation."9

Many Yolmo wa familiar with the Bardo Thedol are aware of its potential to enlighten, either through its very words or through the understandings it generates of the liberating realities that can be perceived during the bardo states. But most know the text to serve as a guidebook to the liminal, dreamlike "between" that a recently deceased person can expect to encounter after dying. In many respects, the text reads as such, for it vividly details, in a day-by-day, vision-by-vision sort of way, what a deceased person undergoes during each phase of death, from his or her last vague moments in life to the soul's entry into a new life form. In offering such a guide, the book depicts the different psychophenomenal states that the deceased's soul passes through, including the diffuse and varied range of perceptions and the sets of peaceful and wrathful deities encountered during the bardo period. One early passage helps the bewildered, itinerant soul brace for the dreamlike world soon to be encountered:

Hey, noble one! At this time when your mind and body are parting ways, pure reality manifests in subtle, dazzling visions, vividly experienced, naturally frightening and worrisome, shimmering like a mirage on the plains in autumn. Do not fear them. Do not be terrified! Do not panic! You have what is called an "instinctual mental body," not a material, flesh and blood body. Thus whatever sounds, lights, and rays may come at you, they cannot hurt you. You cannot die. It is enough just for you to recognize them as your own perceptions. Understand that this is the between.10

"Voidness cannot harm voidness," the text advises. "Signlessness cannot harm signlessness."11 Instructions like these help to explain why the book is also read to and by the living, for it is understood that if a person becomes more familiar with these states and perceptions before dying, and so gains a better understanding of their apparitional, "signless" nature, he or she will not be so frightened by or attracted to them when they are encountered for real in death.

The text's contents also help the deceased to identify and continue along routes that can enable them to attain good rebirths. They also instruct the listener to avoid inopportune paths. "Don't be enticed by that soft smoky light of hell!" the narrator in one version warns:

Hey! That is the path of destruction from the sins you have accumulated by your strong hatred! If you cling to it, you will fall into the hells; you will be stuck in the mire of unbearable ordeals of suffering, without any escape.[12]

Page after page, prayers are sounded, instructions are meted out, the looks of deities are described, and readers and listeners are urged to act in certain ways, to contemplate certain visions, and to avoid some options in death while attending to those that will lead to either liberation or, failing that, a good rebirth in a human body. Finding great value in these narrations, Yolmo lamas read the book to people who are dying in order to prepare them for what they will encounter in the days and weeks after they pass from their bodies. They also read the book during several of the funeral rites for a deceased person, with the understanding that the deceased can still hear their words and so continue to be guided by them. Since the text is written in a Tibetan script rich with esoteric Buddhist terms, family members of the deceased and other laypersons attending a funeral usually understand but a few of its words. But they too understand that the collective, oral reading of the book serves as a guide to the deceased.

Along with reading the text at funeral rites or to others when asked, many Yolmo lamas, especially older ones such as Mheme, read it on their own to add to their understanding of the bardo and to help them to anticipate what can be expected in the death between. When Nogapu and I first asked Mheme about the nature of this text, our elder produced a copy from the cabinet where he kept many sacred texts. He carefully unwrapped the cloth, produced the two hundred or so looseleaf pages of a well-used text, and spelled out the title for us. He said that someone had recently given him this version of the Bardo Thedol, which had been produced by a Tibetan teacher residing in a monastery in Boudhanath: "Someone gave this book to me. Now I'm just looking in it every day [in the hopes that I might glean something from it]." Then, assuming his role as lamaic "teller," he proceeded to recite out loud the introductory passages of his copy, though neither of his listeners could follow along very well, since it consisted of "lama words," to quote Nogapu, who, eager just then to return to some construction work he had to attend to that day but too respectful to interrupt his elder, kept checking his watch as Mheme read for over forty minutes straight, suspending his reading at times with occasional explanations in Yolmo of the text's meanings: "He can't go forward, he can't go backward.... Sometimes we're shocked in the bardo."

"What is the Bardo Thedol for?" I asked Mheme after he concluded his reading and began to return the text to its silk enclosure. "The Bardo Thedol, it's this," he replied, tapping his fingers on the text:

To show the way, when we're trying to go to the land of bliss.[13] What one thinks about in one's mind, and what one says, all the time they [the deceased] are listening [to the lamas' words]. If we remember very well—we'll be very scared when we die—if we remember that this is what the lamas read from the Bardo Thedol, it will be very helpful right then. All the fear will go away, everything will go away.

Bardo Thedol means that, after we die, there's the way [to a good rebirth]. It describes what it's like after we die. If we think about what's in the Bardo Thedol, then everything that gives us trouble then will go away. It's not like we have a body then. There's no body then, only the soul, after dying. Only the Buddha can help us [then]. Our family and friends cannot help.

Without a stable body, without the aid of family and friends, humans are relatively powerless in the death between. "It's not like now, when you can say, 'Don't do like this to me!' That's not possible," Mheme explained. "They give us a terrific fright." But by gleaning what the Bardo Thedol has to say about such things, a person can better prepare for such encounters. Scanning its pages can dispel fears and uncertainties.

Consider now what Ghang Lama's words tell us about his take on the sensory plight of humans in the death between. In dying, a person is deprived of his or her body, a "heap" of matter that decays soon after its soulful inhabitant departs. Everything else also has to be parted with, including one's family. Though the recently deceased can see, hear, and talk to family members, those loved ones cannot perceive the invisible, inaudible soul, and so must go about their mourning without being able to converse with or see the face of the deceased. Visual and verbal copresence cannot be maintained.

Awareness of one's death comes fitfully, harshly. A deceased person travels alone, without the help of friends and family or the agentive abilities that a human body usually affords. He or she is guided only by previously acquired knowledge and the oral instructions of lamas, who read

from lamaic texts as funeral rites are performed. Despite such instructions, opacity and confusion are the mean. Without a body to anchor it,
a person's consciousness is unsteady, flitting, easily distracted. Everything appears as if in a dream. One's thoughts and perceptions lack the
sober, single-minded abilities that usually coincide with daytime realities.
Visual and acoustic images suddenly appear, then disappear or morph
into other images.

All images and deities perceived are projections that emanate from the
deceased's mind. More the substance of dream than reality, such images
appear much more than they exist on their own. All is subjectively rendered; nothing has a stable, secure existence outside self-consciousness.
But while humans are in fact the karmic authors of the images they perceive, they are far from being in command of their senses or of any phenomena perceived after dying. A person's perceptions in the days after
death are dreamlike, altered, radically subjective, obscured, unsteady, ungrounded, immaterial, signless.

Such, then, was Ghang Lama's thanatology, his speculations on death.
It's the name he knew it by, his pale priest. While much of what he had to
say about death drew on understandings shared by other Yolmo and Tibetan peoples, his sense of what would happen then was also particular to
his ways of proceeding in the world. Death to him was a temporal
process, at once disconcerting and transformative. It also offered the possibility of rebirth or escape from sansāra. For Mheme, the death between
was an obscure, phantasmagoric realm, in which humans, adrift and
alone, had to rely on sensory and cognitive abilities quite unlike what
they were accustomed to while alive. Depicted as such, the bardo implies
a graph of sensory alterity, primarily one of altered vision, in which perceptual faculties are inverted or thrown out of kilter. All this is a far cry
from the visual lucidity, self-possession, skilled means, and cognitive and
bodily presence that the lama counted on throughout much of his life.
Perhaps it comes as no surprise then that, until his eyes grew too weak, he
prepared for this realm by training his eyes daily on a text that would help
him to recognize the true nature of the images within the death between
and the routes it offered.[14] A sober, methodical, visual practice enabled
him to anticipate the sights and sounds to come.

To Phungboche, by Force

Some recollections nagged at old wounds. They rehearsed contemptuous deeds, retraced scars, marked a woman's defiance.

The marriage between Rinjin Lama and Kisang produced two children: a first son, who died at the age of five, and then a second son, who soon acquired the name Kānchā. Living in the lama's home in Shomkharka, Rinjin and Kisang stayed together in marriage "for no more than ten years," according to their son Kānchā, and then the husband "quit" his wife. "They didn't get along," their son explained. "Her husband was nineteen years younger than she was," Kānchā's wife, Neela, once noted. "And, after a while, he wasn't satisfied," she added, speaking the last three words in a delicate English.

"Why did my uncle give the divorce papers?" Pramod once asked his aunt.

"He released me, for sure," Kisang answered. "Grudges were made. So he released me, and he said to me, 'You need to take your son with you.' He transferred the responsibility to me. He had another wife. He brought that wife, so he gave me the divorce."

"What did he give?"

"He had the paper, where, where? [I don't know where it is now.] I kept it for a while. That was the divorce paper, it was said."

Writing, associated anew with the skilled actions and knowings of men, again shaped the course of Kisang's life. Much as her brother's painterly "writing" on the interiors of the lamaic temple in Shomkharka led to her transfer in marriage to that village, so her husband's scribing both announced and sealed the divorce. Indeed, while the document had

Figure 10. Kisang Omu in her early fifties. Copy of a photograph owned by Kān-chā Lama, Boudhanath, Nepal.

long since been lost, she knew that it was a divorce paper, not because she read it as such, but because people "said" it was. She relied here on acts of speech as much as her husband had relied on acts of writing.

Her begrudging husband, now with a third, younger wife, then released Kisang and "transferred" to her the responsibility for their son Kānchā. "He did a madman's work," she noted. "They drank a lot of chhang, then they acted crazy. Good did not come of it. I've also been betrayed."

"Yhabu mhayong du" (Good did not come of it). Crazy actions can have sad consequences. Like other women who marry men of bad character or who are tricked into agreeing to arrangements that later bring hardship, Kisang too was "betrayed." As a result, her residential and political status grew precarious once again. "I had to go," she once said of her first marriage. "I needed to hold one tree. So I did. But now there's no tree. Now neither tree is there." In adjoining herself to different family trees she needed to hold onto first one, then a second, husband, but neither support was available later on.

After the divorce, Kisang stayed in Ne Nyemba, where she shared a house with her youngest son from her first marriage, on lands close to the homes of her oldest two sons. Her daughter had moved to Kathmandu, and Kānchā, the only living child from the second marriage, usually lived in Shomkharka with his father, although he did stay with his mother in Ne Nyemba from time to time. Without a husband, without a proper family "tree" to hold onto, Kisang likely soon questioned whether she would or should remarry again. Any such marriage would have had both advantages and disadvantages. While remarrying would have enabled her to find some security in the household of another male line, she would also have had to submit to a new marital bond and difficult labors in a new household. Of such hardships Phur Gyalmu had this to say after being asked if she had given any thought to remarrying after her husband died when he was in his early fifties and she was in her early forties: "Now, who would want to marry this old woman? Me, I didn't think of this. I didn't think."

"Why didn't you think of this?"

"Why think of it? Now, then, I've gotten old as well. Now, with whom would I face hardship? If I go to another house, I have to face hardships again. Now, I didn't think of this. It's not in my sem."

Thoughts of remarrying were apparently not in Kisang's sem either in the years following her separation from her second husband, even though her ability to work hard had skillfully attracted the interest of several Yolmo families who were searching for mates for men whose own spouses had themselves passed on. One such family, from Phung-boche, a village set upon a sloping ridge that lies close to the Malemchi River at the base of the Yolmo Valley, was quite serious about bringing Kisang into their family. Several of its members proceeded to "capture" her in Ne Nyemba and take her forcibly back to Phungboche in order to espouse her to a man whose first wife had died.

Pramod and I first learned of this event toward the conclusion of a conversation with Kisang one day in March 1998, after we had asked her what she thought about having been compelled to marry by her father and brother ("What do I think? They don't let the women stay!"). We followed this question with another, asking what she thought when her father, brother, or husband told her "to do this and that." She asked in response, "What do I think? What's in my sem?" Then she cited some advice about remarrying that others, not necessarily her father or brother, had once given.

I have no feeling about this. I didn't understand anything. The people said this thing, this thing, many things. Then it made me like crazy. It made me like crazy, then everyone was saying, "You need to hold one thing. It's better [to remarry]."

Then they took me also to Phungboche. His father's corpse! [Son of a bitch!] Who set this course? Who made this plan? When I went to Phungboche, my male relatives did not release me [they did not agree to this plan]. They didn't release me.

The conversation then trailed off into other subjects.

Later that same morning, Kānchā's wife, Neela, joined us in the room after she had finished preparing Kisang's lunch. During a lull in the conversation, when Pramod and I had run out of questions to ask, she said, "Even though mother got old, everyone wanted to take her [in marriage]. That's because she did a lot of work. She was very active." Hearing these words Kisang noted, "They also took me to Phungboche. When they took me to Phungboche, I was surprised. I didn't want to stay there." To which Neela added, "Even though she grew old, she did a lot of work."

Two weeks later, after we had a chance to listen to and translate the above passages, we returned to Kisang and asked her what she meant by this "surprising," undesired transport to Phungboche. She didn't understand at first what we were asking about, so we played a section of the tape that contained her words on the subject. Upon listening and chuckling slightly at the recorded sounds of her own voice, she nodded her head and began to talk and gesture with her hands.

Ah, I forgot. They took me to Phungboche, by force, certainly! By force. To the place I didn't have the heart to go. To say, what to say? Our own people had arranged this way, it seems.

Several different Kisangs-in-time, it's worth noting, were implied in this scene of words reheard and renarrated: the woman who was taken to Phungboche; the woman who spoke about these actions some thirty years later; and the woman who then heard and commented on the acoustic recording of a voice she took as her own.

Kisang was saying, upon hearing her earlier words, that she was taken by "force" [N., *jabarjasti*] to a place she did not want to go, apparently as a result of a marriage arrangement unwisely worked out between a family in Phungboche ("they") and members of her "own people." It turns out, I later learned, that she and others came to the understanding that another woman in Ne Nyemba, the wife of a cousin of her second husband, was jealous of Kisang's reputation as a diligent and skillful worker. This woman, who will go here by the fictive name of Pemba Lamini, arranged the marriage in order to remove Kisang from the village and so elevate her own value and status within her husband's family. "My mother was very hardworking," Kānchā later told me, "and she [Pemba Lamini] was jealous of my mother and wanted to send her to another place."

Since Kisang was known as such a hard worker, it was possible to arrange another marriage for her, even though she was already in her midfifties. "My mother was taken not for her youth or beauty, but because they valued her ability to work hard," Kānchā explained. She was therefore to be the woman transferred in marriage, the "new bride," as it were. But if she were to say something about these arrangements at the time, what could she possibly say, especially since a close relative had orchestrated the capture? What could she have said that would change anything? How could she have contested their actions through language? To say, what to say? And yet it turns out that she had a great deal to say, both then and later, if not directly to anyone, then to and about those who took her to Phungboche.

P: *Did this happen before or after your first husband died?*
K: *Ah, after he died. After my first husband died, not the second husband. Maybe I went with the second husband? But I'm not sure. What to do? I don't remember. I don't remember.*

While Kisang's memory was "vague" as to when these events occurred, her son Kānchā told me that he knew them to have taken place when he was around twelve or thirteen, soon after his father had divorced his mother, which meant that Kisang was probably in her midfifties then.

Then, they put the procession in Aunt Pemba's house [in Ne Nyemba]. I was unaware of this. Early in the morning, who opened the door at that time? All the people came inside and seized me.

In ways similar to how her first marriage had proceeded, the marriage procession hid in Pemba Lamini's house and waited until dawn to enter Kisang's home. In this case, however, Kisang was taken in a much more forceful way, without any warning or opportunity to flee. Early in the morning, her door was opened, and "all the people" rushed inside and pulled her outside. Both the invasion of the interior of her home and her forced removal from this space connoted archetypal acts of abduction among Yolmo wa that say a lot about the occasional disregard of women's personhood and volition in those days. If either of these acts had been enacted on a Yolmo man then or on any adult woman or man in the 1990s, they would have been considered acts of violence.[1] "They treat women poorly," Kisang said rather cryptically during a later discussion of her trip to Phungboche.

> P: *From Phungboche?*
> K: *And then. Yes.*
> P: *Who was it?*
> K: *Who? No—the children, nobody was there. Everyone had gone to work outside then.*

As Kānchā later recalled, he happened to be visiting his mother at that time, and he and his half brother, Kisang's youngest son from her first marriage, were sent to work away from the house, so that their mother's capture could be more easily achieved. "My mother was seized when I was in Ne Nyemba," he told Temba and me. "I saw that with my own eyes. I saw it in the sense that, at that time, Pemba Lamini arranged it so that we were sent to work. I was sent to the flour mill, and my brother was sent to a field to cut some grass. It was their plan that, if we were at home, it might be difficult for them, and we might do something against them. So we were sent away. Only later did we learn that our mother was taken. Then I kept crying because I was a small boy."

Pramod and I then asked Kisang another question.

P: Did you stay there, in Phungboche?

K: I didn't! I didn't stay a single night. One of my mother's nieces, my mother's niece, was over there. I spent the night with her alone, putting my head in her lap. I stayed, stayed, stayed like that.

The salience of the passage of time: After being taken bodily east to Phungboche, along a path that mirrored in reverse the route she took when she first married, she did not sleep "a single night" there. Unable to leave, she was physically present in a house through the course of a night, but she remained awake, with her head buried in her cousin's lap, without conversing or exchanging with its residents. The posture described—an immobile body, its face hidden in the lap of a "bride's friend," curtained from the gaze and words of others—resembled an action-form often assumed by Yolmo brides during marriage ceremonies; that position in turn bears affinities with the ways in which Yolmo girls today cover their mouths or hide their bodies behind others when faced with a presence they are unable or unwilling to retreat from fully. When asked about Kisang's actions here, Yolmo people have consistently said that her posture in this situation spoke to the "anger" and "worry" she felt at being forcibly taken away from her home and her children. Yet many also agreed with an interpretation of my own, that by entrusting her body to a familiar, solacing other, visually and verbally disengaged from the world, she created and sustained a makeshift interiority within the home of strangers, and so made clear that she did not accept the new household offered to her. If she were to have resided in the house longer or used her body or speech in more social, transactive ways, her actions could have signaled a complicit agreement to a marriage she neither anticipated nor desired. "It meant that she was not content, not interested. She was feeling sad and worried," Neela said of her mother-in-law's prolonged and unchanging stasis that night.

Then, morning came. During the night I didn't even drink water. At the time I was smoking cigarettes, it was my misfortune. I only smoked cigarettes. I stayed, just smoking. Then, morning came. Someone said, "This child didn't drink a single glass of water since yesterday. So we need to give some tea, or maybe prepare hot porridge." Someone said this to the people who took me there.

As the night wore on Kisang refused to consume anything offered to her, except for some cigarettes only, on which it was her "misfortune" then to be hooked. There were few transfers between her and her hosts and no communal "back and forth" exchanges of words, as would have been the case if she had been with friends. Unnamed people spoke about her but not to her, perhaps because they had concluded that she would not have responded to their queries. The words quoted, relatively considerate ones, were in fact the only time Kisang gave direct voice to the people of Phungboche in relating their actions.

When morning came, my mother's niece took me to her house, after receiving the permission of the family to which I was supposed to marry. At her house she prepared egg porridge and placed it in a bowl. I was ready to eat it, but just then the man who took me came there. I could not swallow the porridge very easily when I saw him. When I saw him, I thought he was like poison. I felt he looked like a black enemy.

I didn't have thoughts [of staying with him]. I told my cousin, "I won't have this porridge while in his presence. Keep it there." I didn't have it, and that person stayed there for some time. Then I declared that I would not live there. "Why did he come here? I can't stay in a place that I never thought about before." I stayed there. He had come there then. I didn't eat. My mother's niece was married to Phungboche [village]. I didn't eat the porridge. That man continued to stay there. I gave the soup back.

After first asking permission to do so, her cousin brought Kisang to her home, then prepared a breakfast meal and offered it to her. But when the proposed husband, a Yolmo man in his late forties, a widower with several children who desired a skilled and industrious woman to help run his household, entered the room where she was staying, Kisang could not swallow the idea of being with someone who struck her as a poisonous "black enemy" *(dha nhakpu)*. "People say that there are two kinds of enemies," Binod told me upon hearing of this characterization. "There are enemies, and then there are black enemies, and these are the worst kind." Staying put, without any thoughts of living with that man, Kisang refused to eat any more of the soup. In giving it back, she terminated the possibility of exchange and symbolically refused the marriage.

Two of them, my cousin and that person, were talking with each other. I heard their talk. "She does not agree and, as she is unwilling to stay, we cannot force her."

After they spoke together, that person went back outside, and only then did I have the porridge.

I was telling people, "Don't be angry with me. Don't do anything to me. I don't want to stay here. Don't have hope in me. My children are not mature. I'm not going anywhere, with anyone! Who made this plan?" Eh, saying this I struggled.

She spoke, finally, to her captors and contested their plans to keep her in their village, at first with pleas to leave her alone, then in more insistent, outraged terms. She "struggled" against the interests of others, through physical and linguistic means more commanding and defiant than she could have achieved when she first married, at the age of twenty. She also asked to be told who orchestrated the "path," or plan, of this marriage. Her question, and the fact that it went unanswered in her account, helped to explain her assertions, when speaking with Pramod and me, that her male relatives "did not release" her, for she seemed to be saying that no male elders of any real authority in her family agreed to these arrangements. So why should she have agreed to stay in Phungboche? It was enough to make her "like crazy."

"If I stay in Phungboche, I won't remain here one day even. 'Phungboche' comes from [the word] corpse. I'll become a corpse by falling." I said this.

Drawing wildly on the fact that the first two syllables of the place name Phungboche sound similar to *phungbu,* a Yolmo word for corpse, Kisang clarified that she too would become a corpse by "falling" intentionally, she likely meant, from a cliff or a boulder. Rather than stay in an unwanted marriage in an undesired place, she would annihilate her own life as well as any plans they had for her to remain in that deadly place. When Temba and I asked his family about Kisang's words, his grandfather answered, "By her words, she meant to say that if they let her go nicely, it would be good, but if they did not let her go, then she would commit suicide falling from the hillside and become a corpse. It was a threat to these people."

Later, I said, "I'm going. If you let me go, let me go in a good way. If you don't let me go, it won't be good. I'll die, in the middle of the way, falling off the cliff."

Without any noted responses from her captors, she continued to plead her case and assert her intentions. If they did not let her go "in a good way," with their respect and goodwill and without any physical force hindering her progress home, she would die a bad death, in a middling, in-between land, in neither their home nor hers. Either way, she would have nothing to do with them, and she would not remain in Phungboche.

Then, after a while, they let me go. Then I went alone.

They decided to release her and permit her to return home, but without an escort. On the move again, she went alone, in a marked show of independence, in a manner similar to how many Yolmo woman have "fled" the homes to which they have been forcibly brought in marriage. Her cousin apparently would have preferred that she not travel alone.

I said to my aunt's daughter, "It's nothing. A relative of mine lives near Dak-pakharka. If I can make it to Dakpakharka, then after Dakpakharka there's the home of a relative, Nakpu Lama."

The route would be a safe one, she explained, since she could visit and take shelter in the homes of relatives along the way, if need be.

I went by myself! From the side by Phungboche, I went up a steep way and then I reached to the top. Then I entered into Nalungkharka. At that time, there was Aa Gyalsang's house. I went there [to this relative's house]. When I arrived, they said, "Oh, the new bride has returned so soon."

Teasing so from her relatives, then a peeved response.

"Who's the new bride?! There, they acted contemptuously toward me. The mother of children, they treated with contempt. What new bride? How can I stay in such a place and be the bride to such a man?"

She told her relatives that her captors had treated her scornfully; literally, they "did contempt" *(helā bhekyo)* to her. Such misdoings she remembered well. "The people who treated me with contempt, it's very present in my sem." A Tibetan proverb advises: "Fighting and disputes, these two do not decay [with time]. Ill words spoken in the summer do not rot; ill words spoken in the summer do not freeze."[2] Ill words remain lodged within the sem.

Some acts of kindness nevertheless resounded within a larger recollection of disdain: her relatives invited her inside their home in Nalungkharka.

"Come sit inside, come sit inside, please drink tea."
"Aboh! If I wait for tea [it's no good]. I came alone."

Since she was traveling alone she needed to step quickly and could not accept the invitation.

Then I came back quickly, quickly, quickly. I walked alone and alone, alongside the vertical face of Laing. Oh, I forget. I forget where I went, the road above or below.

She walked *"phel, phel, phel,"* directly, single-mindedly, without distractions. She moved with a singularity of thought and purpose that rivaled how she thought of death years later. She also proceeded with little social or perceptual interchange with the terrain she crossed, a mode of action that perhaps explains why, when speaking with us, she could not recall which route she took.

In the fall of 2000, however, Kisang related anew her thoughts then after listening to her narration as recorded on tape two years before. "I wasn't frightened," she said. "I wasn't afraid. Nothing [harmful] appeared to me. When I arrived at Baldanda resting place, I gave thanks, saying, 'I'm safe now.'"

Staying Still

Kisang's account of her forced passage to Phungboche parallels other narratives of marriage among Yolmo wa, particularly those tales that speak of a woman's "capture" by unfamiliar others. In many ways, the account stands as a distorted image of Kisang's first marriage, as though the violence enacted upon her during what would have been her third marriage also violated any narrative expectations in such matters. She was taken by force. The good cheer and ritual auspiciousness that accompanied the first wedding went unsounded. She labored against the flow of ritual time. The prospective groom was an unwanted black enemy. She refused to stay in that man's village, then returned home by herself, along the same general route that she had traversed when she first went to Shomkharka. Having already crossed fifty, she derided the absurdity of being called "the new bride."

She also spoke in ways that were unlike the quiet voicings she had adopted when she first married. Her voice throughout was reluctant, defiant, searing. It was impolitic to those who disrespected her. On display here was a strong "interrogative voice," as Veena Das uses that term in speaking of the narrative discourses of women and men in South Asia: a voice, sometimes pronounced by women, that questions the actions of others, displays a skeptical stance toward a society's precepts, and casts doubts on the authoritative, "legislative voice" often assumed by men.[1] Das's analytic concerns lead her to consider the interrogative voice as a general capability and truth of women. Kisang's words lend themselves to another perspective: that such a voice was available to her at some times more than others. While there were glimmers of its tonal-

230

ities in each of her narratives, those same narratives suggested that it emerged most fully in the later years of her life, after she had married and raised several children. Different possibilities for speaking and listening were in effect at different times in her life.

As it was, as she grew older she more often questioned and denounced the authority of others, adult men in particular, to determine where she would live. Her life had been one of movement, but often disagreeably so. From time to time, she voiced words that cut against the causes of these displacements. They did not let the women "stay."

Yet if the bulk of Kisang's life had been marked by relocations, her last years were ones of stasis and stillness. During the years that I came to know her, after frail legs had confined her to her bed, she found that she was dying, but in such a way that death, as the final movement of her life, was itself hard to come by. "I just stay, for sure. I can't move about," she told us. "If I need to go outside, I need someone's help. Heartache. Alas, I'm not dying soon. I wish this breath would just stop, instead of having the sorrowful life, staying."

Other spells of staying proceeded this. She stayed put while playing as a child ("We just stayed and ate"), while hiding with her friend before marrying ("We stayed there. We stayed there"), while waiting out her husband's death ("How many days did it stay like this?"), while refusing to engage with her captors in Phungboche ("I stayed, stayed, stayed like that"), while delaying a return to the doctor ("I just remained still"). Many memories stayed with her still, while her love for her husband had "stayed like that."

Dying brought its own stasis. "I stayed well," she once said of her first marriage. She then continued: "In the difficult time, I did the difficult work. Now, in the time of dying, I need to stay like this. What to do? I did well." Able to walk only with support of some kind, she found that she could not do much more than sit upright in her bed and pray with the use of a mālā. "What do I think about?" she replied when asked. "I just stay here. I do the mani [prayers]. I just do the prayer beads. I just contemplate the gods.... I just stay still [nga choge ji dhekyo]."

She "just stayed still." That's all she did then. There was little movement, no full-bodied actions, nothing that "startled" her, just a few words and gestures, a repletion of stillness. Just that.

Stillness is often a mark of good and proper forms among Yolmo wa. Children, for instance, are taught to be less *chak-chak*, "restless" or "fidgety," and more still and reserved when among others.[2] Physical stillness in adulthood is associated with a respectful presence among others as well as with the peaceful detachment of meditation. An absence of movement, in turn, often implies an absence of suffering. Moments of "sitting, eating" (N., *basne, khāne*) among friends and family members are taken to entail times of painless comfort, especially when compared with a life of work or carrying loads.

Kisang's body was similarly stilled. That stillness was unpleasant, however, because it hinged on a loss of bodily faculties that forced her to stay put. When asked if her current life was one of comfort or hardship, she replied, "Well, I have to say comfort. I can't walk, but they bring me food. I haven't died. It's of comfort, for sure. Now, I cannot die, I cannot live [shyi mhi khu du, so mhi khu du]." When I asked Karma about these words, he suggested that they imply a meaning along the lines of "Yes, this is comfort, but otherwise I'm rotting." Binod, in turn, said that he recalled Kisang uttering the last statement in the company of visiting relatives when she was ill during the 1998 New Year festivities; he took them to mean mostly that she was no longer able to live a healthy life, and, unable to either live or die well, she was "giving trouble" to all of her relatives.

She was "staying while suffering"; she suffered in staying. "Before, I was very active," she once observed, after telling us about the work she did while living in Ne Nyemba. "Now, I can't walk. What was all that?—this thought comes to me," she continued, as if her former exertions were mildly inconceivable to her in her current state. And since her stasis threw into sharp relief the buzz of actions and movements she spoke of when recalling earlier times in her life, I am left to wonder whether her actions earlier in life gave further emphasis to her stasis in old age, or, just as likely, whether she told us so much about her earlier activities because she was relatively still and inactive when we spoke. What was the significance, as well, of the two interlocutors seated beside her being relatively young and active men?

Apparently most Yolmo wa would prefer not to "go" in this way. For one, people fear that, as their powers wane in old age, their children will not listen to or obey them as they once did. "Their children don't agree with them, they don't listen to them, as they once used to do," Nogapu explained in sketching out such a scene for me. "They just say, 'Oh, you old people just sit there and be quiet and let us do what we think.'" While bouts of "quiet sitting" among Yolmo elders are socially constructed in all sorts of ways, comments like this suggest that, at the least, they can be desired and encouraged by others. A person can be stilled by others. Few, in turn, appreciate the idea of a bodily stasis in their final years. When asked in what manner they wished to die, many women told me that they wished to go "while walking" or while "on the road," while still active and useful, since they did not want to suffer from a long, painful illness or be a burden to others. "In dying," Phur Gyalmu asserted, "the way for me is: 'May illnesses not come. May I die while going along a road. Walking, walking may I die, for me....Let my children not have hardship.'"

Movement here signifies able-bodied health until the moment of death. Kisang's demise was an uncommon one in that it was taking her so long to die. Acutely conscious of the social dimensions of the static delay, she was worried that she was giving trouble to others.

"I cannot die, I cannot live," she said in 1998. While her weakened body forced her to remain in bed, Kisang also understood that she was "staying on" in life, hovering between death and an able life in such a way that she was neither fully alive nor dead.

Waiting is a common feature of life in Nepal. People wait for buses or taxis to pass their way. Guests patiently wait for food to be served at social gatherings. Those of lower status must often sit and wait for their superiors to complete some ongoing task before they can gain their full attention. Hindu mendicants stand for long minutes outside storefronts, silently waiting for shop owners to hand them a coin or two. And as Buddhist accounts have it, those reborn into the lower realms must sometimes wait for eons until their bad karma expires to a point where they can finally take a new birth. Kisang likewise had to wait a spell. But her waiting also squared with a specific structure of temporal action common to Yolmo lives. Among Yolmo wa, social engagements often consist of some kind of activity or interaction, followed by a pause of some sort, which is then succeeded by another run of activity. When villagers sing while dancing at festive settings, for example, they usually sing a song or two, then there is a still moment wherein people compose themselves and perhaps imbibe a bit while pondering further couplets. After collectively voicing the next song, they step into another lull in preparation for the next performance. This pattern can continue for hours on end. Most lamaic and shamanic ritual performances also build upon sets of distinct rites, reading a sacred text, exorcising a ghost, with restful pauses in between. Many conversations likewise include flurries of verbal engagement, then moments of silence until another topic arises and people begin to talk again. The silences can go on for quite some time. While I was visiting a tea shop in Gulphubanjang one after-noon, a Yolmo man from a neighboring village, calling himself "joker man," came in and told a humorous, animated story about his recent ex-ploits in Kathmandu while several men and a few children listened and laughed along. Soon after the man ended his tale, he finished his tea, said his good-byes, and walked on home. After exchanging a few words on his performance, those remaining in the room, myself included, then sat quietly for several minutes, sipping tea, looking around, gazing at the pictures on the walls, until someone else entered the tea shop with another flux of words.

Kisang's life similarly consisted of a series of engagements and quiet moments in between, much as stories of hers tended to be composed of distinct acts verbalized in sequential sentences with gaps of time appar-ent between those acts. Her demise was like yet another quiescent inter-val between one set of actions and another. She was biding her time, waiting to "move" again, waiting for actions to resume, for the in-evitable to occur. Yet these actions apparently would have to be under-taken in a field outside the self. Someone or something else would have to get her body going again.

The orientations to time noted above mesh well with how Tibetan Buddhist adepts tend to think and talk about time, in particular the mo-ments of betweenness that, they say, fill a person's life. As noted earlier, they have a word for such intervals in time. That word is *bardo,* a "be-tween-state" of some sort. As the lamas tell it, any intermediate moment in life is a bardo. An interval of sleep between states of waking con-sciousness is a bardo, as is a dream between stretches of sleep. In the stretches of their own lives, however, Yolmo lamas and laypersons most commonly invoke the word when speaking of the between-state that is known to occur between life and rebirth.

When I asked Kisang if she knew what the word *bardo* meant, she claimed not to know in the way that Yolmo women often claim not to know about religious matters: by deferring to the presumed experts on the matter. "The lamas talk about the bardo," she said. "When we die the lamas tell us about the bardo. Then we need to listen, for certain."

While it remains unclear to me how much she actually knew about the concept of the bardo, several aspects of her existence then accorded, at times, with elements of this "between," as Yolmo lamas and others know of it. As with persons traveling in the bardo, she was neither dead nor alive but, rather, liminally in between these two states. And as with those immersed in the bardo, who necessarily possess a dreamlike, hallucinatory consciousness, she found that everything she perceived or remembered was like a dream. "Everything is seen like a dream," she said while looking at several photographs I took of her. Her dreamlike take on the world itself related to the waning of her senses, particularly her inability to see or hear well. "I've become too old. I can't see, I can't hear well." The dissolution of these sensory faculties approximated the process of dying as understood by Tibetan Buddhists, wherein the senses falter one by one and collapse into their metaphysic grounds.[3]

For some, her sensory disengagement from the world put her close to the likes of a corpse. "She can't see. She can't hear. She's like a dead person!" a close relative of hers told me after a visit to her room in 1998. While Kisang probably would have responded to such an assessment by saying that she was neither like the dead nor like the living, but something in between, she did portray herself as largely disengaged, sensorially, physically, socially, from the world of the living, much as a deceased traveler in the bardo interval is said to be cut off from others and the world with which he or she was once familiar.[4] The location of her room then could itself be construed as liminal in nature. Close to the entrance of the house, edging the border between outside and inside, it compared to the interstitial "dying spaces" identified by Lawrence Cohen in his study of cultural discourses of aging in Varanasi, India, wherein aged women and men are set up to live and die in spatially marginal (but often visually central) sites on the threshold of a household.[5] Yolmo women often must inhabit a similar intermediate space, since they hover in marriage between their natal homes and the foreign lands of their husbands' villages. The betweenness in which Kisang waited was therefore a familiar one to her; death was a bit like another marriage. "Going nor staying, neither can be," goes the last line of a Yolmo pain song about the sorrows of travel.

It would not go against Yolmo understandings, then, to contend that Kisang had come to inhabit an intermediate, bardo-like stretch between one life and the next. "I'm saying that I'm not dying, I'm not alive," she observed in 1998. "I might not live much longer." Then again, it was clear that many aspects of her life dealt with betweenness and liminal times and spaces. There was a great deal of movement throughout her life, transfers from one household to the next, from one voice to another, and thus many moments in between, moments when she was startled from one kurā to another or forced from one place to another. She knew well, better than many lamas, perhaps, what it meant to be in between.

Mirror of Deeds

Different lives bring different betweens. For Kisang Omu, the bardoic interval between her present life and her next one was characterized by a moribund stasis. For Ghang Lama, both the "bardo of dying" and the more general "death between" that would transpire just after he died were marked by turbulence, disorientation, and discombobulated states of mind and body. For one, a life of movement ended in a stillness unto death. For the other, a life founded on notions of clarity, legibility, and patrilineal rootedness altered into a spell of unfamiliar, dreamlike uncertainties and a slew of perceptual opacities.

Those opacities related, it need be said, to a diminishment of the deceased's powers in the world. For Mheme, a person's sensory and spiritual faculties in the death between, meager and skittish, were thrown into sharp relief when he or she envisioned an encounter with yet another awesome and terrifying deity: Chhe Gyalbu, the "Lord of Dharma," with whom, Yolmo wa say, the deceased must inevitably contend at some point in the days after dying.[1]

Yolmo wa speak in varied ways of Chhe Gyalbu, or, as his equivalent is known in Nepali and Hindi, Dharmaraja, a name that is itself a propitious term for Yama Raj, the Lord of Death. For some, such as Karma, the name refers to an abstract, nonpersonified reflection of one's deeds, both good and bad, enacted during a lifetime. The nature of those mirrorlike reflections, which a person necessarily confronts after death within the karmic theater of his own mind, helps to determine the nature of that person's rebirth. For many others, however, including Ghang Lama, Chhe Gyalbu is a personified, omniscient deity, as real and unreal as other deities, who observes and records all of the actions a person committed while alive. "He keeps everybody's record, you know," one man told me. "Even now he is watching," said another.

Yolmo wa often speak of Chhe Gyalbu's recording device as being like a written ledger or a television, or, as one lama put it, "like a computer like the ones you have in America." Mheme told me, "Just as we use cameras to make snapshots, so he has the same sort of thing to record our life." Ghaki Lamani observed, "Every deed in our life until death is filmed and recorded like in the movies." Most often people speak of the device as consisting of a singularly powerful mirror, known as the *leki melong*, the "mirror of le," the mirror of deeds or karmic actions. That mirror, Yolmo wa say, serves two vital purposes, one that relates to a person's actions while he or she is alive, and one that bears significance soon after she or he has died.

While a person is alive the mirror reflects that person's actions as they occur, deed by deed, throughout his or her life. But just as a mirror will invert any images facing it—words written on a page, for example, are conveyed backward when held up to a mirror's surface—the leki melong reflects those deeds in such a way that they rebound to their doer. Binod described the principle well one day. "The leki melong," he told me, "reflects our actions in its mirror. Yet because the mirror is 'opposite,' it reflects them in an opposite way. So if we cut a chicken today, then soon we will be cut. If we tell lies, then soon someone will lie to us." So while the mirror reflects actions as they occur, it also foreshadows, in a doggedly karmic fashion, future events that will befall the doer of those deeds, with those later events mirroring what the doer himself did.[2]

As the mirror continues to reflect a person's actions during the course of his or her life, it also retains a record of them, much as a piece of paper preserves traces of any ink that passes its way. Yolmo wa do sometimes stress the scriptive nature of such remembrances. Some say that Chhe Gyalbu employs a host of scribes, who, like a legion of bureaucratic record-keepers, labor tirelessly to register each person's actions in life. Others, drawing on more novel comparisons, say that a computerlike apparatus does this work. In any event, the retentive capacity of this instrument makes possible the second main function of the leki melong: once a person has died and enters into the phantasmagoric, subjectively rendered world of the death between, he perceives that he is brought to the heavenly domain of Chhe Gyalbu, where the mirror, having previously reflected and recorded all of the person's actions, now displays them all in detail, deed by deed, as they occurred in the course of the life that just ended.

As Yolmo wa often tell it, Chhe Gyalbu reveals this mirror to the person in question, sometimes by dramatically opening up a set of curtains that previously hid its features. Before he does so, however, he asks the shocked human about the acts, good or bad, that he undertook while alive (much like the police in Kathmandu "interrogate" suspected criminals, I have been told). The person questioned about this usually tries, as humans are prone to doing, to put on a good front by playing up any good deeds enacted and keeping silent on more than a few misdeeds. Once the person finishes with this self-accounting, Chhe Gyalbu asks, "Are you finished?" As soon as the lord hears a response, which, as Yolmo wa who narrate such a scene suggest, is invariably a quiet "yes," he discloses the mirror of deeds, and this mirror then shows all of the person's deeds, bad as well as good, as the dead man watches his life flash before his eyes. After the presentation concludes, with every deed revealed, then weighed collectively on a scale, Chhe Gyalbu decides what the punishment must be for any sins committed and, in so doing, determines to which of the six realms that person is to be sent in rebirth.

Mheme spoke often of the mirror of deeds, and he had much to say about its postmortem functions in particular. He also spoke often of Chhe Gyalbu, usually without prompting on our part, perhaps in order to advise us about the consequences of our actions and the futility of lying. But I also wonder if he worried about his own imminent encounter with this lord. In talking about this deity, he tended to stress his panoptic, all-seeing abilities and a person's inability to lie or hide in the face of these powers:

Even if one lies, he will know. It will be recorded beforehand, and he will show these are the things one has done. He will show the whole life, like what is seen in the movies today. We mustn't lie. It's very difficult to be a lama.

When we have to go to Chhe Gyalbu, we can't run away. Wherever we go, he can find us. He can know everything. This king [the king of Nepal] doesn't know such things, he can't see like this.

What to do? Dying means the worst thing, for sure. It's good now, we can do anything. With this king, if we do something wrong, we can run away and hide. But we can't hide when we meet with Chhe Gyalbu. He can see us wherever we go. Whether we try to hide in water or in a hole, he can see us.

The lama sends the [deceased] person to the place of Chhe Gyalbu and tells him not to return below. Chhe Gyalbu shows a mirror like this, what deeds the man did. He shows them in this way. Just as we see our face in the mirror, so Chhe Gyalbu also sees things in his mirror, in the place where he lives. This is how he knows things. The people on earth have copied the same mirror that Chhe Gyalbu has. The scientists know all about this.

Some are taken to the deity. And Chhe Gyalbu determines whether the person sinned or not. He has a mirror, the mirror of deeds. Inside the mirror everything is already written. If a person says, "I didn't do any sins," then his shadow [dhipsa] tells on him. Our shadow itself shows everything. What to do, ah?! Whatever we have done, the shadow just tells [on us]. Just like this thing [the tape recorder] does, the shadow repeats as well. The shadow does this thing. A-ba! So even if we say we haven't done anything bad, the shadow tells so well.

"He can see us wherever we go." As many other Yolmo wa do, Mheme underscored what Chhe Gyalbu "sees," rather than what he might hear, and the lord's powers are premised, at least figuratively, on visual rather than acoustic modes of observation, recording, and re-presentation; actions appear as they do in a movie, or they are "inscribed" within the mirror. These cinematographic traces draw from a particular kind of vision: Chhe Gyalbu's gaze has an objective, distanced air to it. Quite unlike any of the mutual and potentially tender "eye engagements" that Mheme knew of in other quarters of his life, Chhe Gyalbu's gaze is one-sided, nonreciprocal, rather faceless, and supremely powerful. Humans are always within the frame of this absolute gaze while alive. This is why, as Mheme put it, it is "very difficult to be a lama," for any infractions of ritual or dharmic protocols, however minor, will surely be noticed and retained.

After a person dies, that person's mind-spun engagements with the Lord of Dharma are rife with fear, trepidation, and a sense of one's meekness while under the deity's sway. A man is utterly on his own, without any of the worldly resources on which he might once have relied. Even one's shadow, one's immaterial double, turns informer on the friendless traveler. Humans are shocked numb during their imagined encounters with this deity. Mheme told us:

When we die, we get so frightened. After dying, we get many fears and shocks. While alive, there's no fears. After dying, many questions are asked, "What have you done? What did you do?" Many things are inquired into. When these questions are asked, we can't answer them. When Chhe Gyalbu asks the questions, we'll be as if fainted. After [we die], we'll faint and be scared stiff. When we go to the king, can we talk to him? In the same way, we can't talk to Chhe Gyalbu. When the fear comes, it overwhelms.

The fear is so overwhelming that a person, rendered powerless in the midst of Chhe Gyalbu's mastery, like a small child overawed by a towering father figure, cannot produce a single word when confronted by him. The old man continued:

This king is not like us. Chhe Gyalbu appears bigger than the sky, bigger than the earth. If he comes near us, we die by fainting, from the fear alone. Chhe Gyalbu looks like Mahaguru and Dhakpotsal [fearsome protector deities]. He's not like our king, and he's not like us. Chhe Gyalbu appears in the land without power [*wang mheba yhul*]. When the important and powerful lamas go to that place, they also go without power. When we arrive in the land without power, we can't talk.

While *wang*, or *dbang* in written Tibetan, refers to an "initiation" into Buddhist practice, the word is usually used in reference to a kind of spiritual "empowerment" that the initiation bestows on the supplicant. In general, such a power refers most to the spiritual vitality that can be attained through religious practice. Mheme was suggesting, then, that such powers are rendered useless when a person enters into Chhe Gyalbu's domain. Even great and mighty lamas go "without power" when they enter into the zone of powerlessness in which this lord appears. Chhe Gyalbu's greatness is sublime; he "appears bigger than the sky, bigger than the earth." A mere human, rendered spiritually impotent, unable to act effectively, could be expected to faint or fall mute when in his terrifying presence.

In contrast, then, to a human's dreamy, short-sighted vision or even an earthly king's considerable, but nonetheless tempered, powers, Chhe Gyalbu can see and know everything. Lies and omissions that a person can get away with among seminescient neighbors are futile when it comes to this dharmic lord, whose panoptic powers stand in stark contrast to a human's limited knowledge of others. Set within the opaque and sunless between of death, fabricated from the deceased's own mental and karmic heritage, all of this is a far cry from the masculine potency, adroitness, clarity of knowledge, and sense of presence and stability that Mheme and other Yolmo men have valued in their waking lives as they have worked and walked about their respective lands of power.

There is a comparison to be made here, a mirror image to be noted, for once I had thought a bit about Mheme's depictions of his imminent engagement with Chhe Gyalbu, I began to sense that this anticipated encounter bore strong and haunting affinities with the on-the-spot review of his life that I had been undertaking with him. What got me thinking about these affinities were Mheme's depictions of Chhe Gyalbu's tools of observing and recording a human's life and the equivalencies the lama drew between those tools and various means of visual and acoustic duplication among humans. As noted above, Mheme held that the deity relies on a set of panoptic techniques first to know, then to reveal, all the actions, good or bad, that a person has undertaken in life. Along with other dizzying elements of doubling evident in Mheme's accounts, such as a person's shadow as unhesitant informer and a mirror that reflects all of one's actions, the lama broached the idea that "the people on earth have copied the same mirror that Chhe Gyalbu has." He also noted that both the mirror and the shadow work just as my tape recorder does and that Chhe Gyalbu shows "the whole life, like what is seen in the movies today." On another occasion he observed: "Now we have these televisions; the deity has a similar kind of thing. That's why they made those things, to teach people to know that god is watching in a similar kind of way. If the deity doesn't have that thing, then how would they be able to make it?"

In listening to Mheme trace these and other equivalencies, I soon came to understand that, for him, the human world was populated by the resemblance of objects also found, sometimes in more powerful and more original forms, in the realms of deities: he made it known to us, for instance, that the king's palace in Kathmandu is "only a very small model" of a buddha's realm in heaven, whereas life in any man-made jail is much the same thing as life in hell: "Some people already get hell here, in this life," he noted one afternoon in a characteristic aside. "Look at the jails. They're beating and killing people. Hell means that." The semiotic cast of such replicas is in line with how he learned much of what he had learned in life—by watching others, then copying what they did—as well as with how he and other lamas have tried to imagine their bodies as resembling the divine forms of great bodhisattvas. Taken as a whole, such doubling acts are on a par with the "homological" or "analogical" thinking of many South Asian and Himalayan peoples, in which images and objects are understood to resemble or ritually stand for other, often sacred, images or beings.[3] Features of Mheme's world often involved such homologies, and mimesis was for him a common, but by no means the only, means of thought and being.

Given the presence of such doubles and copies in his life, I was soon led in 1998 to wonder if our conversations together were faintly mirroring a human's encounter with the Lord of Dharma after death. Mheme's occasional finger-pointing at the tape recorder would spark just this perception of similarity for me. At fleeting moments like this I felt, and thought that perhaps he felt, that through our engagements we were in effect involved in an uncanny rehearsal of the mirror work to come. Was the anthropologist acting like the Lord of Death? Much as scientists had copied Chhe Gyalbu's mirror, the godly existence of which, in Mheme's eyes, made possible the invention of the television, were we somehow simulating the Lord of Dharma's inquisitive, postmortem review of a life?

Eventually I got up the nerve to ask about this. "Mheme," I asked, "we're writing your life story. And Chhe Gyalbu also has a person's life story. Do they look the same?"

"Yes, they're the same," he replied. "Whatever we say, it's in here [the tape recorder]. Now, if we don't say the truth, then Chhe Gyalbu has the record of all our words. What we're recording here, Chhe Gyalbu is also making the record. If good doesn't emerge [during our lives], then Chhe Gyalbu has the record." After a pause, he spoke again. "Here we can lie and then run away. With Chhe Gyalbu, we can't tell lies, because he has the record. If one lies, this buddha knows everything."

Although I am still unsure about Mheme's opinion of how close a fit there is between the two endeavors, he clearly took the methods of recording to be much the same: much as Chhe Gyalbu's observations do, the tape recorder picked up all of Mheme's words when in use and held them in such a way that they could easily be resounded at different times and places. For me, at least, the similarities in techniques have resurrected the ghostly echo of anthropology as an intrusive colonial mechanism of knowledge as control. Armed with suitcases crammed with recording devices—a camera, a video camera, a portable computer, two tape recorders, notebooks, pens and pencils—I collected images, sampled words, charted lives. While I did not engage in these scriptive acts in order to control anyone or to render any Yolmo wa controllable by others, it would be foolish to ignore the fact that, as with Chhe Gyalbu, such observations emerged out of and contributed to a position of relative wealth and power. My interactions with Mheme, from my initial inquiries to my final acts of writing, were always predicated on a differential of power.

Less certain is whether Mheme thought that our conversations mimicked in advance the life review that would took place with Chhe Gyalbu. Be that as it may, the affinities are unnerving and worth noting. We might think of a Yolmo elder's anticipated conversation with the Lord of Dharma as a local "discourse genre" of sorts, as linguistic anthropologists use the term these days: not to name a rigid formal type of text or speech, as formalist approaches often construe the idea of a genre, but to refer to a usually open-ended, ambiguous, routinized schema of linguistic practice, ordering a meal, taking an oath, whose shifting uses and potential meanings emerge through specific engagements between interlocutors.[4] Such schemas can occur in a variety of contexts, including ones not usually identified as being inducive to them. Asking for a friend's help, for instance, can playfully or ironically entail a conversation that approximates how a diner might go about ordering a meal, while that friend's vow to help can echo how a citizen pledges an oath.

So it was with the genre in question here, for it recurred, for me at least, beyond the walls of Chhe Gyalbu's kingdom. Our talk, like the pages of this book, was grafted in mirrors upon mirrors. When I spoke with Mheme about his life and recorded his words on my tape recorder, there were moments when the discourse genres of the-deceased-as-confronted-by-Chhe Gyalbu or the-living-as-observed-by-Chhe Gyalbu (and possibly even a-citizen-as-interrogated-by-the-police) quietly haunted our thoughts. Here and elsewhere, words and actions echoed, at times to Mheme and at times to me, the forms of other scenes and engagements known to Yolmo wa. As would be the case with Chhe Gyalbu, we were engaged in a review and assessment of Mheme's life that could have lasting consequences in terms of his future destiny. Perhaps as a result, our conversation similarly focused on the moral aspects of a life and the ethical value of its actions. Indeed, my guess is that Mheme's understanding of what his life story would or should entail conformed more to Chhe Gyalbu's reputed focus on specific, morally significant "deeds" than to the culturally informed interpretive musings on life and death that I have been generating.

Both engagements drew, in turn, on dialogic inquiries. Much as Chhe Gyalbu interrogates and a human responds, I asked questions and Mheme answered. In responding, Mheme understandably tried to speak well of his life and his actions—as many a human does when faced with Chhe Gyalbu. It appeared, though, that he would have to doubly defend his life's actions, both before and after he died. My understanding is that our talk together prompted a review of his life more thorough than any other act of recollection in which he had otherwise been engaged in his life—until, that is, he would have to contend with Chhe Gyalbu. And since Mheme and his family found, as the months wore on in 1998, that I had asked and he had answered an exhausting number of questions, he understood that a comprehensive life story would be compiled that could pass as a pale copy of Chhe Gyalbu's own ledgers. In a world inhabited by human-made resemblances of divine forms, any book written about him might be the closest thing possible to Chhe Gyalbu's all-knowing biography. Then again, since all of this, we both knew well, was bound for print some day, perhaps I was just a scribe in such proceedings, writing down, like one of Chhe Gyalbu's clerkish attendants, all of the actions a human enacts, with the result that any life story later penned about Ghang Lama would serve as a mirrorlike compendium of his deeds, to be reviewed and judged by any number of faceless readers. Perhaps then it is not so much the biography's author as its readers who are performing a function most akin to the Lord of Dharma's.

As Mheme himself noted, however, a telling difference is that he could easily hide the truth when it came to the life story we were constructing. My gaze, humble and reciprocating as it was, was far from absolute. With Chhe Gyalbu, one could not be so lucky. While Mheme was perhaps "hiding" some deeds and aspects of his life, he understood that he would have to admit to everything later on or stand by abashedly as the mirror of deeds or his shadow did the truth-telling for him. His expectation of such a scene apparently helps to explain some of his fears about dying. "Everything would be shown" after he died, although I never did learn what deeds, if any, worried him, perhaps in part because he was able to put a good spin on his life when talking with us.

Here and There

Words for Kisang could sow memories. They could recall a disgraceful scene or denounce a relative's actions. They could track a mother's displacements or question why things happened the way they did.

In the years following her divorce from Rinjin Lama, both before and after she was taken to Phungboche, Kisang lived in a series of homes in Ne Nyemba, on lands once owned by her first husband but now divided among the sons from her first marriage. By a roundabout course of events, she eventually moved to Kathmandu and later settled in Boudhanath, a few streets north of the chhorten, with Kānchā and his wife.

> P: *Auntie, how is it that you came to [live close to] the chhorten?*
> K: *I came to the chhorten, indeed. In the village we weren't getting along. They quarreled with me. That's to say, I went with your uncle [my second husband], and then my son wasn't getting along with me. Lama Mingmar's father [my oldest son], yes?*

Her first son, "Lama Mingmar's father," was not getting along with her. As Kānchā Lama later told me, he was angry at his mother for marrying another man and so throwing into question the rights to the land and property originally owned by his father, Wangel Lama, before he died. "He gave my mother a lot of sorrow," Kānchā said of his half brother, "and my mother scolded him in return."

Complicating all this was the divorce.

Your uncle gave the signature, yes? He gave the divorce to me.

245

The signing and "giving" of divorce papers made the separation binding.

Then, after giving the divorce, he said to them, "You need to take responsibility for your mother." Kānchā's father, yes?

With this said, significant voicings continued to drive social actions. Sometime after the divorce (Kisang never said when exactly), Rinjin Lama informed Kisang's children from her first marriage that now they, rather than he, needed to care for her. So while she was at first responsible for her children in their youth, they needed to take responsibility for her as she grew older. Otherwise, she would again be left without a familial "tree" to hold on to or a rightful place to live—both very threatening possibilities, especially given that her ability to work productively and care for herself would wane as her age grew "less." "Grandma, you're unimportant, with no share...," Milarepa exhorts an aged woman in one of his hundred thousand songs.[1]

Well, now, if I say something, what can I say? If I don't say anything, still, they will say, "Mother, you are saying the sorrowful talk."

These words were spoken in the present tense, as though Kisang was talking or thinking to herself during the narrative moment at hand. Voiced in response to her husband's statement and to whatever her children might have said (or did not say) in reply, they composed an enigmatic statement that built on the "to say, what to say" phrasing sounded at other times. If she had said something about these proceedings, what could it have been? And yet if she had held her tongue and kept silent on the matter, her children would have said she was complaining, or "saying the sorrowful talk," nonetheless. What words or actions were available to her under these constraints?

> K: *Now, Lama Mingmar's father [the first son of my first husband] was doing a tsog-ya [rite]. Toward that side, where I had lived earlier—do you know where that was?*
>
> P: *Where?*
>
> K: *On the other side of Ne Nyemba, where I built the house. You don't know it?*
>
> P: *I was young then.*
>
> K: *Ah, you might be young. Kānchā's father had given the separation to me. He didn't need to take care of me. His sons weren't obliged to take care of me. He had released me.*

She intertwisted two lines of thought here, evidently because two histories needed to be told at once: one, concerning the consequences of her divorce; the other, relating to the ways her children responded to the charge that they were now responsible for her.

When Rinjin Lama renounced himself of her, his sons from his first marriage were not compelled, by either custom or law, to care for her. As the same could not readily have been said of the children of her first marriage, it became a question of which son or daughter, if any, would take her in. At that time, her two oldest sons from her first marriage were living in Ne Nyemba, and her daughter resided in Kathmandu. Forced to vacate her second husband's home in Shomkharka, she moved on to Ne Nyemba with hopes of staying there, on lands adjacent to the home of her first son. Her situation remained precarious nonetheless. Many Yolmo women achieve a measure of security and authority in their later years, especially if they have a home they can count on inhabiting. For Kisang such a home was hard to come by. Because of the loss of a family "tree" to hold on to and because of the various movements and relocations asked of her, she did not have and could not effectively claim an especially rightful place to live. As a widow, now "released" by a second husband, she remained vulnerable.[2]

As Kānchā told it, his mother did, in fact, live beside her first son's home in Ne Nyemba for a while. But she found that this son was hostile both toward and toward Kānchā when he came to stay with his mother. His family quarreled with her, they did not provide sufficient food, they sometimes took things from her home, and they made it clear that they did not want Kānchā to stay in Ne Nyemba, in part because they feared that, if he did so, he might lay claim to some of the property formerly owned by Kisang's first husband. It was also a question of "pride," Kānchā noted, in that his mother did not want to rely on handouts from her son and "wanted to eat her own food," especially since she found that she was working harder in the fields than anyone in her son's family was. "They also didn't bring their mother any flour [or other food supplies]," Neela added. So a meeting was called, during which Kisang announced that she could no longer tolerate living in Ne Nyemba, and her first son declared that he no longer wanted to look after her.

When Kisang related these events to Pramod and I, her narration suggested that all words and deeds in those moments belonged to her children and her second husband. In contrast with how she depicted herself in other recollections of hers, she did not speak directly in any of this, here or elsewhere, as though, in her reckoning, she had remained silent throughout or had little authority or power then to utter anything of consequence. Her various stories reflect an arch of social and vocal power in her life, in which she said little when she first married, then

spoke strongly and defiantly at crucial times in her adult life, only to return to relative silence in her later years. Then again, as she suggested
earlier on ("If I don't say…"), her silence among her children could
have carried substantial pragmatic force: it could have been construed as
complaining, among other things, or it could have motivated her children to rethink how they were treating their mother.

Then, one of my sons said, "Are you going to take your mother? We're not taking her."
I thought my daughter-in-law advised my son to say this, so they didn't take me. This
daughter-in-law is now dead. She spoke like this to her husband. Then my son said,
"Mother, I won't take care of you. You can do whatever you want to do."

So many significant statements. Her first son, the one who disap-
proved of the second marriage, announced that he would no longer be
responsible for his mother and that she was now free to do as she
pleased, even though her viable options were clearly limited. She believed that this man's wife, now dead, stood behind his words.

Yolmo widows fear such mistreatment at the hands of their sons and
daughters-in-law, on whom they often must depend in their later years.
When talking with Phur Gyalmu about her life, I asked her if she had
worries about growing older. "Sure, now," she answered. "After getting
old, how will my son treat me? How will my daughter-in-law treat me?
If the son is good, then the daughter-in-law is not good. If the daughter-in-law is good, the son is not. That's to say, it worries me."

Then they released me. They released me.
   At that time, my relatives were also there, including Cousin Jamyang. My second
husband was also there then. "I released her before, and I release her now as well. You
need to take responsibility for her, or you need to release her [as well]. Think about
that." Kānchā Lama's father said that, while among the people gathered.

When Rinjin Lama learned while attending the tsog-ya rite in Ne
Nyemba that her first son had similarly "released" his former wife, he
reaffirmed that he had already separated from her and put the matter
back into that son's hands: he needed either to take in his mother or to
pass her on to someone else. That his words were heard by those gathered gave public witness to his declarations. They might also have
proved a bit humiliating for Kisang, who had to abide by whatever was
decided by these men. Ritual as opportunity.

My first son didn't take responsibility [for me] then. He's the father of my grandsons.

The family ties invoked illustrate how shameful the son's slight was. This son could have argued, however, that, because Kisang had remarried and so had already settled into another household, he and the other children of her first marriage were no longer obliged to take her into their homes. And yet these children, now adults themselves, still worried about the situation.

Later, the middle son and [my] one daughter wanted to take the responsibility. Before they were trying to decide. "Abi! At this time we are so many children!"

It would have been a disgraceful thing, indeed, if not one of them took care of their mother. "It must be good," Kisang told us when asked what she thought about being a mother. "It must be good, of course. It must be good....I should say it's good. Again, if I say it's not good, for myself, it's already happened. I've already been a mother."

Then, Cousin Jamyang [my brother's son Jamyang, from Sermathang] said he would take me. "Oh, Auntie, we have the old house that was made by you. Please come! I need to bring you into my home." He was quite eager to take me.

A nephew of hers excitedly invited her to return to Sermathang and live in the house formerly owned by her now deceased father and brother. After all, she helped to "make" this structure years before.

Kānchā Lama told me that, rather than accepting this kind offer, Kisang moved into the home of the youngest son from her first marriage; "I'll keep you," said this son. That arrangement did not work for long, however, because she found that she was still dwelling too close to her first son and feared that they would continue to quarrel. Kānchā, who by then had a place in Ne Nyemba himself, then offered to take her into his home, but the first son was against this. "'If he takes her,'" Kānchā said his half brother said at the time, "'then he can get all the property.'"

Then later on my daughter and [second] son decided to take me. One son said to his sister, "Eh, if we don't take our mother, people will spit on us. We need to care for our mother." The middle son said this to my daughter. So they brought me to Kathmandu. Oh, since then I've never gone back to the village.

Kisang uttered the words quoted above in a slightly hushed voice, as might be used when family members are discussing matters they wish to keep among themselves: her daughter and son, who were both living in Kathmandu by then, agreed to have her stay with them, partly in fear of the shameful contempt that they would be held in if they did not provide well for their mother. Kisang was then "brought" to Kathmandu. She stayed first with her son, then with her daughter.

I gave all my goods to my youngest son [from my first marriage], not my eldest son. The eldest son didn't take responsibility for caring for me. The children of my eldest son are four.... There are four. They didn't care for me. From them, they don't care much for me.

Goods transferred to the good. As for the bad, she named, for the record, the sons of her eldest, who bore the sins of their father. Pramod advised me not to write these names here, for fear of shaming or upsetting them upon the release of any published account of Kisang's life; then later on Karma and I agreed that it would be best to change her first son's name to a pseudonym ("Lama Mingmar's father"). Such are the potential means and consequences of writing and a mother's invocations.

> K: *Lama Mingmar's father [my first son] didn't take the responsibility to care for me.*
> P: *Why didn't he?*
> K: *He took the advice from his wife. He said, "I won't take care of my mother." All the children were there, everyone, at that time. So one daughter and one son took responsibility to care for me, in fact.*

It was a question, here and there, of morally charged utterances, their authors, and those who heard or reiterated such talk.

> K: *Ah, this kind of talk, where, where [to what purpose]? Ah, I don't remember. I don't remember.*
>   *Please drink tea. Oh, please drink tea. Drink.*
> R: *Yes, please.*

While we were drinking tea, and while Pramod was explaining this conceivably "aimless" talk to me in English, Kisang said quietly:

Ah, chatty talk.

Or so she evaluated our slapdash *(thele mele)* conversation with her.

In talking further, Pramod brought me up to speed with these myriad events, and we tried a new line of questioning:

> P: *When you came to Kathmandu, you lived in the house of [your second son] Jho Bharpa?*
> K: *Yes. Before he had the house in Chabahil. I entered in there. Both my son and daughter together brought me. Then, my daughter built a house in Baneswor;*

I was also there then. Oh, now that house has been sold. In that house I lived. They did this [brought me] together.

As a result of these occurrences, Kānchā related, Kisang stayed with her daughter for twelve years. "My daughter does well, my daughter is valuable," she told us on another occasion. "Now she is near [living close by]. Otherwise, if she was far away, then she couldn't do well. She has acted well toward me, my daughter. She is near. Only one daughter I have. There's only one. My daughter is better than my sons."

"The same. It's the same, for the children," she said on another occasion when asked if she liked her children all the same. "Everyone comes to visit me, everyone says 'Mother.' If their mother feels unwell, then everyone worries about her. I like all the same, for sure. It's the same. I gave my milk to them [I nursed them]."

I've had sorrow, ah. Difficulties didn't come to me. My children cared for me. Happiness didn't come to my sem.

Negativities of body and mind: While her living situation was not uncomfortable then, she could not say that she was happy.

Mishmash, for sure.

"Mishmash" here is our translation of *dzan-dzo,* a Yolmo word usually used in reference to a meal prepared by hashing together different foods. "'Everything has happened to me,'" Karma glossed the import of Kisang's words here. Her retellings, and the events, good and bad, depicted through them, involved a hotchpotch history of incongruent deeds and voicings.

> P: *Auntie, in this house, in Kānchā Lama's house, how many years have you stayed?*
> K: *In this house? Since the time when my daughter and me had differences. I didn't have differences with my daughter. My son-in-law gave me over to Kānchā Lama. He handed me over. In that place they handed me over. Why did they give, hey?*

While she referred to her daughter's mate as her "son-in-law," she later explained that he never formally married her daughter. "My daughter did not have a wedding. They went together [without any marriage ceremony]. My daughter did not go to her husband's house by marriage. They just got together." The two had since separated. "Now my son-in-law has not treated my daughter well. He left her behind. I'm angry at him. She went to another place. If she had married with a Yolmo man, it would have been good. Now my daughter has difficulties. She has to do everything herself. There's no problem with eating, there's no problem with a living place, there's no problem with finances. [But] It's troublesome that she doesn't have a husband in her house. My son-in-law divorced my daughter.... It's good he gave it [the divorce]. His heart was not good."

Why did the couple hand Kisang over to Kānchā Lama? "Why did they give, hey?" Kānchā's explanation was that there was a "small dispute" between his mother and her daughter and son-in-law, who subsequently felt that they could no longer house their mother. "We need to hand her over to you," his sister told him. So Kisang moved to stay in with Kānchā, who by then had relocated to Kathmandu. That was in 1980 or so, when Kisang was around sixty-five.

In that house they ate my property. He [my son-in-law] couldn't do what he wanted to do, so he gave [me away], I think. I did the hard work, but I couldn't die in that house. "I'm not going, I'm not going, I'm not going," I've said it!"

Kisang thought that her son-in-law had set the path for her departure, either because he could not live in the manner he wanted to or because he did not get his way in some matter. Although he and his wife had "eaten" some of Kisang's possessions and monies, and though she had labored greatly in their house, she could not live or die within it. Kisang willfully said what might have gone unsaid. But could she really insist on staying?

Her words prompted an unexpected response.

When I said that, my daughter-in-law [Neela] said, "Ibi, I'll take you. Ibi, come to our house. Otherwise, I won't move. Ibi, where you live, I'll live there. If you go into a ditch, I'll go there. Wherever you live, I'll also live there." They [Kānchā and Neela] wanted to have me handed over [to them]. The [other] couple slipped away silently.

Her daughter-in-law told her that she would gladly live beside this "Ibi," wherever she happened to be. These compassionate words stood opposed to the actions of her daughter and son-in-law, who "slipped away silently" from the scene, without others knowing that they were leaving. "If you take me, I'll help to pay the rent," Kānchā said his mother told him at the time. Things worked out, and she resided with Kānchā and his wife in parts of Kathmandu since then, first in a series of houses that Kānchā bought and sold (sometimes with the aid of loans from his mother), then in their present home, close to the chhorten in Boudhanath.

> P: *How many years have you been here?*
> K: *How many years? I don't remember how many years.... Since this house was built, for sure. When I moved from my daughter's house, we rented in another house for two years. Then after we made this house. It has been maybe ten years since we made this house. I don't know.*
>   *...This house was made by my body.*

The last assertion, she labored bodily in helping to build their current residence, recalls the lines of a pain song couplet sung by Yolmo women:

> The pillars beneath the house,
> we daughters build ourselves
> But beneath the roof we build,
> we have no chance to live.[3]

—or die, it seems, at times. While Pramod and I were talking in English, Kisang offered another aside:

Here and there.

What, precisely, was dispersed "here and there" *(phetar ghotor)* here? Her family life, as a result of the various displacements she faced? Her words and recollections? The places in which she had lived? Her body and person? Our questions?

> P: *Do you like to stay here?*
> K: *What is to be done? If I like or dislike it, I need to die here. Now I'm here. Where can I go? Now I'd like to die here.*

One reason Kisang wanted to die in that home was that it was quite close to the chhorten, the stūpa known to bring great merit to those who live nearby or who regularly circumambulate its perimeter. "I would like to die near the chhorten," she said when asked how she liked living so close to it. "We [intentionally] built the house close to the chhorten. So I pray to die near it. We made the house nearby. The chhorten is tremendous.... Having imagined and imagined [that it might be so], I arrived at the chhorten. Before I thought about dying near the chhorten. Now, I think I'm decaying by the chhorten. I should be able to die here. I'll die here."

She preferred to die in Boudhanath rather than in the Yolmo region, as many other Yolmo elders wanted to do. While she said, when asked, that it was "good to die in one's village," she was also of the opinion that a cremation site newly built by Yolmo wa for Yolmo wa on the outskirts of Boudhanath was a sufficiently "pure place." She therefore saw no reason to die in Yolmo. "I want to die here, close to the chhorten," she told us. "Where would I go in Yolmo? The chhorten is a better place. Now that I've come to the chhorten, why should I go to Yolmo to die?"

All this spoke to the geopolitics of cremations. Some bodies are known to pollute more than others. Some sites are thought to be purer than others. Some Yolmo wa are more at home in Yolmo than others: having been displaced from several villages, none of which she could take as home, where in Yolmo could Kisang go to die? Why go there to die at all? Passed on from son to daughter, transferred to one house, then another, she eventually came to feel at home in Boudhanath, close to the great chhorten, with her youngest son and his wife. It therefore made good sense to die there and be cremated there.

"So: Ragged Woman"

"If it's not good, don't show it," Kisang told me late one morning. "If it [my talk] is good, then show it. If it's not good, don't show it. What to do?...What to say? I don't know how to compile my talk well. It's all jumbled up."

She spoke these words toward the end of one of our tape-recorded interviews in 1998, as we sat and drank tea in her room in her son's house. She voiced similar admonishments on other occasions as well, particularly during the later occasions when we met; to me it became clear that she was quite concerned about the quality of her talk, whether it was, or would appear to others to be, "good" or "not good." It was more than just a question of what her words meant or what actions or memories they might effect in life. What also mattered was how well her words cohered, whether they appeared "straight" or "crooked," "clear" or "garbled," as she grew frailer. Others, she knew well, would hear and evaluate those words and in turn convey thoughts, either before or after she died, on how "skillful" their speaker was. At work here was a set of deeply held cultural discourses, ones that centered on ideas of skilled talk and action, that helped to determine what this elderly woman thought of her words and, by implication, her social and moral worth in general.

At the same time, all this put into question what exactly I would be doing with her words, whether I would be "showing" her talk to others, and how and in what form that talk would be shown. In time I came to understand that swirls of cultural sensibilities were informing Kisang's thoughts about my work with her; that a strong measure of responsibility came with this work; that my own efforts would also be evaluated within a criterion of skilled action; and that any treatment or invocation of her words by me would require efforts that were at once ethical and aesthetic in nature. To take someone's words and render them into a "life story" to be read or heard by others, I came to realize, is not just a question of interpreting those words well or translating them correctly; it is also a question, or should be, of minding the speaker's own concerns about the quality or import or social fate of her words. Life history research, like all forms of ethnographic inquiry, is an ethical act, with few easy answers to the issues that arise.

Despite its vagueness, Kisang's aside, noted in the previous chapter, about something having dispersed "here and there" was dense with meaning, for ideas of fragmentation and dispersal are central to Yolmo understandings of matter-in-time. In line with the fundamental Buddhist tenet that all composite forms erode in time, Yolmo wa commonly understand that elements of something once unified eventually decay and disperse. Many would therefore not feel at odds with the sentiments expressed in a verse chanted during a Tibetan ritual for caring for the dead:

O child, the end of collecting is dispersal,
the end of building is disintegration,
the end of meeting is separation,
and the end of birth is death.[1]

Such ideas pattern thoughts near and far. Among other things, Yolmo people worry about the fragmentation of bodies in illness, the erosion of life forces, the disbanding of families, the fission of lineages, the diffusion of communities.[2] "Mhi phetar ghotor ghalsin" (People have gone here and there), Rhidu Pema once said with concern when talking about the recent migrations of people from Yolmo to Kathmandu and parts elsewhere. These dispersals were the inverse of integration and wholeness.

Growing old, as perceived among Yolmo wa, can also be a matter of form and the dissolution of form. Key cultural concerns about the metaphysics of form are invested in the Yolmo word *nhongyo,* a passive participle from the verb *nhongba,* "to be ruined." The word can be used to characterize something as damaged, flawed, ruined, or imperfect. One's clothes can be nhongyo if they have tears in them, as a photo can be if it fails to convey well its subject. Young men can be said to be nhongyo if they drink too much. By and large the word reflects Yolmo concerns for wholeness, completion, and perfection as well as preferences for objects well formed and free of flaws or impurities. Appreciation of tasks that are done skillfully reflect much the same set of values, as do criticisms of activities or jobs that are done imperfectly or only partly. "Form is everything," Karma once observed. Perfection is an ideal. Many Yolmo wa are formalists in thought and deed.

The bodies of old persons can be marked by qualities associated with the word *nhongyo*. Analogies to a moon that first waxes, then wanes, or to an apple that first ripens, then withers, are apt here. Yolmo wa understand that a body can lose its "freshness," while the skin becomes "wrinkled" and "faded out," and it can grow more ragged and imperfect and increasingly prone to illness.

Kisang's words often advanced similar images of decay. Earlier in her life she was "very active," strong, and hardworking. "Nobody did the hard work like me." In recent years, however, she had lost her strength and the ability to work or move about. Staying so, she found her immobile body to be *rulge,* or "rotting": "What to do? I can't walk. Now, I'm going to rot." "What to do? I can't walk. I can't move about. Decomposing, rotting—whatever happens, happens.... My legs are disabled. I'm rotting here, rotting. They treat me well."

The decay affected her ability to think, remember, and speak well, she told us on several occasions: "Now that I've become old, my brain is also damaged. There's no brain as well." "I've become old, so there's no smarts. The smarts are gone. I don't know how to tell a story." "I have no memory, now. My sem has rotted." "What comes now? I don't remember. I've become too old. I can't see, I can't hear well. I've become an old woman, I can't remember the past years."

All this, she said, was affecting her ability to speak well, for she feared that her talk was now without the kind of *rikpa,* or "smarts," required to organize it well. In the course of compelling, wonderfully poetic accounts of her life, she claimed time and again, and despite our protests to the contrary, that her talk was "messy," "unskillful," "garbled," "here and there," "crooked," "topsy-turvy," "haphazard," and "unattractive"; that her voice was "not good"; and that, in her old age, she could speak only "curved talk" and could only "catch loose, unformed words."[3] *"Laso, laso"* (Please, please), she said when asked at the end of one session if we could return to talk with her again. "My talk is not good. My talk is messy," she added, then said quietly in Nepali:

It's the words of a ninety-year-old woman. What to do? I've forgotten everything. I have no memory. Everything is forgotten, I remember only a little bit. If my wits were really clear, I could say continuously. I've told [you] that I only have the smarts for work. I only know the art of weaving. Now I've also thrown these things [lost these skills]. My talk is not pretty. My talk is unskillful.

Hearing such evaluations, I found a woman deeply concerned with how well she was speaking, with how others might evaluate her words, and with how her aging, "decaying" mind prevented her from speaking in the kinds of coherent, fluid ways with which, she recalled, she was once familiar.

To understand these concerns well and how they have weighed in my approach to Kisang's life and words, we need to consider something of great importance in Yolmo lives: ideas of skilled talk and action. In fact, the more I reflect on what I have learned while living on the margins of Yolmo households, the more I appreciate the ways in which Yolmo lives are concerned with questions of skill, style, and aesthetically and ethically proper forms. I think, for instance, of the way in which Ghang Lama spoke proudly of how "skillful" (N., *sipālu*) his three sons had become in terms of their knowledge of lamaic practices. I am reminded of Karma's recollection of the importance that his father, a highly respected lama and politician, placed on skills when raising him and his siblings in the village of Takpakharka: "You're like pencils and I'm trying to sharpen you, and it's for your own good," Karma recalled his father saying to him and his friends. Karma took the simile to mean that his father was trying to "sharpen" their minds and talents so that they would become more steadfastly diligent and conscientious in their dealings in the world. And I recall various offhand remarks made by Yolmo wa on the grace or adroitness displayed by others, including a child's comment to me that she appreciated when a bombo would don a white dress and dance around a client in order to exorcise a demonic force. "How nice it is when the bombo dances," she told me. When asked why she thought this, she said, *"Tesai,"* using a Nepali expression that can be heard in English as "just because" or "just like that." I also remember well that, a few days later, that girl's father insisted I erase and record over a segment of a video tape I had used to film her and her friend giggling through a folk song. "Their clothes are ragged and their faces are black [dirty]," the man told me after viewing the tape. "Later," his wife added, as if tendering a solution, "when they're wearing good clothes and know a good song, then you can take their photo." That same day I recorded over the segment in question. Caution to those who might be portrayed as dark as ghosts, and woe to an observer who acts without skill.

Or without ḍhaṅga, as Yolmo wa might say. This Nepali word, which has come to mean variably "skill, skilled manner, adroitness, know-how" in Yolmo circles, is usually applied to the skillfulness or smarts that people display or fail to display in undertaking certain activities, from hosting guests to taking photographs. "To have ḍhaṅga is to have style in doing something," Karma told me. In contrast, people who are judged by others to be acting without good ḍhaṅga, people, that is, who do "not present in a good style," as Karma once put it, are some-times said, in terms either joking or serious, to be lacking "smarts." To act without ḍhaṅga can therefore be, at times, to be less than fully cog-nizant of how one should act among others.

Presumptions about gender factor into such attitudes. Whereas par-ents generally encourage sons to be courageous and to accomplish good deeds in their lives, daughters are advised, particularly by their mothers, that they should take care in how they talk, walk, sit, and serve others. Talk about skillful action also comes up in discussions of young women, who are often judged on how much ḍhaṅga, or skillfulness, they possess in terms of housekeeping, cooking, and hosting guests. Parents thus of-ten find it necessary to remind teenage daughters that they must learn how to act with ḍhaṅga if they are to secure good marriages and main-tain their families' honor. After they marry, women need to continue to act in skillful ways. As Binod once put it, "When a person does not fol-low the rules of our society, such as a woman who walks in front of her superiors [including her husband], we'll say that she doesn't have ḍhaṅga." Such actions can bring consequences. "She didn't have the right kind of ḍhaṅga," one woman said of her father's first wife, "and so my father divorced her." And when I asked Ghaki Lamani if she thought Yolmo men treat their wives well, she replied, "Some treat [their wives] nicely. Some, if they are mean, beat their wives. And if the wife's ḍhaṅga [manner] is not good, then he starts beating her, saying, 'What did you do?! Why is this dirty?! Why haven't you washed clothes?!' A woman therefore has to be well-mannered. Then her husband won't beat her."

It is likely, however, that a man who harms his wife will also be con-sidered lacking in ḍhaṅga. For men, ḍhaṅga applies less to any house-hold graces they might possess than to how they relate to and work among others. In general, everything in how a woman or man works, sits, dresses, eats, or engages with others can be evaluated in terms of how much ḍhaṅga is invested in the style and manner of those actions. The way in which something is done is as important as the act itself. Since the uses of a body are often instrumental to such actions, an important consequence of this is that, whether chopping wood or hosting neighbors, a Yolmo wa's sense of self and bodily action can be profoundly conditioned by an ongoing and sometimes worrisome awareness of the evaluative perceptions of others. Subjective consciousness implies, in many crucial ways, a constant awareness of the consciousness of others. This is not to say that Yolmo wa regularly find that their selves merge with other selves, nor is it to suggest that they commonly partake in sublime empathies with one other (after all, "one can never truly know what is in another's sem"). Rather, it is to contend that, as Yolmo wa understand it, the consciousness of others, quite distinct from but copresent with one's own in time, can variably be concerned with watching, perceiving, commenting on, and praising or mocking how a person acts in the world. Nogapu put it well when, in trying to convey the logic of ḍhaṅga, he noted, "If you try to do some kind of work, but can't do it, [people say,] 'Ah, ḍhaṅga mhindu!' [Ah, there's no skill!]"

Notice how the very phrasing of Nogapu's sentence suggests a close and immediate affiliation between a person's actions and often critical evaluations of those actions. Actions are observed, then commented on. This, I think, is the case in general for many Yolmo wa: one's skillfulness at select activities is not simply a personal, subjective matter; ḍhaṅga speaks from the start to questions of social regard and critical evaluation, what in effect people say about another's skilled or unskilled manner when undertaking an activity.

Listen, for example, to an explanation offered by Kisang when asked what the word *ḍhaṅga* means. "Eh, *ḍhaṅga*," she answered, then continued:

"No intelligence," one says. "No smarts," one says. If there's no intelligence, if someone doesn't keep it in her sem [maintain knowledge well], then we say, "There's no skill" [*ḍhaṅga mheba*]. Someone who is doing things hastily. Someone who is doing the straight work, everyone says they have good skills. If some are rushing through it, everyone says they have no smarts, these women.

And when asked what it means to have good ḍhaṅga, she replied:

People say that. It means to praise her. If good work is done, then everyone says, "She has good ḍhaṅga." "Her smarts are good," everyone says.

Kisang explained what ḍhaṅga means by giving examples of the social uses of the word, as densely intersubjective speech acts, wherein people decry or praise the degree of skillfulness evident in someone's actions. Ḍhaṅga, then, is as much a matter of social evaluation as it is a matter of skillfulness per se. As a concept, it exists in practical terms only when people are talking about others or fearing the talk of others.

Such talk, Kisang's own narratives made clear, is both crucial and pervasive. "People talk," Yolmo friends have often told me. They talk, in either critical or laudatory tones, about the work one does, good or bad, and of how well one talks or performs certain actions. They talk about whether one flirts or fights with others. They talk about whether someone is known as a drunk or a thief, and they talk about how skillful young women are at doing housework or hosting guests, even when visiting relatives. "Even when you go to your aunt's house," Norbu's sister Tashi told me, "you have to work. After drinking tea, you have to take the glasses and wash them. If you don't, they talk, the people talk, you know: 'She doesn't know how to work.'" In general, one's reputation, or "name," is tied up with how one and one's family act in life and what people say about those actions. Many activities that Yolmo wa engage in or think of engaging in therefore have an intersubjective air (and ear) to them from the start, for there is always the chance that others will comment on those activities, sometimes in quite critical terms. Such critical *gyap-tam,* or "back-talk," which quickly spreads from household to household, applies not just to oneself but also to a person's entire family. If a person acts in what others consider a shameful or sinful manner, it can "cut the nose" of other family members, causing them to be similarly disgraced. "It sounds like Yolmo society is a whole world of people talking," I suggested to Karma once. "Oh yes," he answered. "Oh yes. It's like that. It just spreads—poooh! It just spreads." Good talk also regularly occurs, but it's the gossip that spreads most quickly. Something of the anticipatory, consequential logic of karmic principles resounds in both forms of commentaries, for the moral implications of one's actions can echo in what others later say about those actions: "bad," inept actions incur critical talk, the cultural logic goes, while "good" actions resound in praise.

Of course, intimations of skilled action or of its absence become much more complicated and multiladen once they take form in the realtime pragmatics of everyday social engagements, what with all the rhetorical flourishes, ribbings and denials, boasts and jests, interethnic exchanges, and whispers, recollections, appraisals, and counterappraisals that line the pockets of Yolmo converse. Be that as it may, a criterion of skillfulness pervades many everyday actions and the critical regard of others among many Yolmo wa. People often find it necessary to be present with style, with skillfulness, in an at once aesthetically and ethically good manner. A person is always aware of his or her "relational existence," to quote Karma's words on the subject, with that existence largely founded on engagements with others. The highly interwoven, cross-talking nature of Yolmo social relations has something to do with all of this, as do almost constant comparisons between self and other, the high value given to skilled work and artistic craftsmanship, concerns for personal and familial honor, and the focus in Tibetan Buddhist circles on proper, virtuous comportment, "skillful means" in religious practice, and the ethical import of specific deeds.

The close link between ethics and aesthetics is crucial. As I understand it, among Yolmo wa any distinctions between skillful action and ethically proper action are blurred at best. Virtuousness and virtuosity go hand in hand. While Yolmo wa distinguish between concepts of good in the ethical sense and concepts of good in the aesthetic sense, making a virtuous life something different from a well-made thangka, they understand that many of the actions of everyday life involve a mix of both: to say that a woman "hosts well," for instance, is also to say that she welcomes and serves guests in skillful, ethically sound ways. Morally good deeds often rest on skillful means—people can and should be "skilled in good," as the Buddha reportedly put it—and skilled action usually implies virtuous action.[4]

Without question, understandings of this sort are ideological in nature, for they intimate that certain ways of acting are better than others. It's also the case that, in the 1980s and 1990s at least, some Yolmo wa heeded and promoted these understandings more than others did. In particular, the members of communities affiliated with the main villages along the eastern slope of the Yolmo Valley—Sermathang, Chhimi, and Takpakharka, among others—were concerned with an aesthetics of action more than members of many communities to the west were, in large part because of the heritage that had resulted from the predominance of lineage lamas and kheba, or artists, in these eastern villages for several generations. The members of village communities in the more forested, more agropasturalist, and more shamanic regions to the west and northwest, often known collectively as *ghang mhi*, or "hill people," were also concerned with how their actions appeared to others. But they tended not to act or talk in ways that suggested that well-formed actions were one of the more pressing concern of their lives.

This often came at a cost, however, especially given that, of those living in Kathmandu in the 1980s and 1990s, men who came from the eastern villages held more dominant positions of authority. And since some

social actors, particular those from lama families, from the more prosperous eastern ridge of Yolmo, and from wealthier households in Kathmandu, had a better chance of being "sharpened" in all the right ways,
certain cultural sensibilities set them up to be known as more skillful,
more virtuous beings. Those, in turn, who came from impoverished
farming families or from remote areas in western Yolmo, with little
chance of receiving an education in good schools and with little time or
opportunity to undertake "the lama's work," were often cast by others as
less refined, less virtuous followers of dharma, and so justly impoverished, because they had not engaged in the merit-making practices that
naturally resulted, many say, in prosperity. And while some might have
wished to contest such designations and the cultural and religious notions that supported them, and while glimmers of resistance and alteri-
ties did take form at times, there were few other orientations to meaning and value common to Yolmo lives that had the capacity to counter
or override in any significant way what the lamas and others advocated.
One could always have tried to live outside the social networks and
moral tenets of Yolmo society by making a home elsewhere or by associ-
ating solely with people professing different ethnic identities, but few
chose to do so, and those who were in fact ostracized for wrongdoings
committed were said to live miserable, beggars' lives. Talk about skilled
and virtuous action, or its occasional absence, thus continued to domi-
nate the social scene, with powerful consequences for how individuals,
families, and entire regions interacted and were portrayed.

Kisang Omu, very much a part of this moral universe and from a respected lama and artisan family from Sermathang, with no "caste"
above hers, deliberated often on who was and who was not skilled in
good. Quite frequently she spoke of the former by mentioning how
"well" people did things, usually with the use of the Yolmo word *yhabu,*
an adverb and adjective that mean much the same as the English words
well and *good* do. She said, for example, that she "stayed well" in marriage, that her first husband "did well" with her and "treated" his brothers "so well," and that she "did well" in arranging his funeral. Religious
sponsors "gave well" in support of the gompa in Ne Nyemba, and she
"hosted well" in return. Even after her husbands had died and she had
moved on to Kathmandu, she noted, sponsors sometimes came to visit,
"saying 'Ibi,' doing well." Some people had treated her "well" in her life,
she said, while others had treated her "with contempt." "Go well, stay
well" was her advice to young Yolmo women anticipating marriage,

while "Live well, eat well" was a blessing she bestowed on her children, who, she felt assured, had "done well" in their lives.

Those that did not measure up so well received harsher judgments from her, through words direct or roundabout:

Because of his own actions, he died. Not by the disease.

The man who gave it was also bad.

Our own people had arranged this way, it seems.

If you let me go, let me go in a good way.

The mother of children, they treated with contempt.

It's the shameful thing, she acted jealously toward me.

He did a madman's work. . . . Good did not come of it.

My son didn't take responsibility for me then.

Phrasings like these depicted at once the degree of skill and ethics invested in specific actions. Most acts done well were understood to have beneficial or at least unhurtful effects on others, while acts done poorly could harm the lives and reputations of others. To say that she "stayed well" in marriage, for instance, was to say that she lived in her husband's house in a respectful, well-mannered, skillfully virtuous way that did not bring shame to her elders.

She herself was a woman of skilled means, her words conveyed. She said that she was morally "straight," that she thought only in a "straight manner," having no knowledge of "the roundabout, haphazard ways." She also spoke proudly of her many talents in life.[5] She said she was "greatly talented" as a child—"Before, I could dance, sing, everything"—and she recalled the praise she received when, soon after she had arrived in Shomkharka, she introduced a new technique for the use of feed and manure in the care of water buffaloes:

I brought the skills [ḍhaṅga] from Sermathang. Before then, they weren't doing things skillfully. . . . I did everything. I collected the leaves, and cleaned the shed. I was the Yolmo girl [the girl from the Yolmo Valley], so everyone saw what I did. They regarded my work as an example. . . . When I did these things, everyone said, "We need to do it this way. The Yolmo girl came here, and she set up a system. The Yolmo girl showed us all these things. What she did, we need to do." . . . So everyone said, "You came here, and you did everything like this." They still say that, these days.

She also took pride in her ability to work well. "I was very strong, for sure! A-ma-ma!" she said when asked about this.

Even though my body is like this. I've woven a lot. I've knitted as well. Scarves I've knitted, gloves I've knitted, caps I've knitted! It ended when I came to Kathmandu [fifteen years before]. I've made all different kinds of caps. Eh, who can say anything about my skill?

Who could disparage her skill in knitting? Once again, critical evaluations of a person's skillfulness were swiftly anticipated.

Much the same held for acts of speaking. In relating aspects of her life, Kisang sometimes remarked on how well or how poorly people spoke: "My father spoke well." "Like this they were joking well." "'Don't say whatever you feel like saying. You shouldn't talk like this.'" The presence of such comments made sense, given her acuity for all things vocal and given that Yolmo ideas of skillfulness apply as much to acts of speaking as they do to other actions. How a person talks, which is to say how *well* a person talks, is something that people, including the speaker herself, commonly take note of. We can speak of an ideologically charged and less than unified "aesthetics of speaking" among Yolmo wa, for many abide by and often assert certain values and sensibilities when it comes to how a person should communicate with others. Most generally, people talk about the need to use a soft rather than hard or rough voice. They talk about the need to speak with respect and politeness, without being too arrogant or obstinate, and in ways that sustain sentiments of comradery and goodwill. They also stress the importance of avoiding abusive gossip that "goes against others." Among other things, these understandings imply that people often talk about how others talk— and, in turn, about how some talk about the talk of others.[6]

Different social contexts and relations call for different interactive styles, of course, and a person can talk to a child or joke with a friend in tones that would be highly inappropriate when conversing with a respected elder. Given the many considerations of status in Yolmo communities, to be a competent speaker one must know how, and when, to speak respectfully to others. Since such communicative know-how indicates in part how skillful a person is in her engagements with others, what a person says and how one speaks in general can say a lot about that person's self or character or moral worth. It is therefore important to speak well, for others might later comment on a person's manner of speech and so portray him or her in a certain light. A person can develop a reputation as being someone who "talks well" or "knows how to talk" in the sense that he or she can relate a story well, command an audience, or explain matters in coherent and understandable terms. Others, in contrast, are said to talk in confused or "zigzagging" ways. Some are said to be prudent and clever in verbal engagements with others, while others are disposed toward talking foolishly or ignorantly. Some men are known as effective rhetoricians, able to persuade or "sweet-talk" others, while some are reputed to talk in ways that are overly harsh or direct. Some women are thought to be good hostesses, able to make others feel comfortable when visiting, while others are derided for their lack of skill in this regard.

There is a gendered edge to different kinds of skillful talk, but it does not take a narrowly oppressive form. People understand that women and men can talk knowledgeably about the domains of life in which they have expertise. Men are often said to know about and know how to talk about "outside" business dealings. Women are thought to know how to talk well about "inside" household duties, but not necessarily about what men know well. "Ah, she doesn't know how to talk. If they had asked me, I would have spoken well," boasted a Yolmo man while observing a videotape I recorded of a Yolmo festival in Kathmandu. Watching a segment of the tape that documented the audience's engagement with a television crew that had arrived to film a segment for a weekly program on different folk-song traditions in Nepal, he was commenting on a Yolmo woman's responses to the questions of a mike-wielding interviewer, whose steady advance into the crowd moments before had led several other women to flee their seats in efforts to avoid having to talk on camera.

Another man expressed a similar attitude when I was talking to him and his wife about the layout of Shomkharka, the village to which Kisang first moved in marriage. After the husband gave a long and somewhat irrelevant explanation about the possible meanings of the name "Shomkharka," his wife, who grew up there, told him to "say it briefly." Upon hearing this, the man turned to her and said, "Just keep quiet. You don't know anything. I know about it, I'll explain it." The woman kept silent while maintaining a slight smile. A minute or two later, the wife tried to speak again. When her husband continued to talk, she pointed out that, since he had never been to Shomkharka, she was perhaps more qualified to explain what it was like to live there. "Just keep quiet," he quickly answered. "You don't understand. You have to think first, then speak."

The perspectives on gender invested in comments such as these, which women learn from an early age and sometimes promote themselves, that men know how to think and talk about such matters while women usually fall short in such skills, help to explain why some Yolmo women said that they did not know "how to talk" when I asked them to tell me something of their life stories. More often than not, they held that the language game of talking abstractly and autobiographically about their lives, either within the presence of a tape recorder or not, was quite foreign to them, and this put them at a loss as to how to proceed when questions were posed to them. Once, while Nogapu and I were talking with Ghang Lama, his wife Rhidu Pema came and sat by his side, as she sometimes did when her husband spoke with us. At one point I gestured toward her and asked her what she thought about something. "Ah! No, no. I'm not saying [anything]," she quickly answered. "I don't know how to talk [in this way]."

"She doesn't know how to talk [in this way]," Mheme added.

Even when some women did agree to talk with me, they often laced their talk with self-deprecating asides: "I can't talk." "I can't talk well." "My talk is not good." "I don't know how to talk [in this way]," Phur Gyalmu announced at various times during our taped conversations. "I don't know how to talk," she repeatedly averred, though I wonder still if, given the expectations imposed upon her, this woman's put-downs amounted to skilled talk after all. Another woman, in contrast, asked that I erase the tape recording of an hour-long conversation with her after her niece criticized her manner of speaking. "She talks," said this niece, "as though she's speaking to a deaf person [she talks very loudly and bluntly]. . . . She used to talk quite well, but now that she's gotten old, she doesn't speak so clearly or eloquently." That evening the woman sat quietly and watched as I deleted her words. It was perhaps with similar concerns that Gom Dolma spoke when she came to the end of her taped narration of her life story. "My dear grandchildren, listen to this well, even if I die," she said in closing. "This is all. May all my children and grandchildren lead good and prosperous lives. I don't know how to speak well. Please don't make fun of my words."

When Kisang spoke with Pramod and me about her life, her words hinted at similar discomforts. Her distress appeared to relate in particular to the idea that she spoke better when she was younger. "When one becomes old, everything is forgotten, it's found," she once said in our presence. She then added, "Oh, if I were [still] a middle-aged woman,

Figure 11. Phur Gyalmu, *center*, with her sister and grandson, 1998. Photograph by Robert Desjarlais.

maybe I could have said well." I also think that her comments involved more than feigned or sincere humility, the sort of self-deprecation common to many verbal performances throughout the world, for at other times she spoke proudly of her abilities in other domains of life. Indeed, the pride with which she spoke of these prior but now all-but-lost abilities worked to underscore, for me at least, her worries about speaking poorly when talking with us.[7]

She spoke, for instance, of a failing memory and "rotting words" spoken by a "woman who has no smarts." When asked about something once, she said, "What can be said? From a woman who has no smarts. It's rotting, dying. What is there to say? There's nothing left to say, now. What to do? Now, what to do? In my sem, it has rotted. From here nothing comes."

Other exchanges brought similar voicings:

If I could speak nicely, I would tell a lot of things. Everything from here [my head] has gone.

I cannot say my words in an organized way. It needs to be organized....I cannot say everything like before. There's no memory. It's incomplete, haphazard.

What to say? I don't know how to say anything. I've become without intelligence, now. I can't say anything. If I could say it well...There's nothing, now. Now, leave it. [laughs a bit] I don't know how. I've become without any intelligence. It went through my insides. All the smarts have left from my head, for sure. I can only catch the loose, unformed words. I can't remember the useful words.

When we asked what she thought about the fact that I would be "making" a book about her, she replied, "What do I think? I couldn't compile my talk well. It's all scattered. It's scattered. I didn't keep it well. If I could say it well organized, it would be nice."

"If the book comes out good, can we show it to other people?" we then asked.

"If it's good, then you can. If the words are not good, then what to do? Pointless. It doesn't come good. I can't say it in an organized way. It's scattered."

"What would you like to tell to the people in America? What words do you have for them?"

"The American people haven't come here [so what can I tell them?]. I can't speak well. I don't know anything."

When I later said that I found her talk to be "good," she answered, "Oh, then, [my talk is] unorganized, incomplete. I don't know how to talk. If I had the past stories inside [my sem], then I could talk smoothly."

Several themes recurred in her self-critiques. In her old age her words were scattered, mixed up, bent, haphazard, unuseful. These qualities corresponded to other aspects of her demise. Her dreams were scrambled or mixed up, her memories were vague and unclear, and her thoughts had dispersed and decayed. In dying, different formations of her being were becoming increasingly fragmented, unformed, unsmooth. "The compounded decays," Buddhist texts observe, be it compounded houses, texts, or persons.

Her words also seldom came "straight" then. Yolmo wa tend to value straightness in their lives and speech. They also tend to associate that quality more with the thoughts and actions of men. A longstanding Yolmo symbol of maleness is an arrow. Spindles, in contrast, represent femaleness. While I have never heard anyone speak at length about the reasons for these two symbols, they do tend to conform to the kinds of

activities traditionally associated with men and women: worldly pursuits
and household duties. They also convey ideas, respectively, of linear advances and generative weavings, straight lines and complex patterns.
Similar themes are evident in a range of gendered activities. Whereas
young men can be likened to pencils in need of sharpening, folk songs
voiced by men portray women as opaque, involuted, mysterious beings.
Whereas men when attending religious festivals seat themselves in
"rows" (dhal) of hierarchical status, lining up like so many words on a
page, women cluster together in loosely formed groups. Men usually
trace their heritages through patrilineal descent; the identities of women
are borne of both blood affiliations and marriage alliances.[8] Men's work
is also "one-sided" or "single-minded" (N., *ekohoro*), Yolmo women often say in comparing the straightforward business affairs of men with
their own multifaceted, more diffuse labors.

These sorts of imaginings swirled around Kisang's words. While she
said she was morally "straight" in life and thought only in straight, un-
roundabout ways, her words of late seemed to distort these lines of
thought, for they often zigzagged through a story, or looped back to
earlier statements of hers, or featured uncommon poetic allusions,
while in the presence of two men, no less. It would be simplifying
things too much to say that she was unsuccessfully trying to live up to a
male ideal. But the "curved talk" did worry her.

Her language intimated a disjointed self. When Pramod suggested
on his own that "important people" might want to visit her once they
read her life story, she responded with these words:

I can't talk well, then. I don't know how to talk. The talk appears to be rotten inside [my body]. So: ragged woman [*ole: phimi bindu*]. Don't invite such people.

"So: phimi bindu." While the word *phimi* was used to mean "woman"
here, the Yolmo adjective *bindu* implies something old, broken down, a
remainder of sorts no longer used as it was once. The phrase suggests that
she considered herself a discarded or ragged woman whose former
significance had since expired. "I'm the ragged woman, just wearing the
hat," she said when asked if I could take a photograph of her, and she
donned a new hat in preparation.

She was just the ragged woman then, just wearing the hat, much as
she "just played in the dust" when a child. An arch of significance
spanned the actions of her life, with insubstantial just-dust acts gracing
her childhood, followed by a whorl of consequential deeds and voicings

in her adult life, but then more "justness" in her later years, when she "just stayed still." Buddhist texts often speak of the emergence, presence, and dissolution of phenomena in the world as consisting of sequential acts of "arising," "abiding," then "ceasing." Kisang's life evinced a similar curve. At times she described herself as someone who was jāba, using a Nepali word often applied to someone considered worthless or insignificant, such as a child or an impoverished person lacking social importance. "If someone just knows about talk, he's jāba [a worthless trifle]," Ghang Lama once told Norbu and me. "How would a person like me know? I'm jāba," Kisang once said in response to a question posed to her. The adjective, comparative in nature, implies that others were more significant than she. The perceived worthlessness tied into her inability to act as she once could and so pointed to the way in which, while being transferred from house to house, her use-value as a wife, mother, or laborer diminished as her physical skills waned.

Then along came a man who, finding value in her words, asked if he could record them on tape, then put them in a book that others might read. Kisang agreed to this request. From the start, however, she knew better than I did that any Yolmo wa who heard her words would be inclined to judge their degree of skillfulness and so to evaluate the person who uttered them. A lot was at stake here, of a combined ethical-aesthetic nature, for both the woman who related aspects of her life and the anthropologist who recorded her words. How would a woman's last days be portrayed and perceived by others? How would her words, and person, be modeled on paper?

Asking herself questions of this sort, Kisang was quite conscious of the fact that the tape recorder was picking up her words. "They've recorded everything, even though I don't know how to talk." And while it is likely that the attentive presence of two young men made her think twice about the quality of her speech, she knew well that a much larger audience might also hear or read her words, once they were put on display either in Nepal or in the "foreign land" where I was taking them. "You're taking an old woman like me to show to other people? I don't know how to talk."

Others did in fact talk about her way of talking, both critically and in praise of her words, and while I cite such comments here I do so hesitantly, not to engage in any back-talk but to show how well-founded her concerns were. "It's difficult to understand," Pramod's mother told us when we once asked her to help us decipher Kisang's words as recorded

on a tape cassette. "She can't speak well. She's old, and has no teeth."
Pramod himself said on different occasions while listening to the tapes
that her talk was "noisy, not together," that it was "not very connected":
"She says whatever she wants to say." "But she's saying the zigzag." Another young man who helped me to listen to some of her talk said that
her words were difficult to translate or even understand at all, because
she was not being "systematic" or "straight" in her narrations: "First she
mentions her brother, then she talks about her father, then she goes
back to her brother's work as an artist!" When I later played sections of
a tape recording of a conversation with Ghang Lama, the man said he
could understand Mheme's talk better because it was "straighter."

Those less focused on the tasks of translation and so evidently less
concerned with any narrative flow found her recollections to be
poignant and lucid. "She has said well," one elderly man observed after
hearing several of Kisang's stories. "All the details she has disclosed, the
sad and happy moments of her life. Even though she is of such an old
age, she has a very good memory. In any event, she has related well all
the facts of her life." Another man said, after hearing a section of a tape,
"She spoke well." Moments later, he said, "When you're finished with
this, please give it to me, so I can listen to it. I like to hear the talk of the
old people." Kisang's son Kānchā, in turn, listened intently to an hour's
worth of tape in his mother's absence while commenting on the many
happenings related. "How nice this talk is!" he said at one point, exchanging glances with me. "A-ma-ma-ma! Absolutely *realist. In detail*.
She has a very good memory. Lucid.... Other people cannot remember
like that. But she has remembered everything that people said."[9] His
wife, Neela, added, "She's quite clever. She has spoken very well. She
hasn't made up any stories. It's all straight [direct and honest]." Another
woman, after she and her husband had heard a story or two, said, "She
hasn't twisted the stories [distorted the truth]. Her husband added a
moment later, "She can speak very clearly. She has reached ninety years,
and she can speak clearly." He then pointed to his wife, seated on the
floor beside him, and said, "She, however, she can't even speak clearly."
Karma said, when queried after helping me to fine-tune translations of
her talk, "As I said, I think she's a good talker. A good talker. And the
style in which she talks is, like you said, sometimes the poetic way, with
a lot of metaphors. Few people talk that way."

Kisang knew that others would talk like this, either praising or finding fault with her ways of talking. And since she knew that I would be
shaping how her words appear in print, she took pains to instruct me

on several occasions, usually at the end of a day's conversation, when we spoke of the larger aims of our conversations together, to put her words in "well" in any writings I might compose. Stating that her words needed "to be organized," she asked me to "put the very good things in" and to "put the very good talk [in], while saying 'It's an old person's talk.' If it's not good, then don't show [my words to other people]. If it's good, please show them." She also advised me on what should be included and excluded in any account of her life:

Put the very good [words in]. Don't put the bad, eh? In the book. People will shame me. Now, now, it's a ninety-year-old's, the talk of a ninety-two-year-old woman. It's rotten talk, now.

Don't put the bad things in the book. Put one or two very good things, then release it.

So, the Yolmo language doesn't come well. Just the curved talk. Make the corrections. I've forgotten. . . . Here my talk is crooked. The words don't come. I ate them with rice [I forgot them].

Her words, once they were circulated in writing, could deem her a figure of decay and fragmentation. People might mock or shame her. A technology of writing was at work here, one that she was unaccustomed to, perhaps even suspicious of. While my transcriptions and assessments presented new forms of writing to her, they did bear affinities with a few scripts known to her, such as the fate impressed on her forehead, the divorce papers signed by her husband, or an artist's "writing" of religious images on the interior walls of gompa. As was the case with the last two genres of writing, her life story was being authored by a man, with the aid of other men. As with all three, it would shape her life and "name" in important ways. A script penned by men would again delineate the contours of her life.

Put in the very good. Make any necessary corrections. Rethread loose strands. This was the aesthetic and moral charge put to me. It was not just a question, in other words, of creating an accurate portrait of Kisang's life and death or of analyzing the content or pragmatic gist of our conversations alone. I also had to keep in mind, during the act of writing itself, her concerns about the fragility of her talk and the substance of her social identity, both before and after her death. Since they do not really teach such things in graduate school, and few anthropologists write about them, I have found it necessary to figure out on my own, with some uncertainty, the best way to proceed here. In the months after leaving Nepal

I tried to follow the spirit of Kisang's instructions without infringing on the accuracy of what took place between us. In so doing, I feel I have been able to heed some of her pleas, in part because the textures of thick description help to fill out any possible gaps in her accounts. And since others have also found her words to be quite good, I have not felt compelled to alter either the syntax or the rhythms of her sentences much. In fact, many of the displacements and socially entangled doings of her "mishmash" life seem to call for the kinds of intertwisted story lines that her words stitched together, while her comments on her own "topsy-turvy" speech consisted of a smartly creative poetry of self-disparagement. Finding the right balance between caring portraiture and sober analysis has proved more difficult. I cannot say for sure that Kisang would have been fully pleased with my representations of her. And while one option would be to keep her words locked within a file cabinet and not write about her at all, I do not think that she would have asked for or expected this herself. I have therefore attempted to write about her in ways that attend at once to the substance of our talks together and to the forces that shaped how she herself regarded those exchanges. Others might have gone about it differently.

There is no easy solution to any of this, no set guidelines that show the best way to proceed. What is clear, however, is that, whatever words are fashioned, the skill I convey in fashioning those words will also be evaluated by Yolmo readers, in part because those words have the potential to affect others. Any efforts at writing here, as well as all acts of reading, are ensnared within the complex weave of consequential action that Kisang so often spoke of. In trying to present her words well, I need to act in ethically skillful ways. Like others, I am not immune from either the critical regard or the responsibilities infixed by Yolmo voicings. Several names are on the line. Words, spoken or written, have their effects.

Echoes of a Life

"Shyi mandi mareko hoina. Sareko ho." I heard these words as I drove south along Interstate 84, gliding past Worcester and Hartford and a world of unknown places as the magnetic trace of a voice recorded months before sounded through an unreliable tape deck sitting on the seat beside me. Time and again I listened to the voice and tried to soak up the sounds and grammar of the sentences heard. I wondered about the welfare of the speaker, hoping that the old man was alive and well and talking still.

"Shyi mandi mareko hoina" (Dying does not mean dying). The voice belonged, if a voice can ever belong to its speaker, especially once it is recorded and resounded electronically, to Ghang Lama. The first two words of the quoted utterance, *shyi mandi,* were in the Yolmo language, followed, after a very brief pause, with the remaining two words, *mareko hoina,* in Nepali, as though the inequation noted by the statement, dying does not mean dying, prompted or necessitated a transfer from one language to another.

"Sareko ho" ([Dying] means moving). The words were spoken in the spring of 1998, in the course of an afternoon's conversation with Nogapu and me. At that time, Mheme, I believe, was trying to think of death, his death in particular, in terms that did not involve the complete loss of the "I" known to him or the end of life in a world of familiarity and loved ones from which he did not wish to part. To die, he was proposing, did not entail a complete annihilation but rather meant a re-becoming, a "transfer" or a "shift" into a new life. "When a man dies," he went on to say, "his soul goes inside another person [into the womb of

Figure 12. Ghang Lama, 1998. Photograph by
Robert Desjarlais.

his next mother]. Then later he needs to call those people Father and
Mother."

Dying does not quite mean dying. Fair enough. But does the same
principle hold for a society and culture that have changed substantially
in the past two decades? As noted earlier, this was a question on the
minds of many Yolmo wa living in Kathmandu in the 1990s, when individuals and families were "dispersing" to parts near and far, children
were learning Nepali rather than Yolmo as their first language, and
some were working to preserve aspects of Yolmo culture before they
were lost for good. Ghang Lama was also concerned about the possible
demise of Yolmo culture. And while neither he nor I put it in so many
words, I believe he found that our work together could substantiate
something of his life and time, especially if we conversed not in Nepali
but in Yolmo, a language that, he felt, embodied so much of Yolmo culture. "We should not leave the Yolmo language," he once said pointedly
to his grandson Norbu, who, to Mheme's chagrin, knew but a few
words. To later insist, after Norbu had left for the States, that our con-

versations take place in Yolmo was thus to make a political statement about the value of this language and the need to preserve it as well as the cultural heritage encoded within it.

What is "dying," what is "moving," how does a culture shape the makings of a life or the meanings of a death? What does it mean to generate a life story in a place where people often advance the idea that a life is, by nature, impermanent, forever changing, perhaps ultimately illusory, yet also highly consequential? What does it mean to inscribe a life on paper? How do the understandings of the participants in a biographic encounter figure, substantively and morally, in the production of a life history? What are the short- and long-term consequences of the encounter?

So far in these pages on Ghang Lama, we have focused on aspects of his life, his thoughts on death, and the visual components of his life and death. What remains to be considered more fully is what the lama himself understood was going on when I came to talk to him and his words took form on paper—what, in effect, the act of inscribing his life on paper meant for him.[1] In an attempt to address these issues, I would like to detail the various ways in which, as he saw it, a written account of his life might come to "echo" in his life or after his death. By tracing the possible trajectories of a few such echoes, we can, I think, gain some sense of what it meant for him to speak about a life or to incise elements of it onto paper, especially when that paper was understood to be potentially more durable than the life itself. We must therefore continue our inquiry into the properties of speech, writing, duplication, remainders, reminders, and other acts-in-time among Yolmo wa.

Such an inquiry also requires an attempt to understand something of the "pragmatic" import of people's engagements with one another. It requires an attempt, that is, to estimate the potential effects and real-world significance of various utterances and actions—how people do things with words and how words and actions do things on their own. Anthropological inquiries of this sort usually investigate how certain actions, such as a lengthy pause or a laugh or a sigh, build to certain identities or understandings, with conscious intention or not, in the course of a conversation or two in order to understand more precisely how meanings take form through social engagements.[2] Here, the focus is broader and more diffuse, concerned, as it is, with the meanings that emerged, in the span of a year and beyond, with meanings that are emerging still, out of the heteroglossic invocation of a life. And since what I have come to know of this invocation is similarly tied to the emergence of meanings in time, my writing reflects, in some ways, my shifting awareness of what is at stake, and what my responsibilities might be, in the writing of that life.

As for such meanings, it strikes me that in order to make sense of what my work with Ghang Lama meant for him, one also needs to consider *how* things mean for him and other Yolmo wa. This is to say that anyone who lives outside the folds of Yolmo culture must try to suspend her own notions about how signs signify and explore something of the semiotic sensibilities of these people and how those sensibilities contributed to the ways in which the lama thought of his life and the textual inscription of that life. To do this effectively, one needs to attend to how he, along with other Yolmo wa, thought of the interrelated workings of such matters as language, time, bodiliness, personhood, life, and death and what it meant for an aged man to tell something of his life at a time when he thought that life to be ending.

One rainy afternoon in the spring of 1998, Mheme used a word whose multiple, intershading connotations have greatly influenced how I have come to think about his life and the meanings he and I have invested in his life story. That word is *bhaja*. In trying to elicit the lama's thoughts on good ways to die, Nogapu and I had asked if it is better that family members keep quiet in the presence of a dying person, which is something I heard other Yolmo wa speak of. "It's good, for sure," Mheme said in response, then continued.

If no noises are made, it's good. If it's quiet, we can die well. . . . If it's quiet, we can get the way easily. If the noisy sounds come, then the dead person becomes confused. He gets confused, the poor man [*nyingjwa*]. If he dies and is lost, what can we do?

He then went on to describe what happens to a dead person during the bardo between one life and the next, and he ended by detailing what the soul encounters when it tries to leave the deceased's body: namely, amplified features of that person's body as perceived by the itinerant soul as it journeys through the body.

We need not go somewhere else, far away. After we die, if we have long hair, we can see lice and a bear and tiger. The hair appears like a jungle. We can see a bear and a big tiger. The forehead appears like a plain, and the nose appears like a big hill. When they say the soul goes out, it's our own body that frightens us. Our shadow [*dhipsa*] frightens us. Whatever we do, our shadows do the same thing.

That's called an echo [*bhaja*]. When we make a loud sound, an echo is heard. If we say "wey!" it also says "wey!" That's called *bhaja*. "Good echo" [*bhaja zangbu*] is said: If we've done good, good comes. If we've done bad, bad comes.

After a pause, he continued.

Bhaja is like imagining. If we think good thoughts, then, after we die, they echo in what we see. If we make a loud noise, a bad echo [bhaja] comes. [In the same way], if we pray "om mani-padme hūm," a good echo comes. If people are crying and fighting and making a lot of noise, then it's no good. If one dies when it's very quiet, it's good. Noises are no good.

A cluster of subtly overlapping meanings and examples infused Mheme's uses of the Yolmo word *bhaja*. Mheme first used the word in speaking of echoes. *Bhaja* in this sense means very much what *echo* does in English: the repetition or reverberation of a sound. Its nineteenth-century Tibetan equivalent, *brag-cha*, which also translates as "echo," appears to have literally meant "rock noise" or "rock clamor."[3] As Mheme observes, "When we make a loud sound, then the echo is heard." But for Mheme and other Yolmo wa, visual echoes can just as readily occur; as the soul tries to journey beyond its corporeal abode, features of the deceased's body (hair, forehead, nose) appear as elements of a landscape (jungle, plain, hill). A mimetic principle is at work here, for bhaja, be they acoustic or visual in nature, simulate the phenomena they resound or revision. From this perspective, a person's shadow can be seen as a bhaja, or visual echo, of that person, and a person's thoughts while alive or the cries of grief-stricken family members can resonate in the liminal, phantasmagoric world encountered in the hours after a death. As Mheme put it, "Bhaja is like imagining. If we think good thoughts, then, after we die, they echo in what we see. If we make a loud noise, a bad echo comes." For this reason, bereaved family members should not mourn a loss too vocally, since their cries will be heard as noises by the deceased, with the din of any noises sounding in direct proportion to the intensity of the cries: "How many tear drops, that much rain comes. The sound of crying brings thunder," Mheme explained.

Yolmo wa understand an echo to be something immaterial and unreal. One hears the echo as though one is hearing the actual sound but usually while knowing well that it's not the actual sound. Since the repeated sound is secondary to the original, it is commonly taken to be an illusory, insubstantial trace of the original. Such an absent presence involves the paradox of "there being nothing and yet there being a presence," as the fourteenth-century Tibetan sage Longchenpa put it in likening the sansāric "world of fictions" to an echo.[4]

Mheme sometimes spoke in similar ways. "That's only the sem imag-ining," he once said of phenomena encountered by a deceased person soon after dying. "There's not really a body. It's only an illusion [bhaja], for sure." He might have had the same idea in mind when he observed that "bhaja is like imagining," for, as a good Buddhist, he would at times understand, and encourage his interlocutors to understand, that much of life, including a person's body and self-perceptions, are illusory appari-tions. Echoes, then, are on a par with other illusory phenomena, such as mirages and hallucinations, in that, despite their differences, they all in-volve perceptual phenomena that are understood to be not materially real. As Kisang's son Kānchā put it one day when explaining to me the il-lusory nature of bhaja, "We say from our Tibetan books, '*bhaja tabu, gyuma tabu, migyug tabu*' [like an echo, like an illusion, like a mirage]." The Bardo Thedol relies on similar thinking in advising its listeners to recognize all phenomena of waking life as being "like a dream, a magical illusion, an echo, a fairy city, a mirage, a reflection, an optical illusion, the moon in water, lacking even a moment's truth-status, definitely untrue, and false."[5] For Yolmo wa, bhaja can be understood as an "as though" phenomenon: as an apparition that merely appears to be real.[6]

Yolmo lamas advise, as their Tibetan counterparts do, that the images a person perceives in the hours and days after his or her death are best understood as apparitions of this sort. One passage of the Bardo The-dol, for instance, encourages any recipients of the text's instructions to develop and affirm an understanding that all sights and sounds per-ceived during the death between are one's own:

> May I know all sound as my own sounds!
> May I know all lights as my own lights!
> May I know all rays as my own rays!
> May I know the between's reality as mine![7]

Elsewhere the text advises its readers to recognize that all visions en-countered in the death between are "but empty images," the product of one's "own creations," with one's body itself "born by apparition."[8] Ghang Lama understood that the sights and sounds perceived by a dead person in the bardo are like such empty images. For him and other Yolmo wa, such selfsame manifestations are a bhaja in that they entail mimetic apparitions of a person's actions, thoughts, and karmic her-itage: "Whatever we do, our shadows do the same thing." Both of the key features of Yolmo bhaja, reverberation and illusion, thus pattern what a recently deceased person perceives.

All this helps to explain that, while *bhaja* literally means "echo," Yolmo wa take the word in its broadest sense to mean "illusion." But it is always an illusion of a distinct kind. *Gyuma* is the Yolmo word for an optical illusion in general, in which something that appears to be real is, when it comes down to it, not actually real. Bhaja, in contrast, is best thought of as an "echoic illusion" of some sort, for a bhaja resounds or re-visions, in an immaterial form, something else, most often something that was once present but is no longer in existence. Mheme himself offered several examples of bhaja that fit this criterion. "When someone has been singing at a festival," he told me, "and then goes home to sleep at night, but then still hears the songs while he is drifting off to sleep, we say this is a bhaja." Likewise, when a person eats a fine-tasting meal, the gustatory after-presence of that meal, which can linger on that person's mind and taste buds for hours on end, is a "good bhaja" of the foods eaten. The same goes for a meal that tastes poor, although here the after-taste is a "bad bhaja" of the foods eaten. Dream images as well are understood to be the bhaja of thoughts and actions undertaken while awake.

In each of these situations, features of something once present later appear in more immaterial, ghostly forms. Like an echo, they repeat, in apparitional but still quite significant terms, elements of an earlier phenomenon.[9] Such echoic acts resembled the many other doubles and copies evident in the lama's life. It is important to note, however, that a strong temporal dimension inheres in the concept of bhaja. Certain acts or images repeat or are repeated in turn. As far as the concept of bhaja goes, then, it involves not simply copies or simulations, as many modern Western discussions of mimesis suggest, but repetitions and re-presentations in time.[10] With such repetitions, changes occur. A bhaja is like its original but not quite. In its most basic configuration, a logic of bhaja implies a logic of change, loss, and death in that one sound or form replaces another in time, with the earlier ones dissolving. To repeat is to occasion a death in some way. An echo can therefore signify a loss; it can indicate the absence of something once present, something that can be represented only through a reverberation of some sort.

Yet the presence of such reverberations points to the implication of a logic of traces, of lingering consequences, in the concept of bhaja, for something of an original sound or phenomenon can carry on in subsequent reverberations. An element of mimesis still applies with any bhaja, for the secondary phenomenon simulates, in some respect, an initial phenomenon or action. A bhaja contains traces of its predecessor. To repeat is to continue living in some way. Dying does not quite mean dying.

As it is, the word *bhaja* among Yolmo wa can also imply a remainder of some sort, particularly of something that no longer exists. While the residuum left in an empty teacup, for instance, is literally a shul, or trace, it can also be thought of as a bhaja, or a less-than-material remainder of the tea that once filled that cup. A ghostly presence, in turn, can be thought to entail a bhaja of the person that once inhabited a household. Usually the presence makes itself known through strange occurrences, such as undetermined sounds within a household. Compared with the other kind of ghostly appearances that can result after a death, such a bhaja is a harmless presence. "A bhaja doesn't hurt people," Ghaki Lamani explained when asked about this. But since the presence is nevertheless unnerving and unwanted, a good death is one in which a dead person makes a clean break from the world of the living and does not leave a strong "echo" behind. Yolmo wa do indeed worry that a family member might leave such an unwelcome remainder in his or her wake. When speaking to the spirits of the deceased at funerals, bereaved family members will often tell them not to "leave a bhaja behind." In voicing such concerns, they have in mind the possibility that the deceased might remain attached to his or her former life circumstances and in effect "cling" to cherished loved ones or possessions. Apparitions of the deceased are fitting exemplars of bhaja: they occur after the fact, as ghostly traces of beings once alive, as illusory afterimages of former presences, like the original, but not quite.

Invested in Mheme's understanding of the physics of bhaja, then, were two complementary, characteristically Buddhist messages: the understanding that all material forms are impermanent, that nothing lasts forever, that life is transient, shifting from form to form; and the understanding that traces remain, residues linger, rebirths occur, and actions have consequences long after the actions themselves are completed. Life is impermanent and, some say, ultimately illusory, yet the actions a person undertakes in life can effect powerful reverberations. Milarepa sang of similar notions in a song of his:

> All that which manifests
> Is unreal as an echo,
> Yet it never fails to produce
> An effect that corresponds.
> Karmas and virtues therefore
> Should never be neglected.[11]

Manifestations of a life, unreal as echoes, produce further, corresponding echoes.

The principles of karmic action play an important role in all this. But they do so in rather echoic ways. Actions produce "effects that correspond." As the workings of the mirror of deeds make clear, the consequences immanent in certain actions often entail a kind of temporal mimesis, of "results" echoing in time, for many deeds entail *corresponding* effects later on, what one Tibetan Buddhist text revered by Yolmo lamas identifies as "effects similar to the cause": "Sometimes babies die at birth as an effect similar to the cause of having killed in a past life....To have stolen will make us not only poor, but also liable to suffer pillage, robbery or other calamities...."[12] As Mheme once said of people fated to die at the hands of others, "Before, they did this to others [murdered them], then later the same thing comes to them." The force of karma often involves a mimetic economy of meaning and action. Punishments fit the crimes.

Something of Mheme's understanding of the consequential force of human actions can be heard in his statement, cited above: "'Good bhaja' is said: If we've done good, good comes. If we've done bad, bad comes." That is, if people act in morally good ways, good will result, whereas if they harm others, misfortune will plague them sooner or later.[13] Most often Yolmo wa speak of such causal linkages in terms of the temporal relation between a person's present and next life; if one acts in good ways in this life and steers clear of troublesome situations, then those actions will effect a good bhaja, and one will be reborn into a good life, free of trouble.

Ghang Lama spoke in similar ways. Much of his talk with us seemed to be concerned with what had happened while he was alive and, by implication, what might happen when he dies—how, in effect, his life might echo in his death. Such musings, along with the way in which he went about his life, led me to conclude that his world was very much shadowed by an anticipatory consciousness; his thoughts and actions were geared toward anticipating and preparing for the future, his death in particular. "This is work for later, not for now. This is work for the time of dying," he said in 1998 of the religious texts he was reading daily to augment his spiritual merit and so increase the chances of a good fate after dying: "One reads as much as one can. If one reads more, one reaches heaven." And yet despite all his preparations, all his spiritual practices, and all his efforts to develop a spiritually pure heart, he still feared what might happen. "Dying means something very bad," he said on another occasion.

We might not get this life the next time. That's why we should think, "Don't commit sins," and that's why we should have a pure, bodhicitta heart [*jang chub sem ba*]. If one thinks about [having] a pure sem all the time, it [that thought] will take him to the Buddha after he dies. "He's the bodhisattva" [the gods will say].[14]

In our conversations, Mheme's words often quietly designated him as a spiritual teacher. I think such a role made a lot of sense to him while talking with us, given that many Yolmo wa knew him foremost as a lama, as "one who knows," and given that one of the main forms of biographical representation known to him was the nam-thar, or "full liberation [stories]," of Tibetan Buddhist lore, in which the spiritual development and fruition of a spiritually great person's life is portrayed in writing with the intent that the portrait will serve as a supreme example for others also seeking liberation.[15] While Mheme never said that his imminent life story would in fact be like a nam-thar, I do believe he sincerely wanted to teach us and others something, and much of what he conveyed to us, about his life or life in general, could indeed be heard as a primer on meritorious ways to live, with his words and deeds serving as both model of and model for a good life in modern, spiritually flawed times. So it was with the words quoted above, voiced when Mheme was detailing certain principles of death and rebirth to Nogapu and me: one should maintain a pure "bodhicitta heart" and avoid thoughts of wrongdoing. Yet what the lama's next life might entail, where and in what sentient form he might be reborn, remained a troublesome unknown.

Ghostly echo, illusion, reverberation and manifestation, remainder, reminder, afterimage: *bhaja* carries these many connotations. Any life story told by Mheme or written about him, I slowly came to understand, would effect a similar whirl of echoes. Put most simply if not most subtly, an account of his life, as rendered into print, could effect a bhaja of that life as many Yolmo wa might understand that term: a secondary, illusory echo of something that existed prior to that echo. Much as an acoustic echo repeats a sound, Mheme's words as presented in these pages resound his words as uttered. When speaking of his life in general, we have echoes upon echoes upon re-echoes: any words I write about Mheme's life repeat, in a greatly translated and edited fashion, his words as heard and recorded on tape, which in turn speak of the actions that made up his life, as remembered. And just as different temporalities coursed through the circumstances of his life, so different kinds of echoes emerged during our work together.

A biography could very well include shadowy remainders of the life it indicates. The idea that, through the making of his life story, some traces of his life would remain after he died was a powerful one for Mheme, and he clearly appreciated the staying power of the "talk" that was being put into print. When Norbu and I were concluding our taped conversations with his grandfather in the summer of 1997, we wanted to make sure that our interlocutor was satisfied with our engagements, especially since he had said earlier that thoughts about the past sometimes troubled him and made sleep difficult.

"Mheme, how have you liked this process?" Norbu asked. "We've asked many personal questions, perhaps this offended you?"

"No," Mheme quickly replied. "I can understand what he's doing."

"Perhaps it's been painful to remember such memories?"

"No, I would say. Now, I won't be staying after I die. But this talk/matter [N., kūra] will be staying after I die. Isn't that a good thing?"

Given his apprehension about the end of his life, Mheme found comfort in the knowledge that his words would be "staying" on after his death. His body, clearly, would not be. As noted earlier, this learned lama spoke often of the belief that when humans die their nam-she, or souls, separate from their corporeal abodes, which are then cremated in a day or two, and these souls must then journey into death without the kind of bodily grounds that they were accustomed to while alive: "There's no body then. Only the soul." Also as noted, such a much-anticipated loss of bodiliness was presaged for Mheme by the gradual erosion of his physique through the latter part of his life: in the past few years his body had, to him, become progressively weaker, smaller, less visible; it had grown "down, down, down"; it took him longer to walk places; he often had to use a cane. With absences eclipsing former presences in several domains of his life, he was becoming a shadow of himself, his body now a faint echo of its former size and strength.

The texts that we were producing, in turn, could shore up the forms of his life and fix something of that life within a durable, visible materiality. While his body would be reduced to ashes in death, it is as though he would in some sense remain present after death, in the subtle form of a text. "As though" is a crucial phrasing here, for in speaking of such matters we are dealing not with the principles of real souls or tantric practices but rather with questions of echoic illusions, of ghostly possibilities and wistful, momentary imaginings—questions, notably, from which anthropologists usually shy away, which means that our conceptual tools for thinking through such imaginings tend to be rather poor ones. I very much doubt that Mheme thought his soul or consciousness would continue in any vital form within a set of pages like these. But there is nevertheless something in the formal logic of Yolmo actions and ways of meaning, of residual traces and itinerant spirits, that suggests that some kind of conversion from body to text was at stake in an imagined, "as though" way.

In reflecting on my potential role in this dreamlike conversion, I read with some seriousness Veena Das's observation on the reconstruction of symbolic bodies during Hindu funeral rites: "It is the task of men to ritually create a body for the dead person and to find a place in the cosmos for the dead."[16] By "men" here she means primarily the sons of the deceased. Since Yolmo funeral rites require a similar set of ritual effigies that work to represent the deceased and embody that person's soul, though the direct role of sons is not so important, I ask myself if in some way I am performing a comparable task in Mheme's case, either as a surrogate (grand)son or not, with his life story becoming a kind of "second body" that will linger after his body vanishes in death, one that could give solace even to those trying to come to terms with the death. Perhaps so. But then I also find that talk of a reconstructed body per se is a bit too overt and specific, that when it comes to Mheme's life story what is really in question is a kind of materiality, a tangible afterimage, a kūra, or matter or talk, wherein visible, durable traces of his life could remain.

Ultimately, I think, it was a question of "transferring" certain traces or qualities of a life from one domain to another. "Dying does not mean dying. It means moving," Mheme told us. Although he was speaking for the most part in Yolmo during this conversation, he used the Nepali word *sareko* here, which, when in the form of an infinitive transitive verb *(sarnu)*, means "to move, to shift, to transfer." Yolmo wa often consider movements from one entity or spatial domain to another as a transfer of this kind, and I have heard people talk, in either Yolmo, or Nepali, or English, of transfers of the dharma from teacher to student, of transfers of property and land between generations, of transfer of money between men, of transfers of family households from one place to another, of transfers of "empowerment" (wang) from a lama to his patrons, and, on one occasion, of transfers of young women to Bombay to work as prostitutes. Such transfers often assume a spatial form, in which something is transferred out of the body, from self to other or to some domain external to the body. When a person is dying, a lama or a group of lamas perform a ritual act of *phowa*, a "transference of consciousness," which works to transport the dying person's soul out of the body and deliver it to a heavenly realm. Bombo, in turn, are said to transfer harm and evil forces from a client's body to an effigy or an animal, which is then sacrificed. Mheme drew from the same word when talking about copies he had made of religious texts. "I wrote, I made transfers," he told Nogapu and me when asked if he had ever written Tibetan texts. To "make transfers" in this way was to copy the letters and meanings found in one sacred text into the new one he was inscribing. Such an act (which is thought to accrue great merit for the copier) implies a direct carryover, in which everything supposedly remains the same and no changes are made in replicating the original.

Given that inscription for Mheme typically entailed the idea of a duplicative "transfer" from one domain into another, it makes sense to consider that, within the imaginative frame of his own metaphysics, our work together implied the possibility that something of his life could be transferred or translated from a corporeal body into a textual one. Somewhat akin to the transference of consciousness that can occur at the moment of death, there was a sense at times of a transfer of Mheme's voice and life from his body to the texts that we were producing. The old man alluded to such a textual reincarnation one day when, in the course of a conversation, he spoke of my taking with me the set of transcripts of our taped conversations when I returned to the United States. "I feel myself," he said to Nogapu in my presence, "that when he takes this and goes there, I'm also going there, even though I haven't reached there." Through his words he would go places. Other travels were also afoot. The textual presence of his life story appeared to involve a set of anticipated transfers, each of which took imaginative form at different, passing moments in our talk and in our thoughts. Along with the passage of his "talk" from Nepal to the States, the texts variably implied, or so it impressed me, transfers from transmitter to scribe, from teacher to student, from a grandfather to a surrogate son or grandson, from high to low and inside to outside, from voice to print, from original to copy, from a life to an afterlife, from past to present and present to future, and from a soon-to-vanish body to a set of words that would "stay." Dying meant moving.

The idea that my work with Yolmo elders might lead to certain bhaja-like reverberations of their lives is one that emerged in my own thoughts while I was conducting fieldwork in 1998. But it is also one that has made sound sense to all Yolmo wa I have spoken with on the matter, Mheme included. When I returned to Kathmandu in 2000, I brought the lama up to speed on the progress that I was making on his life story. Until then I had not broached the idea that the words entailed within his biography could be likened to a bhaja. But since I had just completed an earlier version of this chapter and so had a chance to think about the idea in depth, I thought it a good time to check with him on it. So during a second visit to his home that year, I explained to him and his wife that I was planning to write that the book itself could effect a series of bhaja of the lives written about. Upon hearing these words, Rhidu Pema said something like "Ah!" and Mheme's eyes lit up. "Yes, that's it, for sure," he said immediately. "It's a bhaja. All my bhaja, all my traces, will be in the book. And even though I'll be dead, and my body won't remain anymore, my thoughts and words will remain in a book, and that book will be dispersed to all sorts of different countries, and so my thoughts and words will spread."

Much as the Buddha's words, as Mheme sometimes related, had the good fortune to be "spread" throughout the world because they were written down, and then "remain" there for centuries on end because they have been effectively copied and recopied in print, so traces of Mheme's life would disperse to countries near and far, even after that life had expired.

It was highly significant that Mheme's words were being rendered into print. As we have seen, acts of writing among Yolmo wa regularly carry with them ideas of permanence, truthfulness, and tangible visibility. Politically charged understandings such as these help to explain why the tape recordings of our conversations seemed to interest Mheme less than any writings that would result from those conversations, although he and his family did seem to appreciate a set of cassette copies that I gave him upon leaving Nepal in 1998. Indeed, when Mheme said he was pleased that his talk would "remain in a book" after he died, he clearly had in mind the understanding that his words would be put into print and that this print would, by its very nature, convey both truthfulness and durability. Implicit here was a quiet but fundamental metaphysical play, influenced by Buddhist perspectives and common to many Yolmo lives, of ideas of stasis and movement, presence and absence, truth and illusion, permanence and impermanence.

Many Tibetan texts speak of the difficulty of humans leaving a "trace" behind after they die. Milarepa, for instance, rues the death of his father in these terms:

> Today, my good father, Mila Banner of
> Wisdom, is no more, no trace remains.[17]

The Seventh Dalai Lama's poem "Meditations on the Ways of Impermanence" includes the lines:

> ... A young man, with teeth for the future,

With plans for months and years ahead, died,
Leaving but scant traces. Where is he now?
   Gone!
My mind turns to thoughts of death.[18]

Many biographies of Buddhist sages, in turn, remark that the only thing that remains of the sages after they die is their biographies. While an overt purpose of such biographies is to detail an exemplary religious life in order to illustrate to others how to attain salvation, a message rooted in many is that everything, including the lives and bodies of great religious masters, is ephemeral and impermanent. As one Tibetan lama suggests, "You can then meditate on impermanence by thinking about holy persons such as Buddha and his famous disciples, Shariputra and Modgalyayana. All that is left of them now are stories....All we have of them now are impoverished biographies....Of that famous adept Padmasambhava only his biography remains."[19] And then there is Milarepa, contemplating the loss of his mother:

My mother...
Is nothing but crumbling bones.
This, too, is an example of ephemeral illusion,
An example which summons me to meditation.[20]

Yet an oblique implication of such assessments is that, while the subjects of such biographies are soon reduced to ashes, their words need not perish if transferred into writing. Legible traces can remain. Like the "cult of relics" that followed in the wake of the Buddha's death or the symbolic architecture of stūpas, which are said to represent simultaneously the presence and absence of the Buddha, such texts signify at once themes of continuity and discontinuity, permanence and transience.[21] So it is with Mheme's biography. With his life story, there is the possibility of a (foot)print of sorts, even after he dies: it can entail a lasting remainder, an imprint of his existence, an echo that lasts beyond the materiality and livelihood of his own body or voice.

If printed, the old man's words could also serve at times as evidence for actions he undertook in life—what he did, where he traveled, how he labored. The prospect of evidential truths seemed especially important for Mheme when it came to the hardships and sorrows he and others of his generation had suffered in life, from carrying heavy loads to walking long distances barefoot. Yet since such hardships were of a past time and could not be "seen" or witnessed but only spoken of in the present, their existence would always remain in question, especially when an elder was trying to convey them to a younger generation that did not know about or appreciate the significance of such hard work. One day Mheme told Nogapu and me of the "desperate situation" that he had faced after his first wife died and his sons were away from home. He then nodded his head toward me and said to Nogapu, "Maybe he thinks I was always like this before. Rich, and not working. I wasn't. I was in a desperate situation before. I had to work a lot, with all the animals. A ba ba!" A minute later, he looked at me and said, "Maybe people like you think, 'Now this man is staying like this.' They don't know how much I suffered." To "stay like this" meant that burdensome movement and physical labor were now largely unnecessary, making for a life of leisure that was greatly at odds with, but perhaps the karmic fruits of, the toils of the past.

It's true. His interlocutors did not quite know how much he had suffered, and any hard work that today's children face pales in comparison, he thought, to what people of "his time" undertook. But by telling us of his hardships and by having them converted into print, there could be a trace of them in the present and future. If written down, if rendered visible, the cultural logic went, they could gain an aura of truthfulness. His sufferings could echo visually in writing. He therefore found it important to tell us, among other things, of the hardships of his body and encouraged us to record in writing what he took to be the historical reality of such hardships. "Write that," he instructed his grandson Norbu and me early on during our talks, when he was detailing the exhausting, callus-causing prostrations and contemplative austerities he performed in a month's time when he was twelve in order to "cleanse" any sins he had accumulated and to begin a life of religious practice. "*Chag bum.* That means 'one hundred thousand prostrations,'" he said. He then pointed to the notebook I was holding in my lap and said, "That should be written." Heeding his instructions, I jotted the words down and so registered the significance of his knees' long-lost calluses within a very different brood of marks.

To write about a lama's initiations or other cultural practices serves not simply to substantiate one man's sufferings, however. It also says something about how life in general was lived years before. As such, any writings helped to address another concern of Mheme's: that much of "the old ways" could soon be lost, especially since Yolmo society seems to be changing so quickly and so many Yolmo youths in Kathmandu are unable to speak Yolmo well. "Slowly everything will be forgotten," he told Norbu and me in reflecting on the waning use of the Yolmo language and traditional Yolmo customs. Others thought much the same. Writing about a life, in turn, could serve to counter the erosion of memory through the use of a medium that is known to work well against the possibility of forgetting. One Yolmo man, the president of the Yolmo Foundation, expressed much the same idea upon learning in detail in 1998 about my attempts to record the life stories of several elderly Yolmo wa. "This is very good. This is important," he said. "Because though we might not be able to read English well, our children and grandchildren will be able to, and they'll be able to know about the things that would otherwise be forgotten." An older generation's knowledge and memories could transfer, in writing, to a younger generation.

An intergenerational transmittal seems particularly likely to occur in the case of Mheme and his grandchildren. Norbu and his siblings conveyed to me that, since they had spent much of their childhood in India, they were not particularly close to their grandfather, and since he was, by nature, a "quiet" man, they knew little of the details of his life. They were quietly intrigued by my talks with him, however. While Norbu said he wanted to help me because, in part, he could learn about his grandfather's life, his sisters and brother, admittedly "reserved" themselves, read with interest the transcripts of the conversations I was translating into English when I offered them a chance to take the texts for a few days to read through them. "When you gave us the book before," Tashi later told me, "there were many things we learned in reading it that we didn't know before." She then went on to say that her grandfather could "be remembered from that book you're writing. Our children's grandchildren can read that book and know about him." I suspect that Mheme held the possibility of such oblique communications in mind when talking with me. Others were once again counting on him to carry out an important endeavor.

Prospects of permanence and truthfulness (always tricky at best, any good Buddhist will tell you) thus took imaginative form once we began to transcribe the lama's words. His voice, various recollections of his life and time, and perhaps something of his spirit could be cast into a set of physical inscriptions that would remain beyond the voice itself. At the same time, writing about his life could transfer oral accounts of that life and its opaque sufferings into a medium of "print" that many members of his society would find to be relatively evidential and truthful. While I'm sure that Mheme would admit to the unreal, illusory nature of such echoes, what seemed to win out for him over any such thoughts was the idea that fleeting speech could resound in a more durable record, and a scant trace could remain. "This book will come soon, and people will look at it," he observed toward the end of our conversations in 1998. "What we've been saying will come out in the book.... If we can't read, then other people will read and they will think, 'It was this.'"

Mheme knew well that anyone who might have the occasion and skills to "look" perceptively at his life story would also generate a sense that "he was [like] this," and he clearly sensed that the contents of any account of his life would affect his family's reputation once it was published and people had a chance to read or hear or talk about it. As we have seen, such an awareness is a terrifically important one among many Yolmo wa, for one's *mhin,* or "name," is forever tied up with how one's family acts in life and what people say about those actions. People talk, and that talk can have powerful consequences. Negative talk can lead some to feel ashamed or shy around others and so hesitant to "show their faces" in public arenas. A person can also lose the respect of others, who will then be reluctant to associate with, do business with, or marry into that person's family. It therefore becomes crucial for children to maintain the reputations and good names of their parents and thus to "save" or "hold" their noses. People say that sons need to work well, marry someone from a good family, and "do something with their lives," as Mheme put it once, while daughters need to be known as skillful, hospitable, chaste women. Many try to lead morally good lives and encourage or insist that other family members do so as well, in part to gain the respect of others and avoid any "cutting" talk.

Ghang Lama's family, respected by other Yolmo wa, has so far been free of the scabrous talk that has fallen on a few families. And while he and his family are, like other Yolmo families, forever wary about the possibility of such gossip, the old man appeared confident in what others might say or know about him, and he approached our conversations with a certain degree of comfort and candidness. It struck me that he thought his words and actions (and candidness) would bear out that he was, in fact, a good man, and he tried to convey as much when talking with us. "I say that my sons and I are very good," he asserted on one occasion. The phrase "I say that" (Ngai mai) characterizes well his stance in many of our exchanges, for his words had the effect of "saying," usually indirectly, what he and his sons were like: namely, good people who faced a lot of hardships but who continued to practice dharma and act in morally good ways.

What troubled him more, apparently, was how much prestige or honor he and his family might carry through the years. Ultimately, this was a question of what others might say about him and his family, especially if his sons or grandsons were to act or fail to act in certain ways, as he noted on several occasions:

Now, afterwards, some [of my family] are that way, others are that way [they live in different places]. Now there is a worry about what they are doing, whether they are fighting with others. If something happens, people will say he's so-and-so's son, so-and-so's grandson. With this, won't there be sorrow, won't there be worry?

Now our relatives' children [Norbu and his siblings] don't speak our language. When we talk to them, they talk to us in Nepali. If they go up there [to the Yolmo region], people will say, "These guys are not Yolmo."

Among other things, the old man worried over his grandsons' inability to speak Yolmo well, and so they might not be considered ethnically Yolmo by other Yolmo wa. He was also troubled that his grandsons had little interest in learning to become knowledgeable priests, as he, his sons, and his revered ancestors had done, and so had not "continued the tradition." Such eventualities, and the possible demise of the family's prestige that they implied, could damage Mheme's name, since a grandson's (or son's) dishonor is also a grandfather's (or father's) dishonor. This was one of the scenarios implied when he expressed concern about what members of his family were up to and whether they were "fighting with others," for, if they were, people would surely gossip that they were the sons or grandsons of Ghang Lama. More troubling still, some might assume that Mheme was the distant source of such misdeeds, for Yolmo wa commonly understand that the moral consequences of a person's actions can eventually affect that person's children or grandchildren, such that a son's violent or drunken demeanor, for example, can indicate wrongdoings or spiritual failings on the part of that man's father. I first took note of this idea when I asked Mheme how it is that children often assume the habits of their parents, and I heard in his response something quite different than the "like father, like son" psychology that I knew. "Some children become good," my instructor replied,

some become very bad, some become like murderers, some become like thieves.... If their grandfathers and fathers are doing good dharma, then that will help the children become good. If we don't do good before, then later our grandchildren will be negatively affected [ne kyalgen]. These days we're also saying, if someone is affected, if his head is funny or if he steals, we say, "Oh, his grandfather committed sins, so that's why he's like that."

"Mheme yhinju tso-tsamu thu" (from [male] ancestors to descendants), Yolmo wa sometimes say when speaking of the transfer of karmic goods, moral dispositions, or acquired skills through the generations of a family. Some hold that, in particular, karmic effects transfer most from grandfathers to grandsons. Mheme reckoned that others might assume that any good-for-nothing grandchildren were the karmic product of a grandfather who did little good in his life. He therefore worried over the possibility that the demise of his family might indicate moral flaws on his part.

Faced with these potential legacies, the lama sensed that the life story could effect a good echo and so help to shore up his family's reputation. Nogapu and I once asked him what he thought about the fact that his great grandchildren would be able to read the book. "What do I think?" he replied. "It will become very good. Because my grandchildren will say, 'Our grandfather did this work, told all these stories.' Our name will come." A good name could result, that is, from what people read and know about Mheme's words and actions and from the simple fact that such a record exists. Still, the future cannot be predicted, the voicings of others cannot be fully determined. There is an air of slippage and unpredictability in these sorts of echoes. "I'm not the one to decide what people will say about me," Lhatul once told me when asked what he thought others would say about him after he had died. Any account of a Yolmo life is destined for the ears of others, requiring others to speak in that person's name. Much as the Lord of Dharma judges a person's life after viewing what is shown on the mirror of deeds, so Mheme's neighbors would be the final arbiters of his life and reputation within the world of the living.

Given all this, I began to question which doings and tellings to stress in writing the life story, which could influence what people might say about Mheme and his family later on. As I learned of the potential implications of our talk and became more embedded within it, I wanted to ask Mheme what he thought the focus of his life story should be. Nogapu helped me to pose the question one day in March 1998.

"Inside this book, Mheme, people will read. What kind of good things should we write inside? Should 'a good household man' be written? Or should 'good dharma' be written? Or 'good friendships and relations with all the relatives'?"

"For a good read," our elder replied, "you should tell about the good friendships and that there's good dharma. Also, about being close with my family, in the house. Also, that there's good dharma."

Since so much of Mheme's talk circled about themes of sorrow and hard work in his life, themes that I thought would prove crucial in any account of his life, I wanted to know what he thought about including them in the book: "If we talk about suffering [dhukpu], should we put the sorrowful things. What do you think?"

"Why should the sorrowful words be put? What's the point? Suffering means [more] suffering. Why put it in the book? Only talk about the pleasant talk. Then it's good for the book."

"It's good if dharma and the good friendships are put, yes?"

"Oh, that's it. If you talk about the dharma and the good friendships, that would be good, for sure. People will say, 'That man did dharma. He was a good man. But he's dead.'"

Since this assessment still left in question the accounts of Mheme's hardships in life, accounts that I guess I was unwilling to part with, Nogapu and I pressed the matter: "All three should be put together, Mheme," Nogapu said in conveying the gist of my thoughts. "Because you're a man who did hardship, and later you did a lot of dharma. Then, with dharma having been done, happiness now comes."

"Okay, okay. That's also good. Then people will think, 'This man suffered before. Now he has become like this.'"

At first, it seems, Mheme balked at the idea of including his "sorrowful words," since he apparently felt that reading about suffering would induce further suffering; who would want to read a book of hardships?[22] Accepting our logic, however, Mheme changed his mind and decided, apparently, that the inclusion of hardship would make for a morally instructive biography: attesting to the principle of karma, a comfortable, merit-rich life is the eventual fruit of hard work and religious effort. Such a biography, faintly reminiscent of the moral teleologies implicit in the autobiographies of many great Tibetan saints, would speak well of him. People would say that, despite the hardships and sorrows he faced, he was a good man.

Much was riding, in short, on what people might say about the life and actions of this hardworking man. His afterlife will correspond in many ways to his afterimage. That afterimage will emerge, in part, from how others speak of him. For my part, any words I might write about his life and circulate among others could very well feed into such talk in as yet undetermined ways. At the least, I find I need to write well of Mheme's life, to say that he was a good man, which, I should say for the record, is an easy, straightforward thing to do, since, like his children and grandchildren, he is, in fact, a good and virtuous man, without significant sins or moral failings to speak of.[23]

"He was a good man. But he's dead." As was often the case when we spoke, Mheme anticipated what might occur after his death and how his life might echo in his afterlife. In his estimation, his reputation and social identity will be defined even more by what others say about him once he passes from his body and so can no longer speak or act on his own. His appreciation of the lasting legacy of people's talk and of how people can be remembered in death was evident in how he described his father and mother to us when asked what they were like.

People said he was a hard man, but his heart was good. People also said that he was a good man, my father.

All the Tamang people, all, were saying that she was a very good woman. They said this because she would cook food for them.

In characterizing people who have died, he related what others had said about them. Mheme similarly expected people to talk about him after he died, and he anticipated what they might say.

"How will people remember your life after you die?" Norbu and I once asked him.

"Even today villagers remember me," he answered. "They say, 'Don't stay in Kathmandu, come back to the village [and live in Thodong again].' For good people, people will always speak good of them. For bad people, people will always say bad things of them."

"After you die, do you think people will say good [things] about you?"

"I think they will. Because I have never done bad to anyone, never ruined anyone, never talked rudely to anyone. Everyone says I am a straight lama [*theka lama*]. The Tamangs say I am a straight lama, even today."

In effects similar to the cause, people speak good of good people and bad of bad; because of his actions, people will continue to say that Ghang Lama is "straight"—upright, honest, direct. Yet, for Mheme at least, when it comes to talking about a recently deceased person, the import of such words does not simply shape that person's name, or reputation. As with so many other kinds of talk among Yolmo wa, such as curses and the mantras of lamas and shamans, this kind of eulogistic, postmortem talk entails an effective force that can have powerfully real consequences in the world. As Mheme explained it, what people say about a person after he or she dies influences where that person is reborn, for the gods listen to and heed such talk, which can then affect one's fate. "After someone dies," he told us, "if the people talk good about him, then he reaches heaven, because the gods also hear the people talking." He then pointed at the tape recorder and said, "This thing picks [up] when we talk. Similarly, the god picks [up] when people talk about us. It's like that, above." On another occasion, with the tape recorder rolling on, Nogapu and I asked him where a person's soul travels once it separates from the body in death. He said:

If people did good things, then the soul will go to a good place. If people did bad things, the soul will go to a bad place. If people do really good, then the Buddha will take them. If they've done sins, then they'll be taken down to hell. If they've done good, performing good rites [pūjā], talking well of others, then they'll go to heaven. That is our thinking....If someone is bad, Ah! and the people say "He should die, because he's bad!" then he reaches hell, because many people are saying that about him. If someone is good, people will say good things, and then he reaches heaven.[24]

"By oneself it's not enough," Mheme told us, implying that a person cannot reach "heaven" by his or her efforts alone. Though a person travels alone and friendless in the death between, others need to help from a distance. As with the vocalizations of grief that can disturb a person's death if too intense, the voicings of others can, for Mheme, powerfully influence the nature of one's journey and existence after death. The lamas who perform the funeral rites need to guide the soul toward a good "way," and the deceased's family and friends as well as any enemies have to act and speak on the dead person's behalf. Death and the fate of the deceased are social affairs. There are, in fact, several activities that people can undertake on behalf of a dead person in the weeks following a death. Along with performing the funeral rites well, mourners can light chemi (butter lamps) to help illuminate the way after death; they can accept food distributed in the deceased's name; and they can participate in the group chorusing of prayers, known collectively as mani, that occur at various times in the ritual process. The prayers and the wealth distributed increase the deceased's store of karmic merit and so increase the chances of a good rebirth. Mheme also noted that it is important for people to speak well and compassionately of the deceased. "We need to say 'nyingjwa' to the person who is dying, even if he's our enemy," he told us.

Nyingjwa, or *snying rje ba* in written Tibetan, literally means "compassioned one"—one, that is, who is receiving or deserves to receive *nying je,* or "compassion," from others. In contexts such as these, however, its pragmatic import can perhaps be best heard in translation as "loved one," as "poor, unfortunate one," or, to put it more expressly, "I, the speaker, feel love and compassion, or sorrow or pity, for the person to whom my words of 'nyingjwa' are directed."[25] As such, the term, often used when speaking of deceased loved ones or acquaintances, designates the respectful compassion or sympathetic sorrow one feels for a suffering or dying person. "It means he's a good man," Nogapu said when asked what the word meant.

The old man continued:

We need to do some mani [prayers], and pray to the gods—we need to do this. We shouldn't cry. Everyone needs to die. Our enemies also need to die. If we say nyingjwa to our enemy when he's dying, he can reach a nice place [in rebirth]. If everyone says, "He's a bad person," then he goes down, down. If one or two people say he's good, then it helps a bit. If everyone says he's bad, then the gods also believe this. If people say he's a very good person and everyone says [in an expression of their grief], "He's dead," then he can attain enlightenment. If one person tries to pick up a heavy stone, it won't rise. But if many people try to pick it up, it can be lifted. It's the same with saying mani.

There was a lot on the line for Mheme when it came to the voicings of others. What people say about him after his death, he understood, and the extent to which they collectively voice mani, will help to determine the nature of his rebirth. He seemed to anticipate that any writings about him would contribute to such a judgment. He mused, for instance, that people reading certain aspects of his life story, such as his sufferings and his dharmic career, might voice the elegiac, nyingjwa-like statement, "He was a good man. But he's dead." Notice how these words foreshadowed an observation that he expressed a month later, noted above: "If people say he's a good person and everyone says, 'He's dead,' then he can attain enlightenment." His words anticipated the mourning to come. They also suggested how an account of his life might help to shape any laments voiced on his behalf.

One reason Mheme invested in the recording of his life, in short, was to convey that he was an important, morally good person and so to effect good talk about himself before and after he died. Like the many texts he read daily in preparing for death, this, too, was "work for later." "A good read" might prompt people to speak compassionately about him; divine beings would ultimately be listening. As it is, the presumed consequences of such talk lead me to wonder if and to what effect the present chain of words will be heard by the gods. Such are the implications of action in a world of karmic effects, and such are an ethnographer's concerns and responsibilities when local realities and interests are taken seriously. For what it's worth, I do not take my responsibilities here lightly, in part because my life has become greatly interwoven with the lives I am writing about, and certain ethical duties come with those ties. At the same time, through the course of my engagements with Yolmo lives, some recesses of my mind seem to have acquired, in rather visceral, preconscious ways, many of the sensibilities toward action, time, and meaning that I have been trying to understand, such that when I put pen to paper the metaphysics of Yolmo lives echoes powerfully in the soundings of my own thoughts. One consequence of this is that what, and how, the life story work apparently meant for Ghang Lama has converged at points with what, and how, that work means for me. Another, related consequence, one in accord with a logic of karmic echoes, is that I have come to appreciate a wealth of potential, long-term "pragmatic effects" resulting from our engagements together, effects that I did not anticipate before getting involved in such work, given that the inhabitants of my Euro-American world, including its theorists of language, tend to conceive of the significance of acts-in-time in ways quite different from those of Yolmo wa.

For the record, then, and to help with the burden to come: nyingjwa.

The prospect of something tangible staying on after Mheme's death was unusual as it stood, for one of the main messages of Buddhist teachings and practices is that a person's life and body are fleeting and impermanent. Yolmo funeral rites drive this message home in forceful terms. To begin with, the deceased's body is quickly cremated. Then, at the dramatic climax of a merit-making funeral rite known as ghewa, or "merit," often held around the forty-ninth day after a person dies, a date that is thought to coincide with the end of the bardo, a lifelike effigy of the deceased's body is constructed from the person's clothes, along with a funerary "crown" and a white cloth for the face. People then carry the effigy out of the deceased's house into a lamas' temple in order to consummate the transmigration of the deceased's soul into the "heavens above." Once the effigy is set up in an appropriate place in the temple, a sheet of rice paper, supported like a flag on a stick, is placed before it or set within the embrace of its arms. This paper, known as the *jhang bar,* or "purification print," is inscribed with a human figure on one side and prayers to a deity on the other; the dead person's name is written in an appropriate place in these prayers (see figure 13). The print serves as a

Figure 13. The two sides of a "purification print."

material representation, a manifestation even, of the worldly aspects of the deceased's former life.

After a set of preliminary contemplations, the lama summons the deceased's nam-she, or soul, to the ritual proceedings and mentally construes the presence of the deceased within the temple. Family members offer foods to the deceased, as represented by the effigy, but they do so with arms crossed at the wrists, possibly to signify the constraints on exchanges between the living and the dead. The lamas present then enact a series of prayers, mantras, and visualizations that, combined with prostrations performed by the family members, serve to absolve the deceased of any sins or vices committed while he or she was alive. Such sins are further cleansed by having a man pour water from a vase over the image of the purification print and effigy as reflected in a mirror (see figure 14). The head lama then calmly voices an explanation (ngo te) to the dead person to the effect that he or she is dead and can no longer remain among the living. Family members do much the same soon after, through more tearful words and expressions. One by one, family members make such pleas while looking at the effigy's face, opaque and expressionless in its blank whiteness, and so in effect "see" the loved one's face, as they envision it, one last time.

Figure 14. Ritual cleansing of the deceased, Thodong, 1988. Photograph by
Robert Desjarlais.

After these activities conclude, the head lama sets the purification
print on a table before him. He then performs a series of rites that effect
the transfer of the transmigration of the person's soul. Among these
rites is a mantra, uttered by the lama, that dissolves the sensory and
dharmic components of the deceased's existence:

zug mhe	no form (no sight)
dha mhe	no sound
dhi mhe	no smell
rho mhe	no taste
rhecha mhe	no touch
chhe mhe do!	no dharma, period!

The lama then extinguishes the deceased's sins and worldly existence
through a set of forceful mantras and visualizations. In these same moments he simulates the annihilation by holding a small flame to the
purification print and burning it. Just before the paper burns, the lama
undertakes a meditative act of phowa that works to "transfer" the dead
person's soul out of the sansāric world of khorwa and into a realm
"above" and beyond that world. As the paper vanishes to a dramatic

charge of lamaic music, the effigy is quickly dismantled into a pile of loose clothes.

These rites establish several ephemeral images of the deceased's body: the effigy; the effigy's image in the mirror; and the figure of a human body on the purification print. While this series of quite subtle bodies points to the way in which the deceased is recollected in figurative form one last time, each of the images is then dissolved through acts that convey the end of a life. The litany of "zug mhe … ;" no vision, no sound, no dharma, announces the annihilation of the dead person's means of engaging with and acting in the world. The rapid, clothes-by-clothes dismemberment of the effigy parallels the disaggregation of the deceased's body and worldly existence. As I understand it, by being able to view the successive constitution and deconstitution of the deceased's form, the bereaved are aided in their efforts to come to terms with the death. The process bears similarities to the psychovisual operations through which, as Mheme told it, the presence of a dead person's corpse helps the living to understand that a death has taken place. It also brings to mind Robert Hertz's remarks, first published in 1906, on a "well-known belief" at work in mortuary rites throughout the world: "to make a material object or a living being pass from this world into the next, to free or to create the soul, it must be destroyed"; as the "visible object" vanishes, it is "reconstructed in the beyond, transformed to a greater or lesser degree."[26] Among Yolmo wa the material aspects of a deceased person, simulated through visible objects, are ritually destroyed.

That a life has ended is indeed a lasting message here. For many, the incineration of the purification print, whose inscriptions embody a graphic trace of a person's life, and so a biography in the strict sense of the term, signifies the final death of the deceased, the cessation of a singular identity, and the end of a living, public biography. "They burn the dead man's name," Pramod once said with a nervous laugh in summing up the rite. The deceased is denamed, defaced, rendered signless.

Many in fact hold that, once a person dies, any invocations of his or her name should be followed by the word *tongba,* which means "empty." Others insist that, after the purification print is burned and the funeral rites conclude in general, one should no longer mention the deceased's name. As Lhatul explained it to me in 1988, "There's no use in saying such names. A name is only for the living, not the dead." When I asked one man about this taboo, he said, "We do say that also: 'With death the name is lost.' Mhin torsin. We say that. To say 'mhin torsin' means 'his name is lost,' which means he's dead." The word *torsin* relates to the Tibetan verb *'tor-ba*, which can be translated as "to be scattered, to fly asunder, to be dispersed, to decay."[27] The lost name implies that its owner's social identity disperses and flies asunder. "So nothing is permanent. Everything is lost," the man went on to say, underscoring one of the Buddhist lessons of the rite: that not even a person's name should last after death.[28] This, at least, is the message conveyed; more private, familial memories of the deceased readily continue.

When it comes to writing Mheme's life story, there is a similar engagement of paper and a life. It's as though his "name," if not his soul, is being manifested within the paper of a text (again: we toil in a bhaja-esque logic of "as though"). But in contrast with the usual turn of events at Yolmo funerals, wherein so much goes up in flames, Mheme's name, and his life as cast in print, will carry on in the markings of a text. "Dying is not good," he told us. "It's good to live as long as one can." Given that he was afraid of dying and wished to live longer, the texts we were producing together could enable him to extend the duration of his life and his name in an uncommon way. Any remainder would imply a middle way between immortality and complete annihilation. Dying would not quite be dying.

And yet I wonder about all this and about my hand in all of it, because it could be argued that Mheme's desires were in tension with what many Buddhist teachings and he himself advocated: that one should not become too attached to one's life, especially when that life is ending. One reason for this creed is that, since attachments limit the possibility of any spiritual transcendence from a world of suffering and desire, it is better to relinquish one's hold on the world. Another reason, more commonly advanced by Yolmo wa, is that if strong attachment arises at the moment of death, a person risks becoming a ghost that, stuck between lives, haunts its former loved ones and possessions.

Most often Yolmo refer to such attachment as *semjha*, as an "attachment" or "clinging" of the sem among others; the second syllable derives from the word *chhaba*, a Yolmo verb that carries connotations of "to love," "to be attached to," "to cling to," "to desire." Such heartfelt attachments can lead, if they are not effectively ameliorated, to a dead person becoming a *shyindi*, or "ghost." As Mheme himself explained it to us:

If one gives semjha to anything, then he or she becomes a ghost. "Before I had this thing, I had this much of that," the person who thinks like this becomes a ghost. Semjha means that. "I have this much money, I remember this, I have my children, I have my family," that kind of attachment [semjha] comes. If one has attachment like this, one might return as a ghost.

In contrast with the bhaja of a dead person that might recur within a household, a shyindi can harm the living. "His semjha is left behind with his youngest daughter," a sentence I once heard, suggested that a father's ghostly presence was clinging to his daughter; the attachment was threatening to pull the daughter into death as well. When bereaved family members, worried about such deathly bonds, talk at the ghewa to the spirit of the deceased as represented by the effigy, they often tell it not to leave a semjha behind. "We talk to it," Mheme told me. "We say to it, 'Don't give the semjha to many things, don't think about this, don't think about that. Think only about your gods and your lama.' The lamas say this." At times lamas also threaten the dead person, saying that if he sticks around he will be forcibly removed from the world of the living. Unlike what those in Western settings so often think, then, among Yolmo wa these days it is not so much the living but the recently dead who have a tough time coming to terms with the reality of death and who, sometimes unable to let go, linger within damaging states of attachment.[29]

What has concerned me here in thinking about Yolmo attachments is that, while Mheme himself was aching for a good death, one free of attachment and longing for the world, he also appeared to desire that something of his life "stay" on after he died. While one might suppose that there are irresoluble tensions here, Yolmo wa themselves would hold that, since the lama was not necessarily attached to the traces he wished to leave behind or to his life in general, the prospects of a lingering, semjha-like attachment after his death was not really in question here. In fact, the conversion of his speech into print, thus leaving something tangible behind after he dies, could actually lessen his attachment to the world. Something Mheme once said while talking about the need to die in the presence of one's family and to "see their faces" for the last time helps me to comprehend this.

It's better to die with one's family nearby. Then your semjha won't stay with them. If one dies in a different place, just alone, then he thinks, "I own these things, I have that many children." Then the semjha gets attached to the house. So then the lamas need to tell him, "Don't affix the sem, don't act in this manner." If the children are not there, or if they're in a foreign country, then the attachment [semjha] comes. If the children are away when the person dies, then they return after the death and say at the ghewa, "Don't do the semjha to me. I was away before, but now I'm here."

If one's children are absent when one is dying, there can be undue attachment, because one longs for the missing, wished-for loved ones. If they are present, however, there is no need for any lasting attachments to occur, because there is no one absent whose presence is desired. This is one reason why it's important for family members to "see the face" of a dying loved one, for the dying person can also behold these loves ones in turn and so not maintain any lingering attachment to them when passing from life. The same principle applies to the death of those who have a particular craving in life: those who like to drink raksī, for instance, will often be given a few sips of this alcoholic brew just before dying so that their desire for it is sated when they die and they can pass into death without any semjha.

In much the same way, any life story penned about Ghang Lama might diminish, rather than add to, his attachment to the world. Its occurrence might lead him to become less attached to his present life, in part because he will no longer worry so much about his death, and he will no longer need to long so much for a world that he must soon leave behind. With something longed for sated through writings about him, he can be at peace upon dying, and his spirit need not maintain a semjha-like presence in the world of the living.[30]

What I have come to gather, then, is that any written accounts of Ghang Lama's or Kisang Omu's life will likely effect diffuse and as-yet-undetermined remainders/reminders that will work through a complex nexus of temporalities and semiotic principles to establish certain absences, presences, identities, and remembrances. Traces of the "old ways," of Yolmo history and culture, of a lama's deeds and sufferings, of a woman's hardships, and of skillful, virtuous ways to live and die might transfer to and remain among others. Particular, and heavily coauthored, understandings of Yolmo engagements with life and death might also echo through texts such as this, much as novel ideas of biographic writing and its worldly and otherworldly consequences might resound in the minds of non-Yolmo authors and readers. And yet while it now seems clear that writings about the two elders will instantiate an array of echoes for different readers, it remains to be seen if some of these writings will function in more ghostly ways. For some time, in fact, I have been worried that any meanings invested in writings about the two could effect or be understood as "bad," disturbing bhaja among some Yolmo wa, particularly the family members of those written about. This is not an easy issue to think through, since there are some re-presentations of deceased loved ones that are usually welcome, such as photographs, and others that are greatly feared, such as ghosts. Five months after leaving Nepal in 1998, I sent an e-mail note to Karma Gyaltsen. Karma had just then purchased a computer to aid him in his artwork, and I took this opportunity to send him an e-mail letter in which I detailed my concerns to him and asked him to clarify, if possible, the difference between good and troublesome bhaja in Yolmo lives. "Why is it," I asked, among other things, "that people don't want a deceased loved one to come back as a haunting bhaja, but will still keep photographs and other objects that help them remember their relation to that person?"

Karma's response, in English, included these observations:

Regarding your question on bhaja, I don't see any clear demarcation between a good and a bad bhaja. It's the same as distinguishing between good and bad dreams through the different meanings you can best make of images and the way you are involved. Maybe I can say it is psychological. When we talk about the photographs or other things of the deceased, they bring memories of the deceased physically and therefore can bring emotional moments....

Speaking of Mheme Lama's life story, the book itself won't be a bhaja. But reading what he had to say will carry meanings and therefore his words, sayings, will be his bhaja; these interpret into some meanings and as long as they don't mean anything evil, irritating, or bad, they cannot be his bad bhaja. However, if one sees nightmares with the book or what is written there after reading or seeing the book, it will be considered (as any other book) as a bad bhaja, meaning it carries some bad meanings with it.

I hope all this makes some sense to you.

These words did make sense. But they took on greater clarity two years later, when I had a chance to talk in person again with Karma, after I returned to Nepal in 2000. As we sat in his home in Boudhanath and watched his daughter play on the floor before us, Karma clarified what he meant in saying that the book itself won't be a bhaja. As he saw it, any actual book written about Kisang Omu and Ghang Lama could not itself be thought of as a bhaja, because a bhaja, by definition, is something immaterial. "The book itself cannot be the bhaja," he said. "Bhaja isn't really anything material. It's more like an energy or what you in the West would call an aura. But the book could be something that carries a lot of bhaja with it."

Karma went on to relate his statement to the example of a human voice echoing in a mountain range. Much as an original sound produces a series of resonating sounds, so a book could effect a series of bhaja. Talking about it further, we concluded that the book compared better to a cassette player set atop a mountain hilltop: When any taped recordings are inserted into the machine and played, it can produce a series of sounds that echo through a landscape. The tape player itself is therefore not the echo but, rather, a "transmitting device" that resounds previous words in a way that can lead to subsequent, bhaja-like utterances in the minds of anyone listening to them, with people differently positioned in space and time hearing different sounds; those standing quite close to the echo's source are greatly affected by it, while those standing far away might not hear much at all. The book, likewise, would resound a set of voicings that, when read or heard about, could "interpret into" different bhaja among those thinking about the book or any of the words, events, or persons depicted within it.

A bhaja, then, resides largely in the mind of the beholder. While the present book is not a bhaja, it will produce a series of different bhaja among different persons. "The book you are writing is like a solid event, a solid action," said Karma in thinking it through. "It's something you can see. It's not really an action. And yet it is an action." In one sense, the "solid event" of the book is not quite an action, because it is more an artifact of human actions than it is an action in itself. And yet it is an action in the sense that it will inevitably produce effects, possibly quite consequential ones.

Hence the comparison to "good and bad dreams": While a particular dream image can in itself be relatively neutral in significance, different people will find alternative meanings in that image and so be affected by it in different ways; while a person from one society might take a dream about swimming in an ocean to be one of drowning in despair, a dreamer from another society might regard it as portending a future of wealth. The book, likewise, will carry different meanings for different readers, some that could be considered as "good bhaja," and some as "bad bhaja." Among the possibilities for the former, Karma suggested, the book could effect responses that lead to the preservation of Yolmo culture, or it could be seen as an omenlike indication that Yolmo culture should be preserved. "These," he said, "would be good bhaja." The same would hold for a strengthening of Mheme's "name" in the world or any voicings on his behalf that would contribute to a good rebirth.

Yet if the book affects someone in a negative way—if, say, it causes bad dreams among any readers—then the book would be understood to be effecting disturbing, unsettling bhaja for them. "If the book brings really bad moments or bad thinking," Karma observed, "then it brings bad bhaja. For one person, being in the book might not mean anything. For me, it might not mean anything. But if, after reading the book, one of Mheme's sons starts to have bad dreams about his father, then the actual seeing of the dreams and the emotional moments that the book carries with it will be bad bhaja for him."

When I conveyed to Karma my concerns that I might inadvertently write something that could bring "bad moments" to someone and then said that I might be criticized in my own country for chancing such a situation, he shook his head, then countered with a set of observations. To begin with, he noted, as long as I did not say anything purposefully damaging or slanderous about anyone, no Yolmo person would fault me. Besides, he pointed out, it is simply in the nature of any phenomenon to carry the potential for both good and bad bhaja. He then observed that, while a man's life story might in fact lead one of his sons to have unsettling dreams about him after he died, those same dreams might lead that son to give some thought to how he had related to his father while he was alive—whether, for instance, he had spent much time with him or conversed with him much in his later years. Those considerations might in turn prompt the son to perform ritual acts on his father's behalf, acts that could improve the latter's situation in any next life. An initially bad bhaja could thus result in very good effects. Since there is no way to anticipate or predict what would come of the book, Karma concluded, I should simply try to write in good and honest ways, without, however, saying anything "bad" about anyone.

While Karma's receiver-response theory of bhaja has helped me to gain greater perspective on what my writings might entail for different Yolmo wa, and his thoughts in general have assuaged several concerns of mine, our conversations together have further underlined for me the complex responsibilities that the work carries with it. The contents of this book have already transmitted a surge of bhaja, such that the ethnographer of bhaja now finds himself troubled by the meanings that bhaja "interpret into." I feel I can speak well of Kisang Omu and Ghang Lama and so help to effect good echoes of their lives, however illusory they might ultimately be. The prospect of writing about their lives and deaths thus continues to sit well with me. Still, in thinking about what this work might mean for Yolmo peoples, in thinking, that is, about the temporalities, semiotic principles, and moral precepts detailed in this chapter, I find myself increasingly entangled in the meanings emerging from this work. I worry about the potential effects of my writings. I am now accountable to a set of lives powerfully geared to the voicings of others. Caught within a particular engagement with time and meaning, I am haunted, at times, by the words of these good people.

A Son's Death

One more story still. One last meditation, on the occasional need for words to rephrase the past, to suggest how things really happened.

For a time in the late 1970s, while Kisang was living with her daughter and son-in-law in Kathmandu, her second son, a man known as Jho Bharpa, was staying with them as well. He was planning to build a house of his own, and he had asked his mother to join him once he got settled there. Before this could happen, however, he died one night under uncertain, contested circumstances. Pramod and I learned about the death one morning in 1998 as we sat and spoke with Kisang. Pramod asked:

Auntie, how did your son Jho Bharpa die?

Pramod later told me he appreciated talking about this event, because, while he had heard various accounts about it, it had remained unclear to him what had actually happened. Kisang answered:

Jho Bharpa drank a lot of alcohol. Raksī [a liquor distilled from grains]. Then, in Chabahil he gambled with his friends. I don't know what they gambled, I don't know if they played cards. They played chhaka [a game played by tossing cowrie shells]. They drank chhang.

Kisang was clear on some things, but not others: they drank, they gambled.

Then he quarreled with his friends, then he fell off the bicycle. He was barely breathing, and he was taken to the hospital. He wasn't brought to the house.

Late one night Jho Bharpa was found lying in a ditch below a bridge to the west of Chabahil, badly harmed, with his bicycle entangled beside him. To many it appeared that, while drunk, he had fallen off his bike or ridden directly into the ditch when coming down a steep incline that led toward the bridge. Some suspected, however, that he had been beaten and then left for dead in the ditch or pushed into the ditch while he was pedaling along the road, possibly by the friends with whom he had drunk and gambled that night or by some of the enemies he had accumulated during his life. Kānchā, for instance, said, in speaking of these events, that, while it could have been an accident, he thought that foul play was involved: his half brother was gambling with friends, and these people possibly got angry with him and beat him. "He was killed, perhaps."

Jho Bharpa was taken directly to the hospital, which meant, among other things, that his mother neither spoke with him nor saw his wounds before he died, and so she could not readily determine the actions that led to his death. Kisang related to us only what she knew for sure: they drank, they quarreled, he fell off his bicycle. Her use of a "then...then" syntax implied that the actions followed one another. But her words also kept in question the causal link, if any, between the drinking and quarreling earlier in the night and the subsequent fall from the bicycle. Left undetermined were the cause of the death and who was responsible for it. Pramod asked:

Was it an accident? Was he hit by a car?

This is what Pramod had once heard. But Kisang answered:

No, he wasn't hit by a car. The bicycle fell down before the bridge, the bridge by Ghang Uncle's house. Then after he died he was brought to the house. They brought him to the hospital first, and then later to the house.

He was not hit by a car, as others might have said. He fell down a steep decline by a bridge close to Ghang Lama's house in Chabahil. In explaining this to me then, Pramod told me that it was an "accident." Upon hearing this English word, Kisang spoke again while Pramod and I continued to talk in English.

"Accident." Not by the people. By falling. He drank chhang. He got drunk from the chhang. He got drunk from the chhang, it turned out. He drank raksī. What to do? He drank raksī, one should say. T-t. [It's a pity.] He died there, and then he was brought to the house. What to do, then?

"He drank raksī, one should say." That's all one could say, given what was known about what happened. It should not be said, if one were to speak with skill or care, that his death was the result of the malevolent actions of others. He died from his own actions.

Another son of Kisang's, Kānchā's older brother, also died as a result of a chain of all-too-human actions. One winter afternoon in Ne Nyemba, when Kānchā was two or so, he and his brother, who was just five then, were playing out in the fields outside Ne Nyemba and had gotten quite cold. They went to a neighboring house to see if they could warm themselves by a fire, but there was no one at home. They then walked on to their own home but found that their mother was still away, working in the fields. The door to the house was shut tight, with a wooden latch affixed to the frame above the door preventing the door from being opened. The two boys found a basket, placed it at the foot of the door, stood on top of it, and unlatched the door. After entering, they started a fire in the hearth. They were numb from the cold, and when the fire ignited part of the older boy's clothing he did not feel it at first. The rest of his clothes quickly caught on fire, and his body was severely burned. He did not die right away but only sometime later.[1]

In relating these events to me, Kisang spoke in a lamentable, "how sad it was" tone, as though underscoring the sorrow ingrained in a series of actions that led to the boy's death. A precise self-enclosed economy of action was evident in the events narrated. Every action was a consequential one, with causes and effects bound up with other causes and effects. Because the two boys were cold, they sought a place to get warm, because they did that, that happened, and so on, until the death itself took place. That death, to be sure, was not due to a random series of events beyond the means of human beings. As was the case with the untimely deaths of her first husband and second son, a person's self-willed deeds led to his own passing. From such deaths sorrow emerges. "Auntie," we asked later on, "a lot of people have died in your life, your husband, your children. How do you feel about this?"

"I had sorrow. I had sorrow, for sure. Then, after moving to Kathmandu, I didn't feel sorrow. My children cared for me, the children who are [still] alive."

"How did you maintain your sorrow?"

"Aba! I needed to maintain. What to do? If I didn't maintain, it couldn't be. I couldn't throw off [the sorrow]."

One had to bear the sorrow.

Having gained our attention again, Kisang continued:

Nobody inquired about the accident. At that time, his brother-in-law was living with them. He did not say a single word on his behalf. There was no arrest. So, rubbish son-in-law.

So much was implied in so few words. She was suggesting here, Pramod later told me, that her daughter's husband should have spoken up on behalf of her deceased son. Because he did not request a formal inquiry into the death, no one was arrested for any possible crime. Kisang's comments pointed to her son-in-law's inaction and the moral failing indicated by it. But it is also likely that she would have refrained from saying anything directly to this man.

In this way, he was lost. Otherwise, if he had been alive, he wouldn't have handed me over to Kānchā.

"In this way." *Anda bheti.* Literally, "having done like this." Actions all around. Kisang was planning, Kānchā told me, to move into a new home soon to be established by Jho Bharpa. Because this son died, however, the transfer could not take place, and Kisang's daughter instead "handed her over" to Kānchā. It was Kisang's misfortune that another potential happening did not turn out as expected.[2]

More can be said about the statement "He drank raksī, one should say." Kisang was sharply attuned to what she and others took to be the reality-making, reality-confirming dynamics of speech. When speaking about certain aspects of her life, she often relied on phrases like "it is said" or "people say this." Other Yolmo wa do much the same. These phrases often have the effect of underscoring the ways in which certain identities or social realities are founded on how people convey them in speech. When asked to tell us her full name, for instance, she replied, "The full name, what to say, now? 'Kisang,' it has been said." She went by what others called her, just as they went by what others called them. Likewise, when called upon to characterize a concept, she would not simply define it abstractly but would rather describe what people said about it or how it was used in everyday speech. Asked to explain what *ḍhaṅga* means, she replied, "'No intelligence,' one says. 'No know-how,' one says." Asked what *semba tsherke,* or "heart-pain," means, she replied, "'Semba tsherke,' we say this, for sure. Something is felt when the tsherke comes. Something comes inside the sem. 'Semba tsherke,' one says this."

"One says this." Kisang lived in a social world that emerged and was substantiated through talk. Things are what they are, or they happened in the way that they did, because people say that was the case: "Everybody told me later on that I was walking in front of the corpse and cry-ing." "'You're very fortunate,' everyone said....Maybe it's true. So I agreed." People's reputations were founded on what "everyone said": "They still say that, these days." Talk can also have profound effects on a person's life: "The people said this thing, this thing, many things. Then it made me like crazy." Yet people are also wary of the fact that talk can also lead to misperceptions or falsehoods. Given all this and more, Kisang's way of putting things often conveyed a delicate attentiveness to what should or should not be said. "I should say it's good," she said when asked what she thought of being a mother. "Well, I have to say [it's one of] comfort," she once said when asked of her present condition.

So much rested for Kisang on what people said or should say about one thing or another. The "should" often implied moral imperatives. Since a person's words can lead, if they have enough momentum, to cer-tain understandings of past or present, even if some think those under-standings to be false or inaccurate, one has to mind one's words, espe-cially if one wants to be (said to be) skilled in good. For her and others, statements reverberated in enduring moral subterrains.

So: "He drank raksī....He drank raksī, one should say," as though the repetition might drown out any alternative voicings and in time as-sume the force of truth. It was an accident, one should say.

When I asked other Yolmo wa why Kisang might have stressed this conclusion, they told me that any mother would hesitate to say that her son was murdered unless she had firm proof that that was indeed the "cause" of the death. But they also pointed out that, if Kisang herself said that her son had been killed by enemies, it would imply that he was a bad person, which in turn could diminish the family's prestige. "Even if she had proof, she couldn't say he was murdered," observed one man. "That's because it would not be good for her to say this," he continued. "It would mean that he was a bad person, and it would leave a bad im-pression. So if she says, 'He just died,' then people will say, 'Oh, perhaps his time had come, or maybe he was sick.'"w Temba's father gave much the same explanation when I asked him about this: "If she said that her son was murdered by others and had many enemies, the prestige of the family could be degraded. So she might have hidden the real past and given 'raksī' as the cause of the death."

The acutely moral, interpersonal slants to speech in Kisang's life were ev-ident in her engagements with language. In speaking with us, Kisang al-ways seemed to be anticipating how her words might be heard, how her kurā might be received, acknowledged, praised, cut against, derided, resounded. Her utterances were always paired with the wordings of others, in dense fields of enunciation and reception. To my ears there was an "interstitchal" quality to her words, to broach an analogy between knitting and talking. Her words were interwoven, interstitched, with the sayings and doings of others reported in her accounts; and they were interknitted, interfolded, with the potential words of anyone who might hear or read what she told us. This doubly stitched talk set up a fabric of sense founded on an economy of anticipation, fear, sorrow, hesitancy, self-correction, withholding, and pride.

Her words about her son's death thus conversed quietly, intervocally, with other words, other contexts, and other deaths. They related to what others had said, or did not say, about the death, as well as to what she or others thought they should say or think about the actions that led up to it. They also tied into other happenings in her life, including the various places she had lived since Rinjin Lama divorced her, and they helped to explain how, "having done like this," circumstances were such that she came to live with her youngest son, Kānchā. As always, actions bore consequences, both proximate and distant. And since much the same principle held for the actions that can spawn a death, what Kisang said about the means and causes of her son's death formed an intercommentary with the potential moral significance of other deaths in her life, including her first husband's passing and the early death of Kānchā's brother. Indeed, the untimely, painful deaths of her first husband and two of her sons implied more than their own accumulation of sufficiently bad karma that had come to fruition in the manner of their deaths. It also spoke to Kisang's karma, since, as Yolmo theories of causality have it, the deeds she enacted in previous lives would have led her to live a life in which several members of her family were slated to die uneasy deaths. "When a wife dies early on, it's not just the wife's bad karma. It's the husband's past as well," Karma put it when speaking about such matters in general. By this he meant not that the husband's karmic heritage resulted in his wife's death but rather that the husband's own past resounded in such a way that it was his misfortune to marry a woman who was fated to die an unfortunate death.

The same could be said of Kisang's life. She and others understood that the sorrows as well as the joys of her life reflected the different reverberations of her karmic heritage. All this then implied questions about her own imminent cessation. What would be the means of her death? How would they relate to her past? What would people say, what should they say, of her passing?

The End of the Body

Her body was eroding, Kisang's words sometimes implied. Once, when we praised her ability to speak well, she answered in Nepali with a slight, possibly self-effacing laugh, "Jiu chaina. Ani bhāṣā mātrai cha. Jiu siddiyo. Ke garne?" (There's no body. So there's speech only. The body is finished. What to do?)

Unable to get about and act in the world, she no longer possessed an active, skillful, useful body. The remaining strands of her existence were becoming more ethereal than material. All that remained, she inferred, were thoughts of dying and the ability to speak a little. "Now I can't walk," she said on one occasion. "Just a little bit of talking [that's all I can do]. The human body is already dead. The human bones are already dead as well.... I can't even walk a little bit. Just a small bit of talking."

No longer able to act effectively in other ways, Kisang advanced the idea that her actions and engagements in the world rested then on her ability to speak, and she in fact seemed to occupy herself with talk and prayers much of the time. Tibetan Buddhist teachings invoke images of human existence and agency consisting of a tripartite aggregate of "body, speech, and mind," with all actions, virtuous or sinful, being either physical, or verbal, or mental in form. "There are three kinds of merit: by thinking, by speaking, and by doing. There are also three ways of acquiring sin [*dhigpa*]: through body, speech, or mind," Kānchā told me.[1] While Kisang never studied the lama texts herself, her being vaguely appeared to assume a similar tripartite form, although it looked as though speech, perhaps the most substantive strand of her life, would be the last to go. With her body wasting away and her intelligence increasingly "damaged," she was now becoming more voice than matter. "My body has died, but my words are still alive," she told us when I returned in 2000. One might hear in such a presence a voice defiantly resistant and active in the world, talking against death, talk that gave testimony to her life and made this text possible, yet she herself said that she could no longer speak as skillfully as she once could. But since she could continue to act through words, it seems she could somehow relive her former actions and re-engage with time through the stories she told.

Hindus in India and Nepal sometimes speak of death as *dehānt*, a word that literally means "the end of the body" but one that is also synonymous with "end of activities," "cessation," "impermanence."[2] The running idea is that a death involves the dissolution of the body and, correspondingly, the end of a person's actions in the world of the living. While most Yolmo wa take the word *dehānt* to mean simply "death," it is commonly understood that, once bereft of a body, a deceased person can no longer physically act in the world. "You can't do anything after dying," one lama advised in stressing the need to perform meritorious deeds before one's death precludes this possibility. In death, a person is no longer able to be able.[3] Old age as well is associated with increasing inaction in life. Older people in particular often say that they can no longer use their bodies as they once could, so they have to act most through words and wishes. When Temba and I asked his grandmother Karmu Omu what the most important aspects of her life were, she replied, "The dharma work that I have done in my life before is the most important matter in my life, and I think that's the most that I could have done. Now I can't do anything except wishing and blessing." And when we later asked her if she kept her grandchildren in her thoughts, she replied, "I keep remembering their deeds, and I pray for their welfare. This is all I can do." Gom Dolma, who had hurt her legs in a bad fall a few years back, said, "When I was young, I enjoyed so much of my life; I've made so many journeys in my life. But now I can't do anything besides wishing. If my legs were well, I would like to walk, dance, and enjoy my life. But now, besides feeling sad, there's nothing in my control."

Once the body falters, only speech and mind remain. A person's actions then become limited to verbal and mental deeds. An aged person can become dependent on others to act on his or her behalf.[4] A common lament among Yolmo elders is that, while they still desire to act in the worldly ways that they did in their youths, traveling here and there, performing meritorious deeds, their waning bodies now prevent them from doing so. Death accentuates the arrest of action even more so.

Kisang was living out a situation much like this. In talking about her life, she usually spoke in ways that stressed specific actions undertaken and the moral connotations of those actions: "I did well. We did pleasant things, we did joyful things." "Hard work I did, did, did, did." But her words also suggested that most of the deeds of her life had already been completed: "There's no hope of doing this, doing that. My will is broken." "There's no work now. I should go. I'm not interested in staying." "Aba bhayo" (Now it's enough), she once affirmed, invoking a Nepali expression often used when announcing a sufficiently completed task or activity.

Since childhood her life had been one of movement, of quick-paced "deeds" between people, "doing this, doing that," until the stillness of the last few years, where, outside of speech, there had been little action among or engagements with others. With her actions primarily consisting then of just-so acts of sitting, eating, sleeping, praying, talking, and recollecting, she was becoming increasingly insubstantial, inconsequential, devoid of form. It was as though she was living out the consequences of previous actions only, without undertaking any new actions, while waiting for the next life's chain of actions to begin. There was little left to "do" but die.

Yet death itself could not be effectively engaged, it seemed. Though Kisang might have wished to die at times, she could not will the action of her own death. During our first visit with her, which occurred soon after she came close to dying from an abscess in her mouth, she spoke of her great age and her inability to do much of anything anymore. "I can't die either," she murmured with a light wave of her hands, as if to say that it was out of her control. She went on to say that she had done everything that could be done in her life and now wanted to die, but Chhe Gyalbu, the Lord of Dharma, would not let her. "Other people can live and die, but I'm not able to die, it seems," she said when I visited her once in 2000. She did not possess the agency to will her death, to "go," as it were, much as she was denied the ability to stay put earlier in her life.

Her demise involved fundamental cultural themes of action and inaction, engagement and disengagement. In relating various events of her life, she sometimes told of situations where she removed her body and self from the presence of others. Attempting to evade the words and gazes of "so many" others when faced with marriage, she ran off to her elder's house, then slept in an attic at night. She likewise tried to disconnect sensorially from others when brought forcibly to Phungboche for a third marriage ("I spent the night with her alone, putting my head in her lap....I didn't eat the porridge"), then warned that she would "become a corpse" if they tried to keep her there. In her narratives she sometimes characterized others as acting in similar ways. When stricken with dysentery, her first husband isolated himself in a shed built specifically for that purpose: "Leave me alone....I'll stay alone." Rinjin Lama's first wife, meanwhile, refused to "come outside" her home when Kisang "challenged" her there. The woman then "swept up everything" when vacating Rinjin's home, leaving but a bit of ash behind.

Each of these efforts spoke to an almost archetypal action-form common to Yolmo lives, wherein people willfully withdraw from some kind of social interaction. Children curtain themselves behind the bodies of others when approached by strangers, brides hide their heads under shawls when marrying, and adults suspend engagements with others by turning their eyes elsewhere. Such disengagements can assume a more formal cast as well, for many Yolmo men and some Yolmo women try, especially in their later years, to detach themselves from worldly affairs in ways that enable them to focus their thoughts and actions on religious practice. Lamas, for instance, try to find ways to enter into meditative retreat, known in Yolmo as tsham, or "demarcated space," or colloquially in Nepali as *guphāmā basne,* "to stay in caves."[5]

Kisang, staying in her room, was disengaged in comparable ways. She was several steps removed from the doings and interests of everyday life. But she was not willfully disengaged, as male renouncers of the world tend to be, and she was pained because of it. Her state was more like that of someone who has lost his or her la, or "spirit," and cannot act in the spirited ways that he or she once could, though in this case the inactivity was due to an absent body rather than an itinerant spirit.[6]

In Buddhist circles, the cessation of karmic action is a valued ideal, for it can lead to the end of suffering while also enabling a person to achieve the kind of consciousness necessary for an enlightened perspective on the "wandering on" of khorwa, or sansāra. For much these reasons, Milarepa praised the virtues of nonaction in a song of his:

> Like a corpse lying quiet in the cemetery
> Doing nothing and having no worries,
> Happy is the Yoga of Non-action.[7]

Like-minded philosophies recur in other lamaic texts. "...Relax into the experience of nonholding, nondoing!" advises the Bardo Thedol in helping an itinerant deceased person to recognize "the naked, pure, vibrant void" that appears in the hours after death and so be liberated from the sansāric cycle of deaths and rebirths.[8] A similar kind of "nondoing" was an element of Kisang's aged existence, but the cessation was difficult to ease into, for it seemed to bring worries more than any liberation. Buddhists speak metaphorically of such liberation as nirvāṇa, the complete "blowing out" or "expunging" of the "fires" of passion and desire. It is understood as a state of being beyond suffering, so unworldly and transcendent that all language must ultimately fail to depict it, though the concept carries connotations, among others, of absolute rest and cessation, dispassion, stilling, changelessness, the unconditioned, and the "deathless" freedom from the sansāric round of death and rebirth.[9] Kisang's demise involved elements that sometimes made for a ghostly analogue of nirvāṇa: she was oddly still and deathless but not beyond suffering and desire.

Nevertheless, she did not appear to be particularly stuck on the features of her life, at least in the days that I knew her, as though her disconnection from the world then entailed the sort of "nonholding" that Buddhist sages advocate. Most Yolmo wa would say that this is a good thing, for it implies that she was not too attached to the world, especially when it mattered most. Kisang declined to say, when asked, whether a person becomes a ghost if overly attached to the world upon dying: "I don't know. People say the shyindi comes. I don't know about this. I don't know myself." But she did agree that people should avoid any attachments to the elements of their lives.

"Auntie, when people are dying," we asked, "should they refrain from giving their heartminds to things?"

"People say this."

"Why is that?"

"The sem will stay, for sure. The heartmind will stay, certainly. We shouldn't give the sem [to the things]. Semjha will remain."

She also asserted that she would not be attached to loved ones or possessions when dying.

"Is there anything that you feel you will have left behind?" we asked.

"What will I feel?"

"That you will lose this thing or that."

"Maybe it will come [maybe thoughts like that will occur]. I have all my property. The god will take me wherever. I don't give much thought to my life or anything else. I need to leave everything."

"What will you leave behind?"

"I need to leave some goods, some clothes, some jewelry, but that's not much. Even if I leave this behind, I leave it without longing [*phangbu*]."

"And your children?"

"The children are already grown. I won't have semjha for them [I won't be attached to them]....If I die, I'll leave just like that, for sure. What to do? We shouldn't have semjha, it's said. At the time of dying, we shouldn't be attached in the heartmind. We need to go joyfully in the heartmind."

"What things will you miss the most?"

"Eh?"

"Where will the semjha stay?"

"Where does it stay? Now I'm not dead yet, of course. Now, I don't know. I won't give the semjha to anything. Eh, after dying, I'm gone, I'm gone."

Her words suggested that attachment would not be a problem for her in the end, as it so often can be in the displacements of death or marriage. She would be "gone, gone," leaving "just like that," without "longing," or phangbu, a Yolmo noun difficult to translate but one that conveys something like regret, miserly grasping, pining for lost possessions. Apparently, since thoughts of engaging in life had been stilled, overtaken by thoughts of death, she would not cling to the world. She could make a clean break of it, effect a death without remainder.[10]

She spoke well of dying, in fact. "Now, I have no strength," she told us.

Now my heartmind is going slowly, slowly. It's dying. In that way, I'll die lying on the bed. To die is a good thing. We can go to another place. About that, may Phagpa Chen Rezig know. May Guru Rinpoche [Padmasambhava] know. This I contemplate, for sure. I'm contemplating Phagpa Chen Rezig. When we die, that deity takes us. When we die, this deity shows us the way. Phagpa Chen Rezig is the one who takes us to the Land of Bliss [*dewa chen*].

Dewa chen is the buddha land of the West, that of Buddha Amitābha. It is known as a blissful heaven or paradise, "the land of comfort and happiness," where suffering is unknown. Here and elsewhere Kisang affirmed that Phagpa Chen Rezig, a bodhisattva of compassion and responsible, some say, for the liberation and perfection of all sentient beings, would "show her the road" to this heavenly domain.[11] Partly for that reason, she "contemplated" this bodhisattva often while awake (a thangka just above her bed embodied his likeness) in the hope that these and other merit-enhancing, sin-cutting prayers would enable her to obtain a good path and so a good rebirth upon dying. "I do the mani-padme. I do the mani-padme, thinking that I'll get a small way. I'm dying, it's the time of dying. I haven't forgotten to do the mani." To "do the mani" was to vocalize repeatedly and mindfully the sacred, merit-producing mantra "om mani-padme hūm" with the aid of a mālā, as many Yolmo women do when time permits.[12] Other prayers further enabled her to "dwell within practice," as an esteemed Tibetan lama once put it.[13] "What is done?" she said with an exasperated laugh when asked to explain how she prayed.

I pray to the deities, "May good come. May hardship not come." To the gods and goddesses, I prostrate. "May hardship not come in another life as well." Wishing this, I prostrate to the deities. Now, the human life has finished. Now, we need to go where the deity takes us. The human life has finished.

Until her frail legs kept her from doing so, she also used to do kora, semiritualized acts of meditative, merit-producing circumambulations around the sacred chhorten near her home, as many other devout Buddhists regularly do. "I did! Every day!" she said in 1998 when asked if she had undertaken such "turnings." "I've been lying in this bed for the past four months. For four months now I haven't had a chance to do kora around the chhorten. I'm only having faithful thoughts from here."

All this was to increase her chances of a good rebirth. As with many other Yolmo wa, particularly of her generation, she understood that a person's fate after dying is dependent on the actions that person undertook while alive. "Some go to heaven, some go to hell," she told us. "If we do good deeds, we go to heaven. If we do bad, we're going to hell.... We need to meditate on the deities." Yet she also knew that, because the karmic effects of an untold number of actions, good and bad, weighed in at one's death, no one could determine for sure where one would go after dying. "If I have done good things or bad things, he doesn't say. Chen Renzi will judge me."

Even so, Kisang did not express the same degree of fear and worry as some Yolmo elders I spoke with did. Most said they were afraid of dying because they did not and could not know what new life they would assume after being reborn. Gom Dolma, for instance, said that she was afraid of dying, "because I don't know where I'll be or what condition I'll be in after dying. I can't come back [after I die]. I don't know whether or not I'll have the same kind of life that I have now." And Ghang Lama, as we have seen, worried over how Chhe Gyalbu, the Lord of Dharma, would judge his actions in life and so what his fate in rebirth might be. He also appeared at times to mourn the loss of "I," of being alive among others, that death would bring and found in my work with him the important possibility of certain traces of his life echoing on after he died.

Kisang averred, in contrast, that it is "a good thing" to die. She spoke of death not as a time of isolation and disorientation, as Ghang Lama did, but as a move that entails a cessation of pain and hardship. Since she now despaired, for good reason, of living more than of dying, her immobile state apparently made such a "going" appear better to her than her current life. Even when she came close to dying in the weeks before I met her, her recollections of that time hinted at good things to come: "I didn't feel any pain in my body. How pleasant a place I arrived in, apparently." And unlike the shy "embarrassment" she showed for the deterioration of her person and speech while alive, she appeared little concerned with the ultimate dissolve of selfhood that, the lamas taught, would come with death. Nor did she seem interested in leaving lasting traces of herself. Apparently, a life of movement had prepared her for the final, inescapable travel of death in ways in which Yolmo men, who tended to be fated lives of patrilocal rootedness and willed goings, were less well equipped.[14]

She asked only that she go without pain. "Which is a better way to die, by disease or while sleeping?" she was polled in the course of a conversation on good ways to die. "A-ma-ma!" she answered.

If I can die while sleeping, then I'll have come into refuge. We don't feel anything. Iiih! If there were illnesses in the heart or in the body, it would be a painful struggle. In that way, it's suffering, no doubt. Suffering occurs. So I pray to Phagpa Chen Rezig, please let me go while I'm sleeping. Now it's time for me to go.

"Kyapsu chi" (I'll have come into refuge) is an expression of relief that means something like "thank God," and the words *painful struggle* here are a gloss on *sambol-nambol,* a Yolmo singsong phrase used to depict anguished struggles with deadly wounds or ailments, as when a body rocks up and down in pain: "Father is hurting, so he's struggling in pain!" The phrase built on the syllable *bol,* which, when cast as a verb, can mean something like "to struggle, resist, fight, quarrel," as in "Nga bolsin" (I struggled), a sentence Kisang uttered when relating her transfer to Shomkharka in marriage. "Eh, saying this, I struggled." Such efforts correlate with other scenes in Yolmo lives, in which people seek to be free of a force of otherness, as when resisting the demands of others. They also faintly recall occasions wherein people try to be clear of hindrances or nagging afflictions, be it by "binding" themselves against the assaults of demonic beings, "cleansing" their forms of impurities, or seeking refuge in the Buddha.

Many Yolmo wa speak of wanting to die without pain or any felt sense of suffering.[15] Karmu Omu told us, "Some people say that so-and-so has died in bed while sleeping. It would be great if I could also die like that." Gom Dolma, in turn, had this to say: "The best way to die is without any pain and in an unconscious state, because then we don't have to bear any pain and trouble in our bodies while dying. . . . It would be good if I die while sleeping, without any illness or hardship. But will I die like that? I think I'll have so many hardships, then die. It's all my fate. . . . I won't be attached to anyone when I die. I'll just have my eyes shut and die without any thoughts or feelings."

For Kisang as well: no attachment, no pain, no thoughts or feelings. In praying that she die while asleep, without having to "feel anything," she was asking to die without the fullness of suffering that marks some deaths. She wanted to pass into the otherness of death somnambulantly, with the stillest of actions, and so avoid the kinds of struggles and attachments between self and others that the movements of life so often requires.

"Dying is this," Kisang once said. But what, precisely, was that "this-ness" composed of? What, in short, constitutes a death?

A great deal, in Kisang's case. Her dying was all-worldly. Much more than a physiological process alone, it touched every aspect of her life. It affected her body, speech, and mind, her orientations to space and time, her sensing of the world, her engagements with others, the grounds of acting in life. Her dying was, by definition, undoing her world and her means of engaging with that world. It shaped her evaluations of herself and worried her thoughts on how others might be evaluating her speech and form and so her life and death. Thoughts of dying bled into the life story we were trying to elicit. Her life, as recollected, was defined by the ending of that life, much as her dying could be understood only in terms of the life she led before. Death had come to her sem. Elements of decay as sensed by her—a dissolving body, a forgetful mind, imperfect speech—made clear the limits of a composite form.

Nothing was always the same, however, for the moods and lifeworlds voiced through her "little bit of talking" were transient, shifting from moment to moment. Thoughts arose, then dissolved into other thoughts. There was, I think, no single "self" or "subject" to speak of here, but rather various intensities of speech and action—life, death, absence, presence—

which, when strung together, could say something about the complex valences of her world. In trying to come to terms with the features of her dying, I have therefore found it necessary to rely on a rather nomadic, word-bound phenomenology.

In sifting through the formations of her demise, I have been struck by the ways in which fundamental aspects of Yolmo thought and action recurred in her life in novel, re-formed ways. There was, for example, an air of stillness in her lifeworld that had a lot in common with other forms of stillness evident in Yolmo lives, though it was a stillness onto itself. Similarly, the disengagement and inaction that blanketed her body and mind were in close accord with certain disengagements and "nondoings" found in other domains of Yolmo life, such as the meditative retreats of lamas, while her liminal plight between life and death echoed the formal logic of the "between state" of the bardo. It is possible that, in talking about dying, Kisang drew upon her knowledge of religious discourses in either tacit or overt ways. But given that she said she did not know well what, for instance, the term *bardo* meant, and given that she had never received the kind of training that Yolmo lamas undergo that enables them to speak directly about such matters, it makes more sense to conclude that there was something in the formal underpinnings of her world that led her to construe her dying in the ways that she did. Her observations that she was neither dead nor alive, that she thought one-pointedly of death, that the congeries of body, speech, and mind were eroding, that her sensory faculties were collapsing, and that she no longer had the agency to act, including the capacity to act out her death—all this could have come from themes inherent in any sacred teachings she had heard or overheard that were then molded to suit the particulars of her life. But I doubt that this is how her understandings came about. They appeared to emerge, rather, from certain tacit takes on action, time, form, and meaning common to her thoughts. This means that, if one is to understand well what dying entailed for her, the demise must be considered within the contexts of the prevailing circumstances of her life.

Invested in her dying, for instance, were fundamental, culturally honed themes of going and staying, of movement and stillness. After a life of displacements and relocations, one can become bedridden and be forced to "stay still." One can "go" quickly into death, or one can be "blocked" from dying.

There were culturally salient ways of talking. A person can draw on a rhetoric of repletion in suggesting that she thinks only of death and so is preparing for death in all the right ways. Dying can be, in part, a discursive act. A woman's talk can also lead to close-to-home depictions of what she takes to be the phenomenal grounds of dying.

Things can appear full and replete, or they can strike one as being empty and depleted. A person can think purely of death or sometimes cease to think at all. Death can blanket a person's mind just as that mind perceives the "loss" of other faculties of a life.

There were act-based orientations to time and storytelling. Actions can occur, and they can cease occurring, to the point, even, that one's death cannot be undertaken, and one appears faintly deathless.

Actions bring consequences. Within the interlocking circuits of cause and effect that pattern a life, death can be one such "effect." The manner in which a woman dies can reflect how she lived in her present life or any previous lifetimes of hers.

There were ideas of suffering and comfort, of dhukpu and kyipu, and the moral logic of such worldly states. Hardship can lead to comfort later on. Virtuous deeds and mindful prayer can contribute to a good rebirth, perhaps even in the land of "comfort and happiness."

There were basic, culturally patterned understandings of the logic and flow of time. A person can be fated to die at a certain time and perhaps even sense that "the time of dying" has arrived, though such hunches will always be in doubt until one's "life" is truly depleted.

There were moments of active engagement in the world and stretches of time "between" such activities. One can find oneself stuck between life and death and so be considered neither dead nor fully alive.

Motifs of coherence and dissolution often came about. Composite forms—houses, families, bodies, minds, narratives, lives—cohere in certain ways, and they dissolve in certain ways. A person's body can decay and disappear. Her sensory faculties can erode. Her smarts and abilities can wane, leading to the sense that she is becoming increasingly raglike, unskilled, insignificant.

There were different possibilities for status and vocal power. An arch of significance can span one's life, with a daughter's constrained silence forging into a mother's tempered effectiveness, which in turn dim into a widow's marginalia.

There was the welcome, comforting presence of others. A person can spend much of her time alone in a room, listening to a radio, or she can be visited by friends and family who respectfully call her Ibi.

There were the potentially critical voicings of others. A person will inevitably worry about what others might say about her manner of dying and so, by inference, her manner of living. Death can be a sharply intersubjective affair.

There were glimmers of purity, isolation, and nonsentience. A person can grow detached from others and the various holdings of her life, and she can wish to die untouched by pain.

Time. Action. Movement. Causality. Force. Form. Speech. Desire. Sensation. The prepersonal imageries and forces relevant to these and other modalities did not pattern Kisang's world in any singular or deeply structured way, transpiring, as they did, in the odd corners of her thoughts and actions, like veins emerging in a leaf or cracks in a sidewalk. But they did shape how her dying took form or, to put it differently, how her life gave form to her take on dying. She was dying in the ways she was largely because her life had led her to die in those ways. Other forces—historical, ideological, political, social, biological— worked as well to compose her subjective sense of dying. A lasting image in my mind, however, is of a person drawing upon certain images and formal sensibilities in thinking, sensing, and talking with others while those same images and sensibilities shaped the modes of thought and action of the person thinking, sensing, talking. The scene was one of a person approaching death through the means available to her. It so happens that these were also the means that constituted her.

The question What constitutes a death? quickly unfolds then into the question What constitutes a person? or better still, What constitutes a (dying) person? In the Yolmo case, a provisional answer to the last two queries is that a person consists of, among other things, particular footings in time and space, visceral sensibilities of form and formlessness, politically charged ways of talking and acting, rhetorical stances toward the world, a grab bag of action-forms, various ethical concerns and duties, the recurrent regard of others, self-tailored ways of sensing the world, a tracework of memories, intertwinements of word and matter, and conversations real or imagined. There is no true core of selfhood here, no single place to fix a name. Nor are there any clear divides between language and sensation, or action and being, or self and other; each feeds into the other. What forms and reforms in time is a complex tangle of action, thought, speech, sensation.

That tangle de-forms in death. If a Yolmo person is composed of many interwoven, interdependent strands of action and being, then dying can entail the gradual or sudden unraveling of these strands. If we can speak of the emergence of Yolmo selves as a matter of "dependent arising," as Buddhist teachings propose, then perhaps we can speak of a person's last days as a process of "dependent cessation." The aging faculties of body, speech, and mind, long dependent on one another, erode conjointly, interactively.

In the end, complexity, rather than simplicity, is the rule. Myriad dynamics of sense, form, force, voice, anticipation, touch, and gaze work together in the intershaded recesses of a life. Traces of Kisang's dying can inform us about the phenomenal, interaffecting makings of one person's passing and remind us about the transience of any life. They can also give us some sense of what it means to be a person in the world of forms in which Yolmo people live and die.

Last Words

Certain forms recurred, certain ways of talking. "Before dying," Karma told me in 1997, "when a person feels that now he's going to die, he calls his sons and daughters, he says everything to them, he talks about everything, and these are the last words to the relatives."

Kha jhem is the proper Yolmo term for those last words spoken to family members in the hours before dying, when loved ones are often themselves trying to see the face of the dying person one last time. *Kha*, which literally means "mouth," is found in many compound words that signify speech, oaths, or oral actions of some sort, while *jhem* is related to the Tibetan word *chem*, which can connote "roaring noises," "thunderous sounds," "exhortation."[1] When combined, the words denote a "farewell exhortation" or "last will or testament."[2] *Kha jhem zjhagen*, in turn, is the verb phrase for this act, with *zjhagen* meaning "putting, placing, depositing." "*Kha jhem zjhagen* means 'putting the dying person's talk,'" Nogapu explained with a hand-gesture miming the act of putting something down, away from the body. The last words are deposited away from the dying self and presented to others.

The dying person usually voices an oral will of sorts. A father in particular might speak of financial matters with his wife and children, and he might clarify the nature of property owned or the amount of debts owed to or by the family. He might also make provisions for the care of any young children, as Wangel Lama, Kisang's first husband, did while he lay dying in his cousin's lap. An elder might also detail what should take place during the funeral rites to be conducted on his behalf, in part to assure that there are witnesses to any requests made. As Mheme put it when speaking of the different ways that people die:

Some die without saying anything. Some die after having said everything, "I have this, I own that." Some die without saying anything, and then die very easily. Some say at the time of dying, "Keep this thing, put this thing here, perform the funeral in this way." They advise people. Some people are called "weakened speech" [*bol chagen*]. They're like a mute person. He can't speak to us, and when we speak to him, he can't hear us.... Some say, "Give money to this person, get money from this person, arrange the funeral like this, do this thing." Some speak like this. But some die before saying these things. If we can, it's important to talk about such things. If we say these things, then everyone hears about them. If the person's family doesn't arrange for a good funeral [to be performed], then everyone will know and say they haven't done a good funeral.

A dying person, especially an elderly man, might also speak of moral matters. He might advise members of his family to practice dharma, or he might implore them to act in virtuous ways. "Don't fight, because fighting's no good, and don't get too angry.... Don't act in ways that will harm the village" are a few of the utterances that Nogapu told me he has heard the dying express in the village of Malemchi, where he grew up. With such words, "deposited" into the future, a person's knowledge and values can transfer to the next generation.

If there was an air of last words in Ghang Lama's exchanges with us, and I think there was on occasion, his words tended to involve the latter sort of moral counsel. In particular his words advanced thoughts on how to live a good life or, in what amounted to much the same thing, how to prepare well for death. Here, though, such counsel was geared not to his children specifically but to younger Yolmo wa in general. The old man expected to be able to talk with his sons and daughters about personal and financial matters before he died, and so there was no need to do so in his conversations with me. But the life story work, conducted during the final years of his life, enabled the lama to convey what he took to be a virtuous life to a generation of Yolmo wa, who, he felt, could benefit from such advice.

Outside of these general "tellings," certain exchanges between Mheme and his interlocutors invoked a tangible genre of last words. (I did not find this to be the case with Kisang Omu.) "The questions are all finished, Mheme. Is there anything else that you would like to say?" Norbu and I asked him at the end of our final taped conversation with him in July 1997, a week before I was to leave for the States and a few minutes after asking him what major worries he had had in life. The way we phrased our question suggested an end to our talk and a chance for Mheme to contribute any final thoughts, with words and phrases such as *finished* and *anything else that you would like to say* evidently serving as "metalinguistic framing devices" whose significance I was not fully aware of then.[3]

"What to say, now?" Mheme replied, then spoke the following words, quoted in an earlier chapter, as though the genre elicited led him to think of another imminent scene of final words and how successful it might be:

When I die, will everyone [in the family] be together or not? I worry about that....Now, my sons have gone, my daughter has gone, one's own have gone. When a man dies he's cremated. If his children cannot see his face before he's burned, [they ask,] "Where has he gone?! Where has he gone?" Isn't that a worry? We have as many worries as there are worries.

The lama's final words with us worried the possibility of conversing with his children one last time before he died and whether they would all be able to see his face before his body was cremated.

"There are not other things to ask?" Norbu then asked.

"No. What else is there to ask about?" Mheme replied. "That's it. We must do service to the gods, and we must treat our father and mother well."

He then offered some thoughts on living and dying:

Dying is not good. It's good to live as long as one can. If one gets the blessings of many old people, one will also be able to live for a long time. We might not get this kind of life again, in the next life. We might not have this kind of body, in the next life. What kind of life we will get, what kind of food will be available, what kind of place we'll reach—we can't know these things. If one does a lot of significant dharma, then one can have a better life later. Now, if a man sins in this life, oh, he'll be a small [insignificant, low-status] man then.

We then asked if he was pleased with the nature of our talks together, and he said he was. He then continued with his counsel:

Now, what is, what is not? One does this, one does that. One mustn't sin. One has to do a lot of dharma, not just sit around. Otherwise, if one doesn't work, nothing will come of it. One needs to work, one needs to make money, because people won't just come and give anything. To survive, one has to work oneself.

It's possible that the latter words were voiced for the benefit of Yolmo youths, including Norbu, who was then underemployed and who Mheme felt needed to be doing more with his life. A testament to the makings of a successful, virtuous life, these were words to live and die by.

Ten months later, in May 1998, another scene of last words took form. Nogapu and I had come to talk formally with Mheme for the last time, a few days before I was to again leave Nepal. Around this time Mheme and Rhidu Pema were thinking of traveling to Thodong sometime soon in order to avoid the summer heat of the Kathmandu Valley (their daughter Maya doubted that they would actually make the trip). When we arrived in early afternoon, the door that opened to the stairs leading up to their home was locked from the inside, which was often the case when they were napping. We knocked on the door, but there were still no signs of movement above. "Maybe it's their time," Nogapu quipped. We knocked several times more, and Nogapu realized that one side of the door had become very thin and frail. "It's time to build a new house here," he said, poking a finger through the door, then tapping on the walls in the hallway. "This one has gotten old."

He then stepped into the courtyard outside and called up to the second floor. We finally heard footsteps, and Mheme came down the stairs to unlatch the door. He and his wife had been sleeping. Maya had gone out shopping with a cousin of hers. Rhidu Pema, suffering from a feverish cold, apologized for being unable to prepare tea for us. "She's unwell, and I don't know how to make tea," Mheme added in a regretful tone.

The lama looked a bit sleepy at first, and his answers to our questions were initially quiet and subdued. But as we continued to talk he became more alert, his voice grew stronger, and we proceeded to talk at length about a range of topics. As we spoke Rhidu Pema lay atop the bed, often with her eyes closed. At times she contributed a word or two to the conversation, but without much force, and we could not hear her very well.

Two hours later it was time to end our talk by clarifying certain issues pertaining to the materials we had collected.

"Now our talk is finished, isn't it, Mheme?"

"Yes."

"Do you have anything else to say? You can say it. We'll be making this book. Do you want to put anything else in the life story?"

"What can be put in? If I put in [knowledge from] our chhe books, they won't understand. So what can be put in?"

Finding that he could not include passages from his lamaic texts, since they would not be understood by English-speaking readers, Mheme was saying that there was little else of value that he could add.

"Not the books, Mheme. Your talk, for later."

"If I read from the books, saying, 'This thing, that thing,' they can't understand that. They don't know the meanings of the lama writings. If they were Sherpa [Yolmo], then I could say, 'That was this.' But they're not. What to say? I'm just thinking about a bodhicitta mind."

Mheme looked at me and spoke to Nogapu in Yolmo. "Is he coming back or not? Will we meet again or not? If I haven't died, then he needs to come up there [to Thodong]. If I go up there, we can meet. If I'm here, we can also meet. How can we meet if I die? He won't return until after one or two summers."

His eyes then lit on me. "So when are you coming back?!" he asked in Nepali, loudly, as if to alert us to a shift in his target audience—to someone with a less nuanced ear.

"Me?" I asked.

"Yes. After going down there [to America], when will you return?"

"After two years."

"In two years I'll die. What—"

"Ah. You won't die."

"I won't die?!"

"You won't die."

After this rapid-fire exchange ended, I spoke with Nogapu, who transferred my words to Mheme as such: "If you have anything to tell him later, you can have your granddaughters write to him. He'll come after two years, maybe."

"Okay. If I go up there, I'll tell my grandchildren. They'll know [where I am]. If he comes back, and I haven't died, then that will be good."

When Nogapu was conveying these words to me, Mheme began to speak again in the Yolmo language. "After two years I'll die, that's all. My body has already died. My speech hasn't died. Now I myself think that I'm dying. There's been too many years. I can't stand, I can't walk. If I try to walk around, my body staggers. I come close to falling." He then added in Nepali, "Now, I won't last very long."

As Mheme quietly uttered the mantra "om mani-padme hūm," Nogapu and I spoke in English again. "Well," I said to Nogapu, "you can tell Mheme that I still think that he has a lot of strength left and that I think in my heart, *mero manmā*, that I will see him again when I come back."

Nogapu possibly heard me in ways different from how I had intended to be heard, or he wanted to say something different from what I had proposed, because he then said, "Mheme, put strength in your sem and stay, okay? You can meet after he returns."

"Yes, that's right, for sure," Mheme said. "I need to have faith. Only the gods know."

"If the gods support this," said Rhidu Pema, who by then had woken up a bit more and was lying on her side with her face turned toward Nogapu and me.

"If the gods support this," Mheme continued, "then we can meet. He's thinking about it, and I'm thinking about it. What to do, then? I'm thinking of staying one or two years. But what I'm saying might not happen. What do we know? The Three Precious Ones [know only]."

His voice had become shaky and tearful. "Since this year, when I put on clothes...I can't lift up my legs and hands. It's like this, no doubt. When I went to the medical clinic [to receive treatment for a sore back], they said, 'Your time is coming, so why do you need medical care?' I think this is true."

As the old man voiced these concerns and wiped some tears from his eyes, Nogapu twice said "laso," used here as the yes-like affirmation that often serves among Yolmo wa as a respectful acknowledgment of someone's speech. He then responded on his own to the laments just voiced. "Mheme, you don't have to worry. We won't stay [alive] as long as you have."

"Ah! How could that be?"

"Laso, Mheme."

"Even you won't be able to remain standing [as long as I have]. The Tamang also say the same thing, everyone does, about the old people [that they live longer than their descendants do]."

After consulting with me, Nogapu communicated my next concern as such: "Mheme, when writing the book, he'll put in the good things about you, such as that you're a straight lama, that you're a good person."

"It's true," Mheme said, then added after a pause. "I feel myself that when he takes this and goes there, I'm also going there, even though I haven't reached there. There's no knowledge [about America]. What to do?"

"Mheme, your grandchildren and your grandchildren's grandchildren might be able to read this book."

"They can read it. Later, later, the words will stay.... We can read it if we're born here. If we're born in another place, where would it be? Where will we be born? In another country, in Tibet, in India—where, where? Our soul goes outside [of the body]. It's like the air."

"Is there anything that he shouldn't put in the book?"

"Put it in well. If he's going to put it in, put it in well. Everything can be put. If I haven't died, I can also read the book. He'll bring it. I can know what's in there. If I don't understand, my children will."

We spoke a bit more about wanting to give Mheme copies of the tapes that we had recorded. "If you leave the cassette copy," Mheme told us, "then there's a tape recorder in the village. If you make a copy, then all the words will come. It's these words that we need to understand."

"Inside the tape there's the talk between you and me [in Yolmo]," Nogapu noted.

"Okay, okay," Mheme replied. "I don't understand his writing. But I understand the talk between us."

"It's the talk from before, when he asks me, I ask you, you answer me, then I tell him."

"Yes, yes."

With these matters clarified I gestured toward the tape recorder and asked Mheme if our talk was finished. He nodded his head yes, and I turned off the machine, but not before it picked up a final remark by him: "Again, if I go up there, I'll send a message." I then told him that I would try to write to him sometime soon.

As Nogapu and I prepared to leave, Mheme and Rhidu Pema again expressed regret that they could not prepare any tea for us. We told them not to worry about this, because Nogapu had to rush off to do some work. Nogapu then clasped Mheme's hand within his own, looked into his eyes, and said something that I did not catch; I took these gestures to convey sentiments of respect, sympathy, and compassion. There were again tears in Mheme's eyes. I stood next to Nogapu, held Mheme's hand in my own, and exchanged looks with him. When I said goodbye, noting that I hoped to meet them again in two years, Mheme said twice, "We can meet if I haven't died." Soon Nogapu and I were outside. As we walked down the muddy path that trailed away from their house, Nogapu turned to me and said in English, "It's sad. They think they're going to die soon."

I find myself returning to this extended exchange, even though the words sadden me whenever I think through them. Perhaps my returns are a semiritualized way for me to "see" Mheme's form for the last time, as Yolmo wa might say, although I find that I am not trying to remember the aged lines on his face so much as I am interested in tracing the fissures and contact-points of our talk.

Deferral, difference, and promises of mediation and copresence are a few of the elements I hear voiced among us. Most in question was when and if Mheme and I would be able to meet again once I had left for the States and he had departed for Thodong. We were both going home, as it were, and quitting the middle ground of Kathmandu, an impure land of betweenness in which the lama did not want to die and which I could no longer inhabit. His understanding that he, too, was leaving Kathmandu was perhaps a comforting and empowering one for him, since I was not the only one on the move, and my departure was not the only reason for our parting. But these plans meant that displacements and separations were imminent, and we would no longer be able to talk with one another. The workings of movement and stasis, of "going" or "staying," absence and presence, contact and disconnection, again played themselves out in Yolmo lives. Despite the parting to come, we made several tentative promises of future communication that indirectly served as tokens of our respect and friendship. An ethics of contact was intimated. Mheme said he would be sure to leave word for me if he traveled to Thodong. I vowed to return to Nepal and so visit him again in two years time.

"One or two summers" later was a considerable stretch of time for Mheme, given his understanding that he would not last much longer. In talking about this, we were faced with the strong possibility that these were his last substantive words to me. Whatever the case, it was going to be a close call: "After two years I'll die—that's all." The end of our talks together evidently strengthened in Mheme's thoughts the idea that his life would also soon be coming to an end. One end brought another to mind. The passage of time was palpable here. But this was time not simply as some abstract human construct; it was a consequential and somewhat cruel force in the world. Yolmo physics informed Mheme that, the longer he lived, the less time he had left to live. There had "been too many years"; his time was "coming"; he would not "last long." One understanding shared between us was that he would be dying soon. Some things that could be done at the time might not be possible later on.

So the question was when the inevitable would occur and what that timing implied for our conversations together. When would Ghang Lama die? For how long would his "passing" be deferred? Where would he be reborn? Would these be his final words to me? Although there were frightful clues that suggested that he would not last long, such as the words heard at the medical clinic and the increasing frailty of his body, any answers to these questions had to remain tentative. As Mheme himself observed, "What do we know?" Unlike divine beings, humans can know about such matters only poorly, if at all. Much remains uncertain.

Several statements suggested desires to defer Mheme's passing. When he told me that he would die in two years, I quickly responded, "You won't die [before then]." I voiced and revoiced this affirmation, because I felt at the time that we would meet again. But it was also true that I would have liked for his death, and any last words, to be deferred until a later time. I wanted to delay the inevitable. Nogapu and Mheme spoke, in turn, of willed postponements of the elder's death. "Put strength in your sem and stay," the former advised the latter, who responded by saying, "Yes, that's right, for sure. I need to have faith." All of this was wishful speaking, as the old man himself later noted; all that we were proposing "might not happen." Mheme's words alluded to two other deferrals of death that, sustained by thoughts of movement, took a more subtle form. He first advanced the idea that he felt himself to be going to my homeland when I took the transcripts of our talk with me. He then later offered up the uncanny possibility that he might be able to read his own life story in his next life: "We can read it if we're born here." In some way, then, something of his consciousness could remain engaged with the text after he died. Complete annihilation would be deferred either through print or through transmigrations of his soul. Dying would not quite be dying.

But unanswerable questions persisted. "If we're born in another place, where would it be?" Alongside such unknowns are the limits to cross-cultural knowledge involved in our work, which Mheme alluded to on several occasions. He suggested, for instance, that if he tried to include further passages from the religious texts he was reading daily then, people who could not read Tibetan would not understand those passages. He noted that while he could understand the talk between us, he did not understand my writing. And though he felt that he was also going to my homeland when I took his words and voicings with me, he had no knowledge of that place, and little could be done to change that. Such remarks indicated a firm grasp, on Mheme's part, of the cultural and linguistic divides between our worlds and the differences we continued to bring to our meetings together.

This is not to say, however, and I do not think Mheme was saying, that such divides are all pervasive and so hinder any kind of communication or understanding whatsoever. Rather, such knowledge is hard to come by. It requires difficult, dialogic work and a willingness to "meet" and talk with others.

And, often, mediation. Several promises of mediation were implied in our words. Mheme (and Rhidu Pema) noted the possibility of divine mediation in extending his life a bit longer: "If the gods support this, then we can meet." We also agreed that his grandchildren, several of whom can speak and write English fluently, could relay any messages between us once we separated. Finally, he suggested that his children could help him to understand what was in the book once it was written. His successors, the children of a different "time," could transfer information between different places and languages. Communications between him and me, in turn, often required linguistic mediation, especially if we were to converse most fully. Nogapu nicely depicted the tripartite dimensions of our person-to-person transfers when he told Mheme that the talk recorded on the cassettes was "the talk from before, when he asks me, I ask you, you answer me, then I tell him."

Nogapu and Mheme's children and grandchildren thus served as intermediaries between Mheme and me. They were agents of betweenness who helped to mediate the spatial, linguistic, and cultural divides that separated us now and again. Through such mediations, messages could be sent and received. Some things could be known. At times, of course, mediation worked to reword messages, as when Nogapu passed my words on to Mheme in terms at odds with how I meant them: "Mheme, put strength in your sem and stay, okay?" Original meanings could be radically deferred.

Sometimes it was worth skirting the middle man altogether, as when Mheme asked me directly in Nepali when I would be returning to Nepal. When I listen to the section of the tape that registered the exchange that followed, I hear in Mheme's voice and can recall seeing in his eyes a tone of relaxed amicableness. Our expressed affinity for each other can be sensed in the syllables of the latter end of the exchange, especially if heard in the original Nepali.

Dui barsa pachi.	(After two years.)
Dui barsamā, ma marchha. Ke [garne?]	(In two years I'll die. What [to do?])
Ah. Tapāī marnuhunna.	(Ah. You won't die.)
Mardaina?!	([I] won't die?!)
Marnuhunna.	([You] won't die.)

Our words, which did not require pronouns, echoed one another, much as a (grand)son's actions might double his (grand)father's. Such a linguistic duplication among Yolmo wa, which usually coincides with a sustained "eye encounter," as it did with Mheme and me on this occasion, often hints at a wished-for consubstantiality of thought and feeling among speakers. Mheme, perhaps more honest about the inevitability of his death, appeared to doubt my affirmation that he would not die anytime soon; and yet our mirrored words suggested that our minds were in accord with one another, despite their amicable differences. My elder soon acknowledged a mutuality of interest between us and the possibility of empathy when he later said, "He's thinking about it [meeting again], and I'm thinking about it." As the "he" referred to here, I hear in these words the comforting idea that Mheme acknowledged the chance that there could be a "one-semness" between us. We were both thinking about meeting face-to-face again. The term *meet,* which the lama used in several ways, was significant, for among Yolmo wa its physics imply contact between the borders of two objects or subjects, and so promise moments of copresence in a world of change.

Despite the gaps in culture and language, there was therefore the possibility of copresence still, of a shared consubstantiality of thought and feeling at times, through either direct or mediated communication. Yet nothing was certain. There was neither complete ignorance nor perfect omniscience, neither complete absence nor sheer presence. Our engagements together usually involved something in between these extremes. For what it's worth, I take such bardoic "betweenness" to indicate the nature of my ties to Mheme and anthropological endeavors in general. The words and gazes passed between us transpired within the liminal borderlands between cultures, lives, languages, consciousnesses.

This, then, is how I recall Mheme's "face," in dialogue with my own, during my last visit to his home that year. It is the record of an engagement.

On the long, sleepless journey home from Nepal that year, through a numbing blur of airports and jetliners, I had a chance to reflect on what I had come to know about Kisang Omu and Ghang Lama. I thought about the moral sensibilities at work in their lives and the moral dimensions of my work with them. I wondered whether I would see the two alive again. It hurt to part from them.

I also jotted in a tattered notebook a few thoughts on the sensory features of the two elders' lives. In thinking about this further, with several years of reflection to draw from, I find still that the two elders sensed the world differently. Kisang was as acoustically engaged with the world as Mheme was visually attuned to it. Mheme, book-learned, vision-minded lama that he was, often processed the world through visual, readerly perceptions. His environment was largely one of visible signs, sacred texts, mirrors, doubles, mirages, visual echoes. Kisang, who never learned to read and who could see but poorly in her later years, minded most what people said or might say and what she herself should or should not say. She inhabited a world of voices.

Their respective ways of sensing tied into, patterned even, diverse aspects of their lives, from how they thought and talked to how they anticipated their deaths. For one thing, the two appeared to remember the past in dissimilar ways. Kisang's words and narratives indicated that she recalled past events primarily through the voices she heard. The lama said he remembered most scenes once seen, and his recollections often had a strong visual cast to them: "My father was a big man." "I can see all of Thodong now, in my sem." While there were acoustic aspects to Mheme's recollections and visual aspects in Kisang's, there was not the same rush of voices in his recollections that could be heard when Kisang delved into the past. His sem remembered most things once seen. Kisang's heartmind retained deeds and voices that had marked it in some way.

The lama's thoughts, accordingly, often had a visual cast to them. There was an observational, "looking at" quality to Mheme's takes on the world, in that his words often proffered proposition-like statements that described things as he saw them: "To be a lama is difficult." "I've had a lot of dhukpu in my life." These were assertions, but they also had an air of objectivity to them, as though there was an object or phenomenon to be perceived, to be "read," as it were, and Mheme, standing back a bit from what he was regarding, was doing just that through his words. By so doing, he could "show" to others what he himself had observed. In accord with this, he most valued moments of lucidity and clear visibility, kurā that were pure and "straight." He also took pride in his self-willed accomplishments and self-possession in life. His consciousness was predicated on the virtues of perceptual clarity, independent action, and sober, contemplative sight.

Kisang's cognitions, in contrast, were more associative in nature. One thought quickly led to other thoughts, and her thoughts in general were linked to other thoughts, to other kurā, especially the words and deeds of others, as though she was always in the middle of several conversations with those close to her. Indeed, I often had the sense that her inner thoughts, her thoughts to herself, were in effect "spoken" ones, in dialogue with others. There was an interwoven quality to her words and thoughts; they were immersed in tangled relations with the words and actions of others. The stream of her recollected utterances intersected with the voicings of others, but they did so in such a way that those voicings commonly ran against the grain of her own wishes, with the thoughts and actions of others at once integral to, but often at odds with, her own reflections. Her concerns showed how word-conscious she was, how much she fretted about the talk she put forth, how much she anticipated the voicings of others. Her consciousness implied a constant, expectant awareness of the consciousnesses of others.

In tandem with this were differences in how the two spoke of their lives. While Mheme told few stories, tending to couch his words instead in assertions and seemingly detached observations, Kisang's words cohered around subjectively situated, morally pregnant narratives more than they advanced general declarations. The lama doled out straight, authoritative "tellings." Kisang voiced socially vexed utterances. In general, she hesitated to speak in general or abstract terms. Her words were openly subjective in their claims. They pertained to things as she encountered them in her own life, not as they might be in any ideal sense, and her utterances seldom carried the aura of eye-sure objectivity that Mheme's statements did. Different kinds of truth and different means of assessing the truth were thus in play. Whereas the lama looked for stable truths in objects that could be readily seen, such as a footprint or a sacred text, Kisang took as relative, socially established truths what people "said" was the case about something.

As they lived, so they died. Thoughts of frail speech were central to Kisang's later years, while motifs of visibility were prominent in the lama's takes on death and dying. Old age for Kisang was a process of fragmentation, dispersal, jumbled words. Dispersed words indicated a disjointed self. Her body, speech, and mind were eroding; the strands of her life were unraveling; her words were coming less straight; she worried about what others might say about her passing. For Ghang Lama old age was a process of diminishment, uncertainty, and increasing absence in life. His body was getting smaller, less visible, and many features of his life evident in earlier years could no longer be seen. Death appeared to him as a scene of altered, echoic vision.

All this shaped how the two sensed the implications of my work with them. Ghang Lama saw in his talks with me a means to inscribe aspects of his life within a lasting visual medium. To an extent, there was a potential for freedom and transcendence in the texts we were producing, for through them he could transcend the physical and temporal limits of his body and establish lasting visible traces within the pages of a text. Kisang Omu, much less invested in leaving traces of her self, had a more ambivalent, skeptical take on the written words that followed in the wake of our conversations together. As far as I know, she did not find anything liberating or transcendent in our work together. Instead, she voiced concerns about what others might say about how her skill in speaking and how, in turn, that buzz of words might shape her identity among others, either before or after she died.

So, distinct ways of sensing, thinking, remembering, knowing, and talking, and of living and dying more generally, were thus at work in the two lives, for a variety of complicated, interpatterned reasons. Yet while I am justified in saying this, it is also important not to overstate the differences between the two elders. By no means did Kisang know the world only through speech, or Mheme only through vision. Vision, along with the faculties of touch, taste, smell, and "mind," played an important role in Kisang's life, while Ghang Lama's life similarly proceeded through an interplay of sight, sound, taste, smell, and touch. It was a matter of different emphases, different patterns, much as two, similarly designed fabrics can both contain a vital array of colors but with red tints highlighted in one and blue ones prominent in the other. And even when Kisang was heeding the words of others or Mheme was gazing upon others, those voicings and engazements entailed similar themes. Kisang's acoustics and Mheme's optics, distinct in their sensory ways, were both dialogic, participatory, transactive, and reciprocative in means. Both were intersubjective in reach. Both entailed means of communication that could be persuasive, assertive, questioning, praising, critical, or caring in their effects. Both worked to shape and reshape people's actions and understandings. Both were founded on morally and politically charged engagements with others. Both could make or break persons. Both took form in the communicative spaces between people. Both were rooted in time. While the two elders engaged the world through different sensory means, the engagements themselves often had a lot in common. As it was, those engagements said something about the constitution of persons among Yolmo people: Kisang, Mheme, and others were highly mindful of others, transactive in means, act-based, morally engaged, subject to time, sensorially attuned, at once distinct and interrelated.

Observations such as these might tell us something worthwhile about the play of the senses in specific social settings. To wit, *(a)* sensate engagements have both personal and cultural strands to them. Sensory perceptions are profoundly patterned by the technologies, social histories, and cultural sensibilities that contribute to people's lives. At the same time, individuals perceive the world in different ways. They live

out different sensory biographies. *(b)* Distinct kinds of sensory perception take effect at different times in people's lives. They are also valued
differently by various groups and individuals. When it comes to sensory
perceptions, multiplicities, shifting orientations, and changes in time
are the mean, not the exception. *(c)* Sensing is a political act. The ways
in which sensory perception is understood, enacted, advocated, and
learned by individuals or institutions relate in important ways to political relations and social hierarchies in specific settings. How images are
perceived, smells transacted, words uttered, or touch engaged ties into
how certain truths are established, how certain social arrangements continue in time, how some hold power and authority over others, and
how acts of violence or contestation take form. *(d)* Sensory processes
play a substantial role in the formation of cultural subjects. What people
come to sense in their lives and how they are perceived, observed, and
talked about by others contribute to the makings of selfhood and subjectivity. For example, a man who learns to envision the appearances of
sacred beings, then identify with their divine qualities, can change his
ways of perceiving and acting in the world, while a woman who is constantly under the watchful, gossipy regard of others learns to act accordingly. How women and men sense the world and how they are sensed
by others pattern how they live and die. *(e)* Sensory engagements are as
much intersubjective processes as they are personal ones. They regularly
emerge in the course of interactions among people. Any considerations
of a person's sensory engagements in the world must therefore be considered within the frame of a person in reflective action among other
persons and other consciousnesses. More generally, what is required is a
phenomenological anthropology that can account for subjectivities not
simply as private domains of experience but in terms of their cross-cut-
ting standing among other subjectivities. *(f)* The senses are as much
performed as they are experienced. They are employed in specific contexts, and they actively affect the gist and evolution of those contexts
and sometimes alter them altogether. Specific acts of sensory discourse—a stench, a lingering look, the recollection of something once
heard—do certain things, with varying effects and implications, in the
lives of those involved. An anthropology of the senses thus calls for a
study of the pragmatics of sensing as much it calls for a cultural analysis
of sensory forms or a phenomenology of sensate experience. A key aim
of that study is to consider particular acts of sensing as they occur in the
real-time flow of social discourse in order to understand what realities
and understandings those acts enact or invoke. *(g)* Acts of sensing pro-

ceed within culturally constituted flows of time, and they are inherently
tied to ethical ideas and moral sensibilities. If one is to consider how the
senses work in any given society, one needs to give serious considera-
tion to the moral and temporal dimensions of sensory perception.

Altogether, diffuse arenas of life—political realities, social relations,
modes of thought and memory, communicative acts, forms of knowledge, assessments of truths and falsehoods, gender roles and identities—are shot through with diverse forms of sensory semiosis. An intricate mix of biological, political, social, cultural, and linguistic forces
contributes to how people sense the world. All the while, though, those
ways of sensing shape the sinews, the musculature, of that mix of forces.
Culturally established, personally rendered ways of sensing have a hand
in how power is asserted, how stories are told, how truths are established, how subjectivities form and reform, how bodies feel pain, how
people live and die. Anthropological inquiries cannot afford to neglect
this fact. For one thing, all of their subject matter has a sensory component to it, either explicitly or implicitly. The sensorial habits of field researchers shape what they notice, pay attention to, and record as data.
For another, whenever anthropologists busy themselves with ethnographic research in a particular social setting, they are invariably en-
meshed, whether they know it or not, in webs of sensory semiosis, such
that whenever they record a conversation, sip a cup of tea, look someone in the eyes, or write an ethnography, the implications of those
deeds, what they come to mean and the consequences they effect for
those involved, are shaped by local perspectives on sensory perception.
Ethnographic observations, always predicated on some sort of sensate
effort, are thus as much ethical and political acts as they are a means to
acquire knowledge. The very substance of anthropological knowledge is
founded on sensory semiosis.

Mheme never made the trip to Thodong, and I never wrote while I was
back in the States. But I did return, as promised, two years later, in August 2000, at a time when Yolmo wa and other Nepali peoples were
talking nightly about bribe-hungry government officials, an increasingly
corrupt police force, do-nothing politicians, and the violent advances of
a Maoist insurrection in the country's outlands. When I visited Mheme
in his home the day after I arrived in Kathmandu, I found a man in
good spirits but frailer and smaller than before. Soon after we began
talking, the lama recalled something we had discussed during my stay
two years earlier. "When you were leaving before," he said with a gleam

in his eyes, "I said I might not be alive when you came back, and you said you thought we would meet again." Evidently the exchange had struck his sem in some way, for I heard him repeat these words to others in the next few weeks, during subsequent visits to his home.

Temba D. Yolmo, the college student who began to work with me that year, accompanied me on one of these visits. He and I spoke to Mheme about the book that was then taking form, and we showed him the partial manuscript as contained within a loose-leaf notebook. Mheme looked at the pages we flashed before him, then said, "I can't read your language." When we then asked him if we could consult with him on some details of his life, he told us that, in effect, enough was enough. "I can't remember the things of the past anymore," he said. "The work we did before is good." I said in response that that was fine with me, but since there were a few facts I was still uncertain on, I wanted to check with him on them. He nodded a tentative yes. By then his wife had joined us in the room, and as she sat next to her husband, who was leaning back against the wall that bordered their bed, Temba and I proceeded to run through the contents of this book's second chapter. Mheme said, "Yes, that's right," to several things I mentioned but also corrected me on his father's name. He also added a few comments now and then, as Rhidu Pema did. After we had finished, he told us that he found that our questions had refreshed his memory. "I can't remember on my own," he said. "But when you asked the questions, things came to me." When asked if what we had discussed sounded good to him, he replied, "Yes. It's good."

But it was also clear that he had little interest in talking with me further about his life, in part, I think, because he felt that what we had done before was sufficient and good in itself. The tenor of our engagements had changed in the three years since we began working together. Our first conversations in 1997, with Norbu as go-between, presented an ornery grandfather who preached homilies for his grandson's benefit as much as he related accounts of his life, and a biographer who slowly gained his subject's confidence. Then, with my subsequent visits with Nogapu in 1998, a foresighted, death-expectant lama emerged, a man who spoke appreciatively and sometimes joyously about his life and dharmic views as two younger men eagerly listened to what he had to say. "I like to hear the talk of the old people, the talk of the past times," Nogapu told me after a visit to Mheme's one day. "When are you coming again [to talk to me]?!" Mheme beamed at the end of one such visit. When the dialogues came to a close that spring, both biographer and subject were saddened, jolted even, by the end of the face-to-face rapport and sem-to-text transfers that their parting implied. By the time I had returned in 2000, our work together, the intensity of those times, and the texts we had produced were, for Mheme, a thing of the past, waiting only for their final transfer into print. Now that his life story had been written down and passed on to others, he seemed to have grown less attached to that work and the life it chronicled.

Kisang Omu also expressed little interest that year in continuing with any formal conversations about her life. When Pramod and I visited her a few days after I arrived that August, I found her to be in good spirits. The monsoon rains that year had seeped into the room that she had been staying in, and so her son Kānchā had set up a bed for her in the day room where he had constructed his altar and hosted visitors; altogether this struck me as a more hospitable, less marginal room than the earlier one she inhabited. As we sat to join her there, Kisang said that she couldn't see well and so could not recognize me clearly. But she agreed when I proposed that she could now quickly recognize my voice. All told she appeared to be quite well, although smaller still. At some point she said to me, "I thought I might have died by the time you returned to Nepal. But I'm still alive." Later on Kānchā and Neela related that Kisang had been quite sick a few months back and had to be taken to a hospital to receive treatment. While they were bringing her there she was quite upset and angry, and she said gruffly to them, "Why are you taking me to the hospital?! I want to die at home, not in the hospital." She soon recovered and returned home. After these events were related to Pramod and me, Kisang said to no one in particular, "I have to die, it seems." Hearing this, her son laughed a bit and said, "Well, we all have to die."

When I noted during that visit that I was hoping to clarify some details of her life, Kisang said several times, in an insistent but not unfriendly way, that she could no longer remember the kurā of the past. She said much the same a few weeks later, when Temba and I dropped by and asked her if she would be willing to listen to the tape recordings of several stories she related in 1998. And yet she agreed to do so nonetheless. As she turned an ear to the voices she had conjured up two years earlier, she responded to several wordings with additional statements, "That's right.... He did say that," which appeared to be directed more to the recorded voices she heard than to those then present in the room. When the recording of each narrative ended, she said her words were "good" as they stood and required no additions or corrections.

"It's all right. I think this much sounds good. I don't think anything is missing," she said when asked if she wanted to add anything after listening to her narration of her first husband's death. With Kāñchā and Neela she also answered several questions we posed in regard to the import of specific deeds and utterances spoken of. We left it at that.

Temba and I paid another, entirely social, visit in early October, just before I left Nepal again. We had lunch there and talked informally with Kisang and Neela. When it was time to leave, I said goodbye to Kisang and noted that I hoped to meet and talk with her again when I returned to Nepal. Someone suggested that I could continue to "meet" with and remember Kisang through the book. Kisang nodded her head to this, then added, "We can meet in the next life, perhaps."

The next morning, the day before my flight home, I spent some time packing in my room at Norbu's house. I had to sift through my possessions and figure out what to take with me, what to give to others, and what to store in the homes of friends. I soon tired of this and walked out onto the terrace to have a look around. The aromas of a morning's meal simmered in the air. Scanning the rooftops of Boudhanath, hearing the bleats of car horns in the streets below, I considered the fact that I would soon be unable to perceive these things. I was going to miss the place, I thought, the whole bustle of it, the bad as well as the good, the muddy alleyways, the dusty heat, the music, the food, the noises, the people most of all. The thought then came into my mind that Kisang and Mheme might very well be faced with similar sentiments, but in a larger and more drastic way. Sometime soon they would no longer be alive. They had to part with the worlds familiar to them. There was an unavoidable finality to their lives and to their engagements with others. This disturbed me. I felt for their sorrows. I didn't want them to die. I was leaving Nepal without knowing whether I would be able to talk with them again. It seemed unthinkable that there would be a time when one could visit their homes without finding them there. There would be a day when mournful words would reach me.

These thoughts I kept to myself. I think the two knew how much I came to care for and appreciate them, and Yolmo wa themselves tend not to put such sentiments into words. So while I did visit both elders on several occasions in 2000, none of our conversations together had the intensity or seriousness of purpose that earlier ones had. Nor did any "last words" of any significance emerge. But still it strikes me that, as a whole, the book at hand has the markings of a set of last words deposited to others. Kisang Omu's and Ghang Lama's words might be passed on to later generations. It's worth noting, however, that Yolmo wa have been remarking lately that the dying do not pass on the "oral wills," or kha jhem, as often as they once did. There seem to be several reasons for this, Yolmo friends tell me. For one, the living situations of Yolmo people have been gradually improving through the years, such that a dying father is less worried these days about how his children might fare after he expires. Many are also living longer than their parents and grandparents did. This means that, when parents do die, their children are often adults themselves, with families of their own, so the need to exhort them to live morally good lives is less urgent, since they have already learned how to do so. People also often clarify their family's financial accounts and property holdings before the time of dying itself, thus making a dying will and testament unnecessary.

For one reason or another, then, important messages and will-like statements are now often conveyed through other means, if at all, and the moral counsel that once transferred regularly from the dying to the living, and old to young, is not sounded as often as it once was. Last words all around, it seems. This book harbors the final words of two elders within the profile of a speech genre, kha jhem, which is itself on the wane. And yet this is only one of many ways to envision these pages, one of several lasting echoes to bear in mind. First one form appears, then another. An analogy might be helpful.

Once, while Mheme was discussing with Nogapu and me how humans perceive the sights and sounds that transpire during the bardo, he noted that, when Chhe Gyalbu appears on the scene, he often "transforms" into the visage of three other divine emanations, which in turn can swiftly morph into the appearance of any of the other deities, Chhe Gyalbu included.

Guru Rinpoche, Chheku Nangwa Thaye, Longu Thujhe Chhenpo, these three bodies transform [*tulgen*].[4] *Tulgen* means the deities change bodies. That frightens us. Yes, the three gods mix, and that frightens us....Then Chhe Gyalbu changes and goes away, and then we can see Guru Rinpoche again. It's good if these three names can be remembered, because that's what frightens us.

The Yolmo verb Mheme used in speaking of such transformations, *tulgen,* denotes a process whereby a deity or something else imaginatively perceived metamorphoses or "morphs" into another body or takes on a different appearance or incarnation altogether.[5] Since such sudden changes can frighten and disorient any deceased person observing them in the death between, Mheme was saying, it is important to anticipate them as well as the names and looks of the deities that appear. In all, the flow of such transformations points to the apparitional, meta-morphic qualities of the bardo, a temporal state that, lamas say, is but an intensified exemplar of how a life proceeds in general.

Texts can carry similar qualities, for they can invoke for their readers or authors a swirl of different emanations. So it goes with the present one, at least as I envision it. When, within the chambers of my own imaginings, my mind's eye turns to the kurā at hand, what the book appears to be can quickly change form. At one moment it's but a mix of pages, a gloss of voices. But it soon takes on other forms. Most times it stands as a pair of "life stories" that model the strands of two lives that mirror one another in compelling ways: a widowed lamini, twice married, who, after facing a rush of words and displacements, settled in Boudhanath in order to pre-pare well for death; and a widowed lama, twice married, who, after stak-ing out a home and a life's worth of reading in Thodong, settled in Chabahil in order to prepare well for death. And yet, as noted, the book sometimes embodies a set of "last words," the later testaments, moral counsel, and "faces" of two Yolmo elders. At other times the book resem-bles one of the practice tablets that Karma spoke of, upon which Yolmo boys learn to sketch figures and letters: the imprint of certain deeds and memories remain on the sooty face of the tablet, like so many scars on a heart, while other marks have long been covered over with white ash. The book then morphs into a writing instrument that leaves an imprint on the hearts of a few. Soon the text takes the form of a mirror, a mirror of deeds, one that "reveals" some of the actions two people undertook in their lives, acts that will be reviewed and evaluated by others.

As the images continue, the mirror dissolves and another text comes to mind, this one bearing affinities with the Bardo Thedol, the guidebook to the betweens of death. But the compendium at hand, culled from the words of Ghang Lama and Kisang Omu, advances a guide not so much to the death between as to the unsettling terrains of old age, dying, and anticipated death. "The lama needs to tell it very well," Mheme once said of what could be expected in the death between, which a lama tries to ex-plain to a dying or recently deceased person and the living in general through his spoken reading of the Bardo Thedol. These and other com-ments of Mheme's lead me to think that all along this lama was trying to tell well about the arts of death and dying and would have liked nothing better than for this text to convey some of those thoughts. The book then appears, less in any present time than in some dreamlike future, as a body of sorts, a textual corpse, ghostly in its absent presence. A vestige of people and voicings no longer there, it carries the potential for solace, or sorrow, or reincarnated spirits. Yet another heap of words takes imaginative form, for the book appears like one of the purification prints written on and then incinerated at Yolmo funerals. This biographic script contains the looks and names of two Yolmo wa. Unlike the funeral print, however, its destiny is apparently not one of flames. The present text could be around long after its subjects, and its author, have vanished.

In August 2001 I completed a final draft of this book and sent it to the publisher. Events that fall made it necessary to add a few more lines, however. In September I returned to Nepal in order to conduct further research among Yolmo people. A lot had changed in the past year. In June the king and queen of Nepal had been killed in the royal palace, along with other members of the royal family; the government's official report held that the crown prince, the king and queen's son, had committed the murders before taking his own life, although no Nepalis I spoke with believed that story. It was clear, in any event, that Nepal would never again be the same. Through the year the Maoist insurgency had gained ground throughout the country, including the Yolmo region. While representatives of the Maoists did enter into peace talks with the Nepali government in September, friends nevertheless cautioned me that it would not be fully safe for me to travel to Yolmo. I therefore decided to remain and work in Kathmandu.

I stayed for two months but spoke with Kisang Omu and Ghang Lama only briefly. On several occasions I visited the latter in his home. He was usually lying on his bed, with his body curled up, his hands tucked underneath his head, and his eyes closed or resting lightly on any visitors or the images that flickered from the television set in the room. Those images included the attack on the World Trade Center in New York and the subsequent bombings in Afghanistan. Maya told me that her father had been feeling unwell of late, with headaches, dizziness, little appetite, and general physical weakness. "When I try to sit up the room starts spinning," Mheme explained. Therefore he and I did not talk all that much, though I did spend a lot of time in his presence.

Kisang Omu, meanwhile, had relocated in the spring of 2001 to her daughter's home in Chabahil. Apparently she and her children had agreed that it would be good for her to live in new surroundings for a while. Temba and I visited her a few days after I arrived in Nepal. She was sitting in a bright, sunlit room adjacent to the kitchen. When Temba explained who I was, she said that she did not remember me. "I faintly remember talking into the tape recorder, with my nephew [Pramod]," she said. "But I don't remember much beyond that. There's no memory. There's no memory." While she did appear to recall me better as we talked together, I was taken aback, to say the least, by her words. So much for the presumably lasting, unforgettable bonds established between ethnographer and informant. While I had found great meaning in my conversations with Kisang, her own memories of them had apparently faded in the months since.

Several weeks later Kisang returned to her son Kānchā's home. The reasons for the move remained largely unknown to me. Kānchā told me simply that his mother was suffering from a lot of pain in her lower back, and they concluded together that it would be best for her to live again in his home. One more move, then, this time in a taxi.

A few days before I left Nepal, at the end of October, Temba and I paid another visit to Kānchā's home. Throughout our stay, while we talked with her son, Kisang lay flat on her bed, set up then in the main room of the house. Blankets covered her body and the sides of her face. She looked small and frail. Her hands held a white cloth that she used as a handkerchief. From time to time she shifted her body a bit or cleared her throat, but at no time did she acknowledge our presence or talk with us. It was as though she wanted to engage as little as possible with the world or with the pain she felt. When we left we said goodbye to Kānchā, then stepped quietly by his mother.

In late November 2001, four weeks after I left Nepal, while the peace talks in the country were collapsing and the Nepali army was engaging in bloody skirmishes with Maoist militias, Temba sent me a hurried email. "Ibi Kisang died," its subject line read. She had died the day before, he wrote, around 10 P.M. Temba himself was then en route to her home to help console the family and to aid in the preparations for the cremation. Her nephew Binod Yolmo later informed me by email that

she was ill even during your stay in Kathmandu. Indeed, she didn't improve much and eventually she passed away on Friday, 8th day of the new moon on 23rd November 2001 at 9:45 pm. According to visitors on that very day, she was in the same condition—feeble, and unable to speak but in consciousness. She seemed to listen to and understand what others were saying to her. Prior to her death on that day she showed herself to be quite comfortable. She couldn't speak before her death, so her son and daughter-in-law could not get any word from her as a kha jhem.... She passed away on a Friday night, so only a few people, close relatives especially, were present there and other relatives had yet to be informed. The death of the old lady spread only the next morning and many relatives and Yolmo people came to express their deep sorrow and consolation to the bereaved family.

Her corpse was cremated three days after her death, in Jambu Gang, a sacred cremation site south of Kathmandu. Three weeks later a ghewa was performed for her in the Yolmo gompa in Boudhanath. Kānchā Lama sponsored these funeral rites. As his mother had asked, two sets of lineage lamas, Ningma Lamas and Sarma Lamas, led the rites. Kisang's two other living sons arranged for a second ghewa to be performed in the seventh week after her death, in the village of Ne Nyemba.

Such sad news. "Temba told me," Karma wrote in early December 2001, "that he has already written you about the sad news on Ibi Kisang. End to a life and the many stories constructed around it. Nyingjwa."

Compassioned one. A life is impermanent. And yet I hear the tones of her voice still.

Notes

Note on Transliteration

1. Clarke 1980a.
2. Wylie 1959.
3. Turner [1931] 1966.

Kurāgraphy

1. The ages of all persons noted are as of the year 2000.
2. Serematakis (1994:129) also uses the term *sensory biography*.
3. See, respectively, Seremetakis 1991, 1994; Stoller 1989, 1997; and Feldman 1991, 2000. Other works geared toward an anthropology of the senses include: Classen 1993, 1998; Classen, Howes, and Synnott 1994; Desjarlais 1992, 1997; Feld 1982, 1996; Goodwin 1994; Howes 1991; Jackson 1989; Laderman 1991; Mintz 1985; Mitchell 1992; Roseman 1991; Seeger 1975; Taussig 1993; Turner 1980; and Tyler 1987.
4. Herzfeld 2001:242.
5. On person-centered approaches in anthropology, see LeVine 1982; and Hollan 1997, 2000:546–47, among others.
6. Amichai 1993:135.
7. On psychodynamic approaches to person-centered ethnographies, see Levy 1973; Obeyesekere 1981, 1990; and Hollan and Wellenkamp 1994. For phenomenological approaches in anthropology, see Jackson 1989, 1996, 1998; DelVechhio Good et al. 1992; Good 1994; Csordas 1994a, 1994b; Kleinman and Kleinman 1995; Hanks 1996; Desjarlais 1997; Kapferer 1997; and Cohen 1998.
8. See Urban 1991 and Hanks 1996, among others, for overviews of discourse-centered approaches in anthropology.

9. One Tibetan text conveys the idea well in advising practitioners, "On the path of analysis, one must be ever mindful of death. Measure your practice by watching the compounded decay" (Thurman 1995:120). "Death awareness is second to none," observes another text (Mullin 1998:66).

10. For details on social, historical, and cultural dynamics among Yolmo wa, see Bishop 1998; Clarke 1980a, b, 1983, 1985, 1990, 1991; and Desjarlais 1992.

11. See Clarke 1980b.

12. On the concept of "ethnoscapes," see Appadurai 1991. On the politics of ethnicity in Nepal in the 1990s, see Gellner, Pfaff-Czarnecka, and Whelpton 1997.

13. The three most prominent of these organizations in the 1990s were Yolmo Samaj Sewa Kendra (Yolmo Social Service Center), Yolmo Foundation, and Nepal Yolmo Student Association.

14. Behar 1996:42.

15. Geertz 1973:452.

16. While I know Nepali well and developed a good understanding of the Yolmo language through the course of the present study, and so could have conducted most of the interviews on my own, I preferred to engage in most of the life story interviews in the company of assistants, who often asked questions on my behalf in the local language, in part because they helped me to avoid broaching inappropriate topics and usually knew better than I how to introduce certain subjects. They also led informants to talk in greater depth about their lives, since they, rather than a cultural outsider, often served as the most direct interlocutors.

17. James Clifford (1997:56, 351 n. 2) attributes the latter phrase to Renato Rosaldo.

18. See, for example but not exclusively, Turner [1931] 1966:100; and Schmidt and Mani Dahal 1993:108–11.

Hardship, Comfort

1. Conversations with Norbu present were conducted in Nepali, while those with Nogapu as translator were in Yolmo. I usually spoke to Mheme in Nepali, both during our formal interviews and during my visits alone to his home.

2. Jäschke [1881] 1995:383.

3. The other four lineages are Sarma Lama, Lhalungpa Lama, Lama Dhomar, and Lama Terkelingpa. Alongside these lineages are some fourteen clans with which nonlama families are affiliated (Clarke 1980c; Bishop 1998:98–99).

4. Clarke (1980b), in turn, estimated that Nga-chang Shakya Zangpo arrived in Yolmo in the latter part of the seventeenth century c.e. The prefix *Nga-chang* (*sngags chang* in written Tibetan) literally means "mantra holder"; it implies that Shakya Zangpo was a proficient yogi (Clarke 1980b:11, 14). *Zangpo*, in turn, carries connotations of "morally good," "excellent," "beautiful" (Jäschke [1881] 1995:496). Of the numerous stories concerning this founding lama, several hold that Padmasambhava prophesied that Nga-chang Shakya Zangpo would "open" the

"outer, inner and secret" doors of Yolmo Gangra, the snow-covered mountains that then isolated the Yolmo region from Tibet (Clarke 1980b:11). Through this ancestral line, Ningma Lamas link themselves genealogically to the Nyingma, or Old School, of Tibetan Buddhism (Clarke 1980b:11). It is also the case, however, that the other four lineages are Nyingma.

5. Lineage lamas are also often referred to by the Nepali term *thari lama,* "lineage lama," and nonlineage lamas by the term *paḍhi lama,* or "reading lamas." Quite often nonlineage lamas are Yolmo men whose mothers are the daughters of lamas but whose fathers are not lamas; since these men cannot claim a patrilineal link to a lama lineage, they cannot effectively identify themselves as lineage lamas. In accord with this, Yolmo wa today often distinguish between Lama families and Sherpa families: families fathered by a lama and families without such parentage. Accordingly, a person's last name (Lhatul Lama, Nogapu Sherpa) usually indicates to which kind of family he or she belongs.

Beginning in the late 1990s, some reading lamas, arguing that they should be treated as equals, have begun to challenge the privileged status and authority that have traditionally been assigned to lineage lamas. As of 2000, their complaints had been met by responses from lineage lamas that ranged from bewilderment to tentative agreement in words along the paraphrased lines of, "What can we do about it? This is how it always has been done; our system is written in the sacred books."

6. Thurman 1995:103.

7. Khetsun Sangpo Rinbochay 1982:130.

8. *Jhinda* comes from the Tibetan *sbyin bdag,* which Jäschke ([1881] 1995:405) translates as "dispenser of gifts...a layman manifesting his piety by making presents to the priesthood." More generally the term designates a supporter, follower, or donor to a lama lineage. Yolmo wa understand that spiritual merit can be accrued through deeds of gift-giving to lamas and the support of lamaic practices in general, such as by financing the construction of buildings or copying sacred texts (see Clarke 1990:174).

9. See Bishop 1998 for details on dzomo herding in Yolmo.

10. "Burma" is the name often used by older Yolmo wa to refer to areas in eastern India (see Clarke 1980c:97). It therefore remains unclear whether Mheme actually traveled to Burma itself (now Myanmar) or was employed somewhere in India. But in this case it appears that he did travel to and work in Burma, as the members of other Yolmo villages did just before the Second World War (Clarke 1980c:97).

11. Another reason that sons left their parents' homes was the possible limitation of lands that a family could farm and thus the possible limitation of available food as well.

As Lhatul related to me, he left at night with friends, sleeping in the forest at night, and arrived in a train depot in Kathmandu two days later. They took a train to India and worked for six months as manual laborers, "building a road, shoveling dirt." Phur Gyalmu, Mheme's niece, in turn, told me that a brother of hers had run away when he was twelve or thirteen, after their mother died.

"There was no mother, and he ran away." She said he never returned or wrote home after that. "We never even received a letter saying that he was dead."

12. The necessity of such difficult travels was the main reason Mheme found that men had more hardship in life than women in his time. "Women didn't have dhukpu [then]," he said when asked about this. "Men had dhukpu. They had to travel here and there. Men had to work more. Men used to go to Lhasa to get salt. . . . Women also had difficulties. Once they married, they had many jobs to do. But the men had more work to do. They had more hardships."

13. Mheme himself spoke of how he used to drink a lot of chhang. "During the *ghewa* [funerals]," he told us, "I used to drink the whole day. If you drink, then you don't feel shy, and you start singing. Even women start singing if they drink. . . . When I got a bit drunk and saw the people, I would have no fear. Because of the chhang. Then, after the chhang was finished, I would think that I shouldn't have said such things to them." When asked how it was that he came to stop drinking, he said, "I ended it myself. I was getting old, and I could fall down. Nobody told me to stop drinking. I stopped myself."

14. Not everyone would draw the same conclusions as Mheme. When I asked Phur Gyalmu if she would agree that those who did a lot of dharma were the ones who became rich, she replied, "If dharma made people rich, then I would do only dharma. I wouldn't work. . . . The ones who work hard are the ones who get rich. If one could get rich by doing the dharma, then everyone would do it, right?"

Binod Lama, for one, thought it worth noting that many Yolmo families living in Kathmandu have recently found that a family's success can also be measured in terms of the education that family members obtain during their lives, not just the money they manage to accumulate.

15. Norbu in fact, uncomfortable with the high (and, to him, unearned) status that came with being born into a "lama family," had decided by 1997 to go by the then-novel name of "Norbu Yolmo."

16. *Ijjat* is a Nepali word. See Schmidt and Mani Dahal 1993:47; and McHugh 1998.

Twenty-Seven Ways of Looking at Vision

1. On the role and importance of vision in Hindu and Buddhist communities in South Asia, see, for instance, Gonda 1963, 1969; Babb 1981; Tyler 1987; Scott 1991, 1994; Eck 1996; and Jhala 1997.

2. See Desjarlais 1992:55–57.

3. See Gonda 1969; Babb 1981; Eck 1996; Scott 1991; Jhala 1997.

4. See Eck 1996; Babb 1981.

5. See Babb 1981:390.

6. Babb 1981:393.

7. Jhala 1997:50.

8. See Maloney 1976 for a discussion of concepts of the evil eye in South Asia.

9. On the phenomena of witchcraft in South Asia, see Carstairs 1983; Cohen 1998; Kapur 1983; Lamb 2000:228; and Saletore 1981.

10. The concept of unconscious optics comes from Benjamin [1936] 1968:237.

11. Looking into another's eyes can also work to generate knowledge, however. When serving food or tea, for instance, Yolmo wa often look into a guest's eyes to see if he or she really means no in politely declining further servings. Sometimes men also look into another's eyes when talking about something, apparently in order to convince their interlocutor of the veracity of what they are saying. "Earlier on, a lot of hardship occurred," Lhatul once said of his youth in Yolmo, while looking into my eyes.

12. Levinas 1969:23.

13. Gtsan-smyon Heruka 1977:66.

14. Efforts to block the gaze of others also occur. When Karma told me in detail about the death of his father, a respected lama and political leader who, sadly, died in his early fifties, he noted that the funeral pyre was built in an uncommon way. "The cremation was done in a very different way," Karma explained. "I don't know if you've seen the cremations of other people. Usually, you can see [the corpse as it burns in the pyre] from the outside. But my father's was done differently. The pyre was built, and outside was a wall, and his body was placed in it. And over it they placed enough wood and things like that, and then they hid it—it was covered with mud and stone, so nothing could be seen. They just left a small crack for smoke. And so no one could see inside." The construction worked to maintain the corpse's spiritual purity by obstructing any possible visual engagements with it.

15. The differences between the two verbs *thonge* and *tage* are consistent with the different connotations they have in Tibetan, where they are spelled as *mthong ba* and *lta ba,* respectively (see Jäschke [1881] 1995:216, 242; Das [1902] 1986:540, 603).

16. To adopt a suitable word of Robert Ekvall's: "...among the Tibetans, grapholatry is more real than idolatry" (1964:114).

17. Clarke 1990:171.

18. See Desjarlais 1992:159–84 for an account of shamanic divinations among Yolmo wa.

19. As the case was with most other Yolmo lamas of his time, Mheme engaged much more in acts of reading than in ones of writing. His only successful efforts at writing in Tibetan took place earlier in his life when he would make "transfers," or copies, of religious texts. In his later years he found that his hand was not steady enough. "Nowadays I can't write. My hand shakes and makes crooked lines. If I try to write a letter, I need to have someone else write it for me. If I write in one direction, it becomes crooked. If I write another way, it becomes crooked. Nope. Before, before, I could write."

In contrast with his proficiency in reading Tibetan, Mheme knew very little of Nepali script. "I know a little," he said when asked. "I never studied it. I know one or two words. I didn't learn it. I make guesses and catch the meaning." He might have preferred it this way. "The Nepali language is not for dharma," he once observed. "It teaches us to sin. It instructs us about politics only and about stealing. Our Yolmo language teaches us about dharma."

20. Clarke 1990:171–72.

21. For more on this, see Desjarlais 1992.

22. Tsang Nyön Heruka 1982:205.

23. For Yolmo people, the idea that some individuals and families are lower in caste than others is Hindu in origin. While Tibetan Buddhist texts do not advocate ideas of caste hierarchies as Hindu teachings do, many Yolmo families living in Nepal have come to heed Hindu ideas of caste hierarchies and try their best not to engage in what they take to be any spiritually polluting contact with people deemed, by Hindu thought, to be impure.

24. *Kāmi* is a Nepali word used in reference to the Hindu "blacksmith" caste, presumed by some to be more spiritually polluting than, and so inferior to, others.

25. In general, Yolmo wa understand that places of lower elevation tend to carry more impurities than ones of higher elevation, since fewer people step or live among sites of high elevation. That is one reason why cremation sites are situated at the very tops of hills.

26. See Beyer 1992:107.

27. *Chemi* is spelled *mchod me* in written Tibetan (Jäschke [1881] 1995:167).

28. See Desjarlais 1992:31.

29. "His father's corpse," a Yolmo phrase that comes from the words *kho abayi ro* but is pronounced as "kha-ve ro," entails a curse that conveys something like "May his father be a corpse!" It can also carry an import similar to the curse *son of a bitch!* in English.

30. Mheme was reluctant to tell us about dreams that foretold of something that had yet to occur. "No, I shouldn't say the things that have happened [in my dreams]," he said when asked. He likely felt that, if he told us about any good dreams, the good fortune foretold in those dreams would not come to fruition.

31. There is a rich literature on tantric visualization practices among Buddhist peoples in South Asia. See, among others, Beyer 1973; Gellner 1992; Khetsun Sangpo Rinbochay 1982; Owens 2000; Patrul Rinpoche 1996; Powers 1995; Samuel 1989, 1993; Tucci 1980.

32. *Gom* is spelled *sgom* in written Tibetan (Jäschke [1881] 1995:117).

33. Kalu Rinpoche 1999:49. For other accounts of this practice, see Khetsun Sangpo Rinbochay 1982:141–53; Patrul Rinpoche 1996:263–80; and Powers 1995:262–66. Dorje Semba, known as Vajrasattva in Sanskrit, is spelled *rdo rje sems dpa'* in written Tibetan.

34. Karma's sense of the rite's transformative potential fits with what commentators say of it. "This is a powerful practice," John Powers writes, for instance, "because one cultivates the actual state of the deity, rather than merely working at qualities that are concordant with it. Tantric meditation puts one into the situation of a buddha, and one cultivates the understanding that one is in fact a fully enlightened being, endowed with the exalted qualities of Vajrasattva, and one further realizes oneself as engaging in his enlightened activi-

ties, with the result that one becomes progressively more familiar with the state of buddhahood" (Powers 1995:266).

35. The story itself tells of a devout Buddhist man who undertook a pilgrimage to the sacred lands of India. Before he departed from home, his mother asked him to bring back a relic of the Buddha so that she could focus her meditations and venerations on it. Once the man undertook the journey, however, he was so consumed by what he encountered that he forgot his mother's request until he was but a few miles from home. Spotting a dog's skull lying on the side of the road, he wrenched a tooth from its jaw and took the tooth with him. When he arrived home, he presented the tooth to his mother and told her that it was one of the Buddha's teeth. That woman prostrated regularly in front of the tooth with complete faith that this was indeed the case, and over a period of time the tooth began to radiate a brilliant, incandescent light.

Startled into Alertness

1. In the word-for-word representations of conversations that follow in this and later chapters, many of the exchanges in English that took place between Pramod and me have been left out, in part to save space and avoid redundancy and in part to give priority to what Kisang understood when talking with us. On those occasions when my sense of a question differed significantly from how Pramod then phrased that question in Yolmo, the disparities in meaning are noted.

2. The terms *narrated event* and *narrative event* come from Jakobson 1971; see also Bauman 1986:2.

3. See Bishop 1998:100–105 for details.

4. Gérard Genette (1980:252) attributes the terms *narrating I* and *narrated I* to Leo Spitzer.

5. See, for instance, Bennett 1983; Cameron 1998; Harlan and Courtright 1995; Lamb 2000; Narayan 1986; and Raheja 1994. I thank Veena Das for pointing this out to me.

6. In many respects, the situation of women in Yolmo society is similar to the social standing of women in Sherpa communities: as Sherry Ortner puts it, "On a scale of gender inequality across world cultures, the Sherpas are pretty good" (1996:186; on Sherpa women, see also March 1979; and Ortner 1999). Another way to characterize Yolmo gender relations would be to say that they fall somewhere between the egalitarian relations between women and men that Watkins (1996) has documented among the Nyeshangte, a Tibetan Buddhist people who reside principally in northern Nepal, and the strongly hierarchical relations between men and women in many high-caste Hindu communities in Nepal (see Bennett 1983; Cameron 1998).

In general, my approach to an understanding of gender relations and identities among Yolmo wa is informed by the writings just noted as well as other anthropological accounts of women in Tibetan, Himalayan, and South Asian societies (including Aziz 1987, 1988; Cabezón 1992; Das 1995, 2000; Des Chene

1998; Enslin 1992; Gyatso 1987; Holland and Skinner 1995; Klein 1995; Kondos 1991; Lamb 2000; Levine 1981, 1982; March 1984; McHugh 2001; Menon and Shweder 1998; Miller 1980; Raheja and Gold 1994; Skinner 1989; Skinner, Pach, and Holland 1998; Trawick 1990; Vatuk 1987; Wadley 1980; and Willis 1987).

7. The Yolmo phrase "Chi bheche?" is often voiced by Yolmo wa in the course of everyday talk, as is its Nepali analogue, "Ke garne?" by Nepali-speaking peoples. Best glossed in English as "What to do?" or "What shall be done?" the question often signifies that little can, in fact, be done about a particular situation.

8. It is possible that Kisang asked herself why the two men were still in her father's home, because, in the usual course of Yolmo marriage proceedings, once a marriage proposal has been accepted, the groom's party returns home, only to revisit the bride's house weeks later, after all the arrangements for the wedding have been made and an auspicious date for the wedding has been determined. But in Kisang's case, it appears that the wedding took place the day after her father agreed to the union, perhaps because the groom's party had already traveled so far, and they would have had to undertake an additional four-day, round-trip journey on foot had they visited a second time. Or it could be simply that this was how Kisang remembered it or related it to us.

A Theater of Voices

1. The Sanskrit word *skandha* is usually translated as "heap, mass, aggregate." The Yolmo word for such an aggregate is *phungbu*. It is also the word for "corpse." The phrase "aggregates, fields, senses" comes from a Tibetan devotional vow, cited in Beyer 1973:189. See Collins 1982 on concepts of *anattā*, or "not-self," in Theravāda Buddhism. Dependent arising, or *pratītya-samutpāda* in Sanskrit, is best understood, as one commentary puts it, "as an analysis of how the various sense fields and aggregates in the sphere of the conditioned go about grouping, disbanding, and regrouping in various configurations as they influence one another in giving rise to suffering and to the conditioned world as a whole" (Robinson and Johnson 1997:25). For many years Buddhists in South Asia have expounded on such an analysis in attempting to understand and explain the makings of conditioned experience. The ultimate aim of such efforts is to help people to gain insight into such experience and so realize a way out of the bondage of sansāra. While the intricacies of such thinking are quite complex, they all contribute to the idea that conditioned experience is predicated on an interlocking, scaffoldlike set of "twelve preconditions": aging and dying depend on birth, birth depends on becoming, becoming depends on sustenance, and so forth, until the most basic, underlying precondition, ignorance. Yet once ignorance ceases, the formations of consciousness that "depend" on ignorance also cease. This then can lead to the cessation of the preconditions that depend on those formations, and so on, until aging and dying and all the suffering that rebirths and redeaths bring cease themselves (see Robinson and Johnson 1997:25–28).

2. Indeed, while her account of how she came to marry was rich with feeling, she almost always reported not what people felt but what they did. She also re-

frained from discussing any of the possible intentions of others that might have led them to act in the ways that they did. This was in line with a general understanding among Yolmo wa that, since no one can truly know what lies within another's sem, it is tricky at best and usually unwarranted to guess the thoughts and motives of others. Except for one instance, when she reported that Ibi Gorgen "was worried," the only emotions Kisang spoke of directly were her own. Such sentiments usually had the force of deeds: "Saying this, I was angry."

3. The phrasing of my observations draws from Sylvia Vatuk's (1987:28–29) discussion of the social status of girls and young women of Raya caste of 1970s metropolitan Delhi.

4. It is worth noting that, for Kisang, prayers and meditations were not accompanied by mental imaginings, as the case is when Yolmo lamas and bombo envision tutelary deities. Her prayers were first and foremost deeds of speech.

5. "If anybody speaks about bad or sorrowful things," said Gom Dolma as she spoke of her life to us, "that makes me feel sad. That will never benefit me.... I love to hear only the good and peaceful words, which can make me feel good and give me peaceful moments." With a smile upon serving a meal she had just prepared for several visitors, Neela Lama said, "If it tastes good, say it tastes good. If it tastes bad, say that it tastes good anyway, since hearing that will make me happy."

6. The term *social power* comes from Joanna Watkins's discussion of the economic, spiritual, and moral agency of Nyeshangte women in Nepal. Drawing from the writings of Errington (1990) and Gal (1991), Watkins (1996:75) characterizes such social power as having less to do with political autonomy, authority, or control of resources in any direct way than "with 'the ability to define social reality, to impose visions of the world' and 'the ability to make others accept and enact one's representation of the world'" (Gal 1991:177, 197).

7. "If I come to visit my 'sister,'" one woman said in explaining how she thought this works, "and she doesn't greet me well and doesn't offer me food, then I'll remember that. But if she treats me very well, I won't remember it."

8. The catch here is that, while Kisang related to us mostly the times of hardship in her life, she asked on one or two occasions that I refrain from including too much dhukpu in anything I might write of her life. "Put the very good things," she instructed toward the end of our conversations. "Don't put any bad things. People will say I should be ashamed [for talking about such sorrows]."

9. See Jäschke [1881] 1995:561; and Das [1902] 1986:1241.

10. Nietzsche [1887] 1967:61.

11. See Geertz 1973:93–94 on the concepts "model of" and "model for."

"I've Gotten Old"

1. Mullin 1998:221.
2. Khetsun Sangpo Rinbochay 1982:59.
3. Khetsun Sangpo Rinbochay 1982:59.

4. According to Karma Gyaltsen Yolmo, Mheme's idea that a flame lies within each person's forehead is an uncommon one among Yolmo wa.

5. Khetsun Sangpo Rinbochay 1982:36.

Essays on Dying

1. "This is the chapter of sorrows, when the evil acts of previous lives rose up in my path," wrote Lama Merit Intellect, a renowned sixteenth-century Tibetan lama, in his autobiography after recounting a series of hardships he and his family underwent early in his life (Snellgrove 1967:93).

"Dying Is This"

1. While it is best not to assume that every society perforce advances overtly phenomenological means of knowing the world, and while the word *phenomenology* is undeniably a European one with no direct correlate in the Yolmo language, the present phenomenology—or "ethnophenomenology," to some extent—is not necessarily at odds with Yolmo ways of knowing. Yolmo wa, lamas in particular, are quite familiar with modes of observation and inquiry that attend to subjective processes of action, consciousness, and sensation. Indeed, as Robinson and Johnson (1997:19, 24) note in accord with other scholars of Buddhism, the Buddha's approach to questions of human consciousness and suffering was quite similar to the methods of modern phenomenology. (See also Kapferer 1997:xv–xvi, for a like-minded justification of a phenomenologically inclined ethnography of sorcery practices among Sinhalese Buddhists in Sri Lanka.)

2. To put it in more abstract conceptual terms, I am suggesting that her manner of dying was imbricated in her ways of talking. Talk was a primary substance of her dying. Dying for her was, among other things, a discursive act, one that others would take note of. Any easy distinctions between language and experience or rhetoric and reality must therefore be dispensed with. The "matter" (N., kurā) of her dying cannot be readily differentiated from her "talk" (N., kurā) about it. The phenomenal and the discursive, life as lived and life as talked about, were as intertwined here as the braided cords of a rope. There was apparently a lot to her demise, from concerns about growing old to worries about the loss of memories, as well as an ever-increasing diminishment of her senses, particularly of seeing and hearing, and, in accord with this, a continual disengagement from everyday life, such that she had become increasingly occupied with thoughts of death. But while all this was true, what seemed to pattern a lot of these concerns were particular casts of mind and language, ways of thinking and talking that gave certain form to her demise.

We are therefore attending most to what Kisang said about dying, with those sayings suspended in the kind of rhetorical and pragmatic engagements that are invested in any speech. Even here, traces of her utterances lead not to any singularly consistent statement but instead entail a series of shifting musings and intensities that, when conveyed in combination, perhaps give some sense of what she thought, or at least said, was happening to her. When it comes to her various takes on dying, it is better to think of them not as directly mirroring or windowing any "lived experiences" of hers but as engaging existential domains, spun out of spoken words and private thoughts, that she could invoke or inhabit from time to time. One therefore needs to attend to the very real fact of her dying while also keeping in mind the fact that her demise took form within several currents of words.

3. Jäschke [1881] 1995:4.

4. Desjarlais 1992:40.

5. Phagpa Chen Rezig (or Avalokiteśvara, in Sanskrit) is a bodhisattva of compassion, responsible for the liberation and perfection of all sentient beings.

6. Mullin 1998:219.

7. Mullin 1998:222.

8. See Thurman 1995:177, for instance.

9. Mohanty 2000:53–54.

10. Mohanty 2000:135.

The Painful Between

1. As noted in Lopez 1998:49.

2. The latter three bardo states are spelled in Tibetan, respectively, as *'chi kha'i bar do, chos nyid kyi bar do,* and *srid pa'i bar do.* The description of the three bardos here draws upon several writings, including Thurman 1994, in which the three are translated, respectively, as "death-point," "reality," and "existence" betweens, and Lopez 1998:49, in which they are glossed, respectively, as "the bardo at the moment of death," "the bardo of reality," and "the bardo of mundane existence." For exemplary accounts of the bardo states by Tibetan Buddhist adepts, see Tsele Natsok Rangdröl 1987; and Chökyi Nyima Rinpoche 1991.

3. Tsele Natsok Rangdröl 1987:xiii.

4. See Thurman 1994:43; and Tsele Natsok Rangdröl 1987:27, respectively.

5. To quote Thurman (1994:34).

6. Lhatul, for instance, told me that as a person gets older, his or her mind becomes smaller, weaker, like the diminishing bulb of a well-used flashlight. "The very old become like children again. Their sem become very small."

7. Chökyi Nyima Rinpoche 1991:82.

8. Chökyi Nyima Rinpoche 1991:82–83.

9. Obeyesekere 1968:21.

10. While Yolmo lamas understand that the reading of any lamaic text helps to increase a reader's store of merit, two texts in particular—the dhig-shyag and another known as *thung-shyag*—work, respectively, to "cut" a person's "misdeeds" and "shortcomings." By training his eyes on these texts, and reciting them to himself or out loud, Mheme understood that he was lessening any mis-

deeds and shortcomings he might have accrued in this or previous lives. Other texts, including one known as *dorje chepa*, work well to benefit the person who recites them. A person can also increase his or her merit by giving alms to the poor and disabled, as wealthier families tend to do, or by reciting mani and undertaking acts of *kora* (merit-producing circumambulations around the sacred chhorten), as many Yolmo women and men do.

Desperation

1. When different lineages formally participate in the same funeral, which is often the case when a prestigious lama dies, each lineage constructs its own altar and performs funeral rites in accord with its own practices.

2. Some of the factors that contribute to a woman's life in the wake of a husband's death are her age at the time of his death; her financial resources; the property, if any, she can claim as her own; the needs of any young children; the treatment she receives from her children when she grows older; her relations with her in-laws; her physical health; and the loss she suffers from her husband's absence.

3. The verb *khyamge* is also used when speaking of the undirected roaming or wandering about that a bodiless soul must contend with during the between following death: *bardola khyamge*, "wandering about in the bardo."

4. The phrase "shadow conversations" is taken from Judith Irvine: "Rather than multivocal, we might consider a speech situation to be multiply dialogical: it is not just the speaker who is doubled (or multiplied) by other voices, but a set of dialogic relations that are crucially informed by other sets—shadow conversations that surround the conversation at hand" (1996:151–52).

The Time of Dying

1. The phrase "mani-padme" is short for "Om mani-padme hūm," a merit-producing Buddhist mantra often heard among Tibetan peoples. Said to invoke the bodhisattva Avalokiteśvara—known as Phagpa Chen Rezig in Yolmo—it can be rendered in English as "O you who hold the jeweled [rosary] and the lotus [have mercy on us]" (Lopez 1997:14).

2. To me it seemed that, in some reaches of her heart, Kisang could not understand why the gods were doing this to her, much as she could not fathom why her father sent her away in marriage. "Yama Raj won't let me die, it seems," she once said.

3. By "the Three Precious Ones" Kisang meant the sacred trilogy of the Buddha, the *sangha* [community], and the dharma. While Tibetan and Yolmo lamas take these words to refer simply to the Buddha and his followers and teachings, many Yolmo wa, including Kisang, understand the three together as a triad of supernatural beings. They therefore pray to the Three Precious Ones as they would to other deities.

4. There is, in fact, a Nepali proverb of sorts voiced by Yolmo peoples that speaks to this. It goes, "Kāl bhandā niu thūlo ho" (The cause/reason [for a death] is more important than the fated time [of death]). While deaths might be fated, they cannot actually occur unless there is a means or cause for them. But if a death is indeed truly fated to occur at a certain time, a cause will inevitably present itself.

5. "This is really beautiful, this is really good," Karma said upon hearing these words as recorded. "It shows that she is expecting to go to a good place after she dies."

6. Chökyi Nyima Rinpoche 1991:83.

Death Envisioned

1. Most of the phrases cited are from quotations reproduced in Stevenson (1937:373–74). "Bugbear" is from Epictetus. "Sleeping partner" is from Horace Smith. "Pale priest" belongs to Robert Browning. "Black camel" is from Abd-el-Kader. Edna St. Vincent Millay penned the "spongy wall" metaphor. "Ugly fact" comes from Alexander Smith. Joaquin Miller wrote, "Death is but a name"; Wallace Stevens, "the mother of beauty." "Ultimate horror" comes from Jean Giraudoux. Robert Solomon (1998:161) attributes the death is "nothing" assertion to Epicurus. "That possibility..." is Heidegger's well-known definition in *Being and Time* (1962:294), and "the impossibility..." can be found in Levinas's (1987:74) rejection of Heidegger's views on death.

2. Snellgrove 1967:112–13.

3. The phrase *jigten gi jhawa* reads in Tibetan script as '*jig rten gyi bya ba.*

4. Thurman 1994:167, 163.

5. "Lacking an actual material body," a seventeenth-century Tibetan sage advised on this time in the between, "one roams about, here and there, to and fro, like a feather blown in the wind, and experiences a feeling of pain much stronger than ever" (Tsele Natsok Rangdröl 1987:68–69).

6. As cited in Ariès 1981:19.

7. Thurman 1994:44.

8. See Thurman 1994 for a recent translation, and Lopez 1998 for an insightful account of the texts and the varied attempts by translators to convert their meanings into English.

9. Thurman 1994:xxi.

10. Thurman 1994:132.

11. Thurman 1994:175.

12. Thurman 1994:136.

13. "Land of bliss" is a translation of *dewa chengyi shing kham* (*bde ba can gyi zin kams,* in written Tibetan), a heavenly realm to which many Yolmo people aspire to journey after dying.

14. One consequence of Mheme's readings was that he appeared to be more certain than some about what would happen to him when he died. When I tried

to elicit Phur Gyalmu's thoughts on death, she hesitated to offer a sure under-standing.

"In your opinion," we asked, "what happens after a person dies? What happens to the soul?"

"Where does it reach, perhaps?" Phur said in response. "This is what we feel, for sure."

"What do you think happens to the soul?"

"Mm-mm [no]. I don't think anything [about this]."

"After dying, some people go to heaven, some go to hell—do you know about this?"

"I know that this is what people say."

"Is this true or not?"

"Is it or isn't it? Heaven is reached, they say, [and] hell is reached. Either it is or it isn't, this is what I think."

To Phungboche, by Force

1. While some marriages still result from a groom's party "capturing" a bride, these marriages usually have a playful, performative air to them, with the potential bride making a show of her resistance but often having been consulted beforehand (see Bishop 1998:104). In general, arranged marriages are preferred nowadays, in part because capture marriages are known to bring lingering tensions and resentments. "One doesn't do it these days," Phur Gyalmu said of capture marriages. "One can't force [a woman] nowadays. It's not like before."

2. French 1995:139.

Staying Still

1. Das 1998.

2. This Nepali phrase (see Turner [1931] 1966:163) is often accompanied by a shifting finger that indexes the "to-and-fro," *chak-chak*, movements of a child.

3. See Rinbochay and Hopkins 1979; and Tsele Natsok Rangdröl 1987, for instance.

4. Thurman 1994; Desjarlais 1992:104–6.

5. Cohen 1998:180–83.

Mirror of Deeds

1. Chhe Gyalbu, short for "Chhe gi Gyalbu," is often written as *gshin rje chos rgyal* in classical Tibetan.

2. Jäschke ([1881] 1995:417) defines *lekyi melong* as "mirror foreshadowing future events."

3. See O'Flaherty 1984; Smith 1989; Desjarlais 1992; Samuel 1993; Maskarinec 1995; and Adams 1997, for instance.

4. See Hanks 1996:242–46; and Briggs and Bauman 1992.

Here and There

1. Thurman 1995:101.

2. See Das 2000:209 on the vulnerability of widows in Hindu India. As Das rightly observes, "But to be vulnerable is not the same as to be a victim, and those who are inclined to assume that social norms or expectations of widowhood are automatically translated into oppression need to pay attention to the gap between a norm and its actualization" (209).

3. Desjarlais 1992:121.

"So: Ragged Woman"

1. Mullin 1998:210.

2. See Desjarlais 1992 for details.

3. Details on the origins of these approximate translations help to convey further the terms of Kisang's criticisms. "Messy" translates the singsong *thele mele,* "mixed, mixed up, not direct." "Garbled" is *tam cho mhekhu,* "incapable slurred speech," as when a child cannot articulate words properly. "Here and there" is our translation of *phetar ghotor,* and "crooked" and "curved" talk are from the phrase *khyagtang khyogtong.* "Topsy-turvy" is from *tholo gholo,* an adjective often used to describe something in disorder, like a loose-leaf book whose pages are all "up and down" or the "rambling, aimless" speech of someone who is feverish or inebriated. "Haphazard" is the Nepali colloquialism *phasād-prosok,* implying something "partial, not well organized"; it perhaps derives from the Nepali noun *phasyān-phusun,* which Turner glosses as "odds and ends, nothing of great value" ([1931] 1966:403). "Unattractive," in turn, is from the Yolmo *chhenda mhindu,* which literally means "it has no face." "Loose, unformed," finally, comes from *sithil,* a Nepali adjective that means something like "loose, slack, lax" (Turner [1931] 1966:574).

4. That one could be "skilled in good," as Walpola Rahula (1974:97) translates the master's words, is an idea central to the Buddha's teachings. Michael Carrithers points out, as do other scholars, that the Buddha held that one should approach the path to nirvāṇa much like a craftsman, sharpening the skills that enable a person to further his or her mental stance toward the world. Speaking of the Buddha's use of the Pali term *kusala,* whose primary meaning is "skillful," he notes:

> It is a term which the Buddha made his own, and he used it in the first place to refer to skill in meditation. But he also used it widely to apply to skill in moral discipline and in the acquisition of merit. In this application "skilful" also means morally good, as we might say "he is a good man" or "that was a good act." Indeed in many contexts "skilful" is the opposite of evil, and refers to the same kind of sharp distinction

that is made in Christianity between good and evil. But for the Buddha "skilful/good" always had a practical, not a metaphysical or absolute flavour to it. The dead centre of the term is best conveyed by a sense lost to us (but still alive among the ancient Greeks), that just as one could be skilful or *good at* a craft, so one could be *good* at being a sentient being, and hence one could be *good*. (1983:87)

Carrithers goes on to stress that "for the Buddha skilfulness cut two ways: its consequences were good for oneself, but good for others as well" (1983:87).

While any links back to the Buddha's teachings are undoubtedly indirect at best, many Yolmo wa understand skillful actions to entail much the same.

5. Such prideful talk is commonly heard among Yolmo wa, especially among men. As a rule, it does not spark disapproval among others as long as the speaker does not talk excessively or "conceitedly" about his or her virtues.

6. Kisang observed much the same when asked if it was her understanding that people talk about others. "When the women gather," she said, "they talk about the women. When the men gather, they talk about the men. They talk, perhaps. Someone says, 'That woman is bad because she talks about others.' Some are saying, 'That person is bad.' But then we're doing it ourselves. We talk behind about other people. This is the custom. It is the custom from before. It was like this before, and it's like this now."

7. On several occasions Kisang said outright that others could talk better than she could. "If you asked your mother about this, she could talk well," she once suggested to Pramod in the course of a conversation. "The old women who have the superb intelligence, they can say well," she also observed. And when we explained that I would also be writing up the life story of Ghang Lama, whom she knew, she quickly replied, "The Thodong uncle can explain things well, certainly. To tell, I don't know how to tell well. I don't remember, yes? He's seven years younger than me. He can tell smoothly, for sure. How well he can talk about the lama religion." Identities developed through comparisons.

8. See March 1984 for similar observations among the Tamang people of north-central Nepal.

9. The words italicized here, *realist* and *in detail,* were spoken in English.

Echoes of a Life

1. For other anthropological writings on life history research that attend to similar questions, see Crapanzano 1980; Ortiz 1985; Behar 1993; and Frank 2000, as well as the contributions to an issue of the *Journal of Narrative and Life History* (2, no. 1, 1992) devoted to what Margaret Blackman (1992:1) calls "the afterlife of the life history."

2. See Haviland 1991; Crapanzano 1994; and Kratz 2001 for exemplary accounts of the pragmatics of particular life history interviews.

3. Jäschke [1881] 1995:138, 380.

4. The words quoted come from a discourse of Longchenpa's (1976:87), translated into verse:

...Like an echo—there being nothing
and yet a presence—it roams about here.
...Ah! How funny is this paradox of there being nothing
and yet there being a presence.

5. Thurman 1994:185–86.

6. In fact, the word *bhaja* sometimes serves as a colloquial grammatical structure, "it is the bhaja of," that perhaps has the closest affinity with the English phrase "it appeared as though":

Milam du, ngombu yhimba [gi] bhaja; dream-appears to be, real is bhaja [of]
(It was apparently a dream, [but] it seemed as though real.)

Milamla thongdu, dhenparang thugyo [gi] bhaja; dream-in is/was seen, really met bhaja [of]
(It was seen in a dream, [but] it appeared as though we really met.)

Yolmo wa often voice such phrasings when speaking of dreams of the dead: friends or family members will appear in dreams as though they, the dead, were real or as though the dreamer were actually meeting and talking with them.

7. Thurman 1994:III.

8. Thurman 1994:112, 114, and 167, respectively.

9. The words that Kisang Omu said her brother voiced when he realized his sister was to be taken in marriage to the village of Shomkharka ("If one looks at the sky...") resonated in Kisang's narrative and apparently in her mind as well in similar ways.

10. In this regard, Yolmo understandings of mimetic principles differ from many so-called postmodern attitudes that contend that everything is simulation and, thus, that nothing is more or less authentic, original, or unreal than anything else (see Baudrillard 1983; and Adams 1996, for instance). While some well-trained lamas, including Mheme at times, contend that everyday life is itself illusory, most Yolmo wa, Mheme included, nevertheless live in a quite real world where important distinctions are made between fakes and originals: echoes, for instance, can be unreal repetitions of real sounds; Kathmandu, some say, offers "duplicate" foods that are pale, poor-tasting imitations of more authentic foods found in the foothills; "true" stories are sometimes contrasted with "false" ones; and people often distinguish between "true" and "untrue" lamas—"born lamas," that is, who inherit the role through patrilineage, and "reading lamas," who cannot claim such divine inheritance but nevertheless learn to read sacred texts. The last idea, bolstered by the preceding ones, carries important political implications, since born lamas are seen as more authentic than reading lamas and so incur more respect from others. In a land of illusions, some things are more unreal than others.

11. Chang 1977:511.

12. Patrul Rinpoche 1996:112–13.

13. Yolmo wa also use the phrase "good bhaja," or bhaja zangbu, when speaking of omenlike images perceived while dreaming. Any one such image can be understood to be a good bhaja in the sense that it is a positive karmic reverberation of a good deed enacted in the past. While the dream image has no material

substance or force of its own, it does indicate that something good will happen to the dreamer in the future, when the karmic virtues of the good deed play themselves out for real. As Karma said of such a dream image, "It's a sign, a good sign. It's an echo, but it's a good echo, one that means that something good will happen. It's an indication, of something good to happen....Bhaja zangbu is a reflection of the past, indicating the future."

14. According to Chökyi Nyima Rinpoche (1991:170), a bodhisattva is someone who has developed jang chub sem ba, or bodhicitta, "the aspiration to attain enlightenment in order to benefit all sentient beings." Mheme understood much the same, although for him and other Yolmo wa, the term *jang chub sem ba* also entails the idea, simply, of a spiritually pure heartmind.

15. See Gyatso 1992, 1997:6, 103, for instance.

16. Das 1996:78; see also Parry 1994.

17. Gtsan-smyon Heruka 1977:106.

18. Mullin 1998:220.

19. Khetsun Sangpo Rinbochay 1982:58.

20. Gtsan-smyon Heruka 1977:106.

21. See Gombrich 1988:123-24 and Strong 1995:34-41 on the cult of relics, for example, and Robinson and Johnson 1997:80-81 on the symbolism of stūpas.

22. It is also possible, though he never said anything to suggest such an interpretation, that Mheme hesitated to include details of his hardships because they could also be understood locally as a consequence of bad karma incurred in previous lives. Indeed, an elderly Yolmo man told his grandson that he would not want to relate his life story to me, because, if he did, he would feel compelled to tell of the many sufferings he had faced in life, and since those sufferings could be perceived as the karmic "fruits" of previous bad deeds, they could also indicate that he was a lesser man than others. Be that as it may, Mheme might not have worried about potential assessments of this sort, in part because, unlike this man, his later years were ones of relative comfort, leisure, and high status.

23. Vincanne Adams (1996, 1997) has written insightfully about the potential reality-effecting karmic consequences of ethnographic writing as understood by another Tibetan Buddhist people, the Sherpas of the Solu-Khumbu region of northeastern Nepal. Drawing from her ethnographic research among these people, Adams has found that Sherpas understand that the ways in which anthropologists write about them can, in accord with Buddhist principles of karma and mimesis, have a powerful, determining effect on their welfare and personhood. Much as photographs of people dressed, by chance, in ragged clothes can result in a future of poverty for the subjects of those photographs, so, it is understood, certain ethnographic representations of Sherpas can become the reality for those portrayed. Some people that Adams spoke with, for instance, were concerned that a book claiming that Sherpa society was in decline "could actually have produced that very situation for Sherpas" (1997:92). The means and consequences of such reality-effects appear to be different among Yolmo wa: a negative representation of something or someone can be seen as an unwelcome omenlike "indication" *(preda)*, but not quite the cause, of

a negative karmic consequence to come, and the voicings of self and others, spoken or written, tend to substantiate identities and destinies in everyday life more than anything else. And yet I do find, as Adams does, that a heavy accountability comes with any writings one might author in such a world. This accountability can ultimately work in positive, meaningful ways, however, since I, too, can speak well of Mheme and so help to effect good echoes of his life, both now and in his death.

24. From what Karma tells me, Mheme's understanding of the soteriological force of people's talk about a person is not shared by all Yolmo wa. Yolmo wa commonly say that if people say good things about a person, then that person will have a good afterlife. But the implication for many is not that the gods listen to such talk in judging a person or that people saying good things about that person in effect cause a good afterlife. Rather, it is that the talk itself is, like a good rebirth, a karmic consequence of a morally good life and so simply *foretells* a good rebirth to come.

25. See Jäschke [1881] 1995:198; and Ortner 1978:43.

26. Hertz [1906] 1960:46.

27. Jäschke [1881] 1995:246. Mheme once told me, in contrast with what most others advised (see also Fürer-Haimendorf 1964:236 for Solu-Khumbu Sherpa), that all the talk about "the name is lost" was misguided, since the original and correct phrase was not "mhin torsin" but, simply, "mhi torsin" (the man is lost). The original became something else when resounded. Mheme's stance on the matter suggests that he was less attached to the idea that one's identity must be obliterated after death. It has also made me feel more comfortable invoking his name and presence both now and later.

28. The message is much the same as that which takes form in most Hindu funeral rites in Varanasi, India, wherein, to quote Jonathan Parry, "the complete obliteration of the physical remains of the deceased is accompanied by an almost equally radical effacement of his personal characteristics and biography" (1994:210).

29. Piers Vitebsky (1993:236–59) makes much the same observation in his ethnography of mortality among the Sora of eastern India.

30. It is also possible that our talks together enabled Mheme to take the measure of his life and so helped him to come to better terms with the ending of that life.

A Son's Death

1. In relating these events Kisang described a scene in which the older brother, then infected by the burns, called his younger brother to his side. Kānchā, repulsed by the odorous smell emanating from the infection, refused. His brother then promised him that he would give him some new clothes if he sat by his side, but still Kānchā moved no closer. "He loved his brother very much before this," Kisang said of Kānchā. "But he would not go by his side then."

2. Jho Bharpa's death also had important, life-altering consequences for Kān-chā, who was thirty-one at the time. As Kānchā told it, he was earning a living as a taxi driver then and even owned his own car, but he had just passed an exam that enabled him to obtain a license to drive trailer trucks. Because his marks on the exam were among the highest in his class, he was offered a truck-driving route in Saudi Arabia. But then his half brother died and he faced a "choice," as he put it: "Either I would go to the Arab country for the job, or I would stay in Nepal and take care of my mother." He decided to stay and soon rented a room to share with his mother.

The End of the Body

1. The triad is invoked in a different way in the course of a prayer, known to many Tibetan peoples, of long life for the Dalai Lama: "His three secrets [of body, speech, and mind] not disintegrating, not changing, not disappearing..." (Lopez 1995:174).

2. Kakar 1982:230; Parry 1994:86. In Nepali the word derives from *dehako anta*, "the body's end."

3. To paraphrase Levinas ([1947] 1987:74) on what he took to be the debilitating powers of death: "What is important about the approach of death is that at a certain moment we are no longer able to be able."

4. Phur Gyalmu, for example, characterized herself as someone who "did" things. When asked what she hoped to do in the next few years of her life, she replied, "What I think is that I work a lot, I don't stay put. I work. What does this person do? I work, I carry loads, this person. Nothing else. Not to give hardships to my children [is what I hope to do]. The children should study." She then offered some thoughts that worried the possibility that she might not be able to do as much in her later years. "I'm happy [now]. [But] if we don't work, we don't get to eat. So I feel that I'm happy. If I'm able to do things, I'll do them. If I'm unable, but my sons and daughters feed me, then I'll eat. If they don't, I won't [eat]." A person who has lost the ability to act or work in life can find herself in a precarious situation that requires others providing for her if she is to continue living.

5. *Tsham* is spelled *mtsams* in written Tibetan (Jäschke [1881] 1995:455).

6. See Desjarlais 1992, 1996.

7. Chang 1977:226.

8. Thurman 1994:169.

9. See, for instance, Rahula 1974:35–44; Robinson and Johnson 1997:39–42; and Collins 1998. The Tibetan word for *nirvāṇa* is *mya ngan las 'das pa*, "to pass beyond suffering."

10. It is worth noting, however, that Neela once told me, in the absence of her mother-in-law, "The thing with old people is that they also can get quite greedy." She said this happened to be the case with Kisang, who tended to keep track of everything that passed her way and wanted to keep things for herself,

close to her side. Yolmo wa would understand that such tempered greediness could prove to be a problem, since if a person is too attached to someone or something else, he or she might be unable to die.

11. The name "Phagpa Chen Rezig," or "Avalokiteśvara" in Sanskrit, is written as "'phags pa spyan ras gzigs" in Tibetan. "Dewa chen," "Sukhāvatī" in Sanskrit, reads as "bde ba can" in Tibetan.

12. Women who do farming work in the villages, in contrast, tend not to have the free hours needed to undertake such efforts. "Now there's no time," Phur Gyalmu told us when asked if she prayed frequently. "One needs to carry the straps [carry loads]. One needs to thrash the millet. There's no time." Yolmo men, meanwhile, tend to acquire merit more through ritual practices or, if they can read Tibetan, through the recitation of sacred Tibetan texts.

13. Mullin 1998:92.

14. "This is correct. You're right to say this," Binod Yolmo said upon reading this sentence. He went on to note that, as he saw it, women have to face many new situations and relationships in their lives, from moving to new homes and forming ties with their husbands' mothers to later forming relationships with their sons' wives. Men, in contrast, who tend to stay put, have little need to develop strong bonds with any newcomers to their homes. They are therefore less used to facing new situations.

15. Others say that the most important thing is to die in peace but with the clearest consciousness possible, in order to be fully aware of one's passing.

Last Words

1. Das [1902] 1986:425.

2. See Jäschke [1881] 1995:35, 160–61; and Das [1902] 1986:425.

3. Hanks 1996:245.

4. Chheku Nangwa Thaye, or chos sku snang ba mtha' yas in written Tibetan, is known as Amitābha in Sanskrit. "Guru Rinpoche" is another name for Padmasambhava. Longu Thujhe Chhenpo, or tugs rje chen po in Tibetan, is another name for Phagpa Chen Rezi, or Avalokiteśvara.

5. See Jäschke [1881] 1995:336; and Goldstein with Narkyid 1984:66.

Glossary of Terms

All words listed in the left-hand column are Yolmo words except those followed by "(N.)," which designates a Nepali word, or by "(S.)," which designates a Sanskrit word.

Word	Equivalent in written Tibetan, where applicable	Gloss in English
bardo	bar do	intermediate period; intermediate state between death and rebirth
Bardo Thedol	bar do thos grol	"Liberation through Understanding in the Between"; guidebook to the intermediate period that a person enters after he or she dies
bhaja	brag cha	echo, echoic illusion, ghostly appearance
bodhicitta (S.)	byang chub kyi sems	mind of enlightenment; a spiritually pure heartmind; the aspiration to attain enlightenment in order to benefit all sentient beings
bodhisattva (S.)	byang chub sems dpa'	enlightenment being; one who has generated bodhicitta and seeks enlightenment for the benefit of others

Word	Equivalent in written Tibetan, where applicable	Gloss in English
bombo	bon po	shaman
chhang	chang	fermented grain beer
chhe	chos	dharma; religion; religious teachings or writings
Chhe [gi] Gyalbu	gshin rje chos rgyal	Lord of Dharma; Dharmaraja; Yama Raj (Lord of Death)
chhorten	mchod rten	stūpa; "offering base"; sacred shrine containing relics of the Buddha
ḍhaṅga (N.)		skill, style, or know-how in doing things
dharma (N.)		religion, religious practice, religious duties, virtuous action
dhigpa	sdig pa	sin; misdeed
dhukpu	sdug po	suffering, sorrow, hardship, hard work
ghewa	dge ba	virtue; karmic merit; funeral rites undertaken to increase karmic merit of deceased person
ghore		temporary shelter
gompa	dgon pa	monastery; lamaic temple
jang chub sem ba	byang chub sems dpa'	bodhicitta mind; a spiritually pure mind; bodhisattva
jhang bar	sbyangs par	purification print
jhinda	sbyin bdag	sponsors of or donors to a lama or lama lineage
jīvan kathā (N.)		life story; biography
kha jhem	kha chems	last words; final will or testament
khorwa	'khor ba	the cycle of death and rebirth within the six classes of physical beings
kurā (N.)		talk, matter, thing, subject
kyipu	skyid po	happiness, comfort, joy
la	bla	spirit; vital life-force
lama	bla ma	Buddhist priest

Word	Equivalent in written Tibetan, where applicable	Gloss in English
lamini		daughter of a lineage lama
le	las	work, deed, action; karma, karmic action
mālā (N.)		prayer beads; rosary
mani		devotional mantra; prayer; Buddhist shrine
mantra (S.)		a set of words or sounds endowed with spiritual or magical potency
mhi kha	mi kha	"people's talk"; harmful gossip
mi ser	mig zer	romantic jealousy
nam-she	rnam shes	soul, consciousness
nam-thar	rnam thar	spiritual biography
Nga-chang Shakya Zangpo	sngags chang sha kya bzang bu	heroic forefather of the Ningma Lama lineage
Ningma Lama	rnying ma bla ma	a lineage of Buddhist priests in Yolmo society
nirvāṇa (S.)	mya ngan las 'das pa	the state of liberation from the suffering of cyclic existence
nyingjwa	snying rje ba	compassioned one; one who deserves and receives compassion, love, or pity from others
Nyingma	rnying ma	"Old School"; school of Tibetan Buddhism
Phagpa Chen Rezig	'phags pa spyan ras gzigs	Avalokiteśvara; a bodhisattva of compassion, responsible for the liberation and perfection of all sentient beings
pūjā (N.)		ritual worship; religious rites in general
raksī (N.)		liquor made from distilled grains
sansāra (N.)	'khor ba	cycle of existence; round of birth and death
Sarma Lama	gsar ma bla ma	a lineage of Buddhist priests in Yolmo society

Word	Equivalent in written Tibetan, where applicable	Gloss in English
sem	sems	heartmind, mind
semjha	sems chags	attachment
shalgar	zhal kar	ceremonial offering in the form of a container of liquor
shyindi	shin 'dre	ghost; soul of deceased person
thangka	thang ka	Buddhist scroll-painting
tshe	tshe	life; life span; life force
tsher lu	tser lu	pain song; song of sadness
Yama Raj (N.)		Lord of Death; Chhe Gyalbu

References

Adams, Vincanne. 1996. *Tigers of the Snow and Other Virtual Sherpas: An Ethnography of Himalayan Encounters.* Princeton, N.J.: Princeton University Press.
———. 1997. "Dreams of a Final Sherpa." *American Anthropologist* 99:85–97.
Amichai, Yehuda. 1993. *Poems of Jerusalem and Love Poems: A Bilingual Edition.* Bronx, N.Y.: Sheep Meadow Press.
Appadurai, Arjun. 1991. "Global Ethnoscapes: Notes and Queries for a Transnational Anthropology." In *Recapturing Anthropology,* ed. Richard Fox, 191–210. Santa Fe, N.Mex.: School of American Research.
Ariès, Philippe. 1981. *The Hour of Our Death.* New York: Alfred A. Knopf.
Aziz, Barbara. 1987. "Moving towards a Sociology of Tibet." *Tibet Journal* 12(4):72–86.
———. 1988. "Women in Tibetan Sociology and Tibetology." In *Tibetan Studies: Proceedings of the 4th Seminar of the International Association for Tibetan Studies,* ed. H. Uebach and J. Panglung, 25–34. Kommission für Zentralasiatische Studien, Bayerische Akademie der Wissenschaften.
Babb, Lawrence. 1981. "Glancing: Visual Interaction in Hinduism." *Journal of Anthropological Research* 37:387–410.
Baudrillard, Jean. 1983. *Simulations.* New York: Semiotext(e).
Bauman, Richard. 1986. *Story, Performance, and Event.* Cambridge: Cambridge University Press.
Behar, Ruth. 1993. *Translated Woman: Crossing the Border with Esperanza's Story.* Boston: Beacon Press.
———. 1996. *The Vulnerable Observer: Anthropology That Breaks Your Heart.* Boston: Beacon Press.
Benjamin, Walter. [1936] 1968. "The Work of Art in the Age of Mechanical Reproduction." In *Illuminations,* ed. Hannah Arendt, 217–51. New York: Schocken Books.

Bennett, Lynn. 1983. *Dangerous Wives and Sacred Sisters: Social and Symbolic Roles of High-Caste Women in Nepal.* New York: Columbia University Press.

Beyer, Stephan. 1973. *The Cult of Tārā: Magic and Ritual in Tibet.* Berkeley: University of California Press.

——. 1992. *The Classical Tibetan Language.* Albany: State University of New York Press.

Bishop, Naomi. 1998. *Himalayan Herders.* New York: Harcourt Brace and Co.

Blackman, Margaret. 1992. "Introduction: The Afterlife of the Life History." *Journal of Narrative and Life History* 2:1–10.

Briggs, Charles, and Richard Bauman. 1992. "Genre, Intertextuality, and Social Power." *Journal of Linguistic Anthropology* 2:131–72.

Cabezón, Jose, ed. 1992. *Buddhism, Sexuality, and Gender.* Albany: State University of New York Press.

Cameron, Mary. 1998. *On the Edge of the Auspicious: Gender and Caste in Rural Nepal.* Champaign: University of Illinois Press.

Carrithers, Michael. 1983. *The Buddha.* Oxford: Oxford University Press.

Carstairs, G. Morris. 1983. *Death of a Witch: A Village in North India, 1950–81.* London: Hutchinson.

Chang, Garma Chen-Chi. 1977. *The Hundred Thousand Songs of Milarepa,* 2 vols. Boulder, Colo.: Shambhala Publications.

Chökyi Nyima Rinpoche. 1991. *The Bardo Guidebook.* Hong Kong: Rangjung Yeshe Publications.

Clarke, Graham. 1980a. "Lama and Tamang in Yolmo." In *Tibetan Studies in Honor of Hugh Richardson,* ed. Michael Aris and Aung San Suu Kyi, 79–86. Warminster, England: Aris and Phillips.

——. 1980b. "A Helambu History." *Journal of the Nepal Research Centre* (Humanities) 4:1–38.

——. 1980c. "The Temple and Kinship among a Buddhist People of the Himalaya." Ph.D. dissertation, Oxford University.

——. 1983. "The Great and Little Traditions in the Study of Yolmo, Nepal." In *Contributions on Tibetan Language, History and Culture,* ed. E. Steinkellner and H. Tauscher, vol. 1, 21–37. Vienna: Arbeitskreis für Tibetische und Buddhistische Studien, Universität Wien.

——. 1985. "Equality and Hierarchy among a Buddhist People in Nepal." In *Contexts and Levels: Anthropological Essays on Hierarchy,* ed. R.H. Barnes, D. de Coppet, and R.J. Parkin, 193–209. Oxford: JASO Occasional Papers, no. 4.

——. 1990. "Ideas of Merit *(bsod-nams),* Virtue *(dge-ba),* Blessing *(bying-rlabs),* and Material Prosperity *(rten-'brel)* in Highland Nepal." *Journal of the Anthropological Society of Oxford* 21:165–84.

——. 1991. "Nara *(na-rag)* in Yolmo: A Social History of Hell in Helambu." In *Festschrift für Geza Uray,* ed. M.T. Much, 43–62. Vienna: Arbeitskreis für Tibetische und Buddhistische Studien, Universität Wien.

Classen, Constance. 1993. *Worlds of Sense: Exploring the Senses in History and Across Cultures.* London: Routledge.

———. 1998. *The Color of Angels: Cosmology, Gender and the Aesthetic Imagination.* New York: Routledge.

Classen, Constance, David Howes, and Anthony Synnott. 1994. *Aroma: The Cultural History of Smell.* New York: Routledge.

Clifford, James. 1997. *Routes: Travel and Translation in the Late Twentieth Century.* Cambridge, Mass.: Harvard University Press.

Cohen, Lawrence. 1998. *No Aging in India: Alzheimer's, the Bad Family, and Other Modern Things.* Berkeley: University of California Press.

Collins, Steven. 1982. *Selfless Persons.* Cambridge: Cambridge University Press.

———. 1998. *Nirvana and Other Buddhist Felicities: Utopias of the Pali Imaginaire.* Cambridge: Cambridge University Press.

Crapanzano, Vincent. 1980. *Tuhami: Portrait of a Moroccan.* Chicago: University of Chicago Press.

———. 1994. "Kevin: On the Transfer of Emotions." *American Anthropologist* 96:866–85.

Csordas, Thomas. 1994a. *The Sacred Self: A Cultural Phenomenology of Charismatic Healing.* Berkeley: University of California Press.

———, ed. 1994b. *Embodiment and Experience: The Existential Ground of Culture and Self.* Cambridge: Cambridge University Press.

Daniel, E. Valentine. 1966. *Charred Lullabies: Chapters in an Anthropography of Violence.* Princeton, N.J.: Princeton University Press.

Das, Sarat Chandra. [1902] 1986. *A Tibetan-English Dictionary.* Kathmandu: Ratna Pustak Bhandar.

Das, Veena. 1995. "Voice as Birth of Culture." *Ethnos* 3–4:159–81.

———. 1996. "Language and the Body: Transactions in the Construction of Pain." *Daedalus* 125(1):67–92.

———. 1998. "Narrativizing the Male and the Female in Tulasidas' *Ramacharitamanasa.*" In *Social Structure and Change,* vol. 5: *Religion and Kinship,* ed. A.M. Shah, B.S. Baviskar, and E.A. Ramaswamy, 66–92. New Delhi: Sage Publications.

———. 2000. "The Act of Witnessing: Violence, Poisonous Knowledge, and Subjectivity." In *Violence and Subjectivity,* ed. Veena Das, Arthur Kleinman, Mamphela Ramphele, and Pamela Reynolds, 205–25. Berkeley: University of California Press.

DelVecchio Good, Mary-Jo, Paul Brodwin, Byron Good, and Arthur Kleinman, eds. 1992. *Pain as Human Experience: An Anthropological Perspective.* Berkeley: University of California Press.

Des Chene, Mary. 1998. "Fate, Domestic Authority, and Women's Wills." In *Selves in Time and Place: Identities, Experience, and History in Nepal,* ed. Debra Skinner, Alfred Pach, and Dorothy Holland, 19–50. Lanham, Md.: Rowman and Littlefield.

Desjarlais, Robert. 1992. *Body and Emotion: The Aesthetics of Illness and Healing in the Nepal Himalayas.* Philadelphia: University of Pennsylvania Press.

———. 1996. "Presence." In *The Performance of Healing,* ed. Carol Laderman and Marina Roseman, 143–64. New York: Routledge.

———. 1997. *Shelter Blues: Sanity and Selfhood among the Homeless*. Philadelphia: University of Pennsylvania Press.

Eck, Diana. 1996. *Darśan: Seeing the Divine Image in India*. 2d ed. New York: Columbia University Press.

Ekvall, Robert. 1964. *Religious Observances in Tibet: Patterns and Function*. Chicago: University of Chicago Press.

Enslin, Elizabeth. 1992. "Collective Powers in Common Places: The Politics of Gender and Space in a Women's Struggle for a Meeting Center in Chitwan, Nepal." *Himalayan Research Bulletin* 12(1–2):11–25.

Errington, Shelly. 1990. "Recasting Sex, Gender, and Power: A Theoretical and Regional Overview." In *Power and Difference in Island Southeast Asia*, ed. Jane Atkinson and Shelly Errington, 1–58. Stanford, Calif.: Stanford University Press.

Feld, Steven. 1982. *Sound and Sentiment*. Philadelphia: University of Pennsylvania Press.

———. 1996. "Waterfalls of Song: An Acoustemology of Place Resounding in Bosavi, Papua New Guinea." In *Senses of Place*, ed. Steven Feld and Keith Basso, 93–136. Santa Fe, N.Mex.: School of American Research Press.

Feldman, Allen. 1991. *Formations of Violence: The Narrative of the Body and Political Terror in Northern Ireland*. Chicago: University of Chicago Press.

———. 2000. "Violence and Vision: The Prosthetics and Aesthetics of Terror." In *Violence and Subjectivity*, ed. Veena Das, Arthur Kleinman, Mamphela Ramphele, and Pamela Reynolds, 46–78. Berkeley: University of California Press.

Frank, Gelya. 2000. *Venus on Wheels: Two Decades of Dialogue on Disability, Biography, and Being Female in America*. Berkeley: University of California Press.

French, Rebecca. 1995. *The Golden Yoke: The Legal Cosmology of Buddhist Tibet*. Ithaca, N.Y.: Cornell University Press.

Fürer-Haimendorf, Christoph von. 1964. *The Sherpas of Nepal: Buddhist Highlanders*. London: John Murray.

Gal, Susan. 1991. "Between Speech and Silence: The Problematics of Research on Language and Gender." In *Gender at the Crossroads of Knowledge*, ed. Micaela di Leonardo, 175–203. Berkeley: University of California Press.

Geertz, Clifford. 1973. *The Interpretation of Culture*. New York: Basic Books.

Gellner, David. 1992. *Monk, Householder, and Tantric Priest: Newar Buddhism and its Hierarchy of Ritual*. Cambridge: Cambridge University Press.

Gellner, David, Joanna Pfaff-Czarnecka, and John Whelpton, eds. 1997. *Nationalism and Ethnicity in a Hindu Kingdom: The Politics of Culture in Contemporary Nepal*. Amsterdam: Harwood Academic Publishers.

Genette, Gérard. 1980. *Narrative Discourse: An Essay on Method*. Ithaca, N.Y.: Cornell University Press.

Goldstein, Melvyn, with Ngawangthondup Narkyid. 1984. *English-Tibetan Dictionary of Modern Tibetan*. Berkeley: University of California Press.

Gombrich, Richard. 1988. *Theravada Buddhism: A Social History from Ancient Benares to Modern Colombo*. New York: Routledge.

Gonda, Jan. 1963. *The Vision of the Vedic Poets*. The Hague: Mouton and Co.

———. 1969. *Eye and Gaze in the Veda*. Amsterdam: North-Holland Publishing Company.

Good, Byron. 1994. *Medicine, Rationality, and Experience*. Cambridge: Cambridge University Press.

Goodwin, Charles. 1994. "Professional Vision." *American Anthropologist* 96:606–33.

Gtsan-smyon Heruka. 1977. *The Life of Milarepa*. Translated by Lobsang P. Lhalungpa. New York: Dutton.

Gyatso, Janet. 1987. "Down with the Demoness: Reflections on a Feminine Ground in Tibet." *Tibet Journal* 12(4):7–35.

———. 1992. "Autobiography in Tibetan Religious Literature: Reflections on Its Modes of Self-Presentation." In *Tibetan Studies: Proceedings of the 5th International Association of Tibetan Studies Seminar*, ed. Shoren Ihara and Zuiho Yamaguchi, vol. 2, 465–78. Narita, Japan: Naritasan Institute for Buddhist Studies.

———. 1997. *Apparitions of the Self: The Secret Autobiographies of a Tibetan Visionary*. Princeton, N.J.: Princeton University Press.

Hanks, William. 1996. *Language and Communicative Practice*. Boulder, Colo.: Westview Press.

Harlan, Lindsey, and Paul Courtright. 1995. *From the Margins of Hindu Marriage: Essays on Gender, Religion, and Culture*. Oxford: Oxford University Press.

Haviland, John. 1991. "That Was the Last Time I Seen Them, and No More: Voices through Time in Australian Aboriginal Autobiography." *American Ethnologist* 18:331–61.

Heidegger, Martin. 1962. *Being and Time*. Translated by John Macquarrie and Edward Robinson. New York: HarperCollins.

Hertz, Robert. [1906] 1960. "A Contribution to the Study of the Collective Representation of Death." In *Death and the Right Hand*, 27–73. Glencoe, Ill.: Free Press.

Herzfeld, Michael. 2001. *Anthropology: Theoretical Practice in Culture and Society*. Malden, Mass.: Blackwell Publishers.

Hollan, Douglas. 1997. "The Relevance of Person-Centered Ethnography to Cross-Cultural Psychiatry." *Transcultural Psychiatry* 34:219–34.

———. 2000. "Constructivist Models of Mind, Contemporary Psychoanalysis, and the Development of Culture Theory." *American Anthropologist* 102:538–50.

Hollan, Douglas, and Jane Wellenkamp. 1994. *Contentment and Suffering: Culture and Experience in Toraja*. New York: Columbia University Press.

Holland, Dorothy, and Debra Skinner. 1995. "Contested Ritual, Contested Femininities: (Re)forming Self and Society in a Nepali Women's Festival." *American Ethnologist* 22:279–305.

Howes, David, ed. 1991. *The Varieties of Sensory Experience: A Sourcebook in the Anthropology of the Senses*. Toronto: University of Toronto Press.

Irvine, Judith. 1996. "Shadow Conversations: The Indeterminacy of Participant Roles." In *Natural Histories of Discourse*, ed. Michael Silverstein and Greg Urban, 131–59. Chicago: University of Chicago Press.

Jackson, Michael. 1989. *Paths Toward a Clearing: Radical Empiricism and Ethnographic Inquiry.* Bloomington: Indiana University Press.

——. 1998. *Minima Ethnographica: Intersubjectivity and the Anthropological Project.* Chicago: Chicago University Press.

——, ed. 1996. *Things as They Are: New Directions in Phenomenological Anthropology.* Bloomington: Indiana University Press.

Jakobson, Roman. [1957] 1971. "Shifters, Verbal Categories, and the Russian Verb." In *Roman Jakobson: Selected Writings,* vol. 2, 130–47. The Hague: Mouton.

Jäschke, H. A. [1881] 1995. *A Tibetan-English Dictionary.* Delhi: Motilal Banarsidass Publishers.

Jhala, Jayasinhji. 1997. "Speculations on the Concept of Indic Frontality Prompted by Questions on Portraiture." *Visual Anthropology* 10:49–66.

Kakar, Sudhir. 1982. *Shamans, Mystics, and Doctors: A Psychological Enquiry into India and Its Healing Traditions.* Boston: Beacon Press.

Kalu Rinpoche. 1999. *The Foundations of Tibetan Buddhism: The Gem Ornament of Manifold Oral Instructions Which Benefits Each and Everyone Accordingly.* Ithaca, N.Y.: Snow Lion Publications.

Kapferer, Bruce. 1997. *The Feast of the Sorcerer: Practices of Consciousness and Power.* Chicago: University of Chicago Press.

Kapur, Sohaila. 1983. *Witchcraft in Western India.* Hyderabad, India: Orient Longman.

Khetsun Sangpo Rinbochay. 1982. *Tantric Practice in Nying-Ma.* Translated by Jeffrey Hopkins. London: Rider.

Klein, Anne Carolyn. 1995. *Meeting the Great Bliss Queen: Buddhists, Feminists, and the Art of the Self.* Boston: Beacon Press.

Kleinman, Arthur, and Joan Kleinman. 1995. "Suffering and Its Professional Transformation: Toward an Ethnography of Interpersonal Experience." In *Writing at the Margins: Discourse between Anthropology and Medicine,* ed. Arthur Kleinman, 95–119. Berkeley: University of California Press.

Kondos, Vivienne. 1991. "Subjection and the Ethics of Anguish: The Nepalese Parbatya Parent-Daughter Relationship." *Contributions to Indian Sociology* 25:113–33.

Kratz, Corinne. 2001. "Conversations and Lives." In *African Words, African Voices,* ed. David William Cohen, Stephan Miescher, and Luise White, 127–61. Bloomington: Indiana University Press.

Laderman, Carol. 1991. *Taming the Wind of Desire: Psychology, Medicine, and Aesthetics in Malay Shamanistic Performance.* Berkeley: University of California Press.

Lamb, Sarah. 2000. *White Saris and Sweet Mangoes: Aging, Gender, and Body in North India.* Berkeley: University of California Press.

Levinas, Emmanuel. [1947] 1987. *Time and the Other.* Translated by Richard Cohen. Pittsburgh, Pa.: Duquesne University Press.

——. 1969. *Totality and Infinity: An Essay on Exteriority.* Pittsburgh, Pa.: Duquesne University Press.

Levine, Nancy. 1981. "Law, Labor and the Economy: Vulnerability of Women in Nyinba Society." *Kailash* 8:123–54.

———. 1982. "Belief and Explanation in Nyinba Women's Witchcraft." *Man* 17:259–74.

LeVine, Robert. 1982. *Culture, Behavior, and Personality: An Introduction to the Comparative Study of Psychosocial Adaptation.* New York: Aldine.

Levy, Robert. 1973. *Tahitians: Mind and Experience in the Society Islands.* Chicago: Chicago University Press.

Longchenpa [Klong-chen rab-'byams-pa]. 1976. *Kindly Bent to Ease Us,* part 3: "Wonderment." Translated by Herbert Guenther. Emeryville, Calif.: Dharma Publishing.

Lopez, Donald S. 1995. "A Prayer for the Long Life of the Dalai Lama." In *Buddhism in Practice,* ed. Donald Lopez, 170–75. Princeton, N.J.: Princeton University Press.

———. 1997. "Introduction." In *Religions of Tibet in Practice,* ed. Donald Lopez, 3–36. Princeton, N.J.: Princeton University Press.

———. 1998. *Prisoners of Shangri-La: Tibetan Buddhism and the West.* Chicago: University of Chicago Press.

McHugh, Ernestine. 1998. "Situating Persons: Honor and Identity in Nepal." In *Selves in Time and Place: Identities, Experience, and History in Nepal,* ed. Debra Skinner, Alfred Pach, and Dorothy Holland, 155–74. Lanham, Md.: Rowman and Littlefield.

———. 2001. *Love and Honor in the Himalayas: Coming to Know Another Culture.* Philadelphia: University of Pennsylvania Press.

Maloney, Clarence. 1976. "Don't Say 'Pretty Baby' Lest You Zap It with Your Eye: The Evil Eye in South Asia." In *The Evil Eye,* ed. Clarence Maloney, 102–48. New York: Columbia University Press.

March, Kathryn. 1979. "The Intermediacy of Women: Female Gender Symbolism and the Social Position of Women among Tamangs and Sherpas of Highland Nepal." Ph.D. dissertation, Department of Anthropology, Cornell University.

———. 1984. "Weaving, Writing, and Gender." *Man* (n.s.) 18:729–44.

Maskarinec, Gregory. 1995. *The Rulings of the Night: An Ethnography of Nepalese Shaman Oral Texts.* Madison: University of Wisconsin Press.

Menon, Usha, and Richard Shweder. 1998. "The Return of the 'White Man's Burden': The Moral Discourse of Anthropology and the Domestic Life of Hindu Women." In *Welcome to Middle Age! (And Other Cultural Fictions),* ed. Richard Shweder, 139–88. Chicago: University of Chicago Press.

Merleau-Ponty, Maurice. 1962. *Phenomenology of Perception.* Translated by J. Edie. Evanston, Ill.: Northwestern University Press.

———. 1964. *Signs.* Translated by R. C. McClearly. Evanston, Ill.: Northwestern University Press.

Miller, Beatrice. 1980. "Views of Women's roles in Buddhist Tibet." In *Studies in History of Buddhism,* ed. A. K. Narain, 155–66. Delhi: B. R. Publishing.

Mintz, Sidney. 1985. *Sweetness and Power: The Place of Sugar in Modern History.* New York: Viking.

Mitchell, Timothy. 1992. "Orientalism and the Exhibitionary Order." In *Colonialism and Culture,* ed. Nicholas Dirks, 289–317. Cambridge: Cambridge University Press.

Mohanty, J. N. 2000. *Classical Indian Philosophy.* Lanham, Md.: Rowman and Littlefield.

Mullin, Glenn, ed. 1998. *Living in the Face of Death: The Tibetan Tradition.* Ithaca, N.Y.: Snow Lion Publications.

Narayan, Kirin. 1986. "Birds on a Branch: Girlfriends and Wedding Songs in Kangra." *Ethos* 14:47–75.

Nietzsche, Friedrich. [1887] 1967. *On the Genealogy of Morals, and Ecce Homo.* Translated by Walter Kaufman and R. J. Hollingdale. New York: Random House.

Obeyesekere, Gananath. 1968. "Theodicy, Sin, and Salvation in a Sociology of Buddhism." In *Dialectic in Practical Reason,* ed. Edmund Leach, 7–40. Cambridge: Cambridge University Press.

———. 1981. *Medusa's Hair: An Essay on Personal Symbols and Religious Experience.* Chicago: University of Chicago Press.

———. 1990. *The Work of Culture.* Chicago: University of Chicago Press.

O'Flaherty, Wendy Doniger. 1984. *Dreams, Illusions, and Other Realities.* Chicago: University of Chicago Press.

Ortiz, Karol. 1985. "Mental Health Consequences of Life History Method: Implications from a Refugee Case." *Ethos* 13:99–120.

Ortner, Sherry. 1978. *Sherpas through Their Rituals.* Cambridge: Cambridge University Press.

———. 1996. *Making Gender: The Politics and Erotics of Culture.* Boston: Beacon Press.

———. 1999. *Life and Death on Mt. Everest: Sherpas and Himalayan Mountaineering.* Princeton, N.J.: Princeton University Press.

Owens, Bruce McCoy. 2000. "Envisioning Identity: Deity, Person, and Practice in the Kathmandu Valley." *American Ethnologist* 27:702–35.

Parry, Jonathan. 1994. *Death in Banaras.* Cambridge: Cambridge University Press.

Patrul Rinpoche. 1996. *The Words of My Perfect Teacher.* Translated by the Padmakara Translation Group. New Delhi: HarperCollins India.

Powers, John. 1995. *Introduction to Tibetan Buddhism.* Ithaca, N.Y.: Snow Lion Publications.

Raheja, Gloria Goodwin, and Ann Grodzins Gold. 1994. *Listen to the Heron's Words: Reimagining Gender and Kinship in North India.* Berkeley: University of California Press.

Rahula, Walpola. 1974. *What the Buddha Taught.* Rev. ed. New York: Grove Press.

Rinbochay, Lati, and Jeffery Hopkins. 1979. *Death, Intermediate State and Rebirth in Tibetan Buddhism.* London: Rider and Company.

Robinson, Richard, and Willard Johnson. 1997. *The Buddhist Religion: A Historical Introduction*. Belmont, Calif.: Wadsworth Publishing Co.

Roseman, Marina. 1991. *Healing Sounds from the Malaysian Rainforest*. Berkeley: University of California Press.

Saletore, R. N. 1981. *Indian Witchcraft*. New Delhi: Abhinav Publications.

Samuel, Geoffrey. 1989. "The Body in Buddhist and Hindu Tantra." *Religion* 19:197–210.

———. 1993. *Civilized Shamans: Buddhism in Tibetan Societies*. Washington, D.C.: Smithsonian Institution Press.

Schmidt, Ruth Laila, and Ballabh Mani Dahal, eds. 1993. *A Practical Dictionary of Modern Nepali*. Kathmandu, Nepal: Ratna Sagar.

Scott, David. 1991. "The Cultural Poetics of Eyesight in Sri Lanka: Composure, Vulnerability, and the Sinhala Concept of *distiya*." *Dialectical Anthropology* 16:85–102.

———. 1994. *Formations of Ritual: Colonial and Anthropological Discourses on the Sinhala Yaktovil*. Minneapolis: University of Minnesota Press.

Seeger, Anthony. 1975. "The Meaning of Body Ornaments." *Ethnology* 14:211–24.

Seremetakis, C. Nadia. 1991. *The Last Word: Women, Death, and Divination in Inner Mani*. Chicago: University of Chicago Press.

———, ed. 1994. *The Senses Still: Perception and Memory as Material Culture in Modernity*. Chicago: University of Chicago Press.

Skinner, Debra. 1989. "The Socialization of Gender Identity: Observations from Nepal." In *Child Development in Cultural Context*, ed. Jaan Valsiner, 181–92. Toronto: Hogrefe and Huber Publishers.

Skinner, Debra, Alfred Pach, and Dorothy Holland, eds. 1998. *Selves in Time and Place: Identities, Experience, and History in Nepal*. Lanham, Md.: Rowman and Littlefield.

Smith, Brian. 1989. *Reflections on Resemblance, Ritual, and Religion*. New York: Oxford University Press.

Snellgrove, David, ed. and trans. 1967. *Four Lamas of Dolpo: Tibetan Biographies*. Cambridge, Mass.: Harvard University Press.

Solomon, Robert. 1998. "Death Fetishism, Morbid Solipsism." In *Death and Philosophy*, ed. Jeff Malpas and Robert Solomon, 152–76. London: Routledge.

Stevenson, Burton, ed. 1937. *The Home Book of Quotations: Classical and Modern*, 3d ed. New York: Dodd, Mead, and Co.

Stoller, Paul. 1989. *The Taste of Ethnographic Things: The Senses in Anthropology*. Philadelphia: University of Pennsylvania Press.

———. 1997. *Sensuous Scholarship*. Philadelphia: University of Pennsylvania Press.

Strong, John. 1995. *The Experience of Buddhism: Sources and Interpretations*. Belmont, Calif.: Wadsworth Publishing Co.

Taussig, Michael. 1993. *Mimesis and Alterity: A Particular History of the Senses*. New York: Routledge.

Thurman, Robert. 1995. *Essential Tibetan Buddhism*. New Delhi: HarperCollins India.

————, ed. and trans. 1994. *The Tibetan Book of the Dead: Liberation through Understanding in the Between*. New York: Thorsons.

Trawick, Margaret. 1990. *Notes on Love in a Tamil Family*. Berkeley: University of California Press.

Tsang Nyön Heruka. 1982. *The Life of Marpa the Translator: Seeing Accomplishes All*. Translated by the Nālandā Translation Committee. Boston: Shambhala Publications.

Tsele Natsok Rangdröl. 1987. *The Mirror of Mindfulness*. Hong Kong: Rangjung Yeshe Publications.

Tucci, Giuseppe. 1980. *The Religions of Tibet*. London: Routledge and Kegan Paul.

Turner, R. L. [1931] 1966. *A Comparative and Etymological Dictionary of the Nepali Language*. Delhi: Allied Publishers.

Turner, Terrence. 1980. "The Social Skin." In *Not Work Alone*, ed. Jeremy Cherfas and Roger Lewin, 112–40. Beverly Hills, Calif.: Sage Publications.

Tyler, Stephen. 1987. "The Vision Quest in the West, or What the Mind's Eye Sees." In *The Unspeakable: Discourse, Dialogue, and Rhetoric in the Postmodern World*, 149–70. Madison: University of Wisconsin Press.

Urban, Greg. 1991. *A Discourse-Centered Approach to Culture: Native South American Myths and Rituals*. Austin: University of Texas Press.

Vatuk, Sylvia. 1987. "Authority, Power and Autonomy in the Life Cycle of the North Indian Woman." In *Dimensions of Social Life: Essays in Honor of David G. Mandelbaum*, ed. Paul Hockings, 23–44. Berlin: Mounton de Gruyter.

Vitebsky, Piers. 1993. *Dialogues with the Dead: The Discussion of Mortality among the Sora of Eastern India*. Cambridge: Cambridge University Press.

Wadley, Susan. 1980. "The Paradoxical Powers of Tamil Women." In *The Powers of Tamil Women*, ed. Susan Wadley, 61–92. Syracuse, N.Y.: Syracuse University Press.

Watkins, Joanne. 1996. *Spirited Women: Gender, Religion, and Cultural Identity in the Nepal Himalaya*. New York: Columbia University Press.

Willis, Janice. 1987. *Feminine Ground: Essays on Women in Tibet*. Ithaca, N.Y.: Snow Lion Publications.

Wylie, T. V. 1959. "A Standard System of Tibetan Transcription." *Harvard Journal of Asiatic Studies* 22:261–67.

Acknowledgments

This book draws from ethnographic research I conducted in Nepal in 1988–89, 1997, 1998, 2000, and 2001. The most recent field studies were supported by a grant from the American Philosophical Society, a fellowship from the George A. and Eliza Gardner Howard Foundation, and a fellowship from the John Simon Guggenheim Memorial Foundation. Support was also received through several grants from Sarah Lawrence College, including a Hewlett-Mellon Faculty Development Grant, Flik travel grants, and grants from the Ziesing Fund for Research in the Social Sciences. The research would not have been possible without this generous financial support.

I also thank the many people in Nepal who helped with this project. Phur Gyalmu Sherpa, Sen Zangbu Sherpa, Gom Dolma Sherpa, Karmu Omu Lama, and Ghaki Lamani were kind enough to sit and talk with me about various aspects of their lives. Nogapu Sherpa, Pramod Lama Yolmo, Norbu Yolmo, Tashi Lama, Kunsang Lama, Raj Kumar Lama, Dorje Sherpa, Chhewang Yolmo, and Temba D. Yolmo assisted me in the tricky tasks of interviewing Yolmo elders and translating their words into English. They also offered their friendship, for which I am greatly appreciative. K. B. Lama and Hrikchung Lama welcomed me into their home, and they and their family were supremely generous hosts during the months I stayed with them. Lhatul Lama and Mingmar Lama offered their kind friendship, both when I was visiting them in Thodong and when they were staying in Kathmandu. Kānchā Lama and Neela Lama proved to be wonderful hosts whenever I visited their home, as did Rhidu Pema and Ang Maya. Binod Lama Yolmo worked with me on several translations and offered discerning thoughts on several chapters of this text. Karma Gyaltsen Yolmo, friend and colleague since 1989, helped me with every step of the project, from arranging introductions to Yolmo friends of his to reading carefully through an earlier version of this text. The book would be a much poorer one without his considerate help and advice. Finally, two Yolmo elders, Ghang Lama and Kisang Omu Lama, had the kindness and patience to share with me extremely rich and valuable accounts of their lives. Nyingjwa.

Thuje chhe, "thank you," to all the Yolmo people who have contributed to this project. I will be forever appreciative of the warm and enriching friendships with those just noted.

In the United States, friends and colleagues have helped in the development of the ideas advanced in these pages. Theresa O'Nell, James Wilce, Ernestine McHugh, João Biehl, Mary Porter, Lyde Sizer, Sandra Robinson, Chi Ogunyemi, Elizabeth Johnston, and Bella Brodzki read portions of the book in its various incarnations and helped me to take things further. Gregory Maskarinec, Veena Das, Sohini Ray, and Stephanie Viola read the book in manuscript form and offered insightful comments. David Howes, Arthur Kleinman, and Byron Good supported my efforts in beneficial ways. The collegiality of Naomi and John Bishop is greatly appreciated. Colleagues and students at Sarah Lawrence College offered support in ways both general and specific to this project. Tanya Luhrmann generated a set of helpful comments on an earlier draft. Stan Holwitz and Laura Harger served as sustaining editors. Tracy McGarry continued to be a supportive confidante and astute critic through the years we lived with this project brewing in our home.

Portions of the text were presented at several conferences, including annual meetings of the American Anthropological Association; the 28th Annual Conference on South Asia, held in Madison, Wisconsin, in 1999; and the interdisciplinary conference "Uncommon Senses," held in Montreal, Quebec, in 2000. Portions of the text were also presented to the Workshop on Culture, Life Course, and Mental Health at the University of Chicago in 1999 and to the seminar in clinically relevant medical anthropology at Harvard University in 2001. Critical responses to each of the papers presented have been quite beneficial. At the annual meetings of the American Anthropological Association in 2000, Vincent Crapanzano, William Hanks, Stephania Pandolfo, and John Leavitt offered incisive comments on an essay of mine related to this work. The essay, entitled "Echoes of a Yolmo Buddhist's Life, in Death," was published in May 2000 in *Cultural Anthropology* (15:260–93). Another essay of mine related to this work, entitled " 'So: Ragged Woman': The Aesthetics and Ethics of Skilled Action among Nepal's Yolmo Buddhists," was published in 2002 in *Ethnography* (3:149–175). I am grateful to the editors and publishers of these journals for their permission to draw from these works in revised form in the current text.

Index

Page numbers in italics indicate figures, maps, and tables.

action, 119, 135, 138, 141–42, 170, 173–75, 179, 200, 205, 221, 260, 261, 299, 307, 310–11, 312, 314, 316–17, 318, 325; speech as, 139–40. *See also* agency; karma
Adams, Vincanne, 370–71n23
aesthetics, 83, 181, 199, 255–74, 325; and ethics, 262–65, 273–74; of speaking, 265–67
agency, 108, 114, 117, 127, 128, 138, 193, 198–99
Amichai, Yehuda, 5
Amitābha, 320, 373n4
analogical thinking, 241
Ānandavardhana, 181
anthropological research among Yolmo people, 11–19, 22–23, 240–44, 255–56, 271–74, 331–38
attachment, 185, 202–5, 319, 378
Avalokiteśvara (Phagpa Chen Rezig), 364n1, 373nn11,4, 377

Babb, Lawrence, 55
bardo (between period), 182–85, 214–18, 234–35, 236, 324, 338, 347, 362n2, 375; of dying, 183–88, 236
Bardo Thedol (Liberation through Understanding in the Between), *68*, 214–18, 280, 318, 348, 375
behos (unconscious), 210
between, 206, 234, 325. *See also bardo*

bhaja (echo, echoic illusion), 278–308, 369nn6,13, 375
biography, 22–23, 53, 119, 150–51, 255–56, 343–49; as echo, 275–308; as "last words," 329–31, 346–47, 348; as "mirror of deeds," 240–44; Yolmo evaluations of, 52–53, 255–56, 305–8
bodhicitta, 283, 284, 375. *See also jang chub sem ba*
bodhisattva, 55, 284, 375
bombo (shamanic healer), 70–71, 95, 166–67, 286, 376
Buddha Siddhārtha, 26, 36, 288, 289, 367n4
Buddhism, 38, 57, 78, 96, 99, 100, 134, 165, 181, 233, 282, 291, 299, 318. *See also* Tibetan Buddhism
Burma, 35, 355n10

capture marriages, 31, 59, 107–8, 123, 221–29
Carrithers, Michael, 367–68n4
chemi (offering lamp), 92, 297
chhang (fermented grain beer), 39, 376
chhe (religion, dharma, religious writings), 29, 73, 74, 376
Chhe Gyalbu (Lord of Dharma), 236–44, 317, 347, 366n1, 376
chhorten (sacred shrine, stūpa), 5, 76, *77*, 99, 245, 253–54, 376

childhood, 28–30, 113–14
Chökyi Gyatso, 78
Clarke, Graham, 67, 70, 73, 354n4
Cohen, Lawrence, 235
corpse, 1–2, 91, 227, 348
cremations, 87–89, 165, 351; politics of, 89, 254

Dalai Lama, the, 202, 372n1
darśan (sight), 57–58
Das, Veena, 230, 286
death, 6–7, 92, 127, 165–67, 180, 198, 206–18, 227, 275–76, 281, 297, 309–14, 315–27, 335–36, 350–51; absence of body in, 1–2, 212; sensory aspects of, 235–40, 244, 302; and vision, 211, 215–18
deferral, 334–36
dehānt (end of the body), 316
dependent arising, 134, 326, 360n1
dewa chen (land of bliss), 217, 320, 365n13, 373n11
ḍhaṅga (skill), 259–61, 312, 376
dharma, 25, 26, 47, 51
dhigpa (sin, misdeed), 315, 376
dhukpu (suffering, hardship), 37–38, 41–42, 131–32, 356n12. *See also* suffering
discourse-centered approaches, 6
discourse genre, 242–43
disengagement, 61–64, 317–19, 324
divination, 78–79
divorce, 112, 219–21, 245–56
Dorje Semba, 95
dreams, 93–94, 210, 307–8, 369nn13,6; and death, 91–93, 210–11; in old age, 154; as "small death," 93; and vision, 92–94
dying, 6–7, 87, 161–75, 176–81, 201–5, 231–35, 253–54, 276–77, 315–27; cultural features of, 6–7; karmic aspects of, 174–75; rhetoric of, 178–79

enlightenment, 26, 112, 173, 258

face, 83, 90–91, 300, 304–5, 334, 338, 348
funeral rites, 1–2, 29, 34, 127, 165–66, 297, 299–303, *301,* 304, 350–51; and dissolution of the deceased, 302–3

Geertz, Clifford, 14
Ghang Lama, *21, 276*
ghore (shelter), 32, 167–68, 376

gom (to imagine), 95
gompa (lamaic temple, monastery), 11, 164, 376
Gurung people, 43
Gyalwa Kalzang Gyatso, 153, 180, 288

Hertz, Robert, 302
Herzfeld, Michael, 4
Hinduism, 54, 57–58, 181
Hindu peoples, 29, 57–58, 87, 189, 233, 316, 371n28

ijjat (prestige, honor), 48
illusion, 99, 280–82, 284, 369n10
India, 35, 36, 37, 43–44, 46, 235, 291, 355nn10–11, 371n29
intersubjectivity, 326

jan āndolan (people's movement), 11
jang chub sem ba (bodhicitta mind), 283–84, 332, 376
Japan, 35
Jhala, Jayasinhji, 58
jhang bar (purification print), 299–300, *300,* 302, 349, 376
jhinda (sponsor), 27, 52, 161, 163–64, 355n8, 376
jīvan kathā (life story), 1, 22–23, 376

Kāgate language, ix
karma, 111, 131, 134, 174–75, 186–87, 201–2, 314, 318, 321, 370n23; logic of, 25–26, 75, 261; and time, 51–53
kha jhem (last words, final will or testament), 195, 328–31, 346–47, 376
Khetsun Sangpo Rinbochay, 153
khorwa (cycle of deaths and rebirths within the six classes of physical beings), 27, 215, 376. See also *sansāra*
Kisang Omu, *103, 120*
kora (circumambulation), 321
kurā (talk, matter, things), 18–19, 107, 235, 345, 348, 376
kyipu (comfort, happiness), 30, 37, 376

la (spirit), 124, 180, 318, 376
lama (Buddhist priest), 11, 24, 47, 138, 166–67, 213, 234–35, 348, 355n5, 369n10, 376
Lama Dhomar lineage, 354n3
Lama Merit Intellect, 208

Lama Terkelingpa lineage, 354n3
lamini (daughter of lineage lama), 126,
    348, 377
le (act, deed, karma), 25, 170, 377. *See also*
    action; karma
leki melong (mirror of deeds), 237–44, 348
Levinas, Emmanuel, 61
Lhalungpa Lama lineage, 354n3
Lhatul Lama, *88*
Longchenpa, 279, 368–69n4

Mahāyāna Buddhism, 11
mālā (prayer beads), 62, 231, 321, 377
mani padme. See *om mani padme hūm*
mantra, 72, 145, 377
Maoists, 343, 349, 350
Marpa, 62, 78
marriage, 31, 36, 39–40, 51, 75, 83, 106–32,
    111, 191–200, 221–22, 366n1. *See also*
    capture marriages
meditation, 95–98
memory, 349–50; and death, 13, 91; and
    faces, 90–91; and inscription, 146–49;
    and narration, 132, 134–36; in old age,
    154; and speech, 146; and suffering,
    146–49; and vision, 85–86, 146
Mheme (grandfather), 24
mhi kha (people's talk, harmful gossip),
    141, 197, 377
mhin (name), 292, 293, 302–3, 349
Milarepa, 25–62, 246, 282, 288, 289, 318
mimesis, 281, 283, 369n10, 370n23
mi ser (romantic jealousy), 191, 196, 377
mi zinge (eye encounter), 59–61, 337
mi zuge (eye piercing), 58–59
Mohanty, J. N., 181

naasum tupke (cutting the nose), 82
naasum zunge (holding the nose), 82, 292
nam she (soul, consciousness), 51, 377
nam-thar (spiritual biography), 73, 150,
    284, 377
narration, 5, 106–7, 109, 134–38, 142–43,
    145, 149–51, 175, 176–77, 199, 230–31,
    339–40
Nepal, 8, *9*, 44
Nga-Chang Shakya Zangpo, 24–25, 27, 52,
    73, 76, 150, 354n4, 377
Nietzsche, Friedrich, 148
Ningma Lama lineage, 24–25, 26, 27, 34,
    52, 102, 106, 189, 351, 354n4, 377

nirvāṇa, 319, 372n9, 377
nyingjwa (compassioned one), 297–99, 351,
    377
Nyingma sect, 11, 214, 354n4, 377

Obeyesekere, Gananath, 186
old age, 152–60, 184–85, 256–58, 267–69;
    body in, 152–60, 257, 285, 315–17; and
    vision, 153–55
om mani padme hūm, 201, 364n1
Ortner, Sherry, 359n6

Padmasambhava, 214, 289, 320, 373n4
Pascal, Blaise, 213
person-centered approach, 4–5, 6
personhood, among Yolmo people, 81–82,
    83–84, 133–34, 323–27
pe-tam (story), 150–51
Phagpa Chen Rezig (Avalokiteśvara), 76,
    98, 179, 201, 320, 321, 364n1,
    373nn11,4, 377
phangbu (longing), 320
phenomenology, 5–6, 176, 180, 324, 325,
    342, 362n1
phowa (transference of consciousness), 286
Phur Gyalmu, *268*
Powers, John, 358n34
pūjā (ritual), 34

Ranas, 28, 30, 66, 115, 116, 119–20
rasa (mood), 181
repletion: aesthetics of, 178; rhetoric of,
    178–79, 190, 324
retreat, 95, 168
rikpa (smarts), 257
ritual, 109–10, 166, 192, 248
ritual time, 139, 230

sansāra, 27, 207, 209, 215, 218, 279, 301,
    318–19, 377
Sarma Lama lineage, 30, 106, 108, 189, 351,
    354n3, 377
sem (heartmind), 6, 56–57, 60, 74, 76,
    85–86, 93, 97, 99–100, 146–47, 148,
    319, 338, 378
semjha. *See* attachment
sensory biography, 3
sensory perception, 2–3, 34–35, 54, 181,
    209, 235, 236, 338–43; anthropological
    study of, 3–4, 341–43; and gender,
    143–44; intersubjective aspects of,

sensory perception *(continued)*
341, 342; politics of, 342–43; pragmatic features of, 342; temporal
dimensions of, 341, 342
shalgar (ceremonial offering), 31, 40, 83,
117–18, 341, 378
Sherpa people, 12, 370–71n23, 371n27
shyindi (ghost), 303–4, 319, 378
speech, 3–4, 18–19, 139–46, 275, 338–43;
aesthetics of, 255–56, 265–70; and gender, 266–67; and memory, 146–49; as
moral commentary, 312–14, 325–26;
politics of, 167, 246–48; as social action, 139–40, 312–14; as transformative force, 139–42, 149
sponsor, 163–64, 165
stillness, 181, 231–32, 324
subjectivity, 4, 6, 100, 107, 134, 149–51, 177,
342
suffering, 37–38, 41–42, 114, 163, 190, 232,
251, 295, 311, 322–23, 325; Buddhist
perspectives on, 38–39; and narration,
47, 178
Surje Lama, *49, 88*

Tamang people, 8, 11, 12, 40, 43, 45–46,
102, 296, 333
thangka (religious scroll painting), 104,
117, 378
Thodong, *33, 88, 162, 301*
The Three Precious Ones, 333, 364n3
Thurman, Robert, 214, 215
Tibet, 7, 24, 25, 49
Tibetan Buddhism, 7, 54–55, 69, 98, 134,
153, 234, 235, 315, 354n4
time, 23–24, 49–53, 137–38, 172, 203–4, 221,
305, 308, 325, 335, 341; and narration,
135–38. *See also* ritual time
tongba (empty), 302
trace, 288–89
transfer, 97, 286–88
translation, 105, 286–87, 331–32, 334, 336–37
tshe (life, life span), 23, 205, 378
tsher lu (pain song), 74, 113, 126, 157, 196,
253, 378

tulgen (to metamorphose), 347
Turner, R. L., ix

Vajrasattva meditation, 95–97
vision, 2–3, 20–22, 23, 54–101, 143–44,
159–60, 338–43; among Buddhist
deities, 75–78; and clarity, 78,
86–89, 119; and death, 60, 91–94,
187, 239–40, 302; and divination,
70–71, 78–80; and ethics, 61; and
imagination, 56, 94–100; as interpersonal engagement, 57–64, 74,
82–84; as means of knowledge, 65;
as means of truth and evidence,
65–67; and memory, 85–86; as observation, 80–82, 84–85, 124, 130,
207, 236–44, 317; and old age, 153,
155, 157–60; physiology of, 55–57;
and speech, 60–61, 67, 70; in Tibetan Buddhism, 54–55; and violence, 58–59, 84

waiting, 233–34
Watkins, Joanna, 359n6, 361n6
widows, 189–91, 247–48
witches, 58–59, 112–13
women, status of among Yolmo people,
73, 112, 119–21, 138, 142, 161–63, 325,
359n6
writing, 67–75, 114, 131, 144–45, 164,
214–18, 219–21, 237–44, 273; and gender, 219–21, 273–74
Wylie, T. V., ix

Yama Raj (Lord of Death), 104, 179, 376,
378. *See also* Chhe Gyalbu
Yolmo Foundation, 14
Yolmo people, ix, 1, *16–17;* ethnic identities
of, 11–13; history of, 7–8, 11–13, 50–51,
256, 276–77, 290–91; language of, ix;
religious practices of, 11; social life of,
8–11, 133–34
Yolmo region, 8, *9–10,* 87

Text: 10/13 Galliard
Display: Galliard
Cartographer: Bill Nelson
Compositor: Impressions Book & Journal Services, Inc.
Printer and Binder: Sheridan Books, Inc.